ASIAN AMERICAN LITERATURE

A Brief Introduction and Anthology

Shawn Wong
University of Washington

The HarperCollins Literary Mosaic Series
Ishmael Reed
General Editor
University of California, Berkeley

HARPERCOLLINS*COLLEGEPUBLISHERS*

Acquisitions Editor: Lisa Moore
Cover Design: Kay Petronio
Cover Illustration: Rupert Garcia, "For Vincent Chin," Copyright Rupert Garcia and courtesy of artist and Sammi Madison-Garcia, Rena Bransen Gallery (SF), Galerie Claude Samuel (Paris), and Daniel Saxon Gallery (LA)
Electronic Production Manager: Laura Chavoen
Electronic Page Makeup: Kay Spearman/The Resource Center
Printer and Binder: RR Donnelley & Sons Co.
Cover Printer: The LeHigh Press, Inc.

95 96 97   9 8 7 6 5 4 3 2

Asian American Literature

Library of Congress Cataloging-in-Publication Data

Asian American literature : a brief introduction and anthology /
  [edited by] Shawn Wong. -- 1st ed.
       p.   cm. -- (HarperCollins literary mosaic series)
  Includes bibliographical references and index.
  ISBN 0-673-46977-8 (alk. paper)
  1. American literature--Asian American authors. 2. Asian
Americans--Literary collections.   I. Wong, Shawn, 1949-   .
II. Series.
PS508.A8A8 1995
810.8'0895--dc20
                                                    95-9632
                                                    CIP

To
Henry William Wong
and
Patrick William Wong,
father and son

Contents

POETRY

DRAMA

Foreword

by Ishmael Reed, General Editor

I abandoned the use of textbooks early in my teaching career and developed my own "reader." I was frustrated with textbooks in which the preponderance of prose and poetry was written by people of similar backgrounds and sensibilities—the white-settler-surrounded-by-infidels-and-savages theme common to Euro-American literature. In these textbooks we seldom got information about how the Native Americans or the Africans felt. Female and minority writers were left out. There was slack inclusion of contemporary writers, and little space devoted to the popular American culture of our century. These textbooks seemed slavishly worshipful of the past, such that every mediocre line by a past "great" was treated with reverence while the present was ignored.

Of course, there are many worthwhile ideas to be gained from what in our sound-bite culture—in which complicated ideas are dumbed down for instant consumption—is referred to as "Western Civilization." But as Asian American writer Frank Chin points out when referring to the Cantonese model, after the ability of the Cantonese to absorb every culture with which they've come into contact, one doesn't have to abandon the styles of one's own tradition in order to embrace styles from other traditions. As I have mentioned elsewhere, the history of modern art would be quite different had not artists been receptive to or borrowed from the traditions of others. This creative give and take between artists of different cultures particularly characterizes the arts of the twentieth century.

Things have improved over the years, especially with the outbreak of textbooks labeled "multicultural," a term that has become a football in the struggle between the politically correct of the left and the right. However, even the new and improved multicultural texts appear to have added African American, Native American, Hispanic American, and Asian American writers as an afterthought. The same writers and the same—often unrepresentative—works show up again and again.*

The HarperCollins Literary Mosaic Series

The HarperCollins Literary Mosaic Series was created as an antidote to this version of multiculturalism whose fallibility becomes evident when talented writers, well-known and respected in their communities, are ignored. The HarperCollins Literary Mosaic Series includes not only those writers who have made it into the canon but also writers undeservedly neglected in today's crop of texts.

---

* *For more information on the arbitrariness of this selection process, see Michael Harper's excellent <u>Every Shut Eye Ain't Sleep</u>.*

In his autobiographical remarks, *Asian American Literature* editor Shawn Wong makes an important point that teachers should consider when adopting texts for their ethnic literature, multiculturalism, American literature, and introductory literature courses. Wong writes that his study of Asian American literature occurred outside of the university. "At no time," he writes, "in my English and American literature undergraduate education or in my entire public school education had any teacher ever used (or even mentioned) a work of fiction or poetry by a Chinese American or any Asian American writer." This observation could be made by all the editors of The HarperCollins Literary Mosaic Series: Al Young for *African American Literature*, Gerald Vizenor for *Native American Literature*, Nicolás Kanellos for *Hispanic American Literature*, and of course Shawn Wong for *Asian American Literature*. They had to go outside of the academy—which has committed an intellectual scandal by excluding these major traditions of our common American heritage.

The Series Editors: Pioneers for an Inclusive Tradition

These editors are among the architects of a more inclusive tradition. Indeed, this series is unique because the four editors are not only writers and scholars in their own right but are among the pioneers of American literature of the latter part of this century! It's hard to imagine a list of talented insiders who are as informed about the currents and traditions of their ethnic literatures as the editors of The HarperCollins Literary Mosaic Series. These texts provide teachers with an opportunity to employ material in their classrooms that has been chosen by writers who have not only participated in the flowering of their literatures but also have assisted in the establishment of a tradition for their literatures.

Al Young

Al Young is a multitalented artist who has distinguished himself as a poet, novelist, screenwriter, editor, and writing instructor. His presence is very much in demand at writing workshops and conferences. He has taught at a number of universities and colleges, including Stanford University, Crown College, the University of California at Berkeley, the University of California at Santa Cruz, Rice University, and most recently at the University of Michigan. Among his honors are a Wallace Stegner Writing Fellowship, a Joseph Henry Jackson Award, a Guggenheim Fellowship, an American Book Award, and a PEN/Library of Congress Award for Short Fiction. Al Young and I were editors of the Yardbird Reader series, which has been recognized as the first national publication of its kind devoted to presenting new multicultural literature.

Gerald Vizenor

Pulitzer Prize–winner N. Scott Momaday has said that Gerald Vizenor "has made a very significant contribution to Native American letters and also to American literature in general. He's innovative, he has the richest sense of humor of anyone I know, and in addition he's the most articulate person—he's a man to be reckoned with." Among his innovative novels are *Heirs of Columbus* and *Griever: An American Monkey King in China.* An American Book Award winner, Vizenor insists that the story of Native Americans in the United States should be told by Native Americans and not by intermediaries or translators. His *Native American Literature* anthology in The HarperCollins Literary Mosaic Series will provide students and readers with an entirely different slant on Native American literature from the one they have become accustomed to in standard texts.

Nicolás Kanellos

Author of a number of scholarly works and articles, Nicolás Kanellos is the founder and director of Arte Público Press, the oldest and largest publisher of United States Hispanic literature, as well as the *Americas Review* (formerly *Revista Chicano-Requeña*), the oldest and most respected magazine of United States Hispanic literature and art. A full professor at the University of Houston, he is a fellow of the Ford, Lilly, and Gulbenkian foundations and of the National Endowment for the Humanities. He is also the winner of an American Book Award and is a formidable essayist with an unrivaled knowledge of the intersections of African, European, and Native American cultures.

Shawn Wong

It is not surprising that Shawn Wong and Frank Chin, Lawson Inada, and Jeffery Chan have become known as "the four horsemen of Asian American literature" by both their admirers and detractors. One wonders how Asian American literature would look without their efforts. It was they who began the painstaking construction of a tradition whose existence had been denied by the academy. In *Aiiieeee! An Anthology of Asian American Writers* and its successor, *The Big Aiiieeeee! An Anthology of Chinese American and Japanese American Literature,* the four editors gave permanent status to an Asian American literary tradition. Wong is also the author of *Homebase,* the first novel published in the United States by an American-born Chinese male. This novel received the Pacific Northwest Booksellers Award for Excellence and the Fifteenth Annual Governor's Writer's Day Award. Among his many other honors, Wong has also received a fellowship from the National Endowment for the Arts. He has taught writing at the University of Washington since 1984. His second novel, *American Knees,* was published in 1995.

Remapping Our Tradition

Although the four editors are from different backgrounds, the issues raised in their introductions are those with which a few generations of multicultural scholars, writers, and artists have grappled. With *African American Literature*, Al Young has both a literary and humanistic purpose. He believes that readers and writers will be able to learn from their exposure to some of the best writing in the United States that there are experiences all of us share with the rest of humanity. Like the classic critic F. R. Leavis, Al Young believes that writing can make people better. The writers included in Gerald Vizenor's *Native American Literature* are not outsiders writing about Native Americans or colonial settlers promoting the forest as a tough neighborhood full of high-risk people, a threat to civilized enclaves, but rather works by Native Americans themselves, beginning in 1829 with William Apess's autobiography, *A Son of the Forest*. Nicolás Kanellos's *Hispanic American Literature* represents a literary tradition, part European and part African, that existed in the Americas prior to the arrival of the English. The situation in Asian American literature, one of the youngest of American literatures, is as turbulent as that of the atmosphere surrounding a new star. Shawn Wong's introduction addresses the continuing debate over issues about what constitutes Asian American literature and the role of the Asian American writer.

The books in The HarperCollins Literary Mosaic Series give a sampling of the outstanding contributions from writers in the past as well as the range of American writing that is being written today. And the anthologies in this series contain a truly representative sampling of African American, Native American, Hispanic American, and Asian American writing at the end of this century so that students can become acquainted with more than the few European and European Americans covered by traditional texts or the same lineup of token ethnic writers found in the policy issue multicultural books. It should be welcome news to instructors looking for new ways to teach that such a distinguished group committed themselves to producing three-to-five-hundred-page textbooks that can either be used as the primary text in a course, supplemented with novels, combined for a single class, or used to supplement other texts that don't have the desired coverage of ethnic literature. While each book is designed to be brief enough for flexible uses in the classroom, each volume does represent the breadth of major literary genres (autobiography, fiction, poetry, and drama) that characterizes the literary contribution of each tradition, even if—as in the case of drama—the short format of the series would accommodate only a single example. The four volumes of The HarperCollins Literary Mosaic Series constitute nothing less than a new start for those who are interested in remapping our writing traditions.

Writing for Our Lives

> The genius of the United States is not best or most in its executives
> or legislatures, nor in its ambassadors or authors or colleges or
> churches or parlors, nor even in its newspapers or inventors ... but
> always most in the common people. Their manners, speech, dress,
> friendships—the freshness and candor of their physiognomy—the
> picturesque looseness of their carriage ... their deathless attachment
> to freedom (Walt Whitman, "Leaves of Grass," 1855 Preface).

Whitman said that these qualities and others await the "gigantic and generous
treatment worthy of it." Though American authors from the eighteenth century to
the present day have talked about a body of writing that would be representative of
these attributes of democracy, one could argue that "the gigantic and generous
treatment worthy of it" is a recent and critical development because until recently
many points of view have been excluded from United States literature. The Literary
Mosaic Series also demonstrates that, for authors of a multicultural heritage, literature
often provides an alternative to the images of their groups presented by an often-
hostile media.

Of all the excellent comments made by Al Young in his introduction, one is
crucial and strikes at the heart of why the writing is so varied in The HarperCollins
Literary Mosaic Series. He writes,

> and if you think people are in trouble who buy the images of who
> they are from the shallow, deceitful versions of themselves they see
> in mass media, think what it must feel like to be a TV-watching
> African-American male. Pimp, thug, mugger, drug dealer, crackhead,
> thief, murderer, rapist, absentee father, welfare cheat, convict, loser,
> ne'er-do-well, buffoon. Think of these negative images of yourself
> broadcast hourly all over the globe.

When African Americans, Native Americans, Hispanic Americans, and Asian
Americans write, they're not just engaging in a parlor exercise—they are writing for
their lives. The twentieth century has shown that unbalanced images can cost groups
their lives. That is why The HarperCollins Literary Mosaic Series came to be—to trumpet
these lives, lives that are our national heritage. And once these voices have been
heard, there is no turning back.

Acknowledgments

This is a series that has taken the time, talents, and enthusiasm of its editors—Al Young, Gerald Vizenor, Nicolás Kanellos, and Shawn Wong—and I am excited that they chose to be a part of this project. In addition, the editors and I wish to thank those people who helped us prepare the series, particularly those instructors who reviewed this material in various drafts and offered their expertise and suggestions for making the books in this series even more useful to them and their students: Joni Adamson Clarke, University of Arizona; Herman Beavers, University of Pennsylvania; A. LaVonne Brown Ruoff, University of Illinois at Chicago; William Cain, Wellesley College; Rafel Castillo, Palo Alto College; Jeffrey Chan, San Francisco State University; King-Kok Cheung, University of California at Los Angeles; Patricia Chu, George Washington University; Robert Combs, George Washington University; Mary Comfort, Moravian College; George Cornell, Michigan State University; Bruce Dick, Appalachian State University; Elinor Flewellen, Santa Barbara City College; Chester Fontineau, University of Illinois at Champaign-Urbana; Sharon Gavin Levy, University of Minnesota at Duluth; Shirley Geok-Lin Lim, University of California at Santa Barbara; Tom Green, Northeastern Junior College; James Hall, University of Illinois at Chicago; Lynda M. Hill, Temple University; Lane Hirabayashi, University of Colorado; Gloria Horton, Jacksonville State University; Ketu H. Katrak, University of Massachusetts at Amherst; Josephine Lee, Smith College; Russell Leong, University of California at Los Angeles; Michael Liberman, East Stroudsburg University; Paulino Lim, Jr., California State University at Long Beach; Kenneth Lincoln, University of California at Los Angeles; Marcus "C" Lopez, Solano Community College; Shirley Lumpkin, Marshall University; Barbara McCaskill, University of Georgia; Nelly McKay, University of Wisconsin at Madison; Lucy Maddox, Georgetown University; Thomas Matchie, North Dakota State University; Joyce Middleton, University of Rochester; Alice Moore, Yakima Valley Community College; Eric Naylor, University of the South; Jon Olson, Oregon State University at Corvallis; Ernest Padilla, Santa Monica College; David Payne, University of Georgia; Joyce Pettis, North Carolina State University; David Robinson, Winona State University; Don Rothman, Oakes College, University of California at Santa Cruz; Leonard A. Slade, Jr., State University of New York at Albany; Stephen Sumida, University of Michigan; Brian Swann, Cooper Union; John Trimbur, Worcester Polytechnical Institute; Hari Vishwanadha, Santa Monica College; Marilyn Nelson Waniek, University of Connecticut; Shelly Wong, Cornell University; Jackie Valdez, Caspar College; Richard Yarborough, University of California at Los Angeles.

Preface

It has been exactly twenty years since the publication of *Aiiieeeee! An Anthology of Asian American Writers* (1974), the first major anthology of Asian American literature, which I coedited with Jeffery Paul Chan, Frank Chin, and Lawson Fusao Inada. *Aiiieeeee!* was alternately honored and reviled in its twenty-year history—honored for recognizing and naming the canon and reviled, when it first appeared, for simply saying Asian American writing existed and, later, for too narrowly limiting the Asian American identity.

Twenty years ago *Aiiieeeee!* defined the Asian American writer as someone who was born in America of Asian ancestry. This, of course, excluded the writings of first-generation immigrants, which my coeditors and I rectified in our second anthology, *The Big Aiiieeeee!* (1991), in which we wrote that the first-generation immigrants were "literate people from literate civilizations whose presses, theaters, opera houses, and artistic enterprises rose as quickly as their social and political institutions."

As an Asian American kid in the fifties, I was surrounded by stereotypes in the comics, on television, and in the movies that depicted Asians as an enemy with severely slanted eyes and long fingernails; a horn-rimmed, buck-toothed Japanese general; an obsequious houseboy; or as the fleshy, pasty, overweight, and unaggressive detective Charlie Chan, who spoke only in fake Chinese proverbs. In each of these depictions, Asians never said anything beyond a hopelessly stereotypical chatter that didn't exist in the real world. In fact, it wasn't until the seventies when Bruce Lee finally arrived on the scene that Asian American boys had a role model in the popular culture that defied the stereotype, and a role model that even *non-Asian* boys wanted to emulate.

As a kid I wanted to be a football player named Pete Domoto. Not be like but *be* him. Whenever I had my own small football uniform on, I *was* him. Left guard, number sixty, the Berkeley Cal Bears. After the games I and many other kids ran down on the field looking for autographs and the greatest treasure of all, a player's helmet chin strap. Why was Pete Domoto so important? For a young Chinese American boy growing up in America, there were no other role models of Asian Americans doing something heroic, grand, and real in the way a little boy understands. All of us at that time—whether we were Asian Americans or white or African American—also wanted to be Willie Mays or San Francisco Forty-niner quarterback Y. A. Title. But to me Pete Domoto was special because he was Japanese American, he played football, and he played football on one of the greatest Cal teams ever. He was the only real Asian American image in the popular culture.

Having been born in Oakland and raised in Berkeley, in many ways I spent my childhood preparing myself to attend The University of California at Berkeley, which we called Cal. The Berkeley of my childhood in the fifties was thrilling, and a large part of the thrill had something to do with Pete Domoto and the fact that my father had attended Cal as a graduate student in engineering. By the time I got to Cal in the late sixties, the university life I had looked forward to as a boy had disappeared. It was a different period and, in many ways, I couldn't have picked a better time. Berkeley was in turmoil with demonstration after demonstration over the Vietnam War, the civil rights movement, and the creation of an ethnic studies department. Prior to coming to Cal, I had spent two years at San Francisco State University during the tumultuous and controversial administration of university president S. I. Hayakawa. But in that era of strife and strikes, the first ethnic studies departments had been born on that campus and a few others. In the sixties when college students were demanding ethnic studies programs, one's personal political identity changed as colleges changed—negroes became Afro-Americans, Mexican Americans became Chicanos, and Orientals became Asian Americans. This change, this search for identity, puzzled an older generation that grew up in an America that constantly reminded them of their status, their class, and their race. Minority "baby boomers" grew up in the fifties and sixties and were products of a monocultural education that celebrated the "American melting pot."

As an English major in my third year I had decided to become a writer. I had been writing poetry and fiction for three years. Somehow it seemed significant that I made this decision on the Berkeley campus, the school where my father had graduated, and the school where my boyhood idol had played football. These two men were great role models for me. My education was like everyone's American education of the fifties even when I wasn't living in America.

I attended the second grade in Taiwan. Given my last name, this is perhaps not a startling revelation. What was startling about this experience was that I was born in Oakland, California, and I spoke no Chinese, and in Taiwan, I was enrolled in an all-American, predominantly white U.S. Navy school. When my mother and I boarded the bus on the first day of school, the children chanted, "No Chinese allowed!" I thought they were referring to my mother.

My elementary school education began in the fifties in Berkeley, California, and scattered itself all over the Pacific and California—eleven schools from kindergarten to the twelfth grade—and at its most basic level, my memory is dominated by my being the "new kid," followed by the question, "What are you?" I never thought I was much different from my classmates until that first experience in Taiwan. A consistent monocultural education throughout the eleven schools that make up my public school education spoke to our common backgrounds, made us a homogeneous school population, but did not inform us about the kid sitting in the next seat.

Today, I'm an Asian American studies professor and have been for twenty-two years. In 1972, I was hired by Mills College while I was still enrolled in graduate school at San Francisco State University. I was twenty-two and had no teaching experience. Mills College had just started an ethnic studies department and I applied. When asked what I could teach, I said Asian American literature. "You're hired," the dean said.

The beginning of my academic career in Asian American studies was, in many respects, accidental. I was a student of western civilization from kindergarten through high school and throughout my undergraduate years as an English major at the University of California at Berkeley. It was, for the most part, a wonderful education. But it had little or nothing to do with me and it certainly didn't get me my first teaching job. My study of Asian American literature occurred outside of the university. At no time in my undergraduate English and American literature studies or in my entire public school education had any teacher ever used or even mentioned a work of fiction or poetry by an Asian American writer. At age eighteen, I had just started to write when one day I realized I was the only Asian American writer I knew (and I wasn't very good). As a comparison, imagine an American culture without African American writers, musicians, singers, actors, and painters. I knew no Chinese American painters, musicians, comedians, or singers, and I had seen only a handful of actors on the screen playing the stereotyped roles of the soldier who dies, the kungfu expert, the gardener, and the houseboy. While enrolled at Cal, I took it upon myself to embark on two courses of study: my standard undergraduate English undergraduate major, which was a defined field of study within the university with specific requirements, and Asian American history and literature, which was a field of study that didn't exist on the campus. In my public school education, I never learned the Chinese built the Central Pacific Railroad over the Sierra Nevada Mountains, or that they were a major force in establishing California's agricultural industry, or that they survived years of exclusion and anti-Chinese legislation at all levels of government. Some of my Japanese American classmates didn't even know their parents had been incarcerated in Japanese American concentration camps during World War II. When they asked their parents why they were never told, they answered, "You never asked." We had grown comfortable and even accepted in an America where we could stop being Chinese or Japanese. A monocultural education had taught us that silence was love.

I had to teach myself how to learn outside of the academy—how to do research outside of the libraries that didn't house our books and our writers. I wanted to know who the writers were that preceded me, who described the Asian American sense of self of the previous generation. I knew someone must have written and published in the one hundred and fifty years of our existence in America. I eventually found them and read their work. I telephoned those who were still living, wrote them letters after their twenty or thirty years of silence, and asked about their lives as writers. The first writers I found were my own contemporaries, Frank Chin and Jeffery Paul Chan. Chan had been studying in the same graduate creative writing program at San Francisco

State University as I was. Both of us were unpublished writers. He told me about Frank Chin, who had published one short story entitled "Food For All His Dead," which was set in San Francisco's Chinatown. I called him on the phone and introduced myself in this way: "I'm Chinese and I write. I understand you're Chinese and you've actually published a story."

The three of us soon found Japanese American poet Lawson Fusao Inada up in Ashland, Oregon, and together we began our search for the generation of Asian American writers that came before us. It seemed incredible that we were the first to ask, Where are the writers? In 1970, we found nisei writer Toshio Mori's collection of short stories about the Japanese American community in Oakland and San Leandro, California, entitled, *Yokohama, California* (1949), in a used bookstore for twenty-five cents. Inside it, someone had glued a 1949 newspaper review. In the brittle, yellow newsprint, the writer had noted that Toshio Mori lived in San Leandro. Being a trained academic undergraduate scholar, I headed for the library to begin my search for more about this great writer, but Frank Chin stopped me and suggested we look in the telephone book. There, twenty-one years after the publication of his book, were Mori's name and phone number. We called him and went to his home. No one had come to inquire about his writing in all of those twenty-one years. We came back three days in a row and looked at his scrapbook and at the manuscripts for three more unpublished books. We found other writers from the generation before ours who, like Toshio Mori, were simply waiting to be asked—people such as Hisaye Yamamoto, Wakako Yamauchi, and Diana Chang. Because of their untimely deaths, we just missed meeting novelists John Okada *(No-No Boy,* published in 1957) and Louis Chu *(Eat a Bowl of Tea,* published in 1961). This search led to the publication of *Aiiieeeee!* In the introduction, we wrote that *Aiiieeeee!* was "more than a whine, shout, or scream. It is fifty years of our whole voice."

Nearly every Asian American creative work we discovered was out of print. When ten publishers ignored our efforts to reissue John Okada's classic Japanese American novel, *No-No Boy* (1957), my fellow coeditors and I raised funds, borrowed money, and brought the novel back out into print. *No-No Boy* is now published by the University of Washington Press. As an eighteen year old, all I wanted to be was a writer, but somewhere along the way, in an attempt to educate an audience for my own work, I had become a literary historian, literary scholar, editor, publisher, and, with my coeditors, conference organizer of the first Asian American writers conference, held at the Oakland Museum in 1975. We wanted the older generation of writers to know it now had an audience and that a second generation of Asian American writers was preserving its tradition.

In the first few years that followed, there wasn't much improvement. Six publishers turned down my first novel, *Homebase*, until it was finally published in

1979 by African American writer and publisher Ishmael Reed. And in 1979, it was the only novel by a Chinese American in print. Times have certainly changed. I wouldn't have guessed then that today nearly everyone in America could name at least one American novelist. Indeed, in 1991 five works of fiction by Chinese American authors were published in the same year.

Today, there are dozens and dozens of works by Asian Americans in print, and many of the older works that were out of print are now back in print. Indeed, my own novel *Homebase* was out of print for years and, since its reprinting, sells better now than fifteen years ago.

What we need to realize is that Asian American writing has been published here since the nineteenth century, most notably the works of Sui Sin Far. The literature is not new; rather, it was neglected and forgotten. Asian American literature should be considered within the larger context of American multi-cultural literature and American literature in general.

We need to define terms and a sense of history and identity when discussing ethnic groups whose images have been dominated in the media by stereotypes. This anthology is one approach to such definition. It is not a comprehensive compilation of Asian American writing, but rather, one that represents the range, variety, and depth of Asian American literature today. It is meant to be supplemented by the many Asian American works of fiction, poetry, drama, literary criticism, and history in print. Therefore, none of the examples of fiction is excerpted from novels.

A selected bibliography at the end of this anthology lists the various recommended books that may be used in conjunction with the writings collected here.

A thematic table of contents also at the end of the book is meant to loosely categorize the selections in this anthology into four major areas—naming the language, identity, community, and coming of age. Obviously, many of the works have several themes that may cross over into one or more of these thematic areas. "Naming the Language" covers both the definition of an Asian American voice and engages the reader in the act of naming one's sense of self. The stories in "Identity" explore several varied issues, such as self-determination, loss of identity, the classic search for personal identity, and the conflict of clashing cultural identities. The stories, poems, memoir, essay, and play included in "Community" construct for the reader ethnic enclaves, such as Chinatown, the boundaries of a Japanese American concentration camp, and the bridge between generations within a family. Finally, the stories in "Coming of Age" all come to rest on the field of romance. Some stories are about what this section suggests—the classic coming-of-age story—while others explore the romance of ideas like the American dream. For some, the opportunities are realized, but for others, the dream fades.

I am indebted to Russell Leong, Karen Leonard, and Jessica Hagedorn, who were a great help in recommending authors and searching for their addresses and phone numbers. I would also like to thank my students in my Asian American literature classes at the University of Washington for being the test laboratory for these selections. The writings that made it to the final version of this anthology are the works that challenged my students and quite simply, the works they *liked* to read.

Shawn Wong
Seattle, Washington

Introduction

If you examine the landscape of a place called Asian America in the American mind, you will find its boundaries begin somewhere near a familiar stereotype and end with the truth being told in hidden corners of history—somewhere in the Sierra Nevada in a train tunnel built by nineteenth-century Chinese railroad workers in Donner Pass, by a restaurant kitchen door in a Chinatown alley, on a vast and dusty American plain of a now deserted World War II-era Japanese American internment camp, in a corner grocery store, or in an Alaskan cannery. Part of the story is heroic, legendary, and mythic, the other and more familiar part of the story is a media stereotype of fantasy, foolishness, and fakery.

A bumper sticker on a car in Los Angeles depicts the stereotypical cartoon caricature of a slanty-eyed Asian behind a steering wheel enclosed within a red international cancel sign, a comment on Asian driving skills in a city serious about driving. The CEO of an American car company points a finger at the trade deficit between America and Japan and compares the export strategies of the Japanese auto industry to the Japanese attack on Pearl Harbor. In 1990 Japanese Americans received twenty thousand dollars in redress payments with an apology from the President of the United States for their wartime removal from their homes on the West Coast and incarceration in Japanese American concentration camps during World War II. The editorial pages of newspapers are filled with letters from irate people who cannot distinguish between Japanese Americans and the Japanese who bombed Pearl Harbor. In Washington state there are special license plates that read "Pearl Harbor Survivor," followed by a number. With our consciousness of the global marketplace, does anyone think that these license plates might be offensive to Japanese nationals visiting Washington state? Are there license plates in Japan that read "Hiroshima Atomic Bomb Survivor?"

After the bombing of Pearl Harbor, Chinese Americans wore large red buttons that read "I am Chinese." *Time* and *Life* ran articles in the first days after the Pearl Harbor attack entitled "How to Tell Your Friends from the Japs":

> The Chinese expression is likely to be more placid, kindly, open;
> the Japanese more positive, dogmatic, arrogant.... Japanese are
> hesitant, nervous in conversation, laugh loudly at the wrong time.
> Japanese walk stiffly erect, hard-heeled. Chinese, more relaxed,
> have an easy gait, sometimes shuffle.

By 1943, America repealed the Chinese Exclusion Act, officially allowing Chinese to become naturalized citizens, and began admitting 105 Chinese immigrants in per year because China had proven to be a loyal ally during the war, but the quota was targeted at the country of ancestry rather than country of origin. By the Korean War, the Chinese became enemies again. From yellow peril to red menace.

Environmentally and politically correct white liberals in America were promoting boycotts of Japanese products in order to protest the killing of thousands of dolphins in Japanese drift nets and Japanese whale hunting. The editorial letter writer, the Detroit autoworker, and the college professor in a Volvo eating dolphin-free tuna had met and found common ground in bashing Japan. A Japanese corporation buys the Pebble Beach golf course and the Seventeen Mile Drive in Carmel. Another Japanese corporation buys Rockefeller Center in New York City.

In 1990, Japanese Justice Minister Seiroku Kajiyama compared the presence of foreign prostitutes in Tokyo to African Americans moving into white neighborhoods in America. In 1992, Yoshio Sakurauchi, speaker of the lower House of Parliament in Japan, called America "Japan's subcontractor" and said American workers were lazy and illiterate. In protest and out of patriotism, one woman drove her Toyota truck to a scrap yard and had it crushed. Ironically, the scrap metal was probably sold to Japan. In Los Angeles's Koreatown along Olympic Boulevard, there are stores and malls with signs written only in Korean, selling such ordinary goods and services as furniture, stereos, clothes, food, cars, stationery, hair styling, and nail care. There's no attempt to translate what they offer into English—if you can't read Korean, they don't need your business. In aging Chinatowns across America, the stores and restaurants and bars are named Buddha Bar, Confucius Five and Dime, Pagoda Bakery. There is a Chinese restaurant in every small town in America selling "Chinese American Food," a food invented in America to resemble what once was Chinese food. A Chinese person driving through on the interstate in these small towns has to go into the kitchen in the back and speak to the chef about cooking up something authentic, what the cook's family and employees are eating at the back table by the television. Chinatown was invented to be fake culture and make America's pariah race—the yellow peril— less threatening. Fortune cookies and chop suey are American originals.

The Real versus the Fake

In the last twenty years, dozens of books on the history of various Asian America communities have been published. Out of all of these books, few have documented the artistic and cultural history of Americans of Asian ancestry beyond the listing of some artists' names, the mention of a New Year's parade, and the inevitable confusion of Asian culture from Asia. Even Chinese America's own historians were too quick to point out there was no Chinese American culture to speak of and that the best Chinese Americans could do was to imitate or borrow the culture of their immigrant ancestors. Indeed, some Chinese American historians and sociologists have even encouraged invisibility.

[The Chinese] have gone into occupations which command respect and which lessen conflict from competition. The Chinese are not concentrated entirely in one section of the country. More dispersion away from the vortexes of San Francisco and New York should be encouraged. This ought to be a long-range goal of the Chinese because distribution reduces the degree of visibility. (Sung 1967)

The visibility of Asians in America is a much different story in the nineties. In the American media, several images war against each other—the Asian American superachiever, model American minority, teenage Asian gang member, and an unyielding Japanese business empire, the object of Japan bashing. Inside Asian America these images are related. A once homogeneous American-born Asian American population is now in the minority, accounting for only 40 percent of the total Asian population in America. Anti-Asian violence in America is on the rise, the most famous cases being the murder of Vincent Chin in Detroit and the murder of Asian children in a Stockton, California, schoolyard. Japan bashing is increasing. America's early twentieth century fears of a yellow horde of immigrants is now the economic fear of the immigration of a horde of Hondas, Sonys, and other goods at the heart of the trade imbalance. And on a personal level, each Asian American struggles against a media identity that is not entirely true.

America celebrated and encouraged a cultural confusion and cultural silence by inventing a stereotype in movies, radio, television, and print. Depending on our level of acceptance or rejection, the Chinese in America migrated from yellow peril to World War II ally to red scare to model minority. The price paid for this acceptance has been a cultural silence and the sacrifice of an Asian American sense of self. Maxine Hong Kingston ponders this question in *The Woman Warrior* (1976):

Chinese-Americans, when you try to understand what things in you are Chinese, how do you separate what is peculiar to childhood, to poverty, insanities, one family, your mother who marked your growing with stories, from what is Chinese? What is Chinese tradition and what is the movies?

It doesn't take professors and experts to tell America that we live in a "multicultural" society or that our communities are "culturally diverse." Whatever the current buzzword, the catch phrase, or the business seminar of the moment, America has been aware of the changing ethnic identity of America for quite some time.

The 1990 Census and the media are counting the numbers for the twenty-first century and charting the numbers for America's changing ethnic identity. That identity was once a simple matter of skin color—white, black, brown, red, yellow—but it now has become a complex issue. "What are you?" is no longer an easy question to answer. The business community, advertising and marketing agencies, and all levels of education are in desperate need of resources, people, and books that can educate workers and management, teachers, and executives about our changing cultural identity.

Advertisers learned long ago that it was easy and necessary to market products specifically to the African American community and to the Hispanic community—an African American Santa Claus appears in a Kodak commercial or Spanish is used instead of English on a billboard in a Hispanic community. What about Asian Americans? Advertisers and corporate marketing divisions admit they are lost. Why? In some large metropolitan areas there may be over thirty different Asian ethnic groups. The Asian population in America is now 60 percent foreign-born. Is there a collective Asian American identity for this majority as well as for the 40 percent American-born Asian community? Perhaps the literature that follows in this anthology can answer that question.

As America prepares for the twenty-first century, books that focus on culture and tradition in America have become increasingly in demand, particularly in the schools. Colleges and universities all across the country are requiring undergraduate students to fulfill ethnic studies requirements. All of this attention on ethnic studies in the academy trails an educational process that has been in force in the corporate world for years. American corporations have been competing on a global and multicultural level for years while much of America's educational curriculum remains monocultural. To fill the gap, many corporations have been funding major minority recruiting and scholarship efforts in American business schools. The imperative for students, they say by their actions, is to be both multicultural and multilingual.

We need to define terms and a sense of history and identity when discussing ethnic groups whose images have been dominated in the media by stereotypes. A student of literature must approach an anthology of Asian American writings with sensitivity and a willingness to appreciate the history of the language. For example, in order to honor the oral tradition of Hawaiian writing, Hawaii is spelled Hawai'i.

Perhaps playwright August Wilson described the issue best in an October 1991 *Spin* magazine article entitled "I Want a Black Director," which described his attempt to get an African American director hired to do the movie version of his play *Fences*. Before he gets to the issue of the director, he must first take his readers to school in order to make his case:

> As Americans of various races, we share a broad cultural ground, a commonality of society that links its diverse elements into a cohesive whole that can be defined as "American."

We share certain mythologies. A history. We share political and economic systems and a rapidly developing, if suspect, ethos. Within these commonalities are specifics. Specific ideas and attitudes that are not shared on common cultural ground. These remain the property and possession of the people who develop them, and on that "field of manners and rituals of intercourse" (to use James Baldwin's eloquent phrase) lives are played out.

At the point where they intercept and link to the broad commonality of American culture, they influence how that culture is shared and to what purpose.

White American society is made up of various European ethnic groups which share a common history and sensibility. Black Americans are a *racial* group which do not share the same sensibilities. The specifics of our cultural history are very much different.... Those who are opposed to the ideas of a "foreign" culture permeating the ideal of an American culture founded on the icons of Europe seek to dilute and control it by setting themselves up as the assayers of its value and the custodians of its offspring.

There is not only a quality of inclusiveness or, as Wilson puts it, a "commonality," but also a desire to ground his argument in specific cultural terms.

The Before Columbus Foundation, a nonprofit multicultural literary organization founded by *Literary Mosaic* general editor Ishmael Reed, notes in its mission statement that "multicultural is not a description of a category of American writing—it is a *definition* of all American writing."

In the 1991 edition of *Aiiieeeee! An Anthology of Asian American Writers*, my coeditors and I wrote in a new preface entitled "*Aiiieeeee!* Revisited" that

Before we can talk about our literature, we have to explain our sensibility. Before we can explain our sensibility, we have to outline our histories. Before we can outline our history, we have to dispel the stereotypes. Before we can dispel the stereotypes we have to prove the falsity of the stereotypes and the ignorance of easily accessible, once well-known common history—as maddening and pitifully unfulfilling a task as trying to teach forty-year-old illiterates the alphabet and Shakespeare in an hour and a half.

We've done the stereotypes, shall we begin with the literature?

A Brief Literary History

Chinese Americans were the first Asian immigrant group to come to America in large numbers, beginning in the mid-nineteenth century during the California gold rush and later to work on building the transcontinental railroad. Chinese American literature perhaps could have started as early as 1875 with the writings of a group only known now as "Wong Sam and Assistants." Wong Sam and his assistants, whoever they were, wrote an intriguing book published by the Wells Fargo Company entitled simply as *An English-Chinese Phrase Book*. At first glance, one might assume that this bilingual book of phrases served only to provide a way for a non-English-speaking Chinese person to do business with or send telegrams through Wells Fargo offices, but this book is not organized like any logical western reference work. It is not organized alphabetically by subject or given an index by which the user might quickly refer to an appropriate phrase. Instead, the user must read the entire book from cover to cover to use the book—or understand the whole experience of being Chinese in America for the twenty-five-year period from 1850 to 1875. The book utilizes the way Chinese learn by memorization and recitation. Once Chinese readers have memorized the book, they also understand the strategies of living life in the very inhospitable and rough American West. The excerpt that follows is a line-by-line sequence without the written Chinese characters that precede each English sentence and includes the original grammatical inconsistencies:

> He was murdered by a thief.
> He committed suicide.
> He was choked to death with a lasso, by a robber.
> He was strangled to death by a man.
> He was starved to death in prison.
> He was frozen to death in the snow.
> He was going to drown himself in the bay.
> After searching for several days they caught the murderer.
> Did they find anything in his possession?
> They did.
> He was killed by an assassin.
> He tried to assassinate me.
> He tried to kill me by assassination.
> He is an assaulter.
> He was suffocated in his room.
> He was shot dead by his enemy.
> He was poisoned to death by his friend.
> He tries to kill me by poisoning.
> Assault with the intention to do bodily injury.

He took the law in his own hand.
He tried to deprive me of my wages.
I go home at night.
I have gone home.
I went home.
I abode at home.
I abode at San Francisco.
I have lived in Oakland.
I arise at sunrise.

The book goes on to include phrases that describe everything from bargaining over the price for a pair of pants to going to court to settling disputes about having one's mining claim jumped to further descriptions of murder and imprisonment. In the end, the book is not so much a reference work as it is a story in dramatic dialogue, much like a play, in which the reader understands all the experience of Chinese living in the American West circa 1875.

What goods have you for sale?
Plaintiff postponed the case until next Monday.
But the defendant wanted his case to be tried today.
What kind of testimony did they give?
Did his witness give a good evidence?
The defendant's sentence was two years in State Prison.
He had been convicted in Court.
I bailed him out of jail.
I testify what I show.
He believed his testimony.
I cannot wait for you.
He is my enemy.
He was done wrong.
Is this agreeable to you?
He has good fortune.
He is very much disappointed.
Your friend is coming to see you.

In the late nineteenth and early twentieth centuries, Edith Maud Eaton, a Eurasian writer born to a Chinese mother and an English father, wrote under the pseudonym of Sui Sin Far. She wrote sensitive and accurate portrayals of Chinese in America at a time when Chinese, under the hysteria of movements to exclude Chinese and limit immigration, were considered the pariah race of America. She published stories in a variety of magazines, particularly in the American West. In 1912, A. C. McClurg &

Company published her only book, a collection of her stories entitled *Mrs. Spring Fragrance*. Newspapers and magazines depicted the Chinese as rat eaters and low-wage laborers intent on crushing white labor and infesting America with disease. At the other end of the spectrum, many Christian missionaries felt that the only good Chinese was one who had converted to Christianity. In the midst of all this, Sui Sin Far's stories catered to neither side; she told the truth. In her autobiographical essay "Leaves from the Mental Portfolio of an Eurasian," published in the *Independent* magazine in 1909, she writes,

> Why are we what we are? I and my brothers and sisters. Why did God make us to be hooted and stared at? Papa is English, Mamma is Chinese. Why couldn't we have been either one thing or the other? Why is my mother's race despised? I look into the faces of my father and mother. Is she not every bit as dear and good as he? Why? Why? She sings us songs she learned at the English school. She tells us tales of China.... I do not confide in my father and mother. They would not understand. How could they? He is English, she is Chinese. I am different to both of them—a stranger, tho [sic] their only child. "What are we?" I ask my brother. "It doesn't matter, sissy," he responds. But it does.

About the same time Sui Sin Far was writing about Chinese America, Nagai Kafu, an established Japanese writer visiting America between October 1903 and the fall of 1904, discovered Japanese America while living in Tacoma, Washington, and wrote about his American experiences in *American Tales* (published as *Amerika Monogatari* in 1908). As translator Stephen W. Kohl of the University of Oregon writes in "An Early Account of Japanese Life in the Pacific Northwest: Writings of Nagai Kafu" (1979),

> In contrast to the immigrants he writes about, Kafu had good connections and an ample amount of money. Besides he never seriously considered staying in this country; for him it was only a trip.... Frequently he would make the two-hour trip by train to Seattle where he would spend his days and often, apparently, his nights, prowling the streets of the Japanese district.

The fascinating aspect of Kafu's writings was his acknowledgment that the Japanese immigrant in America was very different from the Japanese in Japan even though their emigration and settlement in America was new in the early years of the twentieth century. Kafu writes in his story "Bad Company" that

> As I entered one alley, I was startled to find it filled with Japanese people walking back and forth. There were archery stalls and ball-throwing

games and eating places. These Japanese people had a composure and self-assurance which seemed to say, "We belong here."

Kafu's own words tend to disprove the popular theory that the first generation of Japanese immigrants, like the Chinese, came to America as sojourners, to work and then return home. Instead, the Seattle Kafu observes is a true settlement with stores, businesses, and skid row hotels:

> This narrow alley and these filthy wooden houses were the haunts of Chinese and Japanese people; but in addition to being an Oriental colony, the district was also populated by Caucasian laborers out of work and by blacks who suffered from poverty and oppression.

The Seattle that Kafu visited gave rise later to an American-born second generation, the nisei. Two Japanese American writers came out of the hotels in Seattle's skid row area, now called Pioneer Square. In 1919, Monica Sone, the author of the autobiography *Nisei Daughter* (1953), was born as Kazuko Monica Itoi in the Carrollton Hotel, which was managed by her father who had emigrated from Japan in 1904. Her book begins with her childhood and follows her and her family's life through World War II and their internment at Minidoka, a War Relocation Authority camp in Idaho. The Japanese district Kafu thought was filthy and frightening was also described by Sone:

> I thought the whole world consisted of two or three old hotels on every block. And that its population consisted of families like mine who lived in a corner of the hotels. And its other inhabitants were customers—fading, balding, watery-eyed men, rough-tough bearded men, and good men like Sam, Joe, Peter, and Montana who worked for father, all of whom lived in these hotels.

Another Seattle-based Japanese American novelist, John Okada was the author of the pioneering work *No-No Boy* (1957). Okada was born in 1923 less than a block away from the Carrollton Hotel in the Merchants Hotel. His novel tells the story of Ichiro Yamada, who returns to Seattle just after World War II after first spending two years in a relocation camp and then another two years in prison for refusing to enter the draft after answering "no-no" to the loyalty oath given to Japanese in the camps. For the American-born nisei men, the oath was worded in the following way:

> No. 27. Are you willing to serve in the armed forces of the United States on combat duty wherever ordered?

> No. 28. Will you swear unqualified allegiance to the United States of America and faithfully defend the United States from any or all

attack by foreign or domestic forces, and forswear any form of allegiance or obedience to the Japanese emperor, or to any other foreign government, power, or organization?

The Seattle Japanese American community Ichiro comes home to is fragmented, polarized, and self-destructive. Ichiro is rejected for his disloyalty and praised by his mother for what she perceived as his loyalty to Japan. Her response to his stand, combined with the fact that she thinks Japan won the war, underscores how far apart her world is from his. The novel reveals the void that existed between the issei (immigrants from Japan) and the nisei after the war as the American-born generation began to separate itself from its immigrant and alien parent's age. Death, hopelessness, tragedy, and despair fill his quest to find his place after the war.

The moral and spiritual distance after the war between the issei and nisei betrayed the compact between the two generations in the twenties and thirties. This compact is probably best revealed in Kazuo Miyamoto's autobiographical novel *Hawaii, End of the Rainbow* (1964). A young nisei, Minoru Murayama, is a student from Hawaii working his way through Stanford University when he receives a call from Mr. Kawano, a distant relative. He learns that his relative, an issei, needs his help to counteract the effects of California's recently passed alien land law of 1920, which forbade the leasing of any farmland to a person ineligible for United States citizenship. Kawano and other issei Japanese farmers are immigrant aliens and need to place their farms in Minoru's name. In return for this favor and for working on the farm, the farmers pay for his education.

With the outbreak of World War II and the internment of alien issei as well as the American-born nisei, this bond between the generations dissolved. In the camps, race prejudice and rejection of the issei became camp policy. The use of Japanese was banned in all public meetings and only English-language camp newspapers and magazines were published.

On April 6, 1942, Mike Masaoka of the Japanese American Citizens League (JACL), a nisei organization, wrote an eighteen-page letter to Milton Eisenhower, director of the War Relocation Authority and General Eisenhower's brother. In his letter, he outlined his vision of the relocation camps:

> We do not relish the thought of "Little Tokyos" springing up in these resettlement projects, for by so doing we are only perpetuating the very things which we hope to eliminate: those mannerisms, and thoughts which mark us apart, aside from our physical characteristics. We hope for a one hundred percent American community.... One thing is certain: there should be no Japanese language schools.... Special stress should be laid on the

enunciation and pronunciation of words so that awkward and "Oriental" sounds will be eliminated.

Masaoka, out of a macabre patriotism, goes on to predict that, while in camp, fifty percent of the issei will die as a result of their old age and adjustment to the harsh conditions, thus making it easier to eliminate oriental sounds, thoughts, and mannerisms. Indeed, the compact and promise between the generations had been betrayed.

Camp journals, literary magazines, newspapers, and even private letters were controlled and censored by camp authorities. In spite of this, the issei still continued to write haiku, senryu, tanka, free verse, and prose. Many of their works would not be published until years later.

Filipino immigrants in the twenties and thirties also lived under the same restrictive laws as the Japanese. One writer who documented the harsh realities of their lives working as migrant farm workers and cannery workers from the thirties to the fifties was Carlos Bulosan. His autobiography, *America Is in the Heart* (1946), does not so much chronicle his own life in America as the lives of all Filipinos here. He writes, "I am an exile in America.... I feel like a criminal running away from a crime I did not commit. And this crime is that I am a Filipino in America." Bulosan saw an immense betrayal of Filipinos who tried to pursue the American dream. A generation later, the post-World War II Filipino of Bienvenido Santos's short stories in *Scent of Apples* (1979) was now urban and professional and working in office buildings in Washington, D.C., and Chicago. But still this Filipino lived a lonely and exiled existence surrounded by prejudice and racism.

In Chinese America, the story of the first-generation immigrant bachelor isolated by these same immigration laws in an American Chinatown in New York was told by Louis Chu in his novel *Eat a Bowl of Tea* (1961). Jeffery Chan points out in his introduction to the 1979 edition that

> *Each [character] remains unfailingly that Cantonese peasant warrior, doughty, resourceful, loyal to a sensibility rooted in a China that has already evolved in his absence, dogging the disreputable and notorious Quan Gung, patron deity and guardian of low life in general, of actors, gamblers, and hired assassins, in the guise of waiters, cooks, and laundrymen. Chu's work is a vision of non-Christian Chinese America, certainly the first and perhaps the last portrayal that accurately dramatizes the life and times of Chinese sensibility.*

Perhaps the best-known Japanese American fiction writer to emerge from the relocation camps was Toshio Mori, whose collection of short stories *Yokohama, California* was slated to be published before the war but was delayed until 1949. Mori wrote and edited literary journals and magazines at Topaz, the War Relocation Authority camp in Utah. His stories remain the only collection of Japanese American stories to faithfully describe the pre-World War II Japanese American community nestled in the East Bay cities of Oakland and San Leandro, called by Mori "Yokohama, California." His stories speak to bonds between neighbors and family members. As the poet Lawson Fusao Inada describes it in his introduction to the 1985 edition of *Yokohama, California*, the community is

> an example of moral obligation, of mutual responsibility, mutual trust: The bargain of life works both ways.... the unspoken understanding of the family, that the community will continue to survive, intact.

It is of course ironic that *Yokohama, California* was published after the war when the Japanese American community Mori described no longer existed.

Hisaye Yamamoto wrote and published in the fifties and sixties. Her story "Las Vegas Charley" tells the story of Japanese America through Kazuyuki Matsumoto, who loses his family, his home, and finally his name and is known simply as Las Vegas Charley. In an unpublished essay, novelist Frank Chin describes the Japanese Americans of Yamamoto's stories:

> Using only the facts of victimization and isolated personal experience, Yamamoto's characters destroy themselves slowly, trying to compound a Japanese American integrity and sense of historically abiding dignity out of a history of moral inferiority, failure, and humiliation. They seem to sense a history and vision they no longer have the language to put into words, a history that is no more. They are not released and given meaning by a history they can only vaguely sense but not clarify and recover.

The act of recovery, in terms of Asian American writing, occurred in the late sixties and early seventies when the very works mentioned above were reclaimed and reprinted. The writers themselves were recovered from obscurity and neglect. The editors of *Aiiieeeee! An Anthology of Asian American Writers* (1974) organized the first Asian American writers conference in 1975 at the Oakland Museum where, for the first time, the new generation of Asian American writer could meet those who established the tradition. The literature of both of those generations of writers—and now a third—fill these pages.

AUTOBIOGRAPHY, MEMOIR, AND NONFICTION ESSAY

Frank Chin

(b. 1940)

Frank Chin, a fifth-generation Chinese American, was born in Berkeley, California. In the 1960s and 1970s Asian American writers called Chin both the conscience and the "godfather" of Asian American writing, while others criticized him for being a relic of the 1960s who emulated militant black rhetoric. Whatever the criticism or the controversy, Chin was central to the legitimacy of contemporary Asian American writing. The poet Wing Tek Lum once lamented Chin's absence at an Asian American writers conference as "a meal without rice." Along with coeditors Jeffery Chan, Lawson Fusao Inada, and Shawn Wong, Chin edited two landmark anthologies of Asian American writing: **Aiiieeeee!** *(1974) and* **The Big Aiiieeeee! An Anthology of Chinese American and Japanese American Literature** *(1991).*

In "Rendezvous," the essay that follows, Chin continues to press Asian American literary scholars to be responsible to original Chinese and Japanese texts and the universally known body of knowledge in Chinese and Japanese heroic literature. He calls on Asian American authors to stop believing in the stereotype that Chinese and Japanese culture is forgotten and thought to be obscure by Chinese and Japanese Americans. He writes,

> *Like horsetrading in the marketplace, the value of any information we buy in the marketplace has to be capable of being independently corroborated. Cultures are bodies of knowledge, histories and their varied facts, artifacts, and texts.... if you buy my book to teach Chinese American history, you really shouldn't hang your teaching career on my word alone, even if I gave that word in a work of non-fiction autobiography....*

> *And in case you haven't noticed, there is a war on against the notion of text. If culture has no text, it has no existence.*

Without a doubt he is an essential ingredient and a pioneer. Chin's play **The Chickencoop Chinaman** *was the first Asian American play performed on a legitimate New York stage when it was produced in 1972 by the American Place Theatre. His second play,* **The Year of the Dragon**, *was not only staged at the American Place Theatre in 1974, but it was also filmed for television on the PBS* **Theater in America** *series in 1975. Both plays were published in one volume by the University of Washington Press in 1981. The volume of plays and his collection of stories* **The Chinaman Pacific & Frisco R. R. Co.** *(1988) won an American Book Award from the Before Columbus Foundation. His writing has won numerous other awards and fellowships from the National Endowment for the Arts, the Rockefeller Foundation, the San Francisco Foundation, and the Lannan Foundation. Chin's first novel,* **Donald Duk** *(1991), tells the story of eleven-year-old Donald Duk, an American-born Chinese American kid who hates being Chinese. All he knows growing up in San Francisco's Chinatown is that it hardly resembles "America" at all. Donald hates his name; hates his parents' names, King Duk and Daisy Duk; hates the accent in their voices; hates* *being Chinese; hates living in San Francisco's Chinatown. Donald is eventually freed from self-hatred when he is able to learn the truth about Chinese American history and culture and to distinguish that truth from the stereotypes that he's surrounded by. His father tells him, "You know what is true.... If you say Chinese are ching chong, you have to choose to do it and lie about what you know is true."*

His second novel, **Gunga Din Highway**, *was published in 1994 by Coffee House Press and explores the media stereotypes of Asians. Chin lives in Los Angeles with his wife, Dana, and his son, Sam.*

Rendezvous

America is not a quilt. America is not a tapestry. America is not a mosaic. It is not fixed. The only thing fixed about America is the place. Everything and everyone are moving and changing all over the place.

America is the road. America is a depot, a marketplace. Everyone came to America as a migrant, and has been moving on, sometimes forced to move on, but moving on ever since. American culture is not a fixed culture. There is no one American culture. What we call American culture, like American English, is a pidgin marketplace culture.

American Standard English, the language of newspapers and TV news, is a pidgin English, an ever changing marketplace-depot language.

In the depot, on the road, in the marketplace, we leave our prejudices, grudges, religion, drugs, guns and knives at the gate and come to the depot, the marketplace, go on the road not to understand or sympathize with or even like other people from other cultures, we come to do business, and we assume everyone else comes to the depot or the marketplace or goes on the road to do business, not to convert the heathen, resolve grudges, accomplish revenge of cross cultural understanding.

Toshio Mori, the Nisei fictioneer, wrote up a vision of America as the house of "The Woman Who Makes Swell Doughnuts," and he called her house "a depot." In this world, through this depot, "everyone was moving." This modern Nisei story published in the forties was written as a reminiscence of childhood. The story affects Japanese who read English more deeply than the reader who grew up without the stories of a Japanese childhood. "The Woman Who Makes Swell Doughnuts" is deeper, richer, more eloquent for being modeled on the traditional Japanese story "The Old Woman and Her Dumpling."

"The Old Woman and Her Dumpling" is a folk vision of marketplace crossroads civilization. She makes and sells dumplings at a crossroads marketplace. One of her dumplings drops and rolls. She chases it as it rolls into a hole and into another world. A stone *Jizo*, the god of travelers and children who died in miscarriages, tries to hide the Old Woman from the demons known as *Oni*. The *Oni* find her, take her across their river, give her a magic rice paddle that fills an empty pot with rice merely by stirring, and make her their cook. She steals the rice paddle and a boat to escape home to her world. Halfway across the river the *Oni* come down to the river and start drinking it up to beach her boat so they can walk out and capture her again. While the *Oni* drink all the water out of the river, the old woman stands in the boat and makes faces and tells jokes, and the *Oni* laugh and they laugh gushes of water they've drunk. The more they laugh, the more water gushes out of them and they drown in the waters of their laughter. The old woman gets to the other side of the river, returns home to the crossroads marketplace and makes rice as well as dumplings.

We can remain private in our cultures, in our private lives, and still do business with each other. For some of us, like writers and artists, exchanging the privacy of our cultures for something we value is our business.

In the marketplace of ideas a generation of white kids has grown up feeling despised for being white and can't stand the real world. Every non-white child in America has grown up despised by white official culture for generations, for centuries, and some of us have come to see the racial self-contempt that comes from being despised with either racist hate or racist love (but still despised) is a childhood disease. Whites haven't had generations of being despised by the whole world around them to thwart this disease. The cure is the truth and knowledge. Both are unpleasant. Whites were slavers. Whites waged wars of extermination against the Indians. Blacks, Indians and all non-whites are the bad guys in white religion, white literature, white philosophy and white Hollywood. Chinese are the badguys in the Chicano epic poem "I Am Joaquin!" And the Mexicans rioted against the Chinese and nationalized Chinese property three times in Mexico. Still Chinese live in Mexico. Richard Wright's classic "Black Boy" repeats and uses white racist stereotypes of the Chinese for humor. D. W. Griffith made a classic silent film called "Broken Blossoms" from a story titled "The Chink and the Child." One of the more exciting stories to come from the Chinese who built the railroad is about answering a series of explosions along the right of way, rigged by the Irish of the Union Pacific, by inviting the Irish to drink a local saloon dry. The whiskey flowed, and the Chinese slipped out, nailed the doors and windows shut and burned the saloon down with the Irish inside.

Between non-white American peoples, as between every non-white and white, our histories and cultures are going to cross and clash in some of our most cherished art and literature. Joseph Conrad's *Heart of Darkness* and Francis Ford Coppola's *Apocalypse Now* haunt white souls with a tenacity that distresses me, for they are two rabidly white racist works. The vision of the most extreme non-white civilization as merely a perversion of white Christian civ is genuinely stupid and bespeaks a yucky mind. But whites love it. We have to be able to accept Conrad and Coppola's works as the white racist works they are and still recognize them as great white lit and film.

And I think most writers from non-white peoples can and have been reading racist white lit and recognizing it as great lit.

We all write from specific cultures, times and places. And let's admit it. We are all ignorant of all cultures not white Christian European. So, here we are, brilliant writers of variants and violations of American Standard English in all the depots and variants of the American marketplace telling the world who we are, where we come from, how we see, how we do, what we live for, what we die for, what we tell our kids.

Why should you take my word for it? You might like me personally, and even envy my way with words now and then, but the truth of what is and is not Chinese does not rest on my personality or style. And why should I take your word for what is and is not black, or Afro-American or Latino or Chicano or Puerto Rican or Jewish or Native-American?

Like horsetrading in the marketplace, the value of any information we buy in the marketplace has to be capable of being independently corroborated. Cultures are bodies of knowledge, histories and their varied facts, artifacts and texts. If you buy my books because you like believing cannibalism is commonly and openly practiced in certain ethnic neighborhoods of Boston, Massachusetts, it doesn't matter what people really eat in Boston. But if you buy my book to teach Chinese American history, you really shouldn't hang your teaching career on my word alone, even if I gave that word in a work of non-fiction autobiography. Though I'd never do an autobiography. And the reasons why I wouldn't are easily verified by Chinese texts and literary history.

And in case you haven't noticed, there is a war on against the notion of text. If a culture has no text, it has no existence. The bounty on Salman Rushdie's head and our defense of his artistic freedom distracts us from the contempt for the Koran and Islam Rushdie's work encourages. So we are set to judge all of Islam based on our being too righteous to so much as read any Muslim text. That is very white and nothing but very white of us.

Look around, friends, check around the corner, are there people, your people, out there saying your people have no texts, that it's all oral tradition, anything goes, not verifiable, your people were too stupid to know the difference between the real and the fake of their own culture? Are there people saying the Chicanos have no history? Are there people making war on Brother Rabbit? Have you, in your memory, been told a fairy tale of children's story of your people, your culture, when you were a child?

It's a war to eradicate the basic texts, meaning children's stories, the myths and fairy tales of every non-white culture. Carolyn See in the pages of the *Los Angeles Times*, and her daughter Lisa See in *Publisher's Weekly*, ridicule all the Chinese students who say Amy Tan's portrayal of the Kitchen god is not Chinese in her novel "The Kitchen God's Wife." The racist act is the white ladies saying the Chinese lie about

Chinese culture, and only the Christian Amy Tan, and Maxine Hong Kingston, and David Henry Hwang tell the truth of Chinese fairy tales. No white has ever experienced being despised out of the pages of the hometown paper and a trade magazine with such utter contempt for their race and fairy tale as the Chinese Americans who read the See's and the white reviewers who love the Gunga Dins with racist love, repeating the Kingston, Hwang and Tan versions of Chinese fairy tales that never existed anywhere except in white racist imagination.

The fact is, after consulting every known regional version of the Kitchen god story ever to have currency in China, that Amy Tan fakes it. The answer to her question as to why the Kitchen god's wife isn't honored is: she is. There are double posters of the Kitchen King and Kitchen Queen characteristic of parts of northern China. The Kitchen Queen's birthday is celebrated. Just check your copy of Werner's "Dictionary of Chinese Mythology." It's been a standard reference most of this century. Very difficult to avoid.

As writers who use the myth and fairy tale and storytelling forms and traditions of the immigrant founders of a new and another American people, we have a stake in defending the essential works of the literary traditions we crunch into art in our work. If we lose the works, or lose the notion of text to goofy demagoguery or ideology, we lose our art.

The question of whether or not African and Afro-American culture teaches men to be misogynist brutes and black women to be mystic victims that splits Ishmael Reed and Alice Walker is easily resolved by consulting the Afro-American fairy tales. They either encourage black men to be stupid and beat on women and women to take it, or they don't.

I asked Ishmael Reed to tell stories with his daughter Tennessee to the kids in my family of Chinese and Japanese Americans in Oakland one weekend of the Chinese New Year. He told a Brother Rabbit story and a story from Africa. Who would you trust to tell stories of another people to your kids?

What if a kid goes up to you and asks if "Little Black Sambo" is a real Afro-American kid story, and you don't know what to answer or how to find out? How deep would your appreciation of the work of any black writer be? Most of us know "Little Black Sambo" is an offense to Afro-Americans and a crime to teach kids in school as an example of Afro-American culture. So, what do you say when a kid asks you if the popular kid's book "The Five Chinese Brothers," now "The Seven Chinese Brothers," is a real Chinese story? Don't feel bad. Most Chinese Americans, most Asian Americans, know the story and can't answer the question either. In fact, Asian American catalog houses sell "The Five Chinese Brothers" and "The Seven Chinese Brothers" on their children's book list. If they could answer the question they would never have been fooled by the likes of Kingston, Hwang and Tan, and Gus Lee and on and on, one Christian soldier after the other.

Brothers and sisters of the gallant pen we can write and write and write ourselves into high gah gah, into the sublime, into joys beyond the reach of others, but our meaning, our genius, goes only as deep as our fairy tales. We have an interest in seeing the traditional children's lit—the fairy tales, myths and heroic epics and adventures of our people—reach all American children, our children while they're kids, and be taught in grade school with the children's lit from the European tradition.

If our peoples have no literary tradition, no texts, no body of fairy tales and myth crunching the meaning of ethics, the individual, the family, the state, the world, right and wrong, the real and the fake in stories our kids have understood and taught for a thousand years whether the authorities of the state liked it or not, our peoples have no culture and can't really call themselves a people. The oral tradition is a text, not a license to fake it. To fake these stories is a crime. A *Griot* who flubbed was killed as a criminal. That's the way it is. That's the way it should be. Would you tolerate faking the Brother Rabbit story, "The Tar Baby," of the Gullah people? Brother Rabbit teaches that life is war, and all behavior is tactics and strategy, just like the Chinese fairy tales. Brother Rabbit is an independent individual who makes it on reading the scene for strategic and tactical advantages and dangers. Far from being paranoid about it, Brother Rabbit moves through the world with a friendly wariness, so he is polite and friendly to the tar baby, and not hostile and frightened by this foreigner. The Grimm's "Rumpelstiltskin" on the other hand teaches conformity to a state hierarchy, and that all foreigners are to be treated with suspicion and contempt and are to be taken advantage of, lied to and betrayed and driven away.

It's simple enough for us to make the difference between the real and the fake and make a stand on the real: Tell a fairy tale of your people that can be verified by going to your people's work and history. Tell a few fairy tales you don't want to see forgotten and faked. Take a day off from your ego, your style, your genius and go home to the kid story, and tell kid stories to kids. If our genius, our wit, our licks don't have their seeds in the kid stories of our childhood, we have no people, no history, only the victim culture spawned by the white sociology, and the perpetual Hollywood stereotype of your people and mine. Brother Rabbit is no victim, no sociological animal datum. The Old Woman who chased her dumpling and got the *Oni* to laugh did not hate herself or her people. You know your people's stories. You know what they teach. You know the difference between the real and the fake. Brothers and sisters of the gallant pen, let's get our kids together and rendezvous, swap some home cooking, and tell each other stories till the fire burns down to a smolder, the coyotes sing, and the moon is high. Whaddaya say? Whaddaya know? Kingdoms rise and fall. Nations come and go.

The Old Woman and Her Dumpling[1]

Long, long ago there was a funny old woman, who liked to laugh and to make dumplings of rice-flour.

One day, while she was preparing some dumplings for dinner, she let one fall; and it rolled into a hole in the earthen floor of her little kitchen and disappeared. The old woman tried to reach it by putting her hand down the hole, and all at once the earth gave way, and the old woman fell in.

She fell quite a distance, but was not a bit hurt; and when she got up on her feet again, she saw that she was standing on a road, just like the road before her house. It was quite light down there; and she could see plenty of rice-fields, but no one in them. How all this happened, I cannot tell you. But it seems that the old woman had fallen into another country.

The road she had fallen upon sloped very much. So, after having looked for her dumpling in vain, she thought that it must have rolled farther away down the slope. She ran down the road to look, crying:

"My dumpling, my dumpling! Where is that dumpling of mine?"

After a little while she saw a stone *Jizo*[2] standing by the roadside, and she said: "O Lord *Jizo*, did you see my dumpling?"

Jizo answered:

"Yes, I saw your dumpling rolling by me down the road. But you had better not go any farther, because there is a wicked *Oni*[3] living down there, who eats people."

But she only laughed, and ran on, still crying out: "My dumpling, my dumpling! Where is that dumpling of mine?" And she came to a third *Jizo*, and asked it: "O dear Lord *Jizo*, did you see my dumpling?"

But *Jizo* said:

"Don't talk about your dumpling now. Here is the *Oni* coming. Squat down here behind my sleeves, and don't make any noise."

Presently the *Oni* came very close, and stopped and bowed to *Jizo*, and said: "Good-day, *Jizo-san!*"

Jizo said good-day, too, very politely.

Then the *Oni* suddenly snuffed the air two or three times in a suspicious way, and cried out: "*Jizo-san, Jizo-san!* I smell a smell of mankind somewhere—don't you?

1. This adaptation is taken from Hearn, Lafcadio, trans. *The Old Woman and Her Dumpling*. Mt. Vernon, NY: Peter Pauper Press, 1948.
2. *Jizo* is the god of wayfarers and children. Stone *Jizos* are found along the roadsides of Japan. Women buy little *Jizos* and leave them at *Jizo's* temple, asking *Jizo* to protect their aborted children in the next world.
3. a type of demon

"Oh!" said *Jizo*, "perhaps you are mistaken."

"No, no!" said the *Oni* after snuffling the air again, "I smell a smell of mankind."

Then the old woman could not help laughing—"Te-he-he!"—and the *Oni* immediately reached down his big hairy hand behind *Jizo's* sleeve and pulled her out, still laughing, "Te-he-he!"

"Ah! ha!" cried the *Oni*.

Then *Jizo* said:

"What are you going to do with that good old woman? You must not hurt her."

"I won't," said the *Oni*. "But I will take her home with me to cook for us."

"Te-he-he!" laughed the old woman.

"Very well," said *Jizo*; "But you must really be kind to her. If you are not, I shall be very angry."

"I won't hurt her at all," promised the *Oni*; "and she will only have to do a little work for us every day. Good-bye, *Jizo-san*."

Then the *Oni* took the old woman far down the road, till they came to a wide deep river, where there was a boat. He put her into the boat, and took her across the river to his house. It was a very large house. He led her at once into the kitchen, and told her to cook some dinner for himself and the other *Oni* who lived with him.

And he gave her a small wooden rice-paddle, and said:

"You must always put only one grain of rice into the pot, and when you stir that one grain of rice in the water with this paddle, the grain will multiply until the pot is full."

So the old woman put just one rice-grain into the pot, as the *Oni* told her, and began to stir it with the paddle; and, as she stirred, the one grain became two, then four, then eight, then sixteen, thirty-two, sixty-four, and so on. Every time she moved the paddle the rice increased in quantity, and in a few minutes the great pot was full.

After that, the funny old woman stayed a long time in the house of the *Oni*, and every day cooked for him and for all his friends. The *Oni* never hurt or frightened her, and her work was made quite easy by the magic paddle—although she had to cook a very, very great quantity of rice, because an *Oni* eats much more than any human being eats.

But she felt lonely, and always wished very much to go back to her own little house, and make her dumplings. And one day, when the *Oni* were all out somewhere, she thought she would try to run away.

She first took the magic paddle, and slipped it under her girdle; and then she went down to the river. No one saw her, and the boat was there. She got into it, and pushed off, and as she could row very well, she was soon far away from the shore.

But the river was very wide and she had not rowed more than one-fourth of the way across, when the *Oni*, all of them, came back to the house. They found that their cook was gone, and the magic paddle too. They ran down to the river at once and saw the old woman rowing away very fast.

Perhaps they could not swim. At all events they had no boat and they thought the only way they could catch the funny old woman would be to drink up all the water of the river before she got to the other bank. So they knelt down, and began to drink so fast that before the old woman had got half way over the water had become quite low.

But the old woman kept on rowing until the water had got so shallow that the *Oni* stopped drinking, and began to wade across. Then she dropped her oar, took the magic paddle from her girdle, and shook it at the *Oni*, and made such funny faces that the *Oni* all burst out laughing.

But the moment they laughed, they could not help throwing up all the water they had drunk, and so the river became full again.

The *Oni* could not cross; and the funny old woman got safely over to the other side, and ran away up the road as fast as she could.

She never stopped running until she found herself at home again.

After that she was very happy; for she could make dumplings whenever she pleased. Besides, she had the magic paddle to make rice for her. She sold her dumplings to her neighbors and passengers, and in a very short time she became rich.

The Woman Who Makes Swell Doughnuts

There is nothing I like to do better than to go to her house and knock on the door and when she opens the door, to go in. It is one of the experiences I will long remember—perhaps the only immortality that I will ever be lucky to meet in my short life—and when I say experience I do not mean the actual movement, the motor of our lives. I mean by experience the dancing of emotions before our eyes and inside of us, the dance that is still but is the roar and the force capable of stirring the heart and the people.

Of course, she, the woman I visit, is old and of her youthful beauty there is little left. Her face of today is coarse with hard water and there is no question that she has lived her life: given birth to six children, worked side by side with her man for forty years, working in the fields, working in the house, caring for the grandchildren, facing the summers and winters and also the springs and autumns running the household that is completely her little world. And when I came on the scene, when I discovered her in her little house on Seventh Street, all of her life was behind, all of her task in this world was tabbed, looked into, thoroughly attended, and all that is before her in life and the world, all that could be before her now was to sit and be served; duty done, work done, time clock punched; old-age pension or old-age security; easy chair; soft serene hours till death take her. But this was not of her, not the least bit of her.

When I visit her she takes me to the coziest chair in the living room where her magazines and books in Japanese and English are. "Sit down," she says. "Make yourself comfortable. I will come back with some hot doughnuts just out of oil."

And before I can turn a page of a magazine she is back with a plateful of hot doughnuts. There is nothing I can do to describe her doughnut: it is in a class by itself, without words, without demonstration. It is a doughnut, just a plain doughnut just out of oil, but it is different, unique. Perhaps when I am eating her doughnuts I am really eating her; I have this foolish notion in my head many times and whenever I catch myself doing so I say, that is not so, that is not true. Her doughnuts really taste swell, she is the best cook I have ever known, Oriental dishes or American dishes.

I bow humbly that such a room, such a house exists in my neighborhood so I may dash in and out when my spirit wanes, when hell is loose. I sing gratefully that such a simple common experience becomes an event, an event of necessity and growth. It is an event that is part of me, an addition to the elements of the earth, water, fire and air, and I seek the day when it will become a part of everyone.

All her friends, old and young, call her Mama. Everybody calls her Mama. That is not new, it is logical. I suppose there is in every block of every city in America a woman who can be called Mama by her friends and the strangers meeting her. This is commonplace, it is not new and the old sentimentality may be the undoing of the moniker. But what of a woman who isn't a mama but is, and instead of priding in the expansion of her little world, takes her little circle, living out her days in the little circle, perhaps never to be exploited in a biography or on everybody's tongue, but closed, shut, excluded from world news and newsreels; just sitting, just moving, just alive, planting the plants in the fields, caring for the children and the grandchildren and baking the tastiest doughnuts this side of the next world.

When I sit with her I do not need to ask deep questions, I do not need to know Plato or The Sacred Books of the East or dancing. I do not need to be on guard. But I am on guard and foot-loose because the room is alive.

"Where are the grandchildren?" I say. "Where are Mickey, Tadao, and Yaeko?"

"They are out in the yard," she says: "I say to them, play, play hard, go out there and play hard. You will be glad later for everything you have done with all your might."

Sometimes we sit many minutes in silence. Silence does not bother her. She says silence is the most beautiful symphony, she says the air breathed in silence is sweeter and sadder. That is about all we talk of. Sometimes I sit and gaze out the window and watch the Southern Pacific trains rumble by and the vehicles whiz with speed. And sometimes she catches me doing this and she nods her head and I know she understands that I think the silence in the room is great, and also the roar and the dust of the outside is great, and when she is nodding I understand that she is saying that this, her little room, her little circle is a depot, a pause, for the weary traveler, but outside, outside of her little world there is dissonance, hugeness of another kind, and the travel to do. So she has her little house, she bakes the grandest doughnuts, and inside of her she houses a little depot.

Most stories would end with her death, would wait till she is peacefully dead and peacefully at rest but I cannot wait that long. I think she will grow, and her hot doughnuts just out of the oil will grow with softness and touch. And I think it would be a shame to talk of her doughnuts just after she is dead, after she is formless.

Instead I take today to talk of her and her wonderful doughnuts when the earth is something to her, when the people from all parts of the earth may drop in and taste the flavor, her flavor, which is everyone's and all flavor; talk to her, sit with her, and also taste of the silence of her room and the silence that is herself; and finally go away to hope and keep alive what is alive in her, on earth and in men, expressly myself.

Maxine Hong Kingston

(b. 1940)

Maxine Hong Kingston was born in Stockton, California. Her book about her female Chinese ancestors, **The Woman Warrior: Memoirs of a Girlhood among Ghosts** *(1976), won the National Book Critics Circle Award for nonfiction, and* **China Men** *(1980), a study of male ancestors, won the National Book Award for nonfiction. Her first novel,* **Tripmaster Monkey: His Fake Book**, *a novel essentially about literary Asian America, was published in 1989. She graduated from the University of California at Berkeley in 1962 and lived and taught in Hawaii before returning to Berkeley where she presently teaches.*

King-Kok Cheung notes in her book **Articulate Silences** *(1993) that,*

> *The forms of double-voicing noted in* **The Woman Warrior**—*her overlapping awareness of gender and race and her mediation between facts and fiction—do have parallels in* **China Men**. *Even at the moment she portrays the emasculation of her Chinese fathers, she hints at patriarchal abuses within Chinese culture. She shuttles between facts and fantasies in both books, but whereas the strategy is used in* **The Woman Warrior** *to forge a matrilineage through the female tradition of talk story, here it is used to challenge the authority of "facts" and to reclaim through imagination a buried cultural biography.*

The Making of More Americans

With no map sense, I took a trip by myself to San Francisco Chinatown and got lost in the Big City. Wandering in a place very different from our own brown and gray Chinatown, I suddenly heard my own real aunt calling my name. She was my youngest aunt, my modern aunt just come from Hong Kong. We screamed at each other the way our villagers do, hugged, held hands. "Have you had your rice yet?" we shouted. "I have. I have had my rice." "Me too. I've eaten too," letting the whole strange street know we had eaten, and me becoming part of the street, abruptly not a tourist, the street mine to shout in, never mind if my accent be different. She had been talking with a couple of women, to whom I said, "Hello, Aunt. Hello, Aunt," mumbling because there are different kinds of aunts depending on whether they're older or younger than one's mother. They'd tease you for being too distant, for addressing them as Lady or Mademoiselle, affectations, and also for being familiar.

"Who is this?" the women asked, one of them pointing at me with her chin, the other with her rolled up newspaper. This talking about me in the third person, this pointing at me—I shoved the resentment down my throat. They do not mean disdain—

or they *do* mean disdain, but it's their proper way of treating young people. Mustn't dislike them for it.

"This is my own actual niece come to visit me," my aunt said, as if I had planned to run into her all along. The women were to understand that I was not just somebody she called a niece out of politeness, but a blood niece. "Come see my new apartment," she said to me, turned around, and entered the doorway near which we were standing.

I followed her up the stairs, flight after flight, and along a hallway like a tunnel. But her apartment need not be dismal, I thought; these doors could open into surprisingly large, bright, airy apartments with shag carpets. "Our apartment is very small," she warned, her voice leading the way. "Not like a regular house. Not like your mother's big house." So she noticed space; I had thought perhaps people from Hong Kong didn't need room, that Chinese people preferred small spaces. Some early mornings if we went down into our basement, we found two straight-backed chairs facing one another, blankets and shawls still cupped in shapes of the women who had sat there. The cord of the electric heater rose to a ceiling socket. Coffee cups and footstools sat on the floor. Our mother and this aunt had stayed up all night talking again. I might have known from the good times they could have in the basement that it would be the smallest apartment I had seen in my life. The door didn't open up all the way because of a table, which had stuff stored on top and underneath. The half of the table away from the wall was cleared for eating and studying.

"Coffee? Tea?" Auntie asked.

"Coffee," I said. "Black."

"How can you drink it like that? How about some meat? Fish?"

"MaMa has started drinking it black," I said, giving her the news. "MaMa has switched to black at her age."

Big and medium-sized blonde dolls sat and stood on tops of stacks of things. Their pink gauze dresses fluffed against the cellophane windows of their cardboard boxes. They were expensive dolls with little socks and gloves, purses and hats. I felt very relieved that my cousin, who was about ten or twelve years old, did not have to share one doll, the naked kind that one had to make clothes out of scraps for; she had two bride dolls. My relatives were not bad off, not as poor as we used to be. They had luxuries.

Auntie went into the kitchen, which did not have room for another person. I snooped about at the desk in one corner of the living room; looked at the desk calendar and the statuettes of the guardians of Happiness, Money, and Long Life, read the appointments pinned among the cut-outs of flowers on the wall. It was this aunt who had given my mother a nice set of the guardians mounted on wood and red velvet. There were some Christian pamphlets on a shelf over the desk; I couldn't remember whether this was the aunt who had converted to Christianity and was sending my parents tracts and Bibles or whether it was another aunt in Hong Kong who was sending to both of them. Or maybe she'd been accosted by a missionary working Chinatown. ("Are you a Christian?" my mother asks periodically. "No, of course not." "That's good. Don't be a Christian. What *do* you believe in?" "No religion. Nothing." "Why don't you take the Chinese religion, then?" And a few minutes later, "Yes, you do that," she'd say. "Sure, Mom. Okay.") Next to the telephone were notebooks, pads, very sharp pencils, a pencil sharpener, another luxury. They had shaving lotion and hand lotion, toiletries on the shelf too.

"The bathroom is over there," she shouted as if it were a huge house. I went into the bathroom, which was the closet next to the kitchen, to spy some more. They had built shelves with stores of sale toilet paper and soap, which was in fancy shapes prettily boxed. They aren't so poor, I thought. They are above subsistence; we have been worse off.

I stood by the kitchen door and watched my aunt cut cake. A corner of the floor was stacked with shiny gallon cans without labels. "My husband baked these cakes," she said. *Hus-u-bun*, she called him, a clever solution; some wives get so embarrassed about what to call their husbands, their names and *husband* such intimate words (like *rooster*—or *cock*), that they call him So-and-so's Father. My uncle worked at a famous bakery whose name is stamped on pink boxes that people carry about Chinatown.

"Cake?" asked my aunt. "Pie? Chuck-who-luck? Le-mun?"

"I just ate," I said, which was true, but took a plate anyway. The biggest difference between my aunt and my mother was that my mother would have forced me to eat it. I sat on the sofa, facing the front door. There was another door near the desk; it must have been to the next apartment.

Auntie got herself some chocolate cake and lemon pie and sat next to me. I enjoyed looking at this aunt, who was how my mother would have been if she were the youngest instead of the oldest, the city woman rather than the peasant. She was wearing a white blouse with sharp lapels; I also liked the straight gray skirt and intelligent glasses.

"I saw those hoppies they tell about in the newspaper," she said. "Some of them talked to me. 'Spare change?' What does 'spare change' mean?" "They're asking if you have extra money." "Oh-h, I see," she said, laughing. "'Spare change?' How witty." She was silly compared to my mother. She giggled and talked about inconsequentials. "Condo," she would way. "Cottage cheese. Football? Foosball?"

But here I was alone with her, and no adults to distract her; maybe I could ask her things, two equal adults, talk the way Americans talk. Talk grown-up. "Is it hard to endure?" I asked like an old Chinese lady, but because I was not brave enough to hear the answer, quickly said on top of it, "Where did you go? Were you grocery shopping? Going for a walk? Visiting neighbors?"

"I was coming from the beauty parlor, getting my hair done," she said, and I wished that I had noticed to compliment her on how nice she looked, but her hair looked the way she always wore it, in stiff black curls. "Otherwise, it wouldn't be this black," she said. "It's really white, you know." She went to beauty parlors. Another luxury, I enumerated. Leisure.

"Are you working?" I asked because it was odd that she was having her hair done in the middle of a workday. "Is it your day off?"

"No. I'm not working any more."

"What happened to your hotel job? Didn't you have a hotel job? As a maid?" I said *maid* in English, not knowing the Chinese word except for *slave*. If she didn't know the word, she wouldn't hear it anyway. Languages are like that.

"I've been fired," she said.

"Oh, no. But why?"

"I've been very sick. High blood pressure," she said. "And I got dizzy working. I had to clean sixteen rooms in eight hours. I was too sick to work that fast." Something else I liked about this aunt was her use of exact numbers. "Ten thousand rooms per second," my mother would have said. "Uncountable. Infinite." Half an hour per unit, including bathrooms. "People leave the rooms very messy," she said, "and I kept coughing from the ashes in the ashtrays. I was efficient until I fell sick. Once I was out for six weeks, but when I came back, the head housekeeper said I was doing a good job, and he kept me on." She worked at a famous hotel, not a flop house in Chinatown. She'd given us miniature cakes of soap whenever she came to visit. "The head housekeeper said I was an excellent worker." My mother was the same way, caring tremendously how her employer praised her, never so hurt as when a boss reprimanded her, never so proud as when a forelady said she was picking cleanly and fast. "He said I speak English very well," Auntie said. She was proud of that compliment.

"What do you do all day long now that you aren't cleaning hotel rooms?"

"The days go by very slowly. You know, in these difficult times in the Big City mothers can't leave their children alone. The kidnappers are getting two thousand dollars per child. And whoever reports a missing child the FBI turns over to Immigration. So I posted ads, and one in the newspaper too, that I wanted to mind children, but I haven't gotten any customers. When the mothers see the apartment, they say No." Of course. No place to run, no yard, no trees, no toys except to look at the dollies. Being poor in Stockton was better than this Big City poverty; we had trees and sloughs and vegetable gardens and animals. Also there were jobs in the fields. "I could mind four or five children," she said. "I'd make as much money as cleaning the hotel. They don't want me to watch their children because I can't speak English."

"But you do," I said. "You know lots of English." When I could not think of the Chinese for something, she always knew the English word.

She was flattered. "No, I don't," she said. "Now, *you* speak Chinese well," but I was speaking well because I was talking to her; there are people who dry up language.

"You speak like your mother. She used to sound like a city person, but American people speak peasant accents, village accents, so she talks that way now."

"Do my mother and father speak alike?"

"Why, yes," she said, but maybe she couldn't hear the difference; being a city person she lumped the village accents together.

"My own son doesn't talk to me," she said. "What's *nutrition*?"

"It has to do with food and what people ought to eat to keep healthy."

"You mean like cooking? He's going to college to learn how to cook?"

"Well, no. It's planning menus for big companies, like schools and hospitals and the Army. They study food to see how it works. It's the science of food," but I did not feel I was giving an adequate derivative of *magic*, something like *alchemy*. "He could work in public health, and that's a field that has lots of jobs right now. He could work for cafeterias and college dormitories, restaurant chains, mass production food plants that make frozen TV dinners, canned foods, cake mixes."

"And *engineering*?" she asked.

"Building things, designing them, like designing bridges and mines and electrical things. Do you know what kind of engineering he's studying?"

"No, they shout at me and tell me I'm too stupid to understand. They hardly come home, and when I ask them what they're doing, they say I'm dumb. Oh, my sons have turned out very bad, and after all I've suffered for them."

I did not want to hear how she suffered, and then I did. I did have a duty to hear it and remember it. She started by telling me how my mother had suffered. "Oh, the suffering," she said. "Think of it. Both of your mother's babies died. How painful it must be to watch your babies die after they can walk and talk and have personalities. Aiya! How hard to endure."

"What did they die of?"

"Firecrackers. The village women exploded firecrackers to scare germs and bed spirits away, but instead they scared away the babies. They filled the air with smoke so the babies couldn't breathe. And then a few years later, it happened again; when you were a baby, you suddenly stopped breathing, and she pounded on the floor for the downstairs neighbor to help. The fire trucks and the police came, and they revived you. She wrote to me about that."

"Probably all the babies, having recently been nothing, have a tenuous hold on life," I observed. MaMa would have sat on the floor and held the babies to her or laid them on blankets in the middle of the house. I remembered the floor, the linoleum patterns and smells of it. Under the linoleum I had hidden milk bottle caps, flattening into lovely disks.

In the falling afternoon, I looked out the windows at the neighbors' windows. For a short while light had pushed through the curtains making little suns and a haze. We faced west and caught the last pale sun. The fog rolled between the buildings, and the foghorns were sounding already. My aunt made no move to switch on the lights. Her eyes were very bright. It aggravated me how easily tears came to women her age, not hardened at all by the years. "I suffered terribly too," she said. I would never be able to talk with them; I have no stories of equal pain.

Now she was telling her part of the story: When she was born, the blind fortuneteller said that she would be alternately very rich and very poor many times but end up rich. Sure enough, they were poor until her father went to the Gold Mountain, whence he traveled three times; each time he got richer and twice brought back wives. He hired teachers for his daughters, who learned to read and write. Between his trips they were poor. He died when she was ten. She was poor from then until she married a rich man. When Communism transformed the villagers, they chased her family out of their house. She hid with her two boys in the pig house. It was winter, and all they had on were cotton clothes. The boys knew better than to cry, learned instantly. The next morning, she found her husband. He said that the Communists had assigned them to a place to live—the leper house. "That's where you belong," said the Communists. Lepers, the "growing yin" people, who have too much cold wind in them, died in there. The rest of the family had disappeared; his mother had run away alone with the gold and jade. They never saw her again. The Communists kept an eye on them in the leper house, waited for them to make a false move. One day her husband caught a pair of doves and hid them to feed the family. "And do you know how the Communists killed him?"

"I think my mother said they stoned him in the tree where the birds were."

"They pressed him between millstones," she said.

Of course. In stories, stones fall crash bang crash bang like pile drivers. It was the sound of harvest and executions. After battle, no matter what farmhouse or courtyard a villain or hero used, when it was time for executions, he always had a device handy—the millstones.

"Aiya," I said. "That's horrible. How hard to endure."

Then she escaped to Hong Kong. She gave her wedding ring to get on the ship, her earrings for food, her necklace to get off the ship. She and the two boys slept on the sidewalks; they ate the rice they begged though the Communists threw sand into it, saying "Have some salt." The oldest boy, Big Baby she called him, and her second son, Little Baby, got angry at her when they were hungry or too hot or too cold. "What did you do today?" she asked them after separating to beg on different streets. "What do you care?" they said. "What do you know?"

She noticed a man who was selling shoes alone in a stall. She bade him "Good morning" daily and thus made his acquaintance. He let her sit in the customer's chair under the awning in rain and in the noon sun. Whenever he shared his lunch with her, she hid some for the boys. One day she said—she said it for me with a giggle— "Sir, why doesn't your lady come help you work these long hours?" (Hong Kong people are more refined than us and don't say *old lady* for *wife* or *old rooster* for *husband*.)

"I don't have a lady," he said.

"I'll help you then," she said, and did so. Soon they got married, the first self-matched marriage in the family. They built the stall up into a store, then added a wholesale outlet, then a factory, and she was rich again. They had a boy and a girl of their own, much younger than the other two.

But she did not forget the accurate blind fortuneteller: a downfall imminent. The people who lived in crates on the hillsides and the boat people who had never touched land would soon rise up and kill the rich people and the British. There are rich people who don't see poor people, but she never stopped seeing them. She took varying routes from home to store so the beggars wouldn't recognize her and mark her. "The Revolution is coming," she kept saying, and her husband agreed, "Yes, it's going to happened," but went on building his business. Each downfall had been worse than the last—the Japanese, then World War II, then the Revolution. "The Hong Kong Revolution will be fought with nuclear bombs," she predicted. Her husband called her a superstitious peasant.

At last she said, "My name is at the top of the Refugee List. Let's leave for the United States." But her husband did not want to go; the business was doing very well. He told her that if she went, she would have to go alone. She took the two older boys and left him with the daughter and son. "Badger him to bring you to the Gold Mountain," she instructed these two youngest, and left.

"Father," they said with their little arms out supplicating, the boy especially naughty, "take us to the Gold Mountain. We want to see Ah Ma. Why won't you take us? Do you want us to get killed by Communists? Ah Ba, take us to America and buy us some American toys. You're a selfish father not to take us traveling. All right then. When we're old enough, we're leaving you. We'll go find her. You're cheap, that's why you won't take us."

My mother showed her the street corners where she was to wait for the farm buses to take her to the tomatoes and grapes. Yes, life in America was meaner, but no signs of revolution; the beggars in the street were young and fat "hoppies," who begged for fun. She hoped that this Gold Mountain poverty counted for the next fall in her fortunes. Her husband wrote that he was definitely not about to leave his homeland and his family. And didn't she miss having servants and friends talking her own language? She suggested that he not sell the shoe store but export the shoes to the United States, send them to her here. She had already gotten her American relatives to promise to take cases of sample shoes from store to store. She said a war in Indochina was going to spread to other Asian countries, and the Pentagon would bomb China. She outwrote him. He said, "All right. I'm coming to the United States, but only to have a look at it and to bring you back."

He brought the two younger children with him. What luxury, I thought. World travel. No more deciding once and for all on a country sight unseen. He took one look at the Los Angeles International Airport, and said, "Let's go back." But she said to give the Gold Mountain a chance. Be a tourist. Take a vacation. For a couple of months he complained how there were no jobs, then how hard he had to work, and how he had to obey a boss. Both of them complained about doing hard work for only a fraction of the money they were making in Hong Kong.

I remember they rented a house with peeling and flaking paint; they did not plaster the cracks, did not hang curtains. They slept on the floor until my sister brought them mattresses. They used their suitcases instead of dressers. Chinese people are like that, we sisters and brothers told one another—no frills, cheap. My sister bought them sheets, then a bedspread. The two older boys, whom we refused to call Big BiBi and Little BiBi, did not talk to us but looked away if we caught their eyes, answered direct questions Yes or No, and never asked us questions in return. Like old uncles, they talked to our parents in Chinese. They were F.O.B.'s all right. Fresh Off the Boat.

The youngest boy was more sociable. He opened our refrigerator door and stood there and ate; he knocked over furniture and sassed his mother in two languages. He asked us questions, and his hair spiked up all over his head as if every hair were listening. "Why do you look like that?" "How do they do instant replay so fast?" "How much money do you make? Yeah, what's your salary?" But when we asked his name, he suddenly stood still. He and his sister looked at one another and down at their shoes. The girl, who was older, pointed to her brother and muttered something, and he turned red. "What?" I asked. She said it again. It was his Chinese name, and we could hardly hear it. "Her name is Lucille," he said. And *Lucille* was easy for him to say and easy to hear. He was proud to be able to give an American name though it wasn't his. So, they'd already learned to be shamed by a Chinese name.

When I Fu, Aunt's Husband, said, "I'm going back. You do as you please, but I'm going back," Auntie went with him. They took the two younger children. Our older cousins decided that they would stay in the United States; they were never going back; they would finish school, apply for citizenship, risk getting drafted—it was worth it. How foreign they were. Another generation of heartless boys leaving their family. Only my mother and aunt showed regret at leaving each other.

My mother nagged her nephews if they took any time off from work and study whatsoever. "My own children study all the time," she scolded, to which the F.O.B.'s replied, "They must not be very bright if they have to study that hard." She told us that retort, stirring up suspicions, establishing a pecking order, which must have been the way in China. They lived down in our basement with a bare light bulb. They were not to put their belongings in our closets or drawers, nor to ride our bikes or watch our TV or listen to the radios. MaMa said, "They're not my children." When they come home from school or from the grocery store, where they worked for twenty-five cents an hour, they were to go to the cellar.

Meanwhile in Hong Kong, Auntie was enjoying another one of her high fortunes. But one day I Fu stood up from a customer's feet and told a clerk to finish up. A surge of chemicals or light had rushed through him. He went back to his office and unlocked his desk. He walked to the bank. The walk he took was magical: Inanimate objects glowed, but, oh, the animate—the trees and flowers and bugs and dogs were spraying colors. Human beings flared haloes around their heads and the rest of their bodies. Bands of light connected couples. He explained later how he understood the stopping quality of red light and the go of green. The city was not making a general roar or hum. His ears separated out the sounds of various motors, the gas pipes and water mains under the city, each bicycle wheel, the way the rubber peeled off the asphalt. It was a good thing it had been a sunny seaport day and not San Francisco; a foghorn would have melted him with sorrow. He passed a bookstore. Jets of colored lights jumped along the books' spines; he wanted to stop and see whether *Red Chamber Dream* and Communist books were red, the Clear River poems blue and green, Confucius's writings a white light, and the *I Ching* yellow or saffron, but he had to hurry on. The seats, handlegrips, and pedals of the pedicabs and bicycles pulsed like fire. The newspapers were aflame in reds and oranges. He passed a drugstore and saw the little drawers leaking squares of light.

At the bank, he filled out a withdrawal slip with the very figure that was the last balance in his account. He said later those digits had had a numerological significance. He took the money in cash—and money had its own brilliance. It was so much money, the bank let him keep the canvas bag to carry it in. The teller and manager asked if he were certain he didn't want a check or money order, and he said Yes. He liked the feeling of the Yes escaping warm out of his body. He also liked voices warming his ears. He would have to remember to go to the theater more often. He carried the money through the streets. He was certain that thieves would not snatch it; he was choreographing the movements of people and the weather. Time and fate were his invention and under the control of his will. He walked into a part of Hong Kong where he had never gone before, but he knew where to go. Fences made out of air guided his way. He entered the correct building and in the elevator knew which floor to choose. He walked through a particular door into a particular room. There were several men he had never seen before, but he knew just which one to approach and what to say. He gave this man all the money he had in the world. He walked out. Free of money. Free of burden. Purpose fulfilled. He flew home. "I can control the weather," he said earnestly. "You can too." His wife and the employees kept asking if he were all right. They planted in him the possibility of his not being all right.

"You look sick," his wife said.

"Stop saying that," he said, and he crashed down to normal. "I've been robbed," he said. "I've been robbed. I was drugged by the bandits that prey on Gold Mountain Sojourners. They slipped a drug into my lunch. And their post-hypnotic suggestion was for me to take all the money out of the bank. I gave it all to them. We're ruined. Why didn't you stop me?"

"What are you talking about?" my aunt asked. "That's impossible. A drug, you say? Hypnosis? How could I have stopped you? Is there such a drug? You gave all our money away? All of it? It wasn't gambling?"

"It was like sleepwalking," he said. "I could see everything; the world was the same, but the story behind it was different. I thought strangely. I thought it was a friend I gave the money to, that he was doing me a favor taking it." According to the passbook, which he found in his pocket, the account had been closed out. "Our life savings."

Husband and wife dashed outside trying to trace where he had walked. They ran about asking if anyone had seen him come this way. "Did you see me go by a little while ago?" "The bookstore," he said. "I remember it. And that drugstore." The unknown neighborhood had disappeared as if the bandits had set it up, then taken the buildings away. They ran to the bank, which was closed. They went to the police station, though they knew that the police were themselves crooks.

They and a policeman were at the doors when the bank opened in the morning. The teller who had waited on I Fu confirmed that he had been at that window the day before, and he had withdrawn all his money. "Was there anyone with him?" his wife asked. "Did you see anyone behind him? Could there have been someone behind him with a gun?" The tellers had not seen anyone. I Fu told the bank manager that he had been drugged or hypnotized to take out all his money and give it away. The bank manager could do nothing about that. "We don't insure against that," he said. Hong Kong was full of criminals, tricksters, shysters, cheaters, con artists, plotters. People made their living by eating other people, by catching pigs. At lunch, a customer who followed him to the back room might have waved a hand over I Fu's food, and the drug had poured down a sleeve or slipped out of a button or hinged ring. "Maybe so," said the policeman. Pig-catching was a game among the southern people. The shoe clerks and his relatives were probably in on it too, and the police too.

"We shouldn't have left the United States," Auntie complained. "American police and American people are honest."

When I Fu made change for the last customer of the day, when the bell dinged in the cash register, the spell came over him again. He scooped up the bills and put them in a shoe box. "Where are you going?" cried Auntie, alarmed at his pinpointy, jumpy eyes. "Where are you going? Stop it. You're doing it again. You told me to stop you. It's come over you again. Snap out of it. Put the money back. Give it to me. Wake up." She clapped her hands and shook him, but he pushed her aside "with superhuman strength," she said. "hold him," she called to the customers and employees. "He's under a spell. Don't let him go. He's got all the petty cash we have left in the world."

"Leave me alone," he said. "It's my money." He broke from their grasp and ran through the streets. The after-work crowds moved aside and closed behind him.

"Stop him. Stop him," Auntie and the employees called, but the people did not want to grab the wild man. Auntie hunted for him, but he had entered a side street into another world. She went back to the store, terrified at what the thieves were capable of.

I Fu returned, walking slowly; he looked fatigued, having been run about like a puppet. "Let's sell the shoe business," he said, giving in at last, "and go back to the United States." "Return," he said. "Return to the United States."

"Be warned not to travel to China," Auntie told me. "Chinese are crooks. Travelers disappear and are never heard of again."

My aunt and uncle sold their businesses before someone could trick them into signing them away. With that money, they went for the second time to the Gold Mountain, where they arrived no better off than other immigrants. They would never go back; they said good-bye properly, good-bye forever.

"He got the job at the bakery, and I got the one at the hotel," said Auntie. "But I've been sick and can't work any more."

"You look well."

"I get dizzy when I work. By the time I carry my vacuum cleaner and linens up the stairs, I'm so dizzy I have to lie down on the landing. High blood pressure. I'll not fly in an airplane again."

"Do you keep seeing a doctor?"

"Yes."

"The doctor gave you some pills?"

"Yes, but I'm not taking them. It's not the blood pressure that makes me dizzy; it's the pills. I've discovered a cure. The Chinatown women, who all have high blood pressure, say that fresh, unprocessed, pure honey is good for hypertension, and I've been drinking it by the quart. I'm going to get your mother started on the pure honey cure too. I feel so much better on the honey than the pills. Too many side effects with the pills."

"Is that honey in the cans in the kitchen?"

"Yes, I like to stock up when a fresh supply comes into Chinatown. It comes from a special farm with special bees."

"I think you ought to keep taking the pills," I said. "How does the honey have that effect?"

"I'm not sure. Maybe it smoothes out the blood so it takes less pressure to move through the veins."

There was no use talking her out of it. I would have to persuade my mother to continue taking the pills along with the honey.

"I'm glad you've decided to quit your job," I said. "You're lucky to be able to stay home and be a housewife."

"But I need a job badly, very badly. My husubun insists on one thing," she said. "He makes six hundred dollars a month. Exactly three hundred goes to China. He's a rescuer. Out of our three hundred dollars, we have to pay rent, food, clothes, everything. So you see why I have to get a job. He's been saying that I don't know how to save money, that I spend too much. He's so stingy; ever since I lost my job, he's been doing the grocery shopping himself. I had to refuse to cook until I got control of the grocery money again. I went on strike." She laughed. "Sometimes when the two of us are carrying the groceries home, he puts his bag down on the sidewalk and walks away swinging his arms free. I have to hurry home with my bag and run back for his before somebody takes it. Men from Kwangtung are arrogant like that. Independent."

"I'll cook if you stay for dinner," she added.

"I have to go," I said.

"Well, I know there isn't much room to play," she said, as if I were a child, or perhaps she meant "stroll" or "tour."

"No, it's not that. I have some tasks that I have to do. Was your apartment in Hong Kong bigger than this one?"

"No. No. About this size." Oh, such relief that the Chinese life they keep regretting leaving is no better than this.

"Do you want to move outside Tang People's Street?" I asked.

"No. No. Here my husubun can walk to and from work. He can wake up five minutes before the bakery opens and get there on time. And I can talk to the neighbors. The children walk across the street to Chinese school." I hoped that she was drawing the conclusion that she and her family were well off, that they were living in this room by choice, in a way.

"Stay for dinner," she urged. "There won't be good food, but stay."

"I can't," I said. "I have work to do."

"Then let me phone my husubun to bring home a cake for you."

"No, thank you. You don't need to do that. I just ate some cake."

"You can give it to someone, your brothers and sisters." She picked up the phone (another luxury, I counted) and called the bakery. "Bring a cake for my niece," she said. "The best kind—lemun kuk." "The bakery is just around the corner," she said to me. "He'll get off work in five minutes and be here in another minute or two."

It would only be polite to stay and say hello to my uncle. Also I wanted to take a good look at him after what I had heard about him. I did feel nervous that he would walk in angry at me for causing him to have to carry a lemon cake through the streets. A request right before closing time. What if he had to whip together a lemon cake on his own time or humble himself to ask the boss for a remainder cake, or worse yet, if he had to take it out of his pay? My mother would want me to protest a gift, argue and tussle, my aunt and I trying to give the cake away, running back and forth, her yelling, "All right, then, I take it back. No cake for you," tucking it into clothes, hiding it in bags, throwing it in and out of windows, pushing the windows up and down, pulling the box back and forth until I gave up and took it. Being rude because young and American, taking advantage of that, I planned to say "Thank you" and take the cake.

I Fu arrived at the front door at exactly 5:05, as I could see by the alarm clock on the desk. Watching the knob turn, I thought, What if he were filled with years of gall, furious from kneeling at people's feet and carrying groceries? He would be mad at me for making my aunt sit all afternoon, no dinner started. But he seemed ordinary, handing over the cake box, a man not particularly burdened by money, smiling, not wide-eyed on drugs, the *Gold Mountain Times* under his arm. I stood up, old enough to have manners without being told. "How do you do, I Fu?" I said, shaking his hand. He did not look like a tough businessman who had built and lost a shoe empire or one who could marry a flirtatious beggarwoman from off the street or dash through Hong Kong giving away bags of money. He asked me what I was doing in the Big City. He sat down, rolled the rubber band off his newspaper, shook it open, and began to read, exactly as my father would have done. He looked just like my father behind the newspaper, the very same newspaper, skinny legs and hands sticking out.

"Why don't you come visit my parents at Christmas time?" I invited my aunt, figuring out a way to leave.

Just then the door opened again, and my girl cousin came home. She glanced at me, startled, and headed straight for the locked door, which I had thought led to the next apartment. She bent and unlocked it with one of the keys on the chain around her neck. I could see inside; it was the children's room, larger than the rest of the apartment, girl's stuff in one half, boy's stuff in the other.

"Lucille," scolded my aunt. "Say hello to Big Sister."

"Hello," she said, her whole body leaning to get into her own room.

"Lucille is returning from Chinese school," said Auntie.

The only times I had ever gotten Lucille to sit down with me was when playing games; she methodically set out to win everything on the board, only talking to clarify a rule.

"I was trying to explain to Big Sister what your brothers are studying at college," said Auntie.

"Nutrition and engineering," said my cousin.

"I see," I said, wishing my aunt would let her go. I Fu could have said something from behind the newspaper, like "I'm a baker and didn't have to study nutrition," but he didn't.

"Where's your youngest son?" I asked my aunt, and while she answered, Lucille went quickly inside her room and locked it.

"In the streets I guess," Auntie said. "Sometimes he doesn't come home until all the stores and restaurants are closed." He was only about ten years old.

"What does he do out there all night?"

"I don't know. Explores."

"Aren't you afraid of kidnappers and gangs getting him?"

"Yes, of course, but there's nothing we can do about him."

I asked her, "Will you walk me a short distance and point out which way I ought to go?" I said good-bye to my uncle who looked up and said, "Leaving so soon?" My cousin did not come out of her room. Auntie and I walked for a block and a half until I recognized where I was, though the night and the street lights were coming on. We stood on a corner and shouted good-byes, me carrying a box of food with a red string, so Chinese, shouting and carrying food, shouting good-bye.

Amy Tan

(b. 1952)

*Amy Tan was born in Oakland, California, and was raised in Fresno, Oakland, and Berkeley. Tan is the author of two best-selling novels, **The Joy Luck Club** (1989) and **The Kitchen God's Wife** (1991). The Joy Luck Club was made into a movie in 1993, produced by Oliver Stone and directed by Wayne Wang. She is also the author of two children's books, **The Moon Lady** (1992) and **The Chinese Siamese Cat** (1994). The essay "Mother Tongue," reprinted here was selected for inclusion in **The Best American Essays of 1991** edited by Joyce Carol Oates.*

In the essay that follows, Tan legitimizes Chinese American English, the language spoken by her mother, as simply another American dialect and says that it should not be called "broken English."

> *To me, my mother's English is perfectly clear, perfectly natural. It's my mother tongue. Her language, as I hear it, is vivid, direct, full of observation and imagery. That was the language that helped shape the way I saw things, expressed things, made sense of the world.*

Mother Tongue

I am not a scholar of English or literature. I cannot give you much more than personal opinions on the English language and its variations in this country or others.

I am a writer. And by that definition, I am someone who has always loved language. I am fascinated by language in daily life. I spend a great deal of my time thinking about the power of language—the way it can evoke an emotion, a visual image, a complex idea, or a simple truth. Language is the tool of my trade. And I use them all—all the Englishes I grew up with.

Recently, I was made keenly aware of the different Englishes I do use. I was giving a talk to a large group of people, the same talk I had already given to half a dozen other groups. The nature of the talk was about my writing, my life, and my book, *The Joy Luck Club*. The talk was going along well enough, until I remembered one major difference that made the whole talk sound wrong. My mother was in the room. And it was perhaps the first time she had heard me give a lengthy speech, using the kind of English I have never used with her. I was saying things like, "The intersection of memory upon imagination" and "There is an aspect of my fiction that relates to thus-and-thus"—a speech filled with carefully wrought grammatical phrases, burdened, it suddenly seemed to me, with nominalized forms, past perfect tenses, conditional phrases, all the forms of standard English that I had learned in school and through books, the forms of English I did not use at home with my mother.

Just last week, I was walking down the street with my mother, and I again found myself conscious of the English I was using, the English I do use with her. We were talking about the price of new and used furniture and I heard myself saying this: "Not waste money that way." My husband was with us as well, and he didn't notice any switch in my English. And then I realized why. It's because over the twenty years we've been together I've often used that same kind of English with him, and sometimes he even uses it with me. It has become our language of intimacy, a different sort of English that relates to family talk, the language I grew up with.

So you'll have some idea of what this family talk I heard sounds like, I'll quote what my mother said during a recent conversation which I videotaped and then transcribed. During this conversation, my mother was talking about a political gangster in Shang-hai who had the same last name as her family's, Du, and how the gangster in his early years wanted to be adopted by her family, which was rich by comparison. Later, the gangster became more powerful, far richer than my mother's family, and one day showed up at my mother's wedding to pay his respects. Here's what she said in part:

"Du Yusong having business like fruit stand. Like off the street kind. He is Du like Du Zong—but not Tsung-ming Island people. The local people call putong, the river east side, he belong to that side local people. That man want to ask Du Zong father take him in like become own family. Du Zong father wasn't look down on him, but didn't take seriously, until that man beg like become mafia. Now important person, very hard to inviting him. Chinese way, came only to show respect, don't stay for dinner. Respect for making big celebration, he shows up. Mean gives lots of respect. Chinese custom. Chinese social life that way. If too important won't have to stay too long. He come to my wedding. I didn't see, I heard it. I gone to boy's side, they have YMCA dinner. Chinese age I was nineteen."

You should know that my mother's expressive command of English belies how much she actually understands. She reads the *Forbes* report, listens to *Wall Street Week*, converses daily with her stockbroker, reads all of Shirley MacLaine's books with ease—all kinds of things I can't begin to understand. Yet some of my friends tell me they understand 50 percent of what my mother says. Some say they understand 80 to 90 percent. Some say they understand none of it, as if she were speaking pure Chinese. But to me, my mother's English is perfectly clear, perfectly natural. It's my mother tongue. Her language, as I hear it, is vivid, direct, full of observation and imagery. That was the language that helped shape the way I saw things, expressed things, made sense of the world.

Lately, I've been giving more thought to the kind of English my mother speaks. Like others, I have described it to people as "broken" or "fractured" English. But I wince when I say that. It has always bothered me that I can think of no way to describe it other than "broken." as if it were damaged and needed to be fixed, as if it lacked a certain wholeness and soundness. I've heard other terms used, "limited English," for example. But they seem just as bad, as if everything is limited, including people's perceptions of the limited English speaker.

I know this for a fact, because when I was growing up, my mother's "limited" English limited *my* perception of her. I was ashamed of her English. I believed that her English reflected the quality of what she had to say. That is, because she expressed them imperfectly her thoughts were imperfect. And I had plenty of empirical evidence to support me: the fact that people in department stores, at banks, and at restaurants did not take her seriously, did not give her good service, pretended not to understand her, or even acted as if they did not hear her.

My mother has long realized the limitations of her English as well. When I was fifteen, she used to have me call people on the phone to pretend I was she. In this guise, I was forced to ask for information or even to complain and yell at people who had been rude to her. One time it was a call to her stockbroker in New York. She had cashed out her small portfolio and it just so happened we were going to go to New York the next week, our very first trip outside California. I had to get on the phone and say in an adolescent voice that was not very convincing, "This is Mrs. Tan."

And my mother was standing in the back whispering loudly, "Why he don't send me check, already two weeks late. So mad he lie to me, losing me money."

And then I said in perfect English, "Yes, I'm getting rather concerned. You had agreed to send the check two weeks ago, but it hasn't arrived."

Then she began to talk more loudly. "What he want, I come to New York tell him front of his boss, you cheating me?" And I was trying to calm her down, make her be quiet, while telling the stockbroker, "I can't tolerate any more excuses. If I don't receive the check immediately, I am going to have to speak to your manager when I'm in New York next week." And sure enough, the following week there we were in front of this astonished stock-broker, and I was sitting there red-faced and quiet, and my mother, the real Mrs. Tan, was shouting at his boss in her impeccable broken English.

We used a similar routine just five days ago, for a situation that was far less humorous. My mother had gone to the hospital for an appointment, to find out about a benign brain tumor a CAT scan had revealed a month ago. She said she had spoken very good English, her best English, no mistakes. Still, she said, the hospital did not apologize when they said they had lost the CAT scan and she had come for nothing. She said they did not seem to have any sympathy when she told them she was anxious to know the exact diagnosis, since her husband and son had both died of brain tumors. She said they would not give her any more information until the next time and she would have to make another appointment for that. So she said she would not leave until the doctor called her daughter. She wouldn't budge. And when the doctor finally called her daughter, me, who spoke in perfect English—lo and behold—we had assurances that CAT scan would be found, promises that a conference call on Monday would be held, and apologies for any suffering my mother had gone through for a most regrettable mistake.

I think my mother's English almost had an effect on limiting my possibilities in life as well. Sociologists and linguists probably will tell you that a person's developing language skills are more influenced by peers. But I do think that the language spoken in the family, especially in immigrant families which are more insular, plays a large role in shaping the language of the child. And I believe that it affected my results on achievement tests, IQ tests, and the SAT. While my English skills were never judged as poor, compared to math, English could not be considered my strong suit. In grade school I did moderately well, getting perhaps B's, sometimes B-pluses, in English and scoring perhaps in the sixtieth or seventieth percentile on achievement tests. But those scores were not good enough the override the opinion that my true abilities lay in math and science, because in those areas I achieved A's and scored in the ninetieth percentile or higher.

This was understandable. Math is precise; there is only one correct answer. Whereas, for me at least, the answers on English tests were always a judgment call, a matter of opinion and personal experience. Those tests were constructed around items like fill-in-the-blanks sentence completion, such as, "Even though Tom was _____, Mary thought he was _____." And the correct answer always seemed to be the most bland combinations of thoughts, for example, "Even thought Tom was shy, Mary thought he was charming," with the grammatical structure "even though" limiting the correct answer to some sort of semantic opposites, so you wouldn't get answers like, "Even though Tom was foolish, Mary thought he was ridiculous." Well, according to my mother, there were very few limitations as to what Tom could have been and what Mary might have thought of him. So I never did well on tests like that.

The same was true with word analogies, pairs of words in which you were supposed to find some sort of logical semantic relationship—for example, "*Sunset* is to *nightfall* as _____ is to _____." And here you would be presented with a list of four possible pairs, one of which showed the same kind of relationship: *red* is to *stoplight, bus* is to *arrival, chills* is to *fever, yawn*s is to *boring*. Well, I could never think that way. I knew what the tests were asking, but I could not block out of my mind the images already created by the first pair, "*sunset* is to *nightfall*"—and I would see a burst of colors against a darkening sky, the moon rising, the lowering of a curtain of stars. And all the other pairs of words—red, bus, stoplight, boring—just threw up a mass of confusing images, making it impossible for me to sort out something as logical as saying: "A sunset precedes nightfall" is the same as "a chill precedes a fever." The only way I would have gotten that answer right would have been to imagine an associative situation, for example, my being disobedient and staying out past sunset, catching a chill at night, which turns into a feverish pneumonia as punishment, which indeed did happen to me.

I have been thinking about all this lately, about my mother's English, about achievement tests. Because lately I've been asked as a writer, why there are not more Asian Americans represented in American literature. Why are there few Asian Americans enrolled in creative writing programs? Why do so many Chinese students go into engineering? Well, these are broad sociological questions I can't begin to answer. But I have noticed in surveys—in fact, just last week—that Asian students, as a whole, always do significantly better on math achievement tests than in English. And this makes me think that there are other Asian-American students whose English spoken in the home might also be described as "broken" or "limited." And perhaps they also have teachers who are steering them away from writing and into math and science, which is what happened to me.

Fortunately, I happen to be rebellious in nature and enjoy the challenge of disproving assumptions made about me. I became an English major my first year in college, after being enrolled as pre-med. I started writing nonfiction as a freelancer the week after I was told by my former boss that writing was my worst skill and I should hone my talents toward account management.

But it wasn't until 1985 that I finally began to write fiction. And at first I wrote using what I thought to be wittily crafted sentences, sentences that would finally prove I had mastery over the English language. Here's an example from the first draft of a story that later made its way into *The Joy Luck Club*, but without this line: "That was my mental quandary in its nascent state." A terrible line, which I can barely pronounce.

Fortunately, for reasons I won't get into today, I later decided I should envision a reader for the stories I would write. And the reader I decided upon was my mother, because these were stories about mothers. So with this reader in mind—and in fact she did read my early drafts—I began to write stories using all the Englishes I grew up with: the English I spoke to my mother, which for lack of a better term might be described as "simple"; the English she used with me, which for lack of a better term might be described as "broken"; my translation of her Chinese, which could certainly be described as "watered down"; and what I imagined to be her translation of her Chinese if she could speak in perfect English, her internal language, and for that I sought to preserve the essence, but neither an English nor a Chinese structure. I wanted to capture what language ability tests can never reveal: her intent, her passion, her imagery, the rhythms of her speech and the nature of her thoughts.

Apart from what any critic had to say about my writing, I knew I had succeeded where it counted when my mother finished reading my book and gave me her verdict: "So easy to read."

Traise Yamamoto

(b. 1961)

Traise Yamamoto, a sansei *or third generation Japanese American, was born in San Jose, California. Her poetry and essays on Asian American literature have appeared in several literary journals and anthologies, and she is at work on a book entitled* **Writing, That Other Private Self: The Construction of Japanese American Female Subjectivity**. *She is presently an assistant professor in the English department at the University of California at Riverside.*

In **Different Silences**, *Yamamoto addresses the issues of race, ethnicity, and gender and the willingness to make oneself heard or to address these definitions of identity with silence. She writes, "In a society that does not expect articulate speech, let alone articulate silences, from Asian American women, the act of writing becomes the broadest stroke towards speech."*

Different Silences

Last night, dinner with friends. At some point, we decide to go for a walk because it is a beautiful evening, and because the rhythms of walking bring out the rhythms of talk; speech syncopated between steps. There are four of us. We are all dressed in the easy sloppiness of the middle class. There is a baby strapped to the stomach of one of the two men.

We walk through a neighborhood where poverty is nonexistent, then through one where Hondas and fancy import cars, flower gardens and freshly painted housefronts give way to older American cars, low-maintenance shrubs, shabby window casings and faded brown front doors.

Paired off and talking movies, the four of us move slowly down the street. As we approach a yard in which three young boys are playing, I hear, "Look!" (the long drawn out "oooo" of childish fascination) "A Chinese lady!" The boy who has spoken, the youngest of the three, is about nine. And he is African American. The other two stare dutifully; they are also African American.

To speak or not to speak? How many times have similar things been said within my hearing, shortly followed by the yo-yo-ed vowels parodying "Oriental" speech? How many times has the next question been, "When did you get off the boat?" To be silent is to give in, to not-face and so to lose face; to be silent is what is expected of "a Chinese lady." But to speak is to risk intensified "chink talk."

To speak is to risk losing my temper and having to see the satisfied grins, the mean pleasure of having gotten a reaction. It hardly matters that I am almost twenty years older than the boy who has spoken. The space into which I have suddenly been flung—keenly conscious that I am not simply one of four friends, but one Asian American with three white friends—is non-temporal: it could be a scene from anywhere between the time I was five to now. The neighborhood resembles the one I grew up in; the boys are the boys that were inevitably part of every school year, the boys that have become the men fascinated by the erotic exotic.

We are not yet past the house. To speak or not to speak? The boy is young. Is it simply a statement that he has noticed my difference? Just one of those things kids bravely call out from the safety of their own front yard, an honest inquiry? Is there an Asian kid at school whom he picks on, whom he is identifying with me? "Not Chinese," I say, "Japanese. I am Japanese American."

I have to say it twice because he asks again; this is a new angle on the universe. "I am Japanese American." Then: "What are you?" "Oh," he answers, surprised, "I'm Black." I say, "Yes. You are not Chinese either, I take it." "Oh no," he giggles. Suddenly, he is just a child again. "Not me," he says as we—finally—pass by. My friends, silent this whole time, wait the space of a two-beat pause. Then, movie-talk.

You ask me to speak. You tell me at parties how lucky I am to be Japanese (always forgetting "American") how you wish you could be Japanese so you too could "be so graceful," or so you could have straight black hair, or because you always *have* liked kimonos. You tell me in classes that you are glad I talk because when I do, you learn something—about yourself. You tell me in clothes stores that I should get the red blouse because "Orientals look so nice in red," that I should get the A-line dress because it makes me look "so doll-like." You suggest that housecleaning is a good way to make extra summer money, then say I'm a snob when I tell you that my grandmothers did not clean other women's toilets, other women's children, other women's dirtiness so that I could grow up and do the same thing. You ask me to speak. Sometimes, I do. And sometimes when I do, you say, "You're so unlike most Japanese women. You are very articulate (funny, loud, strident, etc.)." And if I speak in anger, you are surprised, call me bitter, tell me I'm lucky I'm not Black, Chicana, Native American; or, worse, you apologize for all whites of all time, want me to "forgive" and "absolve" for all Asians of all time. Or you tell me you feel you can talk to me (the comparative implicit) because I am not threatening.

But there are other things besides frustration and fear that keep me silent, that keep me stuck between speaking and not speaking. If you grow up Japanese American, you grow up with the intense insider/outsider mentality that the Isseis[1] brought from

---

1. first-generation Japanese Americans who were born in Japan and emigrated to the United States

a country where therapy is still not widely practiced or participated in. The boundaries begin with oneself, then ring gradually outward: the family ("This is family business," my Nisei[2] mother would say, "and you are not to go blabbing it around to the outside."), the Japanese American community, the Asian American community. What belongs within must stay within: don't lose face, don't spill your guts, don't wear your heart on your sleeve. Fifty years after the war, most of those interned in the "relocation camps" will not speak of it. Boundaries. Self-containment: don't bother other people.

Shikata qa nai. It can't be helped. There is nothing to be done. Its goodness lies in a certain acceptance, a giving of oneself to the world as it is. But it can modulate into resignation, passivity. So one doesn't speak because there is no use in it, *shikata qa nai*, no use to calling so much attention to oneself, to one's family; no use to shame others, both inside and outside.

Between the impulse to speak and the impulse to not speak is the desire to not be said, the desire to not speak others—which means speaking to them so that they can speak for themselves, so they can speak themselves—the desire to work through what is most fraught in myself and in my relations with others. But between silence and speech the skeins, the angles tangle and blur.

Some of those skeins and angles involve the attempt to speak over differences that work like the floating x. Between Isseis and Niseis and Sanseis[3] there are differences of culture, of history; generational blips difficult to speak over. Between Japanese Americans and Chinese Americans. Established Asians and newly arrived Asians. There are Asian Americans I speak to who do not understand why I am interested in the liberal arts; liberal arts folk who ignore or overemphasize "the Japanese stuff" in my poetry, in me. Feminists who don't understand that silence is not always a bad thing, that it doesn't always signify passivity. Asian men who feel rejected because I live with a white man. Lesbians who tell me that my life with another woman is "canceled out" because I now live with a man. Women who say my writing is not feminist enough; Asian writers who say my poetry is too white. Non-writers who tell me what I write is impenetrable; one, who told me it was "inscrutable."

And there is that in me that silences others. There are angles in me that turn others away, gaps in my understanding. Within myself there is a voice that turns another into the Other, a voice that shouts over the painful particulars of people's lives. A voice with whom I make a deal: I'll let you rage inwardly if you will not speak through my mouth, which I will keep closed, in which I will keep you closed. And the dishonesty of that act becomes inseparable from the fear that if I speak, I will meet that voice in someone else.

---

2. second-generation Japanese Americans
3. third-generation Japanese Americans

In my life now, the boundaries are still there, though I am trying to push them outward. I speak with other women of color about what it is like to grow up, to live as a woman of color in a racist and sexist society; about the problematics of (white women's) feminism and its assumption that gender is extractable from and to be privileged over race, ethnicity and class. I speak to Coleen about the distances between Japanese Americans, about the silences or tension-relieving jokes that often make dialogue between Japanese American women impossible. I speak to Eileen about the similarities and differences between African Americans and Asian Americans, about the often fraught relations between African American and Asian American women. I speak knowing that each step from silence is a risk, and that I must understand it as a good one, not as one that betrays the principles I grew up with, that betrays myself.

I speak, knowing that to speak is to begin trust. But to speak at all, there must already be trust, or a reason to believe trust will be possible. You ask me to speak: I am telling you what keeps me from speaking. I am telling you that, for me, silence is part of speaking; silence is also habit, protection. I am telling you that your desire for me to speak, to tell you where I am, is synonymous with asking me to take a risk that I have taken too many times before, with asking me to repeat and repeat and repeat myself without getting anywhere. Endless repetition is not simply to say, and then to say again. It is language circling round its own opacity. To say and not be heard, to say and have to say again is to be silenced, to be spoken, to be made invisible in a skein of language not one's own. Who has access to the what and wherefores of articulation also has separate, make distinctions, make selves and others.

And with the power to name and shape speech comes the power to name and shape silence. My desire to speak, that I will speak, means that I am taking that risk for myself, for the sake of those connections I sometimes feel are impossible, for the sake of the possibilities I feel exist.

In a society that does not expect articulate speech, let alone articulate silences, from Asian American women, the act of writing becomes the broadest stroke towards speech. But sometimes that stroke is too difficult against the current of self-doubt, the belief that what one has to say isn't important or "universal" enough.

Mine is not the individual talent Eliot had in mind when he spoke of its relation to literary tradition, and I sometimes wonder whether Whitman addresses me when he calls out to the poets of the future to look for him under their boot-soles. I do know that when I tell people I write poetry, they often go on to tell I me how much they like haiku, as if it were inconceivable that I might write in Homeric dactyls[4] or Dantean *terza rima*. I know that I don't like it when a poem or manuscript is rejected

---

4.   traditional Western poetic forms

with what is thought to be a helpful bit of advice: write poems on "the Asian American experience." I think of Paul Laurence Dunbar: when he was invited to read his poetry, the audience wanted to hear only his dialect poems—poems of the "Negro experience" in "Negro tones" —and drowned him out when he attempted to read his non-dialect poetry. It's not that I don't write about and out of my experience as a third-generation Japanese American woman, but that I don't feel compelled to trot out the particulars of "Asian stuff" on demand and for display.

And yet, those particulars are what I respond to when I read Asian American writers. When I read the section in Maxine Hong Kingston's *Woman Warrior* where she tries to bully a silent classmate into speech, I know what it is like to be both the silent girl and the girl frustrated by the stereotype of the quiet Chinese female. When I come across the Japanese words in David Mura's or Garrett Hongo's poems, there is always for me a pleasant thrum of recognition; I feel a sense of a shared past, that we share the language of our grandparents. Every internment camp poem speaks my parents' and grandparents' past, speaks their silence. Every short story, novel, memoir guides me and tells me what I knew but could not know enough: we have something to say and we have ways to say it.

Every poem I write silences those who assume my aptitude in nonverbal fields (I first came to understand the use of the collective "you" when math teacher after puzzled math teacher would say, "But you're usually so good at this kind of thing.") or my limited abilities in what must surely be my second language ("Where did you learn to speak English so well?")

But every poem I write also testifies to what has increasingly become the uneasy relationship between the desire to speak the invisible mysteries that move my inner life, and the desire to speak what Blake called "the minute particulars" of which my daily life is comprised. I suppose it is much the same for every writer, the struggle to balance the timeless and the temporal. But for me, whose experience of daily life is inseparable from my identity as an Asian American woman, there is always the question of whether gender and ethnicity will become the filtering lenses through which my work will be judged, by which my work will be obscured. Yet, to write out of some "universal" mode in an attempt to avoid those lenses would be to erase myself with each stroke of the pen. "She who 'happens to be,'" writes Trinh Minh-ha, "a (non-white) Third World member, a woman, and a writer is bound to go through the ordeal of exposing her work to the abuse of praises and criticisms that either ignore, dispense with, or overemphasize her racial and sexual attributes."

For me, none of this can dampen the pleasure of articulation, the sensual satisfaction of words on the page and, most of all, the sense that to speak is necessary—

because the alternative is the silence that comes from without, the silence that cannot speak through fear, frustration, doubt, and the words of the other. But I must also remember that speech for the sake of speech only works to keep me tied to those who would assume my silence. It means forgetting, too, that mine is a heritage that knows the beauty of silence, the many ways in which it articulates what speech cannot. There is a silence that comes from within, what the famous Zen koan[5] calls the soundless sound of one hand clapping. There are silences of difference, different silences.

---

5. A young monk reaches a state of enlightenment when he finally realizes that the sound of one hand clapping transcends all sounds and is thus louder that the sound of two hands clapping.

Connie Ching So

(b. 1964)

Connie Ching So was born in Kowloon, Hong Kong, and, along with her parents and five siblings, came to the United States in 1969. She grew up in Seattle's Asian enclave, Beacon Hill. Her mother works as a seamstress and her father worked as a cook until he passed away in 1992. So received bachelor's degrees in English and communications from the University of Washington in 1987, a master's in public and international affairs from Princeton University, and is currently a doctoral candidate in ethnic studies at the University of California at Berkeley. She is completing work on a dissertation that focuses on the political identity of Asian Pacific Americans. She has taught at the University of California campuses at Berkeley and at Davis and at the University of Washington.

In the essay that follows, So explores the working class background of her immigrant Chinese parents, the family's cultural identity as rooted in the family, language, education, marriage, and sense of self.

The Color Yellow: Working Class Asian American Women and Feminism

October 14, 1989

Dear Mom:

I write to you because I was thinking about your childhood, your teenage years interrupted by war, your womanhood, your marriage, and your motherhood. But most of all, I was thinking about your life as a woman of color in America. I just read Chalsa Loo and Paul Ong's "Slaying Demons with a Sewing Needle: Feminist Issues for Chinatown's Women"[1] for a graduate course when I was reminded of your life. I had been pleased and excited about the prospect of reading the article. Yet, as they described garment workers in Chinatown who were left out of the feminist movement because of language barriers, ethnocentrism, class barriers, and cultural barriers, I thought of you and your feelings toward feminism. These Chinatown women they "interviewed" shared many similarities with you; yet I was disturbed. They did not

---

1. In Ron Takai, ed., *From Different Shores: Perspectives on Race and Ethnicity in America*, New York: Oxford Press, 1987. I was reading this particular article in a graduate ethnic studies course at U.C. Berkeley in the fall of 1989.

seem to be like you at all. I am not certain why I am bothered. Perhaps if I shared with you some of their observations, I will start to understand:

Overcrowding

Many of the problems plaguing Chinatown are tied to the low-income status of the residents.

Like the women interviewed in Chinatown, you are also an immigrant. As of last December, you are 52 years old—just a year older than the mean age of the study. Although we never lived in Chinatown, we lived in crowded conditions for most of our American life.

I recall our first rental house in 1969. I was only four then, but our entire family of eight, plus grandmother, grandfather, and second uncle, got lice from the leaky roof. I think oldest sister got lice first, then it spread to everyone else. Since we could afford the house, it did not have adequate bathroom facilities. I remember each of us sitting on top of a stool with newspaper wrapped around our hair to catch the pesty insects which made our head itch. I recall you pouring a solution in my hair and that I was to sit still—even though the acid from the liquid hurt my cheeks. I remember this occasion well, even though it was our first week in America.

We moved to another residence within two months. It was also a rental house, but this time in Beacon Hill, Seattle's Asian enclave. There were only three bedrooms, so you and father shared a small room with little brother and little sister, grandma and grandpa took another, and youngest uncle took the last. I slept with my three older sisters in the dining room. I remember always going to sleep with the aroma of "good, home-cooked food" filtering through the night air. Since father and grandfather were cooks, they often brought leftover food from the restaurant to feed us. I remember sleeping on the lower bunk bed and kicking the bottom of the top bunk to annoy two of my older sisters—it was fun. I remember once, the bed collapsed from all the movement. You were quite cross with us when you heard our weak explanation. I remember sometimes falling asleep to the sound of "mah-jong" in the living room. The lights were dimmed, but in the dark, I heard the click of the tiles, the clang of the coins, the drops of the dice, and the excited voices which shrieked, "Jong!" when the tiles matched.

Temperament and Mental Health

Besides being in poor housing, residents also face severe health and mental health problems.

Through our family network, you found work as a seamstress. This was a new experience for you since you did not work in Hong Kong. And when you had worked, it was

during the Sino-Japanese War when grandma and grandpa left you in Toisan while they, along with Youngest uncle and Oldest uncle, departed for safety in Hong Kong. Being a woman, you were seen as less important than your two younger brothers. Alone in the village, you found some money teaching others mathematics. Although you only went to grade school for five years, you knew more than most of your peers. Feeling guilty, grandma demanded that grandpa return to Guangdong province to fetch you.

The experience of being left alone made a deep impression on you. I remember your angry, hurt look whenever you told me the story. Yet, you did not linger on feelings of abandonment. Instead, you insisted that the moral of the story was "the need to have a strong family." Dad agreed.

When father was young, he was forcibly separated from his mother. He lived in Shunde, just outside Guangzhou. After the death of his father and two brothers, his wealthy grandparents exiled his mother, whom they never liked. According to them, my father's mother was responsible for the death of all these men and, if father, the only remaining child, remained under her care, she would also kill him. Thus, they exiled her from the village. But a few years later, during the Japanese invasion of South China, his grandparents passed away. So at the age of twelve, father became an orphan.

At fourteen, father wandered to Guangzhou for work and considered joining the Chinese Communist Party when he heard their promises for a liberated China. Yet, as an organization operated by northerners, he felt they would discriminate against him, a southerner, a Cantonese. With nothing to do, he hopped on the Canton railroad and went to Hong Kong in search of work. In Hong Kong, he found a kindly merchant who appreciated my father's neat handwriting and had him calligraph the scrolls in his leather shop. Impressed by father's diligence, the merchant made my father his apprentice. In nine years, my father was able to open up his own leather shop.

Many years later, a visitor came into the shop and mentioned the name of a woman named So. My father told the gentleman that he was also a So—an uncommon surname, even in China. As they spoke, my father realized that they were from the same village and that the man was his maternal uncle. At long last, my father was reunited with his mother who had adopted a new identity, remarried, and was the mother of four other children. Yet, she had retained the surname of her first husband, So. It was the end of a good story.

I have heard from friends and from you, mother, about a confident man who never smoked or drank in Hong Kong. When you met, you had no idea how he would change.

You met while you were in Hong Kong. You were standing around at a corner and he came by. He paused and began a conversation. You were impressed by his generosity, his high morals, and his impeccable taste in clothes and restaurants. You were poor in comparison. When you and grandma and grandpa slept in shacks at the "bottom of the hill," dad would come by and bring dinner to feed the family. He offered your brothers jobs at his leather shop and bought gifts for your parents. You said you had two other proposals of marriage, but dad seemed the most promising, the most generous....

The leather business declined in the late sixties. (Were people resorting to vinyl?) As believers in good education, you wanted to send us to "private schools," despite our declining wealth. After third sister was born, dad turned to drinking and gambling to escape his problems. By the time a fifth daughter was born, his gambling was constant. Like many men, he wanted a son to carry on the lineage. Although I do not recall father demeaning my sisters or me because we are females, we know he felt that since he was the last of his line, he wanted to ensure continuation of the So family. He was so relieved when little brother was born in 1969. About two months later, we left for America. As father and you have often explained, "You have relatives in America and they will help us out."

In America, dad found a job cooking for a man who had once been an employee of his in Hong Kong. His pride was devastated. Dad had always been so independent and proud. In the face of adversity, dad had always seemed to triumph. But America was different. In a new country, he witnessed those who were less fortunate than himself in Hong Kong faring better than he. In comparison, dad must have felt he was a failure. He often said to deaf ears, "Ah, if I knew English, then..." The children groaned because we knew we would be subjected to fantasy stories of grandeur that would never occur. Dad was a true "dreamer" whose dream escaped. As a result, he took to more gambling, drinking, smoking and eventually suffered cirrhosis of the liver.

In the late seventies, dad got into an argument with the other cooks. They called him "ngah-chat So" or "toothbrush So"—a Chinese symbol of conceit. Father lost his job and resorted back to gambling, drinking, smoking. It was embarrassing listening to other children taunt father by calling him "jyou mau gwei" or drunkard. He did not want to work in Chinatown. He refused to cook for people who once knew him as a store-owner. He did not want to "serve" them. He had too much pride. Instead, he went on unemployment insurance for two years until the benefits and his self-esteem dried out.

You scorned him. I remember the constant arguments, the clashing of dishes on the floor, the tears and the hurtful words. You once bought him some new gray slacks to cheer him up. You fought that day…and many days after that. I also remember you walking out on him because he was so "lazy" to not work wherever work was available. You left for two days. When you came back, you said you knew that he couldn't help. But I've always thought that you were talking about yourself.

Marital Sex Roles and Life Satisfaction

I wouldn't get married to the same guy that I married.

Like Loo and Ong's subjects, there were times when you "wished you married someone else." Then you would reminisce about your two other suitors. As you told us, they were both very middle-class. One was a businessman in Montreal while the other had a successful restaurant in Chicago. During these difficult times, you repeatedly said, "If I had married them, I would not have to work."

Mom, you were the primary breadwinner. In 1979, like Loo and Ong's subjects, you only made $3.25/hr. But you had a large family to feed and there was no way out. You went to work even when you had the flu, you went to work even after you carelessly sewed on your finger, and you went to work even when your kids were sick. You even lied about your age, reducing it by five years, to find employment. At times, feeling extremely tired, you cautioned your daughters "to not marry young, be educated. I never had the chance and you do, go to school, work hard, have your own income and don't rely on men."

Meanwhile, father's situation worsened. An experience I never forgot occurred when I was in seventh grade. I had an assignment for my Chinese language class. I had to use an ink brush and write the character "I" ten times on parchment paper. I was excited. But so was dad. I suppose the calligraphy must have brought back memories of Hong Kong to him. He insisted that I let him show me the proper way of writing. I told him my teacher said we had to do it all by ourselves. That's the assignment and I don't cheat. He insisted and so did I. In a fury, he picked up the ink and threw it at my face. I ducked and it hit the wall, staining the map of the world in the dining room where I began my homework. I realized then that he was crazy. I ran off to the bathroom and cried out of anger and disappointment in my father.

Perhaps fifteen minutes passed before I returned to the dining room. Dad was sitting on the floor, staring at the wall with a vague, yet vulnerable expression on his face. Then he whispered, "I don't like what I've become." In 1984, an old friend in ·Renton, Washington, gave father a job and another chance to rebuild his life.

Education

The belief that women should not receive much education, in conjunction with the fact that most Chinatown immigrants are from poor families probably explains why the median level of education for Chinatown women was a grade school education.

During the early period of my childhood, while you and dad worked, grandma took care of all of us. One afternoon, while grandma was preparing dinner, oldest sister walked into the kitchen to get a drink of water. As oldest sister sipped her water, grandma turned to her and told oldest sister that we—the females—should all get jobs to put little brother through college. She recounted how difficult it was to put Youngest uncle through college. But oldest sister felt differently. Oldest sister was in sixth grade and many of her teachers had commented on her aptitude for mathematics and science. Grandma's advice insulted oldest sister.

Oldest sister told all of us what grandmother said and concluded that it was little brother's fault. I don't know when it began, but as long as I can remember, oldest sister resented little brother.

That same day, we told father what grandmother said. He told us to ignore her while you, mother, said "We don't have the money to put all of you through school." Meanwhile, you told us you only had the opportunity to complete elementary and some middle school while dad completed middle school. You added that it was a great amount of education for people caught in the war in China. But your response seemed irrelevant to us.

Oldest sister was determined to go to college. In the seventh grade, she began working as a waitress in Chinatown. Later, she joined the Seattle Work Training Program for lower-income students and worked at the University of Washington's research laboratories. Second sister followed in her footsteps and worked; so did third sister and so did I, the fourth sister, as well as little sister and little brother.

Eventually, we all went to college on scholarships. When that happened, no one was disappointed. It was economics. Not gender. On the contrary, I recall that one of your biggest disappointments occurred when second sister gave up engineering jobs for marriage and domestic life. You quarreled with her. You screamed. You cried. You kept saying, "What a waste of money. We should have saved it." Then she reminded you that you never spent a cent on any of our educations. Then you said, "It's not the money. It's the opportunity."

Language Barriers

Eighty-five of the employed women saw language as a major barrier to a better job.

It has been twenty years now. Dad and you do not speak English. When you first came to America, you both wanted to learn English. But with sewing and housework, you were too tired to continue the lessons. You worked at least six days a week, sometimes seven when you wanted overtime pay at Calvery Manufacturing Company. Meanwhile, dad worked in the evenings, came home at 3 in the morning and was too tired to continue the lessons. During the 1970s and 1980s, you and dad raised six kids while earning a combined income of less than $20,000. But even though money was tight, dad always subscribed to the Chinese *Reader's Digest*, two Chinese newspapers, and the *Seattle Times*.

Although you both complained about not knowing English, you both survived for more than twenty years without it. Your children were able to interpret news and letters for you. And you lived in Beacon Hill—Seattle's Asian enclave, just across the Jose Rizal Bridge from Chinatown. Even in 1974, after grandmother, grandfather and youngest uncle moved out, they still lived less than a mile from us. With the exception of Youngest uncle, they do not speak English either. But you really don't need to in Beacon Hill where many people are Chinese.

I suppose these are reasons why it still infuriates me when people can't believe you do not speak English. I know you try, I know dad does, but few Americans of any ethnicity understand the circumstances you live under. Besides, I know that even when you are trying to speak English, most people do not realize it. Mom, in this country, the accent means you are "unassimilable" and people are too lazy and intolerant to take the time to try to understand. A Chinese accent just does not have the same social status as a French accent in white-dominant America.

Still, I'm not sure if language is the primary barrier for a better occupation. In 1986, you had a chance to get a better job at Helly Hansen's in Kirkland, Washington—just across the bridge. Helly Hansen would only require working 4 days a week at $6.25/hr. You rejected this offer because of "transportation." Since you did not speak English, you felt uncomfortable taking the bus and refused our offers of teaching you to drive. You did not feel confident alone in a car. But most of all, you wanted to be in an environment with other immigrant women who are your friends. Unlike Ong and Loo's subjects, you have an unofficial professional association with whom you play mah-jong and go shopping around Beacon Hill and Chinatown. So not only do you have the real barrier of transportation, but you did not want to leave this group, this community, who understood your "language" and accepted you.

Low Self-Esteem/Lack of Self-Assertion

Low self-esteem was related to low income level and foreign-born status.

You took our advice and exercised: You walked to the local supermarket. An hour later, you came home visibly upset. I asked what happened. You said that a young Asian American boy stole the coupons in your grocery cart and gave it to his mother. His mother looked at him and, without questions, accepted the coupons and bought the goods. You said he made you mad and you stared at him and he laughed and sneered.

I was angry. I asked you why you didn't grab the coupon back from him. I asked you why you didn't say to his mother that "he was a bad boy and took this." You said you didn't like his mother—a woman who wore a dress and high-heels, spoke English, had a fancy hairstyle, used make-up, and just would not understand. I knew you were describing socioeconomic differences, but I wondered at the "sister" and "brother" who did not notice your hurt and anger. And actually used it to their own advantage.

Barriers: American-Born versus Foreign-Born

Even within their race, there was discomfort felt by the foreign-born toward the American-born.

When we first arrived in America, grandma, grandpa, youngest uncle, oldest uncle and oldest uncle's Chinese American wife met us. They took grandma and grandpa and youngest uncle home to rest, while oldest uncle and his wife "showed" us around. You expected your younger brother to welcome us. He did not. We looked different from them. We wore clothes from Hong Kong. Our hairstyles were of Hong Kong. But most of all, we were foreigners more than we were "relatives." Or so we were treated.

They took us to Southcenter, the largest shopping mall in Seattle. Our aunt never looked at us. She continually walked a few yards ahead, then told us to wait for her in front of the directory while she went shopping. Not being familiar with America, we listened. Perhaps an hour passed before we saw her again. Then she told us it was time to go home. As we paced the mall, she walked several yards ahead of us. You told us that "to chi gweis" were all like that—they looked down on foreign Chinese just because they can speak English and had more money.

Time and time again, mother, this incident comes to my mind. It comes to my mind whenever I hear American-born Asians making fun of immigrant "F.O.B.'s"; it comes to my mind when I see poorer Asian immigrants and others living in the projects or what most Americans called the "ghettoed" neighborhoods, which is really another way of saying an "ethnic neighborhood"; it comes to my mind when I hear the ignorance and embarrassment of upper- and middle-income Asian American kin, who may be only one or two generations removed from the projects or were "fortunate" enough to live next to suburban whites fleeing people of color because of the struggles of those deemed "less fortunate" than them; and it comes to my mind whenever people mistake me for an American-born—which I did not correct when I was in grade school. At that time, I had been taught that assimilation was right and proper, not knowing that it actually meant white and preferred.

Women's Movement

Thirty-seven percent believed that "the Chinese are treated worse than whites," and 28 percent believed that "the Chinese in America are discriminated against by white society."

If I were to simply reflect on your life, it would seem to be another "Chinese woman oppressed by Chinese men and society" story. But it is not. If I were to simply reflect on your life, I would think the only reason you are not involved with the Women's Movement is because you do not feel you will be accepted. This is not true. If I were to simply reflect on your life, I would not think you had an opinion on the Women's Movement. This is not true.

In 1981, we were sitting in the living room watching the made-for-TV movie "The Women's Room" about Myra, a bourgeois housewife who eventually becomes an emancipated women's studies professor. As I was translating and editorializing the movie for you, I asked for your opinion of the movie. You said, "Choon sai-gai, nam yen dou ha nyu yen," or "Women are universally oppressed by men."

Having grown up in a society which teaches American students of the sexism of Asia, I asked if you thought Asian men were worse than American men? You looked at me as if I were crazy, then said, "No, your father has always encouraged you to go to school, work hard and get a good job even when he did not. He and I have always told you to do whatever you want in life as long as you get some money for it. Yes, he talks too much sometimes, but that's because he's sad. Not because he's sexist."

I persisted, "What about grandma and grandpa?"

"Your grandmother has treated you very well. How can you say anything else? She's as strong as the white woman on the movie. She raised all of you, your cousins, your uncles, your mother and takes care of your grandfather. You should not speak poorly of her.

"Your grandfather, on the other hand, is too old to know any better. He's too old to change. But aren't all old people are like that. It's not because he's Chinese. Look at your brother, look at your father, do they seem more sexist than those men to you?" You motioned toward the TV set.

Then you asked me, "Is this what they teach you in America? That whites are always better than Asians? How do they know. White women never have to work. Their husbands make more money. What do they know? I worked, not my maids. Give my husband a better job, then I'll have time to stay home and complain."

This may not be the actual conversation. But it is how I (like to) remember it. I know the translation is not the best; in fact, I know that without the proper translation, then this conversation becomes fiction. Yet it seems to me this conversation is very real to me.

I am still not certain if I have yet explained my unease with Chalsa Loo and Paul Ong's essay. Loo and Ong's Chinatown women sound like you and your friends, but at the same time, they are not like you at all. Mom, I think Loo and Ong do a good job of reporting on the problems of working-class Chinese women, but they are cold and distant. Perhaps it is because they really do not know you because they do not understand you: they don't see you. Perhaps like most well-intentioned academics, they do not come from the working-class environment that they describe. So they treat you like a statistic or a victim, not as a woman who survived World War II, raised six children, and provided us with the best role model for feminism while we were growing up. I know you never called yourself a "feminist." Yet, at the same time, you seemed proud of us, your daughters, when we embraced the term.

For me, growing up as your daughter, I do not recall feeling like I am the daughter of a simplistic, ignorant woman from a "backward" society. Instead, if anyone was simply stupid it was the teenage me—growing up and trying to pretend to be a typical "American" who liked Shaun Cassidy and McDonalds (when I actually preferred Chin Han and spiced chicken feet). Mom, it's a credit to you and grandmother that I grew out of my "self-hatred" stage relatively early.

Mom, I think you and grandmother are among the strongest women I have ever met—stronger than many of the white women professors and classmates who always try to universalize their own Eurocentric brand of feminism through use and abuse of Chinese footbinding, and stronger than those assimilated "academic" Asians who pretend to worry about your affairs in the hopes of now appearing to be "in touch" with the "community." This is particularly ironic when we both know that many of them had ignored us "F.O.B.'s" while we were younger and poorer. Now many aspire to appear fashionably compassionate. I know you are no longer hurt by this dismissal; we have gotten used to it and, sometimes, we may even desire it. Isn't some attention better than none at all?

So I do not fault Loo and Ong. I still find their article practical, even if it is cold and uninspiring. Yet I cannot help wondering who their audience is. If it's an academic community, then isn't some attention better than none at all? If their audience is an English-reading Asian American community, then isn't some attention better than none at all? If it's a community of women scholars, then isn't some attention better that none at all? As Martin Luther King, Jr., once said of "quasi-acceptance" and "quasi-approval" by white liberals,

Shallow understanding from people of good will is more frustrating than absolute misunderstanding from people of ill will. Lukewarm acceptance is much more bewildering than outright rejection.[2]

Mom, people may interview you, they may even physically sit by you, but it oftentimes seems that you don't exist except as a pathetic statistic or a victim in need of *their* help. But am I any better?

Nowadays, I also find myself continually contemplating my role as an ethnic studies graduate student. In ethnic studies, racial oppression is typically the focus of discussion. Yet, it is acknowledged that gender oppression, classism, heterosexism, xenophobia, ageism, religious oppression, to name a few "isms", all simultaneously dominate American society and individual consciousness. I suppose, mom, that this is the real reason I am writing to you. I feel I am at a turning point in my life. I am no longer the young working-class immigrant girl from Hong Kong, but a woman who has attended colleges and received degrees. I do not sew garments, I do not have to clean anyone's bedsheets but my own. My only duty at ethnic studies graduate school is to read and write and think about Asian Americans (and other people of color). It is a position of relative privilege. At the same time, it is a position of necessity and survival. Something I know you and dad have always known. Compared to your life, my current situation—with educational debts and all—is still one of ease. But still, I sometimes ask myself, have I become what I did not want to be? Have I become an outsider to my community? What is or has become my community? Even now, I know that in reality, this letter written in English is merely a form of fiction. I know that my Chinese reading skills are barely adequate for an elementary schoolchild in China. So who am I now writing to? Who am I writing for?

As in my younger days when I did not have the answers, I find myself again turning to you; only now, I am not certain if it is the real you, or the one I imagine in

---

2.   Martin Luther King, Jr., "Leter from Birmingham Jail," April 16, 1963, p. 58.

my memory. So I ask "you," how I should represent my community? How I should represent my family? How I should represent you? Should I even try to represent anyone but myself? And what about my children? Will they share my uncertainties? Will they be sensitive to my working class family? Or will they be the stranger that I fear I might become.

Love,
So Wai Ching

FICTION

Sui Sin Far

(b. 1867–1914)

Edith Maud Eaton was born to a Chinese mother and an English father. In the late nineteenth century Eaton chose to be Chinese American instead of passing for white at a time when America was in the heyday of anti-Chinese legislation. Her stories, written and published in American magazines under the pseudonym of Sui Sin Far were sensitive and accurate portrayals of Chinese American community and family life in San Francisco, Seattle, and New York. **Mrs. Spring Fragrance** (1912) is her only collection of stories. Eaton's sister, Winnifred Eaton, born in 1879 to the same parents, also wrote, yet she chose a Japanese identity and wrote under the psuedonym of Onoto Watanna. At the time, her work, unlike that of Edith Eaton's, was received with acclaim, and she enjoyed a financially successful writing career in New York and Hollywood; Winnifred published fifteen novels and worked on several feature films between 1921 and 1930 (about the time she died). Winnifred sold herself as having Japanese instead of Chinese ancestry, which, at the time, would have been more "acceptable" to Anglo Americans. Professor S.E. Solberg speculates that Winnifred may have had a hand in writing Edith's obituary in the **New York Times** on April 9, 1914:

> Edith Eaton, author, known in the East as Sui Sin Far, the "Chinese Lily," died on Tuesday at her home in Montreal, Canada. She was the daughter to Edward Eaton ... [who] went to the Orient. He became fascinated with the East, and after a year married a Japanese noblewoman who had been adopted by Sir Hugh Matteson as a child and educated in England.

Proof of her ancestry is in Edith Eaton's own autobiographical essay "Leaves of a Mental Portfolio of an Eurasian" (1909):

> When I look back over the years I see myself, a little child of scarcely four years of age, walking in front of my nurse, in a green English lane, and listening to her tell another of her kind that my mother is Chinese. "Oh Lord!" exclaims the informed. She turns me around and scans me curiously from head to foot. Then the two women whisper together. Tho the word Chinese conveys very little meaning to my mind, I feel that they are talking about my father and mother and my heart swells with indignation.

The dominant theme in the lives and careers of the two Eaton sisters as writers and as Eurasians of mixed ancestry was one of choice. The student of Chinese American literature is fortunate that Edith made the choice to tell the truth.

The Americanizing of Pau Tsu

I

When Wan Hom Hing came to Seattle to start a branch of the merchant business which his firm carried on so successfully in the different ports of China, he brought with him his nephew, Wan Lin Fo, then eighteen years of age. Wan Lin Fo was a well-educated Chinese youth, with bright eyes and keen ears. In a few years' time he knew as much about the business as did any of the senior partners. Moreover, he learned to speak and write the American language with such fluency that he was never at a loss for an answer, when the white man, as was sometimes the case, sought to pose him. "All work and no play," however, is as much against the principles of a Chinese youth as it is against those of a young American, and now and again Lin Fo would while away an evening at the Chinese Literary Club, above the Chinese restaurant, discussing with some chosen companions the works and merits of Chinese sages—and some other things. New Year's Day, or rather, Week, would also see him, business forgotten, arrayed in national costume of finest silk and color "the blue of the sky after rain," visiting with his friends, both Chinese and American, and scattering silver and gold coin amongst the youngsters of the families visited.

It was on the occasion of one of these New Year's visits that Wan Lin Fo first made known to the family of his firm's silent American partner, Thomas Raymond, that he was betrothed. It came about in this wise: One of the young ladies of the house, who was fair and frank of face and friendly and cheery in manner, observing as she handed him a cup of tea that Lin Fo's eyes wore a rather wistful expression, questioned him as to the wherefore:

"Miss Adah," replied Lin Fo, "may I tell you something?"

"Certainly, Mr. Wan," replied the girl. "You know how I enjoy hearing your tales."

"But this is no tale. Miss Adah, you have inspired in me a love—"

Adah Raymond started. Wan Lin Fo spake slowly.

"For the little girl in China to whom I am betrothed."

"Oh, Mr. Wan! That is good news. But what have I to do with it?"

"This, Miss Adah! Every time I come to this house, I see you, so good and so beautiful, dispensing tea and happiness to all around, and I think, could I have in my home and ever by my side one who is also both good and beautiful, what a felicitious life mine would be!"

"You must not flatter me, Mr. Wan!"

"All that I say is founded on my heart. But I will speak not of you. I will speak of Pau Tsu."

"Pau Tsu?"

"Yes. That is the name of my future wife. It means a pearl."

"How pretty! Tell me all about her!"

"I was betrothed to Pau Tsu before leaving China. My parents adopted her to be my wife. As I remember, she had shining eyes and the good-luck color was on her cheek. Her mouth was like a red vine leaf, and her eyebrows most exquisitely arched. As slender as a willow was her form, and when she spoke, her voice lilted from note to note in the sweetest melody."

Adah Raymond softly clapped her hands.

"Ah! You were even then in love with her."

"No," replied Lin Fo thoughtfully. "I was too young to be in love—sixteen years of age. Pau Tsu was thirteen. But, as I have confessed, you have caused me to remember and love her."

Adah Raymond was not a self-conscious girl, but for the life of her she could think of no reply to Lin Fo's speech.

"I am twenty-two years old now," he continued. "Pau Tsu is eighteen. Tomorrow I will write to my parents and persuade them to send her to me at the time of the spring festival. My elder brother was married last year, and his wife is now under my parents' roof, so that Pau Tsu, who has been the daughter of the house for so many years, can now be spared to me."

"What a sweet little thing she must be," commented Adah Raymond.

"You will say that when you see her," proudly responded Lin Fo. "My parents say she is always happy. There is not a bird or flower or dewdrop in which she does not find some glad meaning."

"I shall be so glad to know her. Can she speak English?"

Lin Fo's face fell.

"No," he replied, "but,"—brightening— "when she comes I will have her learn to speak like you—and be like you."

II

Pau Tsu came with the spring, and Wan Lin Fo was one of the happiest and proudest of bridegrooms. The tiny bride was really pretty—even to American eyes. In her peach and plum colored robes, her little arms and hands sparkling with jewels, and her shiny black head decorated with wonderful combs and pins, she appeared a bit of Eastern coloring amidst the Western lights and shades.

Lin Fo had not been forgotten, and her eyes, under their downcast lids discovered him at once, as he stood awaiting her amongst a group of young Chinese merchants on the deck of the vessel.

The apartments he had prepared for her were furnished in American style, and her birdlike little figure in Oriental dress seemed rather out of place at first. It was not long, however, before she brought forth from the great box, which she had brought over seas, screens and fans, vases, panels, Chinese matting, artificial flowers and birds, and a number of exquisite carvings and pieces of antique porcelain. With these she transformed the American flat into an Oriental bower, even setting up in her sleeping-room a little chapel, enshrined in which was an image of the Goddess of Mercy, two ancestral tablets, and other emblems of her faith in the Gods of her fathers.

The Misses Raymond called upon her soon after arrival, and she smiled and looked pleased. She shyly presented each girl with a Chinese cup and saucer, also a couple of antique vases, covered with whimsical pictures, which Lin Fo tried his best to explain.

The girls were delighted with the gifts, and having fallen, as they expressed themselves, in love with the little bride, invited her through her husband to attend a launch party, which they intended giving the following Wednesday on Lake Washington.

Lin Fo accepted the invitation in behalf of himself and wife. He was quite at home with the Americans and, being a young man, enjoyed their rather effusive appreciation of him as an educated Chinaman. Moreover, he was of the opinion that the society of the American young ladies would benefit Pau Tsu in helping her to acquire the ways and language of the land in which he hoped to make a fortune.

Wan Lin Fo was a true son of the Middle Kingdom and secretly pitied all those who were born far away from its influences; but there was much about the Americans that he admired. He also entertained sentiments of respect for a motto which hung in his room, which bore the legend: "When in Rome, do as the Romans do."

"What is best for men is also best for women in this country," he told Pau Tsu when she wept over his suggestion that she should take some lessons in English from a white woman.

"It may be best for a man who goes out in the street," she sobbed, "to learn the new language, but of what importance is it to a woman who lives only within the house and her husband's heart?"

It was seldom, however, that she protested against the wishes of Lin Fo. As her mother-in-law had said, she was a docile, happy little creature. Moreover, she loved her husband.

But as the days and weeks went by the girl bride whose life hitherto had been spent in the quiet retirement of a Chinese home in the performance of filial duties, in embroidery work and lute playing, in sipping tea and chatting with gentle girl companions, felt very much bewildered by the novelty and stir of the new world into which she had been suddenly thrown. She could not understand for all Lin Fo's explanations, why it was required of her to learn the strangers' language and adopt their ways. Her husband's tongue was the same as her own. So also her little maid's. It puzzled her to be always seeing this and hearing that—sights and sounds which as yet had no meaning for her. Why also was it necessary to receive visitors nearly every evening?—visitors who could neither understand nor make themselves understood by her, for all their curious smiles and stares, which she bore like a second Vashti—or rather, Esther. And why, oh! why should she be constrained to eat her food with clumsy, murderous looking American implements instead of with her own elegant and easily manipulated ivory chopsticks?

Adah Raymond, who at Lin Fo's request was a frequent visitor to the house, could not fail to observe that Pau Tsu's small face grew daily smaller and thinner, and that the smile with which she invariably greeted her, though sweet, was tinged with melancholy. Her woman's instinct told her that something was wrong, but what it was the light within her failed to discover. She would reach over to Pau Tsu and take within her own firm, white hand the small, trembling fingers, pressing them lovingly and sympathetically; and the little Chinese woman would look up into the beautiful face bent above hers and think to herself: "No wonder he wishes me to be like her!"

If Lin Fo happened to come in before Adah Raymond left he would engage the visitor in bright and animated conversation. They had so much of common interest to discuss, as is always the way with young people who have lived any length of time in a growing city of the West. But to Pau Tsu, pouring tea and dispensing sweetmeats, it was all Greek, or rather, all American.

"Look, my pearl, what I have brought you," said Lin Fo one afternoon as he entered his wife's apartments, followed by a messenger-boy, who deposited in the middle of the room a large cardboard box.

With murmurs of wonder Pau Tsu drew near, and the messenger-boy having withdrawn Lin Fo cut the string, and drew forth a beautiful lace evening dress and dark blue walking costume, both made in American style.

For a moment there was silence in the room. Lin Fo looked at his wife in surprise. Her face was pale and her little body was trembling, while her hands were drawn up into her sleeves.

"Why, Pau Tsu!" he exclaimed, "I thought to make you glad."

At these words the girl bent over the dress of filmy lace, and gathering the flounce in her hand smoothed it over her knee; then lifting a smiling face to her husband, replied: "Oh, you are too good, too kind to your unworthy Pau Tsu. My speech is slow, because I am overcome with happiness."

Then with exclamations of delight and admiration she lifted the dresses out of the box and laid them carefully over the couch.

"I wish you to dress like an American woman when we go out or receive," said her husband. "It is the proper thing in America to do as the Americans do. You will notice, light of my eyes, that it is only on New Year and out national holidays that I wear the costume of our country and attach a queue. The wife should follow the husband in all things."

A ripple of laughter escaped Pau Tsu's lips.

"When I wear that dress," said she, touching the walking costume, "I will look like your friend, Miss Raymond."

She struck her hands together gleefully, but when her husband had gone to his business she bowed upon the floor and wept pitifully.

III

During the rainy season Pau Tsu was attacked with a very bad cough. A daughter of Southern China, the chill, moist climate of the Puget Sound winter was very hard on her delicate lungs. Lin Fo worried much over the state of her health, and meeting Adah Raymond on the street one afternoon told her of his anxiety. The kind-hearted girl immediately returned with him to the house. Pau Tsu was lying on her couch, feverish and breathing hard. The American girl felt her hands and head.

"She must have a doctor," said she, mentioning the name of her family's physician.

Pau Tsu shuddered. She understood a little English by this time.

"No! No! Not a man, not a man!" she cried.

Adah Raymond looked up at Lin Fo.

"I understand," said she. "There are several women doctors in this town. Let us send for one."

But Lin Fo's face was set.

"No!" he declared. "We are in America. Pau Tsu shall be attended to by your physician."

Adah Raymond was about to protest against this dictum when the sick wife, who had also heard it, touched her hand and whispered; "I not mind now. Man all right."

So the other girl closed her lips, feeling that if the wife would not dispute her husband's will it was not her place to do so, but her heart ached with compassion as she bared Pau Tsu's chest for the stethoscope.

"It was like preparing a lamb for slaughter," she told her sister afterwards. "Pau Tsu was motionless, her eyes closed and her lips sealed, while the doctor remained; but after he had left and we two were alone she shuddered and moaned like one bereft of reason. I honestly believe that the examination was worse than death to that little Chinese woman. The modesty of generations of maternal ancestors was crucified as I rolled down the neck of her silk tunic."

It was a week after the doctor's visit, and Pau Tsu, whose cough had yielded to treatment, though she was still far from well, was playing on her lute, and whisperingly singing this little song, said to have been written on a fan which was presented to an ancient Chinese emperor by one of his wives:

"Of fresh new silk,
All snowy white,
And round as a harvest moon,
A pledge of purity and love,
A small but welcome boon.

While summer lasts,
When borne in hand,
Or folded on thy breast,
'Twill gently soothe thy burning brow,
And charm thee to thy rest.

But, oh, when Autumn winds blow chill,
And days are bleak and cold,
No longer sought, no longer loved,
'Twill lie in dust and mould.

This silken fan the deign accept,
Sad emblem of my lot,
Caressed and cherished for an hour,
Then speedily forgot."

"Why so melancholy, my pearl?" asked Lin Fo, entering from the street.

"When a bird is about to die, its notes are sad," returned Pau Tsu.

"But thou art not for death—thou art for life," declared Lin Fo, drawing her towards him and gazing into a face which day by day seemed to grow finer and more transparent.

IV

A Chinese messenger-boy ran up the street, entered the store of Wan Hom Hing & Co. and asked for the junior partner. When Lin Fo came forward he handed him a dainty, flowered missive, neatly folded and addressed. The receiver opened it and read:

Dear and Honored Husband,—Your unworthy Pau Tsu lacks the courage to face the ordeal before her. She has, therefore, left you and prays you to obtain a divorce as is the custom in America, so that you may be happy with the Beautiful One, who is so much your Pau Tsu's superior. This, she acknowledges, for she sees with your eyes, in which like a star, the Beautiful One shineth. Else, why should you have your Pau Tsu follow in her footsteps? She has tried to obey your will and to be as an American woman; but now she is very weary, and the terror of what is before her has overcome.

> Your stupid thorn,
> Pau Tsu

Mechanically Lin Fo folded the letter and thrust it within his breast pocket. A customer inquired of him the price of a lacquered tray. "I wish you good morning," he replied, reaching for his hat. The customer and clerks gaped after him as he left the store.

Out in the street, as fate would have it, he met Adah Raymond. He would have turned aside had she not spoken to him.

"Whatever is the matter with you, Mr. Wan?" she inquired. "You don't look yourself at all."

"The density of my difficulties you cannot understand," he replied, striding past her.

But Adah Raymond was persistent. She had worried lately over Pau Tsu.

"Something is wrong with your wife," she declared.

Lin Fo wheeled around.

"Do you know where she is?" he asked with quick suspicion.

"Why, no!" exclaimed the girl in surprise.

"Well, she has left me."

Adah Raymond stood incredulous for a moment, then with indignant eyes turned upon the deserted husband.

"You deserve it!" she cried, "I have seen it for some time: your cruel, arbitrary treatment of the dearest, sweetest little soul in the world."

"I beg your pardon, Miss Adah," returned Lin Fo, "but I do not understand. Pau Tsu is heart of my heart. How then could I be cruel to her?"

"Oh, you stupid!" exclaimed the girl. "You're a Chinaman, but you're almost as stupid as an American. Your cruelty consisted in forcing Pau Tsu to be—what nature never intended her to be—an American woman; to adapt and adopt in a few months' time all our ways and customs. I saw it long ago, but as Pau Tsu was too sweet and meek to see any faults in her man I had not the heart to open her eyes—or yours. Is it not true that she has left you for this reason?"

"Yes," murmured Lin Fo. He was completely crushed, "And some other things."

"What other things?"

"She—is—afraid—of—the—doctor."

"She is!"—fiercely—"Shame upon you!"

Lin Fo began to walk on, but the girl kept by his side and continued:

"You wanted your wife to be an American woman while you remained a Chinaman. For all your clever adaptation of our American ways you are thorough Chinaman. Do you think an American would dare treat his wife as you have treated yours?"

Wan Lin Fo made no response. He was wondering how he could ever have wished his gentle Pau Tsu to be like this angry woman. Now his Pau Tsu was gone. His anguish for the moment made him oblivious to the presence of his companion and words she was saying. His silence softened the American girl. After all, men, even Chinamen, were nothing but big, clumsy boys, and she didn't believe in kicking a man after he was down.

"But, cheer up, you're sure to find her," said she, suddenly changing her tone. "Probably her maid has friends in Chinatown who have taken them in."

"If I find her," said Lin Fo fervently, "I will not care if she never speaks an American word, and I will take her for a trip to China, so that our son may be born in the country that Heaven loves."

"You cannot make too much amends for all she has suffered. As to Americanizing Pau Tsu—that will come in time, I am quite sure that were I transferred to your country and commanded to turn myself into a Chinese woman in the space of two or three months I would prove a sorry disappointment to whomever built their hopes upon me."

Many hours elapsed before any trace could be found of the missing one. All the known friends and acquaintances of little Pau Tsu were called upon and questioned; but if they had knowledge of the young wife's hiding place they refused to divulge it. Though Lin Fo's face was grave with an unexpressed fear, their sympathies were certainly not with him.

The seekers were about giving up the search in despair when a little boy, dangling in his hands a string of blue beads, arrested the attention of the young husband. He knew the necklace to be a gift from Pau Tsu to the maid, A-Toy. He had bought it himself. Stopping and questioning the little fellow he learned to his great joy that his wife and her maid were at the boy's home, under the care of his grandmother, who was a women learned in herb lore.

Adah Raymond smiled in sympathy with her companion's evident great relief.

"Everything will now be all right," said she, following Lin Fo as he proceeded to the house pointed out by the lad. Arrived there, she suggested that the husband enter first and alone. She would wait a few moments.

"Miss Adah," said Lin Fo, "ten thousand times I beg your pardon, but perhaps you will come to see my wife some other time—not today?"

He hesitated, embarrassed and humiliated.

In one silent moment Adah Raymond grasped the meaning of all the morning's trouble—of all Pau Tsu's sadness.

"Lord, what fools we mortals be!" she soliloquized as she walked home alone. "I ought to have known. What else could Pau Tsu have thought?— coming from a land where women have no men friends save their husbands. How she must have suffered under her smiles! Poor, brave little soul!"

Toshio Mori

(b. 1910–1980)

Toshio Mori's collection of short stories, **Yokohama, California** *(1949) is the pioneering Japanese American work of fiction. Slated for publication in 1941, this important collection of writing—indeed, the first collection of short stories ever published by a Japanese American writer—was delayed due to the escalation of the war by the Japanese, then the onset of World War II, and then the relocation camps. Finally, eight years later,* **Yokohama, California** *was published by Caxton Printers of Caldwell, Idaho. Despite the ten-year wait, it was still the wrong time for a Japanese American to be the first of anything—including the first author to show how remarkable and unique Japanese American communities were in the East Bay of the San Francisco Bay area. Following the war, Japanese were understandably unwilling to praise and applaud an effort that would again make them stand apart from mainstream American society.*

The stories in **Yokohama, California** *for the most part describe Japanese America before the war and a community whose wholeness no longer existed after the war. Following the publication of* **Yokohama, California,** *Mori sat down at his desk to become a writer; he wrote every day but was unable to publish a single piece of writing for the next nine years.*

In 1970, Jeffery Chan, Frank Chin, Lawson Inada, and Shawn Wong, the four editors of **Aiiieeeee! An Anthology of Asian American Writing** *(1974), found a copy of* **Yokohama, California** *in a used bookstore for twenty-five cents. A 1949 newspaper article nestled in the twenty-one-year-old book noted that Mori lived in San Leandro, California. "Literary research" (confined to looking up his name in the current Oakland phone book) yielded Mori's name and number. His rediscovery in the early seventies by a younger generation eager to find an Asian American literary tradition led to a restarting of Mori's literary career in his sixties and the publication of his novel* **Woman from Hiroshima** *(1978) and a collection of his short stories called* **The Chauvinist and Other Stories** *(1979).*

1936

There is something in the way I feel toward the year 1936 that I shall be sure to remember. Perhaps it may be that I am living today, that I am alive and am striving toward my hope, that I feel so strongly the tang and the bracing weather of today and the more todays to come. It is the year I shall recall later as the time of change in the conduct of life and outlook. I like to explain away the change and the song of it here but that is a hopeless task just now. I must simply say it is the year of 1936 and was the year and let it go at that. But if I should tell you how I feel today about 1936, I might be able to do something about it.

I began suddenly or slowly, it does not matter, to want, to desire, to sink my teeth into everything I could grasp, to everything I see, hear, smell, taste, etc. I wanted to do everything, I wanted to know women, I wanted to know the white people, the minds of my generation and people, the Nisei, the nature of our parents, the Issei, the culture of Japan, the culture of America, of life as a whole. I wanted to go from the country to the city and from the city to the country. I began to move, I began by joining the Eden Japanese American Citizens League, I went to the girl's homes, I went to see the boys, listened to the lecture of Dr. Alfred Adler, the psychoanalyst, listened to Kagawa in English at the Oakland Auditorium, and also in Japanese at Wanto Gakuen. I listened to the Japanese girl talking about her beautiful girl friend, Tsuyuko, who is wealthy and unhappy; the Tsuyuko I could not forget. I heard her speak of another girl who had been raised and educated in Japan, called over by the parents to join them in California. I heard of the girl who had ruined her chance for marriage and livelihood in America by her temperament and objections, and was now returning to Japan on the next boat. I heard my friend speak of her friend as strong-willed who finally broke down and wept before the sailing day. She was afraid of her friend's rash nature and of her decision to return to Japan and the consequent fate. As I listened to the girl, of her life, gossip, experiences, talks, rumors, I saw how much I did not know of life, the limitations of my life, and how much more she was close to the life of the people and of herself. This girl (I have been grateful to her ever since) drove me restless with her knowledge and her life, to seek, to experience something of my own.

I do not know when I began or perhaps, I do not know when I began to really notice the lives and the people inhabitating today in the year of 1936. I do not know exactly who or what event was the first experience; the lives and the people of 1936 are so assembled together, alike in usefulness, that I cannot place one individual or the individuals above another but must recall them together, hand in hand.

From the morning I began visiting the Japanese dentist in the heart of downtown district, to have my teeth fixed, the every day, the days that come around simply and plainly every day, became my interest and love. I thought it lovely that each day became an adventure; I thought it lovely enough when I realized that every day, plain and simple, was unlike any other day. One day I would meet the white elevator girl who would take me up to the dentist's floor and she would say something about the weather, or about the dentist visiting, or about the tasty smell coming into the elevator shaft from the candy kitchen in the basement, and then I would not meet her for days.

On another day I might be riding home on the bus and would sit alongside a middle-aged man and a college student as I have precisely done. I would find out as I watched the middle-aged man striking up a conversation with the college student, that he was a writer, a writer of cowboy stories, who sold a half-dozen stories or so to the magazines. And I would listen to his theories and his battles with writing in the evenings and listening, I would begin to think about his office (presumably an office man) and his family. I did not meet the same college student again but listening to that one conversation just before noonday, I found out he was once interested in writing but now had quit. He was a quiet youth, gentlemanly and of generous nature. The day and the meeting, and the impression would end just that way and I knew it was the end of another day. And with the weather of the days I found it the same. One day it would be warm, another day too hot for comfort, some days cloudy, another time windy, cold or raining, foggy, drizzling. To go further, it is true that a single day is a variation of temperature, light, etc., and I thought this was a lovely way of prolonging interest in life, to desire something that is yet to be and is not so sure about becoming that way, that uncertain as our lives may be we have come more to love the days that are ours.

While I was crazily pursuing everything, everything in life, wanting to know, wanting to experience, wanting to see the spark and the lives of men, wanting to see the spark of life and spark of individuals. I could have been a poet. I could have claimed the stars and the universe, the earth, the soil, the birds, and the gentlefolks. Today I am not the same; I am still pursuing, still crazily lusting, but I do not and cannot claim the stars and the universe, the earth and the like, or even more so claim the women, the nations, the wealth, the patents, and the life. I cannot claim, when I come to think of it, even the petty things and I cannot claim the tools, I cannot claim the materials and the art of life. This is so I cannot claim the year 1936 though I am in love with it, though I am glad I am living today. I simply sit here in my den, in the presence of the year 1936, present with its shortness, death, and variation, and also, conscious of the rarity, 1936, the only year to be 1936. This leads me to the ending, to the finish of this piece and the commencement of the brother years 1937, 1938, 1939, 1940, and so on, wanting to know, everything, restless, hungering, seeking, crazily....

It is just as well to end anything like this on Monday of his life as well as on Saturday. It is the same, the ending and the beginning, and I shall take one day, Monday, the representative of all Mondays, and the representative of Tuesdays, Wednesdays, Thursdays, Fridays, Saturdays, Sundays, and of the year 1936, as the spokesman, the chronicle, the record, and as perhaps, a farce.

I will begin easily for myself, thinking from the time I rise for the flower market to work, thinking as I go along, remembering, tasting, visioning the faces I've seen and the events that were to be Monday. I will go to the market to sell flowers from 7 A.M. to 8:30 A.M. and finishing that I am through at the market, free to go home and turn over the soil, water the plants, cut the flowers, etc. On Mondays I cannot go home early; it is the day of adventures, because I am going to the dentist, and because there are many hours to fill between the market work and the dentist's appointment. The first thing I do when I am free for the morning (I notice) is to go to the public library on Fourteenth and Grove. It is fascinating to see people reading, and it is fascinating to realize that here one can become learned and be up-to-date as anywhere else. But meeting the man, the incident that happened today on Monday that makes Mondays memorable, did not happen upstairs or downstairs in the reading room nor in the fiction room, the non-fiction room, but down the hall on the first floor in the men's rest room. I do not remember precisely the beginning of our chat with this man, the custodian of the library halls. He was leaning against the wall puffing his cigarette rapidly, taking time out for a smoke when I entered the place and our conversation began. He was my size, a small man, quite bald, a man you would not believe had gone a foot out of California or Oakland even. He began talking, and the minute he opened his mouth I knew he was anxious to have someone to talk to. He began talking of his days at sea and I was surprised at the news, surprised that the custodian of a public library could ever think of such an adventure of life.

"I have been on the sea for twenty years," he said. "I have been to many ports of the world, Bombay, Liverpool, Marseilles, Yokohama, everywhere, coming in, going out, around the world. For twenty years I saw very little but the sea."

"Twenty years is a long time," I said. "You must love the sea very much."

"I did not love the sea," he said. "I was much more afraid to starve on land. I was afraid I could get no job of any kind, I was afraid of knowing nothing, and I was afraid of starving."

I shall not make up anything of the meeting; I will leave it alone. It happened as I told you and it ended briefly without the usual rounds of drinks. In fact there is nothing unusual to this meeting and there is nothing unusual about his twenty years on the sea; only the fact that we talked and were simply alive and warm, to talk, and to listen, wanting to know, wanting to give, that the incident became memorable, that I should be able to remember it today.

I was ten minutes late for the appointment and the Japanese dentist was waiting for me. I have been going to this dentist for almost a year and every time I step from the waiting room to the laboratory, I am reminded, not of teeth-fixing, but something of the experience and the sensitiveness of this artist of molars. He is, what Sherwood Anderson would call, an old craftsman. I have listened to the philosophies of the philosophy, from the books to the philosophers, the scholars, priests, and the masters of the past and they are all right; I do not junk them. But coming here in the laboratory, in the presence of this small Japanese, I forget many things, I forget philosophies, the books. It is an experience like a moth flying toward the red-hot lamp; myself leaping kangaroo-like to shake hands and derive some good and warmth from this man, an alive one. With this in mind I forget my teeth and the dentist begins to possess my teeth, till the teeth, my teeth, belong back and forth, from one to the other, belonging to the wanting-to-know, belonging to the wanting-to-give, till the teeth of the world (becoming the material) becomes one taken possession of, taken care of, becoming relative one and all.

This is not what we talk of, the dentist and I, but if we were able to grease our tongues smoother and nobler, I think, since we are men, and alive today, it would be how we feel about the teeth, about love, about work, about hope, about life.

Every time I visit my brother's shop in Oakland I remember the unidentified day when I had a haircut at Tony's in the presence of two customers. This was out in the suburbs. There are times when I see Tony out on the sidewalk walking back and forth, wearing the barber's apron, smoking a cigar. He would wave his hand when he saw me. Sometimes when I went slow he would shout, "Hello, boy! Where are you going?"

"Hello, Tony," I said, "Oakland."

He would wave his hand again and smile. The day I am particular about was such a day as this. I went in for a haircut. Before I was there five minutes two customers came in a minute apart. I remember this meeting at the barber shop because Tony and his two latest customers, and myself were present and responsible for the effect. It is why I also remember that the event has something in common with my brother in his new rooms above his shop. The four of us at the barber shop did not talk about anything important, I remember. The Spaniard was kidding Tony about the warmth of the shop. (This was in December and Tony had a tiny coal oil stove burning for heat.) All the while the two, the Spaniard and the Italian, kidded back and forth. In the corner a big Mexican was smiling and I, Japanese, sat in the chair smiling. I could not make up the nationalities present there that afternoon at the barber shop. The moment I caught on to the bizarreness of the meeting, the novelty of four nationalities assembled in one tiny shop, I began to think of America. This was not a new thing to the old stock of America but to me as a Japanese American, it was something. If one tiny barber shop could have four nationalities at one time, how many does America house? Then, I could believe the vastness and the goodness of America's project; this is the place, the earth where the brothers and the races meet, mingle and share, and the most likely place, the most probable part of the earth to seek peace and goodwill through relations with the rest of the world. It is for this reaction I think of my brother, living in his new surroundings, in the city, among the peoples of the earth, rooming in the same house with half-a-dozen nationalities, among them a Russian doctor, his best friend. I think of his life ahead in the city of America, I think of the thousands of untouched relations between the nationalities, the colors, the creeds, and the hour, the time and his opportunity of being.

I met Sheldon Brown's father in the morning of a Monday in 1936 and I shall end my day, my 1936, with the remembrance of Sheldon's dad because it is fitting, and for the reason that the meeting took place in the morning of my 1936 which is the afternoon, the evening of my piece and also the morning again. I had known Sheldon and his brother Bob since grammar school days in Oakland. That was fifteen years ago; it does not concern here, today. I want to say something of Sheldon's father who came to see me, a friendly visit, and we began talking about his sons, my friends. And the father of these two boys, now grown, twenty-seven and twenty-four respectively, laughed and chuckled as he related the uncertain and certain, an interesting career of the younger son. Bob, he related, believed he had found the medium, the business of his life, in acting, to be an actor. "After three years of college," the father chuckled and was amused at his son's notions, "he wants to be an actor. He is today, studying dramatics, earning his bread as an art model in San Francisco."

"That is fine," I said to the father. He laughed heartily and one could see he had taken fancy to Bob's ambition. The family, he said, would not interfere. It is no use; Bob tried his hand at carpentry (his father's trade) and was indifferent in interest and work. The father was skeptical of Bob's life, career, and the last I saw of him (the father), in 1936, with his amused, chuckling face, he was fancying and thrilling at the new generation with their struggles, soberliness, loneliness, that is, of 1936.

All this will be forgotten, about Sheldon's father and how Bob rose or fell, how at one time such and such a thing happened and that there ever was a year called 1936, and that there ever was a writer for its days, and that the people of 1936 were once living. All this will be forgotten; this is logical, this is not important. But what I am trying to get at, to put over to you, is that in 1936 once there was a youth wanting to know, wanting to know so badly he wanted to stab at everything, everything in life. He was living once, the youth of 1936, and is living again in 1937, 1938, and so on, till the time of man is no more. I am not weeping for him; I am glad for him, I cannot weep and feel sorry for something that is living and will be living long after our death.

—1936

Bienvenido Santos

(b. 1911)

Bienvenido Santos has had a long and distinguished writing career in America and the Philippines beginning in 1955 with the publication of a collection of stories entitled **You Lovely People**. *This book was followed by the publication of several short story collections, including* **The Day the Dancers Came** *(1979),* **Scent of Apples** *(1979),* **Dwell in the Wilderness: Selected Short Stories 1931-1941** *(1985), and the novels* **Villa Magdalena** *(1965),* **Volcano** *(1965),* **The Praying Man** *(1982),* **The Man Who Thought He Looked Like Robert Taylor** *(1983), and* **What the Hell for You Left Your Heart in San Francisco** *(1987). Santos was a distinguished writer-in-residence at Wichita State University in Kansas from 1973 to 1982. Upon his retirement, he was awarded an honorary doctorate of humane letters.*

In **Scent of Apples**, *Santos tells the story of a Filipino generation that came to America just before, during, or just after World War II. Despite having proven their loyalty to America during World War II, America still kept them isolated and ostracized from mainstream America. This new generation of men was not the migrant farmworker or cannery workers of Carlos Bulosan's classic autobiography* **America Is in the Heart** *(1946). Instead, these Filipino immigrants were educated, urban, and professional. They worked in Washington, D.C., and Chicago, yet remain as lonely and as rejected as the working-class generation that came before. With the memory of their people's sacrifice during World War II in the Phillipines still fresh on these young immigrant's minds, America's broken promise of access and opportunity may be even greater than the poverty, racism, and prejudice described in Bulosan's* **America Is in the Heart**

Quicker with Arrows

For both of them there would be no fumbling for lost dates, no turning over the pages of the calendar for the particular year, the definite month and day, no searching the memory for echoes that now belonged to the past. Always, when their minds turned to the first day, their first day together, like this, together alone and in love, there would be no crashing of cymbals and a thunderous beat of drums and trumpets blowing, sudden and frightening, as it was on that day in summer, was it two or three years ago? It did not matter. Crowded Washington was stifling in the heat, there was a war going on, oh, yes, it had just begun, and lovers who had since long perished yet lived and loved, the same war that had already ended in Europe and would soon end all over the world after Hiroshima.

It was a late afternoon, but the sunlight lay glaring still over the heads of the lugubrious figures on the wall of the upper story of the brown building across the way from the *Bayou*, where Val had lived in an apartment since his arrival from New York. The scene had not altered through the changing seasons and faces.

From the open window, the lovers watched a raucous parade of negroes attired in many colors like characters in a costume play, clowns without their masks, toreadors[1] without their *muletas,*[2] or gypsies grown weary with lying. All marched to the loud music, their black, oily faces shiny in the sun, dark, wet spots showing under their arms.

What was it all about, the blaring music and the marching men and women with hard, unsmiling faces?

It could be that these paraders belonged to a sect or a cult professing a faith others denied, fighting for a cause so flimsy that the voice had to be loud acclaiming it, and these drums and trumpets could be a renewal of courage slowly dying. Or maybe, this was to mark a day of triumph or perhaps the anniversary of a loss—the lovers never knew; they did not truly care.

Now long afterwards, suddenly remembering, Fay asked, "Those colored folks that day, remember? What were they really up to, do you think?"

"Maybe they were celebrating for us," Val replied. Fay took up the banter in his voice, saying, "But they looked so serious, they should have been gay and laughing."

"Think so?"

"Of course, Val, unless, perhaps, you regret all this?" The lightness in her voice was gone.

"Now, don't be silly, I was only joking," he said, drawing her close to him, the dampness of her flesh, a welcome coolness of his own.

Ever since that first day two or three years ago, there had been desperate moments in his life, only he knew, but not even he quite frankly admitted, for which he hated and cursed himself, his wanting Fay so much, delighting in the things she said and did for him without any thought of getting anything in return, or just happily content with her presence in the apartment. But there were times when he wished she would forget and leave him because, well, it did not seem right, it was not right. He was all so confused, sometimes he felt he was going mad ... what did it all mean? was it love? what was it, really, but why find out? Just go on and on till the time came for parting. He was going home and leaving all this behind him. Perhaps even his tenderness, his passion, was just that, a manner of saying, Fay, this cannot last forever. I must return to my country, I must leave you behind. My people won't understand, I don't understand, darling, I'm confused. Help me, help me, whoever you are who could help me.... Hence, every embrace was a last embrace, every burning kiss, the searing end.

---

1. bullfighters
2. spears

Among the Filipinos and their American friends in Washington, Valentin Rustia was the brown prince, always impeccable dressed, always smiling and kind. But Val's kindness was the kindness of the weak. He could not stand suffering in others and he gloated over his own as though self-pity were the ultimate ecstasy. Sometimes he talked tough. Once, he was heard to say that, at least for the duration of the war, there should be a moratorium on feeling, an off-limits sign for all hearts.

Just returned from New York City where he was studying before the outbreak of the war, Val had many friends both among the Americans and the Filipinos. He was often seen in dances escorting pretty, clean-looking American girls, and, now and then, the daughters of Filipinos prominent in the homeland, studying in New York or in New England, in exclusive colleges for women.

The youngest son of a wealthy landowner from Pampanga,[3] Val was sent to America to prepare him to take over his father's place at the sugar central which his family practically owned. There had been rumors linking his name with that of the accomplished and lovely daughter of a wealthy Visayan[4] family, distant relatives of his mother who was once herself a beauty from the Visayas.

But Val was free and did not seem to feel the burdens and inconveniences that the war was imposing on everyone in America. Soon after the declaration of war between the United States and Japan, however, his regular allowance from home was cut off. He took on jobs nobody back home would have thought him capable of doing, until he met a former American senator, who was the spokesman for the sugar block in the Philippines, and a friend of his father's. Without difficulty, the former senator got him a job with the Washington Office of War Information. The job was classified essential and Val did not have to get into a uniform. There had been times, though, when he did not relish the sinecure he had landed. He wanted to get into the army and fight, or get wounded maybe, or even die, why not, so many young men who had as much right to remain alive and whole were getting all maimed in mind and body, and dying. Nothing lasted, anyhow, even life, especially life, such as it was.

When he met Fay, he expected her to go out of his life, just like so many others before, without regret, even without memories. Fay Price had not yet finished high school when she left her home in Virginia to work in the wrapping department of Hecht and Company in Washington. She attended high school, graduating at the outbreak of the war. When they met, Fay worked nights as cashier in a government cafeteria on Constitution Avenue. She was such a simple girl, she would every now and then speak out her fears to Val, in their early days together, asking what sort of spell he had cast upon her. She had met other men, handsomer and taller, and, like her, white, and you are brown, she would say, and not so tall, and your eyes disappear

---

3. central Philippines
4. province or dialect

when you smile, but I love you, Val. This must be love, this wanting to be near you all the time, this thinking of you all day and feeling famished and missing you something awful and all broken up inside me till I see you and I am in your arms again.

She had spoken about it to her friends who advised her to forget Val, the sooner the better, for he was going to bring nothing but sorrow to her life. But that was not true, Val had not brought sorrow to her life. She was happy with him. Now there was some sort of meaning to her life, instead of living one dreary day after another, without hope, without something real to hold on to, an anchor, or something that says to you early in the morning when you wake up, now this is another day, and there will be a smile in his eyes as you look into them, and his arms will be strong, and his touch so gentle, you will feel all weak and trembly and lost, but alive, yes, alive, and wishing to live on and on, for him, whom you have found, for him whom you love.

Fay was understanding. When Val didn't feel like talking, she kept quiet, doing whatever she felt like doing, reading perhaps, or tidying up his things, he was so messy with his belongings. When he felt like talking about things she could not understand, she pretended to be interested and listened on. Now Val was also a good listener. When she talked to him about her life, the poverty of it, a shiftless, good for nothing father, who, on a violent day, clubbed her mother to death, the terrible life in an orphanage, she saw tears in his eyes. Val felt truly and deeply about such things and wondered why they should happen to a lovely creature like Fay. Part of his sadness must have been due to the realization that there was such a gap in their lives.

For her part, Fay felt that Val needed someone like her, to talk to, to love. There were times when he looked so helpless. He was so lonesome for home, he looked so radiant talking to her about his country and his folks, his beautiful mother, and his wealthy father, and the vast stretches of sugar cane fields, and the men at work, the private railways leading to the fields and the mills, how the cars were loaded with cane and the children of the tenants would pull at them as the box-cars passed their shacks; the Pampanga river, swollen and dark during the months of rain, the festivals, Easter and Christmas. During Easter, the fish was cooked in eggs, all eggs, you could hardly find the fish. During Christmas, for three days everybody ate and ate. To climax it all, his father threw coins in front of their mansion and the children, including some adults, fought for the shining silver.

Val had even taught Fay a song she could now sing. The tune was easy, but pronouncing all those jumbled words was difficult. She had fun stumbling through the phrases. He had to write it down for her:

O kaka O kaka, kabalat kapaya
Sabian mu nang patas nung ena ca bisa,
Keta man kekami dakal lang baluga,
Mangayap la keka, biasa lang mamana.

"All those K sounds," she complained. "What's this, a password to the Ku Klux Klan?"

"You should know," he said jokingly.

"And you call this a love song?" she asked, ignoring his remark.

"It is a love song," Val insisted.

When she asked him to translate it into English, Val hesitated. Not that he did not know the meaning; it was clear, but somehow, the words did not make sense, not the way they had to be said in English. Or perhaps they made sense, only he had already forgotten a lot of things about his country, like the meaning of this song. With a war on, the homeland seemed so far away it belonged to another world. No ordinary ship or plane could take one there. But first, there had to be peace.

"Well, it's got to have some meaning," Fay said while Val looked for extraordinary ships in his mind and peered at corners for the peace he could not find; there was no peace anywhere, "unless it's really not intended to have a meaning like 'Mares eat oats and does eat oats and little lambs eat ivy,' but even this nonsense has meaning. And you claim this one's a love song. Perhaps a G.I.[5] tempting a native girl with his K-rations?"[6]

"It's the girl singing," Val explained, ignoring the levity in her voice and words, and thinking of the shadows of hills around the peaceful valley he knew as a child; the little black men who came down to the plain to barter with the lowlanders, their funny way of talking, their appetite, their laziness, their devotion to their masters. "She's asking her beloved to tell her the truth, whether he still wants her because, she says, she will not mind the truth at all. Where she comes from in the nearby mountains, there are many other little black men, better than her lover, who were quicker with their arrows."

Fay was amazed at Val's explanations.

"Goodness gracious," she exclaimed, "is that what it means? I think the girl in the song is nuts. If my man doesn't want me any more, I'd know, he doesn't have to tell me."

"Well you're different," Val said, feeling that he had not quite succeeded in translating the true meaning of the song.

"Besides," Fay continued, "I don't think the girl was sincere. I think she just said that because it was the brave thing to do."

"Our women are a brave lot. They know how to take it. I imagine they have been taking quite a lot since the Japanese came."

Fay said, "If I believed you, your women have all the virtues. I bet, one day you're going to marry one of them, but of course. I have seen quite a few of them, doll-faced, pearly smiles, cute pretty numbers, fragile, handle with care ... "

"None of them would have me, Fay. Besides ... "

---

5.   American soldier
6.   food issued by the U.S. Army

"Now you're being funny, Val. The few times you have taken me to some parties, don't think that I didn't notice the way the girls looked at you. I'm not that blind, sweetheart."

"No, of course, not. They just envied me, I guess, because you're always the prettiest in any crowd, Fay, believe me."

Fay was really an attractive girl. She dressed well and walked like a queen. Her complexion was radiant, especially in winter when the cold winds touched her cheeks. In a well-lighted room, it seemed her eyes gathered all the sparkle from the dazzling chandeliers and the lighted bulbs in America. But she had eyes only for Val.

The truth was, as much as possible, Val did not want his Filipino friends to see too much of Fay, although he felt good and proud standing beside her in a crowd with everybody looking at her. He was afraid some fresh guy might insult her or him in one of these dances and parties where the men drank heavily and the girls talked too much or his friends might come upon the two of them alone in his apartment. He lived in that constant fear, which he had not been able to hide from Fay.

When he was alone with her, in his apartment, he was always listening for doorbells. Even the ringing of the neighboring apartments' doorbells startled and annoyed him.

"What are you so fussy about?" Fay would ask. "If you don't want anybody to know we are here, then don't answer the bell."

"But it will keep ringing. Besides, it might be something important."

"Then answer it. I'll stay in here and won't bother you."

"I just don't want doorbells ringing. They drive me crazy," he said.

One day Fay told him, "Val, you are ashamed of me."

"Oh, no, Fay, I'm not," he protested, feeling deep in his heart that he was telling the truth because it was not really shame that he felt: it was something also he could not quite define. He wanted Fay around. Alone in the apartment, waiting for her to come, as she would sometimes promise, he imagined every footfall on the outside corridor was Fay's, and he would walk towards the door and wait until the footfalls sounded past, dying away in the distance, and a door would open and close somewhere, far away. He tried to read and smoked incessantly till his throat got sore and he would start drinking. He always had a bottle of gin in the apartment. He liked gin very much. Fay hated it. Once he forced her to take a sip and she clawed at her throat as she choked and tears came to her eyes. "It's like fire," she said, "it burns me, it turns my insides out."

Or he would turn on the radio, very low, so that he could hear footsteps on the corridor outside, the clack, clack, clack of high heeled shoes that did not stop at his door. He felt the heels stamping on his breast, strange doors closing in on him like a vise, and he would drink some more, or put some clothes on and walk outside even in deep winter. He would just walk and walk, imagining every tall, slim girl was Fay coming towards him. When he got tired of walking, he would return to his apartment and imagine all sorts of things, that Fay was hiding somewhere to surprise him. Ever since he had given her a key to the apartment, he would sometimes hope that she be around when he came. Once or twice this happened and he had been so delighted with her presence, he could not hide his happiness. She was sitting in the living room when he came in and he had rushed towards her, burying his head in her lap, letting her pass her fingers through his hair, fondling him like a child. "Thank God, you're here, Fay, I want you so," he had told her. But coming home to an empty apartment, he would mumble out her name, Fay, Fay, he would cry, picking up a tune that somehow fitted to the words, come, come, darling, I need you so, believing that wherever she was, she was going to hear him and come. There had been times in Fay's absence when he had to drink himself to sleep, but even then he would wake up before the dawn, hating himself, hating life, hating the world.

No, Val was not ashamed of her. If he only had his way, he would marry her and show her around to his friends with loving pride. But Val was weak, he was a coward, he knew he was a coward, he felt that he couldn't do anything, he dared not do anything without his father or mother, or the great family council, passing judgment on what he should do. Perhaps it was the way he had been brought up, but Val knew that he lacked strength. The fears that preyed on his mind had mostly to do with the great Rustia family, what they would think of a girl like Fay. Not that Fay was objectionable because she came from a broken-up family or that she herself had spent a few years in an orphanage, but they would object to his marrying anybody, just now, when they were out of touch. He remembered his father's words, "The greatest offense you could do would be to lose your head in America." And his own mother had expressed the same opinion.

One evening, the doorbell rang. Val jumped from the chair where he sat reading. "Fay, someone's at the door," he said. "Shall I open it?"

"Go ahead," Fay answered as she combed her hair before the mirror in his bedroom, "I don't care. I'll soon be through and I'm going." At that time she still worked nights on Constitution Avenue.

Val opened the door. It was the old doctor, Val's professor in economics in the University of the Philippines and a dear friend of his father's.

"Oh, come in, Doctor," Val said, wondering how he was going to explain Fay's presence in his apartment. Or should he? Dr. L. P. Mendoza used to be frequent visitor in the apartment and there had been times when he spent the night there. They would cook native dishes. He also enjoyed sipping gin fizz which Val could make very well. But that was before Fay came. His visits had not been too frequent since. The first time he came, Val was alone, but Fay was supposed to come, and he was so worried about it, he nearly told the doctor the truth, then. He wanted to. He wanted to find someone who would understand.

Val was happy to see the doctor. Yet he was afraid. He didn't know what to say or do about Fay's being there alone with him. Of course, he could take the old man to the living room or to the kitchen till Fay slipped out. But he would hear. Besides, Fay was not the sort who would slink away. She was honest about the whole affair; it was he who was the blithering coward. He had called himself many names.

"Chilly outside," the doctor said as soon as the door had closed behind him. Winter was straying early over the Potomac. The elms in the parks and in the circles had not yet completely shed their leaves; a little gold still remained on the promontories and hillocks.

Now, what was he going to tell him? Fay was coming out any minute. How was the doctor going to react to her presence? Would he act the way his father would, furious and merciless and completely lacking in understanding, thinking of nothing but family connection and money and the power that goes with it, the prestige of the hundred-year-old Rustia name?

Val remembered the days in New York when he practically supported the old man while he was sick and jobless. Then Dr. Mendoza would caution him about the girl whom he escorted around. He remembered his saying, "Be careful, Val, be very careful in this country. You're not just anybody." Spoken just like his father. "An indiscretion could be very costly. Not that you can't afford such things. I'm not thinking of that. I'm thinking of the greater price one has to pay at times, not necessarily in specie, but in something else. Then there's the matter of hearts. You just can't go around breaking hearts, Val. Your own couldn't be too immune, could it? Besides, everywhere, hearts are still on the gold standard, I suppose."

Now the doctor had removed his coat, shrugging his shoulders and stretching his arms as though to shake off the cold from the outside.

"The news seems good," he was saying, but Val was listening to the movements in his room, wondering what Fay was doing, what he himself was going to do.

Suddenly, he heard a door open, it was the bedroom door, and before he could think any further of what he was going to do next, there was Fay walking towards them in the living room.

The old man turned and bowed in greeting, showing no surprise at all. Fay was lovely, she was radiant.

"Dr. Mendoza, this is Fay. Fay Price. Fay, my good friend Dr. Mendoza," Val managed to say.

The old man acknowledged Fay's greetings and her smile with another courtly bow.

"Glad to have met you, doctor," said Fay after the briefest interval of silence, which extended, could have been awkward, but as it was, it seemed no interval at all except in Val's mind. "I was just going. Good evening."

"Good evening," said the doctor.

Fay threw Val a glance that said goodbye and strode out of the room, her head high, her manner of walking away, almost regal.

Val seemed to wake up from a trance and then quite impulsively he ran after her, catching up with her as she was about to open the door leading outside. He took her in his arms and kissed her rather passionately as he whispered, "Fay, darling, please try to understand."

Fay looked into his eyes and fondled his cheek with a gloved hand, saying, "You worry too much. Everything's all right. Now go back and talk to the doctor. You're such a boy. 'Bye now, sweetheart."

Val felt silly. She was so cool, so composed, why couldn't he be a little like her, frank, and good, and honest?

The old man was in the kitchen lighting the stove when Val returned.

"I guess, sir, I owe you an explanation," he said, feeling that now was the time to tell the old man about their affair.

"Maybe you don't," said Dr. Mendoza, putting the percolator over the fire. "I've known all about this, Val. You've not told me, but I know."

"You mean, everybody knows?" the coward in Val kept speaking up.

"Oh, no. I mean, your friends know you have a girl friend. They suspect you have several girl friends. This girl is one of them. That's what they say. But they don't know that she ... well, your friends don't come here often, do they?"

"No, sir," Val answered, "not too often."

"The boys understand, I guess, but the girls don't. And they can be very mean about it. You know why. They feel that one of them should marry you, that is, you should marry one of them. Something like that. You know how superior they feel about themselves. At least, each feels superior enough to think she's worthy of you, every blessed one of them. They believe that you have no business getting into a mess with some American girl whom you're not going to marry anyhow."

"Why, the little fools!" Val cried with some heat. "How do they know what my intentions are?"

Soon after saying this he felt ashamed thinking that they could be right. Perhaps that was what made him speak too strongly. They knew what he himself kept refusing to admit.

"Well, you see, they are prejudiced," the doctor was explaining. "Prejudice is a funny thing. A brown girl is as much prejudiced against a white girl as a white girl is prejudiced against a brown girl. The whole thing really cuts quite deep, you know."

"Yes, I know," Val said, helping the doctor with the cups and the saucers rather mechanically, while his thoughts strayed deeper than what the doctor called prejudice. Prejudice wasn't involved in his case, prejudice was of the mind, and this was not a simple matter that could be thought out. This was a matter of feeling, a terrific mix-up that involved a pampered heir to millions, who was taking time to grow up, who perhaps would never grow up, a weakling, a blithering coward. There, he said it again.

"But how is it with you, boy? Tell me, who is the girl? Fay Price, is that her name? Are you going to marry her?" The doctor's voice sounded strangely familiar. Who spoke like that? Who called him boy?

"I really want to talk to you, sir," Val began.

"Go ahead, talk," the doctor said.

"Often, I've wanted to come running to you. I really need help, sir. I don't know what I feel towards Fay. Maybe it's just passion, maybe lust, I don't know; it could be love. I really don't understand myself, sir. There are times when I feel like running away from her, never to see her again, but there are times when I feel I cannot live without her. We say we love each other. We believe we do. But I don't know. I really don't know. When she's not with me here, I miss her. I feel like shouting or going crazy. Maybe I'm crazy already. I see something she owns and I put it to my lips, a ribbon, an underthing, even a pin. Her fragrance, the smell of her flesh, is in the room, she's everywhere in the apartment. I long for her terribly. I know no peace till I see her. It's the same way with her, she says, and she calls herself a fool, too, for feeling the way she does for me. Sometimes, she says, stepping out of the apartment, she vows never to come back, but she comes back, she says she cannot live without me. I hope this doesn't sound funny to you, sir, because it isn't funny at all. True, other women have said the same things to me, practically the same things, but there's a difference here, sir, but just what that difference is, I can't tell. I think I really love her, sir, only, I'm not man enough to admit it. I'm afraid, but I don't know what I'm afraid of ... maybe, I know. Oh, doctor, please help me, help us."

"I think I understand," said the doctor, "I understand too well to offer any remedy."

"You mean there isn't any remedy?"

"I'm afraid not."

"You mean it will just blow over, sir?"

"I'm not even certain about that."

"Suppose I marry her?"

"That's your own problem, son."

Dr. Mendoza was unusually tight-lipped. As he had said, he was not in a position to offer any remedy. Yet he was grateful that Val had taken him into his confidence. After that evening, he was a frequent visitor to Val's apartment. The three of them dined together, went to the movies together. Fay soon became quite attached to the old man, and it appeared that the doctor developed a fondness for her that surprised not only Val but the doctor himself.

"She's a jewel, Val," Dr. Mendoza told him some months later. "She's devoted to you. While she often admits that she has no illusions, that she's too realistic to have any illusions, I know it will break her heart if you leave her, Val. I don't think she'll ever recover from it. She keeps asking about the Philippines, the people out there, your family, its position in the country. She knows and it's part of the burden she bears from day to day that she knows. You're in deep, boy. Remember what I told you. The trouble with hearts, they haven't gone off the gold standard yet. No, sir, not even in this country."

Dr. Mendoza was a great help, though, to the couple, in some ways. Val and Fay used to have many awkward moments of silence together when it seemed as though everything had been said, but there still remained a need for talk and nothing that they said meant sense. Sometimes they turned on the radio and the apartment filled with loud, strident songs, *Rum and Coca-Cola*, suggestive melodies, sentimental ditties, like *When the Lights Go On Again all over the World,* or the white cliffs of Dover with the valley blooming again ... and then news, soon the war was going to end, there would be more shooting, the doves of peace are in the air and the hunters have laid down their arms ... Now, being a much travelled man and a very interesting talker, Dr. Mendoza often told the couple stories of many lands and all sorts of ways of life, to all of which Fay was the more interested listener. Her reactions impressed the doctor, not so much the intelligence of her comments and questions, but the feeling, the deep human feeling and understanding which she showed.

"Don't get fooled by that bold, uncaring exterior, Val," the doctor warned, "Fay's extremely sensitive."

"I know," Val answered.

"Why don't you marry her, Val?"

"Do you think I should, sir?"

"If you love her. You say you do. I think you do, only you're afraid. You're older than your years and yet you have not learned to face things ... What do you know about her? Has she told you that she grew up in an orphanage, that she didn't have a decent childhood, that she has been practically alone all her life?"

"Yes, sir, I know."

"You're the best thing that has happened to her, or the worst. Don't think she doesn't know what sort of person you are. She's not dumb. She's a very good girl, noble, and honest. She's white through and through. I'm convinced that she loves you, Val. But whether you do, as you say, I'm not sure; maybe, you yourself don't know. One of these days, you have to do something about it. This cannot go on and on, the way things are."

That day Dr. Mendoza left Val's apartment without saying good-bye. Val did not seem to notice it. For a long time he thought that truly, one day, very soon perhaps, there was going to be an end to what Dr. Mendoza called "the way things are."

In August, on Val's birthday, he was alone with Fay in his apartment, unaware that somewhere about the same time, a city in the East was burning and men were dying horrible deaths by the thousands. As a severe contrast, there was rejoicing in their part of the world. To the two lovers that mattered little, for in all the world that day, there were just the two of them. A little while back, she had given him her gift of love and none of her own fears. These she covered up with gentle thoughtfulness and a gaiety that hid tears, or if they showed, could have been mistaken for tears of joy. She had even drunk to him, a toast in gin, his favorite. She had felt the fire burn her throat, and she clutched at it, laughing as she said, "It's wonderful. A little more of that would kill me, but I won't mind. Val, I love you, I love you." She wept on his shoulder, stifling the words she did not want him to hear, "Don't leave me, Val, don't ever leave me, darling."

They were preparing to go out to celebrate some more. Fay seemed composed, she didn't look too disturbed at all as she said, "Well, I guess this peace-around-the-corner prospect calls for a double celebration, doesn't it, Val? It seems that soon, you'll have to go home."

Val turned quickly to look at her. She was standing before the dresser, looking at him in the mirror. There was Fay, real and alive, between him and the Fay in the mirror, no less real and looking just as sad no matter how sweet the smile on her face was and how casual her manner of asking, as though nothing depended on the answer.

But before Val could find the words to say, the doorbell rang, shrill and continuous, as though someone had leaned on it and would not budge until the door was opened.

Val stared at Fay, his heart pounding, his hands suddenly turned clammy.

"Well, don't stand there, answer the bell," Fay said with impatience, addressing his image in the mirror.

"I hear voices, many voices," Val muttered more to himself than to the girl who had not even turned to face him.

"Don't be a fool. Open the door," Fay shouted as though her anger, such as it was, could only be vented on the image of her lover.

Val turned to go, but came back to her and took her hands, drawing her to him as she faced him..

"I think I know who they are, Fay," he spoke low as though afraid to be heard, "I'll have to get rid of them . . . if I can. Meanwhile, please stay in here first . . . and . . . wait."

"Your . . . your Filipino friends?" she asked, sitting on the bed.

"Yes, I guess so, Fay," Val answered.

"And you don't want them to see me, is that it?" Fay asked in such a low voice, he could hardly hear her in the din of the ringing bell.

"Well ... " Val could not think of what to say, "I mean, it's better you stay in here, huh, darling? It won't look good if they find you here with me, alone."

"Oh?" Fay had turned to the mirror and now bowed her head as though she could not stand what she was, if there was anything to see, like the familiar suddenly becoming strange; but there was so much to hear; there was something wrong in what the voices said, about the continuous ringing of the doorbell.

"You just stay in here for a while, I'm coming back. I'll just talk to them and then I'll come back," one of the voices said. It was the nearest voice, the gentlest.

Fay did not turn nor look at him in the mirror as she heard the bedroom door close behind him. It seemed there were other bells, other sounds in the air.

Val had the main door hardly opened when they pushed in, barging in like a wave of invaders committed to take an island at designated time. There were so many of them, one would think all the Filipinos in Washington had concentrated on this one door on this particular day. They were carrying bags of food and wrapped-up bottles of liquor, and they were singing, "Happy birthday to you ... "

He recognized some of them, Sev, Joe, Mike, Eric, and Vincent, but the others just swept past him as though their objective was farther inland and there was no time to lose. The singing, broken up and off key, continued. The girls stayed behind and not till Val had smiled at one of them, did they stir. They stood there as though undecided whether to join the party or not. Some of them were leaning on the wall on the far end of the corridor, as though they were not with the party.

"Oh, Pitang, it's you, come, come in, all of you," Val was saying in a voice that surprised him, it was calm and sincere.

Pitang said, "Happy birthday, Val," and the others followed saying the same thing, the two Marias from Ann Arbor, Anita, Pilar, Helen, Angela; and the last, bringing up the rear, one of those leaning on the wall in the corridor, was Cielo, heiress to the Barranco millions, richer than the others, lovelier, and deeply in love, as everybody knew, with Val, and proud, prouder than gold. She didn't greet Val, just walked past him.

One of the girls said, "Kiss him, you said you were going to kiss him, now let's see you do it."

The girl referred to protested, "Look, I didn't say that. You were the one who promised to do it. Now, come on, I dare you."

Val stood by pretending to be interested, but all the while he kept listening to sounds, if any, from the bedroom. He knew, how well he knew, that whatever conversation went on in the living room, where they were now all gathered, could be heard in the bedroom.

"Safety in numbers," cried Helen. "Let's all kiss him at the same time!" The girls made ready to swoop down on him, but Val went among the boys, crying, "Help, help." The cry sounded meaningless. No, he could not act. How was he going to tell them, look, there's a girl in the other room, I love her, but what do you know about love, what will you think of her and me if you knew about us?

Some of the boys challenged the girls to direct their kisses to them. "You won't ever get to Val," he heard one boy say, "the fellow's getting a full diet."

The had spilled all over the hall and the kitchen, and talk and laughter went on simultaneously. Cielo sat in a corner, surrounded by the boys, listening to them and smiling, but she was watching Val. Every time he glanced towards her, she was looking at him.

Val didn't know what to do or how to compose himself. He could hear and understand only bits of what was said to him. He was thinking of Fay. How was she taking all this, would she remain where she was or would she come out and defy them all? Great God, she should not ... and talk and smoke floated on about him while he managed to say something now and the and pretend how overwhelmed he was ... happy birthday, Val, isn't it wonderful that your birthday should almost coincide with the dropping of the atom bomb ... the Japs are cooked, we're going home ... let's all get drunk, and that includes you girls, you should all get stinko ... *bastus,*[7] *bastus!* Oh where's the old doctor, Dr. Mendoza, where's he? Not around yet, but coming, you say? He should, after all, it was he ...

Soon after, Dr. Mendoza appeared. Somebody had opened the door for him. Val had not even heard the doorbell. He didn't care for doorbells ringing now ... Fay, Fay, I'm coming in soon, I'll explain, darling ...

When their eyes met, the old man looked away, but fleetingly. He was smiling when he turned to Val again after acknowledging the greeting of those who had noticed his presence. He kept watching Val as though to say, now is the time, this is the moment, Val. There was pity in the old man's eyes as he watched Val trying to smile and get into conversation in a voice that had no life in it.

Everybody was talking about the future, the Philippines, the letters that they had been receiving from home, the great, golden opportunities for making money out there, the things to do and bring. They were going to spend all the cash they could get hold of, even borrow, sell jewelry just so they could have enough cash to buy the things the country had so long been without, and net handsome profits, many, many times the original investment.

Take advantage of the situation, guys, the voices seemed united in that one refrain—*aprovechar*[8]—and you, Val, ask your old man to send you all the cash he can,

---

7.   asshole, fucker
8.   take advantage

then buy all the cheap trinkets from Woolworth and you can sell them over there for real. They fall for such things, anything that glitters or shows the color of gold. We know one guy who has bought practically all the cheap watches in town, and shoes, summer wear particularly, boy, we can make a fortune on those things ... Cielo, Cielo, dear, may I sign a promissory note, or you don't believe in notes, ha? ... Write your old man, Val, he has money, surely you have heard from him?

Oh, yes, Val had heard from him. Father isn't too well, but he's going to live, but Fay, how are you going to fit into this madness, my lovely Fay, what are you doing now as I stand here like a petrified fool? You have been lonely all your life, Fay, you have worked for everything you own, you owe nobody. I have had everything all my life, Fay, everything, now I realize it, everything, but courage, give me courage, give me my own voice, not the echo of my father's, who will give me my own voice, who will give me courage?

The talk and the smoke and the noise swirled about him ... Fay ... wait a while, I'll be with you ... Hey, Val, I bet your girl friend in the Philippines is just dying to see you now, have you heard, who's she, which family? what? oh, oh, Cielo ... I had forgotten, *mea culpa,*[9] *mea maxima culpa* ... say, where's that lovely brunette we sometimes see you with ... man, you sure know how to pick 'em. What are you going to do with her? No worry, man, you can always leave her to Vincent. That guy gets all the leftovers, he majors in handouts, garbage ...

Vincent didn't hear this at once, but when he was told what had been said about him, he threw an empty can of beer at the talkative guy. The noise grew louder. Some of the girls were screaming and laughing hysterically.

Then Mike said, "You look sick, Val, you're pale, what have you been doing. Nobody told us you've been sick. And what are you doing, alone, on your birthday?"

One girl said, maybe it was Anita, "He was waiting for us, silly, he knew we were coming. Didn't you, Val ... no?"

Val stood before them speechless as Dr. Mendoza tried to help by saying, "I was coming to fetch him, we have an appointment to eat out, but, I guess, there's no need for that now."

"I'm all right," said Val as Mike approached him to find our whether he had a temperature.

"He's okay," the doctor said, "He's just overwhelmed, aren't you, Val?"

"Yes," said Val, his voice truly an echo, "I'm just overwhelmed."

Now this could not go on and on. He must do something. Val walked away from the front room with some sort of just acquired stealth and a sudden cunning. Swiftly, he turned towards the bedroom. Then he looked back, hearing footsteps behind him.

---

8.   take advantage
9.   latin; my fault

Dr. Mendoza caught up with him at about the same time the bedroom door opened and Fay came out, walking towards them. Val ran to her and seized her hands, crying "Fay, where are you going?"

What he saw amazed him. No doubt, she had been drinking. Her flushed face showed under the makeup, but it seemed she had touched her eyebrows anew and her eyelashes. Her eyes shone; there was a shimmer in their depths like tears. Her black hair, held back by a net, was a contrast to the smooth whiteness of her brow.

"Fay, darling," Val whispered, "what have you been doing?"

Fay shook herself free, ignoring his question, and went to the old man. "Hello," she smiled at him, "Please ask Val to let me join the party. I can't stand it any longer in the room."

Val and Dr. Mendoza looked at each other. Fay was dragging the doctor by the arm towards the sala.[10] Yet he didn't move till he saw what he must have been waiting to see in Val's eyes. Meanwhile, some of those in the party, wandering by, had seen them and had hurried in to pass the word, so that when the three appeared at the door, there was no more surprise in the eyes that watched them.

"Good evening," Fay greeted the strangers, her voice clear and firm, almost with some sort of authority, like the voice of an honored guest or the hostess herself.

There was no immediate answer, but finally the crowd found its voice with some fellow saying, "Welcome, welcome."

Fay started to say thank you, but Cielo cut in.

"Correction, please," she cried from her corner, her voice sharp, almost metallic, as she waved towards the boys, "Don't be improper, *caballeros.*[11] *Que urbanidad!*[12] We have no right to welcome the lady. Instead, we must ask, lady, are we welcome?"

It was not just what she said; her tone was a two-edged knife. Val wanted to put his hand on his breast where there was this sudden pain. He felt the blood drain from his face. He looked blankly in front of him. Where was Dr. Mendoza? Why didn't he say something?

"Look," Val began, wondering what he was going to say next. He had taken a step forward to call attention to something important he had in mind, but there he froze as though struck with stage-fright, having forgotten his lines. The faces before him shrivelled and shrank back, dissolving in mist. In the haze, he heard Fay's voice.

"Why, of course, darling, you are most welcome," she was saying, her tone too sweet, her accent cloying with dramatic over-emphasis, "But am I not too late to do the welcoming?"

---

10. living room
11. gentlemen
12. what good manners

Pitang had emerged from the mist of moving figures, huddled in corner. Now she was saying, "Doctor ... Val ... who will do the introductions? What happened to the men suddenly demobilized? The war's still on, fellows, come on, introduce yourselves."

The doctor's voice came through edge-wise in the sudden talk and movement all over the sala. "Friends, this is Fay Price. Fay, these are Val's friends from the Philippines. They've come to give what they call an *asalto*, a surprise birthday party for Val."

"How nice," Fay answered, her accent still deliberately cloying and over-dramatic, "How sweet! I'm glad to meet all of you."

At the sound of the doctor's voice, the mist lifted, and now, Fay's ... the figures in the room had assumed reality, the constriction in his breast didn't seem too painful any more, but still, Val searched his mind for what he wanted to say, something important, something everybody here should know. Val closed his eyes briefly.

Each of the boys gave his name as Fay looked towards each of them. The girls also introduced themselves, but Cielo simply looked at Fay, a half-formed smile in her lips, without giving her name. The old man was quick.

"Fay," he said, "this is Cielo."

Fay smiled, swinging a little towards the corner where Cielo stood. "How sweet you look," she beamed, standing a shade taller as they stood face to face like goddesses before a shepherd king, "how very sweet, just like your name."

"Oh, I didn't know you spoke Spanish," Cielo said, her teeth flashing as she smiled sardonically.

In Val's mind, the idea of a shepherd king vanished like a quick change of slides.

"Oh, no, I don't speak a word of it," Fay answered with a chuckle, adding as she whirled away to face another group, "but your name reminded me of the musical instrument."

There was a loud guffaw from one of the boys which started a chain reaction of other bursts of laughter and the hall was gay again. The doctor was smiling. Val sighed deeply as though all he needed to remember what he was trying hard to remember was laughter like this.

Fay was talking to the boys. They were all around her. Suddenly, she said, "Who's Vincent here? Come, Vincent hold my hand."

Val swallowed hard. He looked around, seeking the doctor's eyes. Now he will never remember what he wanted to say. It was no longer important, whatever it was. There was only one thing to hope for, that the party come to an end. Meanwhile, no bruises, please, no wounds ... not salt, but salve ... no further wounds.

The boys were silent, drink in hand, but not too drunk, no doubt, to miss the implication of what Fay had just said. Vincent's head was bent. Now he looked up, searching the faces around him, his mouth working into a grimace. Someone beside him held his arms, pressing it gently.

"What? No Vincent? Who then will take care of me?" Fay asked, still in the dramatic pose and accent of the amateur, the novice trying hard, too hard.

Val rushed to her side and took her hands. They were deathly cold.

"Fay ... " he began, but there were other voices shouting now, saying something happy; it was a song, "Happy birthday to you ... "

Pitang approached Fay, shouting amidst the din, "Join us, join us!"

Fay joined in, her voice lost in many voices, but just in time for her to sing the last chord, "Happy birthday, dearest Val, happy birthday to you," as she pressed Val's hand. Val wanted to kiss her right in front of them ... by God, why not?

Someone tapped him on the back and shook his hand.

"Speak up, *hombre*,[13] speak up," another fellow was saying.

"Speech, speech!" A chorus took up the cry.

Val smiled at them, shaking his head. "Thank you, thank you, everybody," he said.

Pitang walked to the center of the hall and raised her hand. As the noise subsided, she said aloud, "I'm happy to announce that the girls have prepared a few numbers for our entertainment and we challenge the boys to contribute 'counterparts.' "

Everybody applauded. There was some laughter, too, over the last word Pitang used, a common enough word in wartime Washington, and in this instance sounding so funny, yet apt.

The boys held an emergency conference. It was quick, decisive. Val smiled the ghost of a smile possible in a whirl of thoughts that came in and out of his mind as he sat on the rug at the foot of the chair where Fay sat. Mike accepted the challenge in the name of the boys. The girls booed him and he withdrew quickly for another conference of strategy with the boys.

"Oh, this is good," Fay smiled at Dr. Mendoza.

She was the only girl among the group of boys, but it was not too obvious because the three of them, Dr. Mendoza, Val, and Fay, sat a little forward, as though, indeed, they were the honored guests. All through the program, Fay sat with her elbows on the arm of the chair, leaning back comfortably, her fingers touching her temples. She changed position only when she clapped her hands or turned towards the doctor to say something or to listen to what he was saying. Once, she put down her hand and Val leaned close till her fingers touched his cheek. They were cold. Slowly, he moved his face till his lips touched her fingers. She withdrew her hand a little, but while everybody laughed and clapped, she moved her fingers close to his cheek again and

---

13. hombre

fondled it with her finger tips. Val felt a current of fire go through his body sweetly, painfully. Will the party ever end?

The numbers were short and funny. One of the Marias sang *Ay Kalisud*, a plaintive love song from the Visayas. She looked toward Cielo as she sang as though the song was dedicated to her. As "counterpart," one of the boys sang "Pistol Packing Mamma" with slight variation in the lyrics to suit the contemporary Philippine scene as they read about it in the newspapers. Helen did an imitation of Carmen Miranda[14], swaying her hips while she sang, "Ya, ya, ya, ya, I love you very much ... " It was terrific. Val turned to look up at Fay to see if she was enjoying herself. It was at this point she allowed her fingers to touch his cheeks in a caress.

The boy's contribution was even better. Sev did a solo imitation of an American boy dancing a boogie woogie with an imaginary partner, while he chewed gum as his face, all through the dance, assumed the stony look of one in a trance or in the grip of an ecstatic experience. He moved his feet to the rhythm of his jaws, he swayed and turned, pulling up his trousers, and losing his partner in the crowd of imaginary dancers. Without changing expression, he gyrated through the crowd looking for his partner, then finally he saw her, took her hand, and watched her go through the same motions, the expression in his face remaining the same, his jaws in perpetual motion. It was uproarious. Fay's laughter reached Val through the alien noise like a hail of welcome, as though it were the only voice, the only sound he could tell by heart.

During the buffet dinner that followed, Fay sat among the girls. She was telling them, "You're a happy people."

"We're trying hard," Pitang answered, "but as you can see, we're still exiles."

"And that isn't too easy, you know," one of the girls was saying.

"I know," Fay answered, "But that's over now, isn't it? Soon, you'll all be home."

"I don't think some of the boys are happy about going home," Cielo remarked as she jabbed at the little mound of food on her paper plate, "they are having such a grand time here."

Fay choked, spilling some of the food on her plate.

"Pardon me," she said, coughing softly into her hand.

Mike offered Fay an empty glass. He gave another to Cielo.

"Now," he said, "I'll pour each of you a drink, okay?"

A group had gathered around them. Val stood behind Fay's chair, searching the crowd for the doctor. He was right there, standing close to Mike, right beside where Cielo sat. As Mike was about to pour from a wine bottle into Fay's glass, she withdrew the glass and said, "If you'll excuse me, I'll be back." She walked away towards the

---

14. actress, singer, and dancer

door of the hall. In the sudden silence that followed, the clack, clacking of her shoes sounded like a knuckle blows.

As soon as she was gone, everybody talked at the same time. All voices, a jumble of words. Val felt like leaving, too, and following her, but suppose . . . He had no idea what she was going to do. But she was not gone long. As soon as she appeared, the voices subsided, but Val heard someone telling Cielo, "Now, promise, be a sport."

Fay had returned with the bottle of gin in her hand. It was less than half full. God, no! Val thought.

"Here, let's drink from this," Fay suggested, giving the bottle to Mike, "I can't mix my drinks, that's the trouble."

Mike offered to pour, first into Fay's glass, but Fay demurred saying, "Cielo first, if you don't mind."

Cielo shrugged her shoulders and allowed Mike to pour.

"Enough," she said after a while.

Fay looked at the amount she had taken, then got as much.

"Now," said Mike, "let's have a toast. Everybody!"

Everybody stood up. At a signal from Mike, Dr. Mendoza moved slightly apart, holding up his glass.

"*Salud!*"[15] he cried, "To your health, Val, from all of us."

Everybody drank. The two girls watched each other above the rim of their glasses. The others watched the two.

Fay finished her drink, but Cielo did not.

"It's like fire," she complained, coughing a little.

"That's what I said, too, the first time I tasted it," Fay said with a smile, "But you'll learn to like it. It won't take long."

"I don't think I ever will," Cielo replied, "I can't even drink champagne."

"Oh, that's different," Fay argued, "Gin's the real thing, it's the supreme test, that is, if Val's to be believed."

"Oh, then if Val said so, you must believe him, indeed, you must," Cielo said, her accent just as affected as Fay's, just as spurious.

"Indeed, I believe him," Fay answered, matching Cielo's accent, "I have learned a lot from him. He has taught me to drink, among other things. As you can see, the gin's almost gone. What you have drunk is practically our leftover."

Cielo's eyes flashed and, for a moment, they were on Val. Much to his surprise he found himself staring back. Everybody watched as though this were the second part of the program, in a different mood.

"Don't tell me," Cielo sneered, "you've just learned how to drink from Val."

---

15. to your health

"That's a fact, believe it or not," Fay smiled as though amused that she should sneer and disbelieve, "Tell her, Val."

"Yes, yes, I did, I taught her that, I taught her a lot of things" Val answered quickly. He did not grope for words. They were there. He felt bold and adequate, master of the situation suddenly. Even as he spoke, a surge of warmth pervaded his body and he wanted to move and gesticulate, he wanted to take on anybody. He continued, "Yes, I taught her that, but she hasn't learned. Right now ... right now ... but that's not what I want to say."

He went to Fay and took the plate from her hand. Then he gripped her arm and walked her to the window, near the radio, then turned her around, so that the two of them faced the crowd.

"Here," Val announced, his voice assured and firm. "This is what I have wanted to say all evening. Please listen. It's important." His voice faltered as his eyes fell on Dr. Mendoza. It didn't look like Dr. Mendoza. It was his father standing there, looking at him. With one hand still holding Fay by the arm, he gesticulated with the other, but the words didn't come too easily now. He looked again and it was no longer his father watching him, but Dr. Mendoza indeed. Val smiled as he saw encouragement in the doctor's eyes.

"I wish to make this announcement to all of you, my friends," Val began, the smile still broad on his face. "This lady, Fay Price, is my betrothed. She's the girl who will one day, very soon, be Mrs. Valentin Rustia."

In the wild applause that greeted his announcement, Val could not tell who was happy, truly happy about the new and who was not. He did not care. He looked at Fay, who was smiling, while tears stood in her eyes. Even as he looked at her, Fay made a sudden motion of holding up her hands as though to call attention; she wanted to say something. After a while, there was silence again as everybody waited for what she, the chosen one, had to say.

"I thank you all," Fay began, her spurious accent, completely gone. "And I thank Val for so honoring me today. But as you can see, and as you will agree, I wish also to be heard. After all, I have not been asked, until today. No, no, I mean I haven't been asked yet. Therefore, I cannot give an answer."

There was murmuring over the hall.

"Fay," Val said, turning to her, "I ask you now in their presence, I beg you to, please, be my wife."

It seemed, Fay had not expected that. The answer she wanted to give choked in her throat on which she now pressed her fingers.

"Oh, Val," she cried, facing her lover, "Why did you have to do this now?" She spoke and looked as though for the moment she had forgotten the many eyes upon her.

"Answer, answer!" some fellow from the rear were shouting.

"Good heavens! *Que estupidos!*"[16] it was Cielo's voice, exasperated, impatient, "What answer are you waiting for? Could there be another answer?"

"Oh, yes, there could be," Fay replied, looking straight into Cielo's eyes, then half-turned to Val and said, "Thank you for all the fine times, Val, thank you for this gesture, but, sorry, I'm not buying. Good night."

Before anybody realized what she was going to do, Fay had walked out of the hall. Val stood rooted on the spot, his eyes searching those upon him. Everybody talked at the same time. Their voices came to him like a suffocating wave and he felt like going under. Suddenly he felt a great need to cry, father, father! Just then, above the voices, rose one voice, shouting, "Go, follow her, you fool!"

At the sound of the voice he turned around and ran towards the bedroom. Just as he passed through the door, he heard the radio. Someone had turned it on. A voice was saying that there were rumors in the air, everywhere, that Japan had surrendered. An official statement from the White House was forthcoming. There were no other voices from the hall.

Fay was not in the bedroom. Her gloves and bag were not there. Val ran out fighting back a desire to scream. When he finally caught up with her, Fay was opening the door downstairs. He rushed to her and seized her hand. For a while they stood wedged between the swinging door.

"Darling," Val began, putting his arms around her, but Fay pushed him away and ran down the steps into the night. Val ran after her, but stopped under a lamplight and peered into the dark. It was the first time he had seen Fay disappearing in the darkness. Always, his memory of her was Fay, getting into the light, emerging out of the shadows, a radiance, a beautiful body aglow, against a dissolving darkness. This was different.

On his way back to his room, he saw the doctor standing near the door and for a while he thought it was his father waiting for him. In the hall, the party still waited for the final word for the White House about the surrender.

---

16. what stupidity

Carlos Bulosan

(b. 1913–1956)

Carlos Bulosan was born in the Philippines in the town of Binalonan, Pangasinan. He came to America in 1930 at the age of seventeen. Like other immigrants, he was not immune to the American dream and the promises of security and wealth. Bulosan later wrote about his journey to America and his life in America in his autobiography **America Is in the Heart** (1946). In an essay entitled "My Education," Bulosan writes:

> Now that I was in America I felt a vague desire to see what I had not seen in my country. I did not know how I would approach America. I only knew that there must be a common denominator which every immigrant or native American should look for in order to understand her, and be of service to her people. I felt like Columbus embarking upon a long and treacherous voyage. I felt like Icarus escaping from prison to freedom. I did not know that I was coming closer to American reality.

> I worked for three months in an apple orchard in Sunnyside, in the state of Washington. The labor movement was under persecution and the minorities became the natural scapegoat. Toward the end I was disappointed. I had worked on a farm all my life in the Philippines, and now I was working on a farm again. I could not compromise my picture of America with filthy bunkhouses in which we lived and the falling wooden houses in which the natives lived. This was not the America I wanted to see, but it was the first great lesson in my life.

The American dream, the fabled land of opportunity, would always remain only in the "heart" of this Filipino in America. In Bulosan's lifetime, he would never see Filipinos accepted by the larger society, even after they had "proven" their loyalty in World War II. Through his poetry, short stories, and essays, Bulosan at least made his people visible in a country that did not want to see them and legitimized their labor and existence in America. A worker himself from the first day he stepped foot in America, he dedicated himself to the lives of his fellow Filipino workers by organizing labor unions. Besides **America Is in the Heart**, Bulosan is also the author of **Letter from America** (1942), **The Voice of Bataan** (1943), and **Laughter of My Father** (1944). Having never returned to the Philippines, Bulosan died in Seattle in 1956.

The Romance of Magno Rubio

Magno Rubio. Filipino boy. Four-foot six inches tall. Dark as a coconut. Head small on a body like a turtle. Magno Rubio. Picking peas on a California hillside for twenty-five cents an hour. Filipino boy. In love with a girl he had never seen. A girl twice his size sideward and upward, Claro said ...

I was listening to their heated discussion.

"I love her," he said.

"But how could you?" Claro asked. "She's twice your size sideward and upward."

"Has size got anything to do with love?"

"That's what I've heard from my uncle."

"Your uncle could be wrong."

"My uncle was never wrong, God bless his soul."

"Was he an educated man?"

"Not in the book sense but in the life sense."

"I don't know," he said, screwing up his fish-eyes. Then he saw me. "You went to college, Nick?"

"Yes."

"How many years?"

"Enough to understand a few things, Magno."

"Now tell me," he said. "Has size got anything to do with love? I mean real love, an honest love?"

"I don't think so."

He brightened up. He turned to Claro. "That's what I thought," he concluded.

"But," Claro protested, "he hasn't seen the girl he's supposed to be in love with?" He looked at me hopefully.

"The object of love may be an idea, a dream, a reality," I explained. "The love is there. And it grows—depending, of course, on the ability of the lover to crystallize the beloved."

He opened his black mouth, showing rotten teeth. He jumped to his feet like a monkey. "That's it!" he cried. "I don't understand all your words, Nick. But I get it that it's possible for me to love a girl I've never seen!"

"That's exactly what I mean, Magno."

"Nick, you saved my life!"

"It's all wrong," Claro said, grabbing the long neck of his jug of red wine on the table. His throat gargled. His stomach rumbled. "Words, words, words! They don't mean a thing. My uncle couldn't be wrong: he was a gentleman!"

They were sitting directly opposite each other. They were pushing the jug of wine back and forth across the bare dining table in the smoky kitchen of our bunkhouse. It was early spring and the sun outside was glittering on the dew-laden hills, where the royal crowns of eidelweiss, the long blue petals of lupines and multicolored poppies were shaking slightly in the wind. It was morning and we had no work. Some members of our crew were sleeping in their straw beds, some playing cards in a corner of the bunkhouse, some playing musical instruments on the porch. We were pursuing the daily routine of their lives when we had no work. But the three of us were thinking of Magno Rubio's romance with a girl in the mountains of Arkansas. A girl he had been corresponding with but never seen.

"Will you help me, Nick?" he asked suddenly.

"Sure, Magno."

He looked at Claro with displeasure. "Please go away," he told him.

"This illiterate peasant tells me to go away," Claro said contemptuously. "This ignoramus tells a man who has gone to the second grade to go away! Listen, peon—"

"Here's a dollar," he said, disregarding the insult. "Now go away. Drink the wine in your room. I was crazy to pay for it anyway."

"Look, Igorot—"

"Here's two dollars. Be a gentleman like your uncle."

Claro looked tentatively at the money. He picked up the crispy bills on the table. He grabbed the jug of wine and went to his room.

"What is it, Magno?" I asked.

"I like you to write a letter for me, Nick."

"Where to?"

"My girl in Arkansas."

"I thought you've been writing to her."

"In a way."

"I can't express your feelings, Magno."

"Sure you can. I'll dictate in our dialect and you translate it into English." He looked in the direction of Claro's room, where a bed was squeaking like a dozen little pigs. He turned to me and frowned. "You see, he has been writing my letters. But he's very expensive. Very, Nick."

"You paid him?"

"And how!"

"How much per letter?"

"No, no, no!" he protested. "It's very complicated. At first there was only a gallon of wine. Later he thought of making some money. I don't know where he had stolen the idea, but it must have been from the movies. He demanded a flat rate of five dollars per letter."

"That's reasonable, Magno. After all he spent some money when he went to the second grade."

"But it's not that, Nick! You see, I wrote to my girl every day. I earn only two dollars fifty cents a day. Still, I had to write to her. I love her. You understand, Nick?"

"I understand. I was in love once."

"You see what I mean?"

I nodded my head. I said, "Five dollars per letter. That's more than I earn a day as a bookkeeper for our crew."

"That's not the end of it, Nick." He leaned toward me, his fish-eyes shining like mud. "Realizing that I truly love the girl, that I can't live in the world without her, he demanded one cent per word!"

"One cent per word? It's robbery!"

"Yes! And do you know what, Nick! He wrote long letters that I couldn't understand. And he used big words. How would I know if he wasn't writing for himself?"

"It's hard to say."

"However, I'm not worried about that part of the deal," he said, showing his protruding rotten teeth. He bit at a twisted chunk of chewing tobacco, rolled it from cheek to cheek and said: "I've confidence in myself. But some men use their education to enslave others. I thought education is meant to guide the uneducated. Did some educated man lie about this thing called education, Nick?"

"I don't think so, Magno. Education is what you said: for the educated to guide the uneducated. And it's more than that. Education is a periscope through which a common ground of understanding should be found among men."

He coughed up the slimy wad of tobacco in his mouth, licked the brown shreds of saliva dripping down his thick lips with the tip of his serrated tongue. He banged the splintery table with a fist and said, "The thief! He acts like an exploiter, always squeezing the last drop of my blood! You know what he did to enslave me for a lifetime if you didn't come along, Nick?"

I looked at his coconut head. I looked at his turtle neck. "No," I said.

"Later he charged me ten cents per word!"

"What?"

"You heard me right, Nick! I paid him twenty dollars per letter! Sometimes more! There!"

I studied his monkey face. I said, "It's unbelievable, Magno!"

He bit another chunk of tobacco, swallowed his saliva and bared his ugly teeth. He said, "I didn't mind paying him that much money. But the words were too long and deep for me. And again I say: how would I know if he hadn't been writing for himself? Do you think he's that low, Nick?"

"Some men are capable of anything, Magno. Some men could crawl on their bellies on human filth to earn a dollar."

"I didn't know that, Nick." He was disappointed. "I thought we were all born honest."

"We were all born honest, Magno. But along the way some of us lost our honesty."

"I didn't lose my honesty."

"Keep it, Magno. Honesty is the best policy."

"That's what I've heard. Still ... "

"You heard right, Magno."

"I will, Nick." He brushed off a scab on his flat nose. "But I'm free now because I've you. Will you write for me from now on, Nick?"

"Sure, Magno."

"What would you like to have? You don't drink like Claro. You don't go after girls like our foreman. You don't gamble like the hoodlums in the poolroom in town. You don't smoke like the whores at the Elite Hotel. You don't chew tobacco like—"

I stopped him. I said, "Don't start anything, Magno. I'll do it because I like to help you. Maybe I'll need your help some day."

"That's what I like about you, Nick. You use your college education in the right direction."

"By the way, Magno," I said. "How do you know your girl in Arkansas is tall and big on the beam?"

"She wrote to me about the matter."

"You mean Claro told you that's what she wrote?"

"Exactly."

"Did she send you a picture of herself?"

He fumbled in his pockets and produced an old wallet. He extracted a snapshot from a bunch of bills and magazine clippings.

"This is it, Nick."

I looked at the snapshot. It was faded due to too much handling. It was impossible to determine the girl's age and shape and height.

"How tall is she according to Claro?"

"Five-foot eleven inches," he said. "But I don't mind. I really don't. I like tall girls."

"Everybody does, Magno," I told him. Who is short like you. I almost added. Instead I asked him, "And how heavy is she, according to Claro?"

"One hundred ninety-five pounds on bare feet," he said. "But I don't care about that either. I like heavy girls. I really do."

"Everybody does, Magno," I said. Who is a featherweight like you, I almost added. Instead I told him, "It doesn't really matter how tall she is and how much she weighs if you love her."

His flat nose flared up. "I love her, Nick," he said.

"I know you do."

"Will you write a letter now?"

"Sure, Magno."

He ran to his room. He came back with a pencil and a pad of notepaper. Plus a big dictionary, I didn't know why. He put his hands behind his back, walked around the table a few times, stopped in front of me and screwed up his monkey face. Then he began to dictate in our dialect.

Magno Rubio. Four-foot six inches tall. Dark as a coconut. Head small on a body like a turtle. Filipino boy. In love with a girl five-foot eleven inches tall. One hundred ninety-five pounds of flesh and bones on bare feet. A girl twice his size sideward and upward, Claro said ...

"How did you know Clarabelle?" I asked him.

"I found her in a magazine," he said.

"How?"

"You know, one of those magazines that advertised the names and addresses of girls for one dollar."

"A Lonely Hearts magazine."

"I guess so."

"But you can't read, Magno?"

"Claro read it for me."

"And he found the name for you?"

"He did."

"And of course you gave him the dollar."

He nodded his turtle head. He inserted a finger in his hairy nostril to extricate a slap of dried mucus. He made a face when he pulled it out, looked at a minute, flung it aside and wiped his hand on his trousers.

"How long have you been writing to her?" I asked him.

"Three months. Do you remember the time when we were picking tomatoes and I didn't want to work? That was the time when I found Clarabelle."

"I remember, Magno."

"For a long time I had nobody to work for, Nick," he explained. "But when I found Clarabelle ... " He grunted because he had swallowed the wad of tobacco in his cheek, bringing tears to his dull eyes. "You know what I mean, Nick."

"I do."

"Well, that's why I've been working every day ever since. And I don't regret it, either."

"That's the spirit, Magno."

He put his chin between his hands. I looked at him and wondered what was transpiring in his bird brain. But I recalled about three months before, he used to stay in the bunkhouse all day. I saw him looking dreamy eyes at the pages of dime magazines. I knew he couldn't read, but the magazines were illustrated with the photographs of nude and semi-nude girls. I was tempted to teach him the alphabet, which I did for a few days, but he lacked concentration. And his memory was bad because his mind was taken up by the enticing photographs. So he made excuses that he was either ill or too busy to study.

But he was not ill. Of course, he was ill with love. The foreman scolded him once for staying out of the work, but he complained that he was suffering from arthritis. The foreman left it at that because, if Magno Rubio had the illness that he claimed, it would be dangerous for him to work in the cold weather. It was winter then, and the tomatoes were almost frozen. But the crop was saved by our industry and endurance.

And he was not busy, either. He had nothing to do in the bunkhouse, because we had a cook who cooked our food and cleaned the place. Magno Rubio seldom washed his clothes, if he ever did. He had the same rags on him all the time, even when he was in bed. It was insufferable to sit beside him at the dining table. He smelled of mud, sweat and filth, and more, he smelled like a skunk. He was not lazy of course, but he just didn't know how to be clean. He had forgotten that some human beings had a sensitive sense of smell, and unlike him, he who had been a peon and a companion of pigs and goats all his life.

But now he had Clarabelle. He was in love for the first time in his life. And also for the first time in his life the filthy rags clinging on his back were discarded. I recalled that when he burned them in the back yard, I dashed out of the house to the foothill for fresh air. But even then my stomach betrayed me, and made me curse the ugliness of some human beings. However, it was all over. Magno Rubio was human being again. And he was in love.

It was in the middle of spring and we were picking peas on the hillsides near our bunkhouse. Magno Rubio and I were working side by side, astride neighboring rows that began from the slope of the hills and ended atop a stony plateau, where goats and sheep were let loose by farmers to eat the destructive loco weeds. We worked up and down the hills, crawling on our knees like brown beetles.

I threw a handful of pea pods into my can and looked at him. "What are your plans for Clarabelle?" I asked.

"I want to marry her, Nick," he said.

"Would you like to say that in your next letter?"

"That's what I've [been] planning to tell you."

"Well, you should propose to her. How much money have you already spent on her?"

He counted it on his fingers, his thick lips moving the while.

"A little over two hundred dollars, Nick. There was the engagement ring. Seventy-five dollars. The wrist-watch. Eighty dollars. A pair of suede shoes, some clothes, a diamond bracelet. One hundred twenty-nine. It's over three hundred dollars, Nick!"

"That's plenty of money, Magno."

"It's worth it."

"If you think so."

"I spent every cent I earned for her. I also borrowed some money from the foreman with interest."

I studied his flaring nose. It was caked with dirt and mucus.

"But it's worth it, Nick."

"Of course, Magno. Would you like me to write a letter of proposal of marriage tonight?"

"Yes, Nick. The sooner the better."

"Suppose she'll change her mind when she arrives in California?"

There was a flicker of momentary doubt in his monkey face. "I don't think Clarabelle will do that. She's a good girl."

"I hope you are right."

"I've confidence in her."

So I wrote the letter of proposal. She answered immediately saying that she was accepting his proposal, but, unfortunately, she had to stay home for a while because of her sick mother. However she urged him to send her the ticket money and some extra for expenses, in abeyance, since she expected the old woman to get well.

The money was sent. Several days passed. Two weeks passed. Three weeks, and a letter arrived from Clarabelle. I read it and gave the translation to Magno Rubio. Clarabelle said, in resume, that her mother died from a lingering disease and she had to spend the money on her funeral. And not only that, she wrote sobbingly: now she had to take care of her little brothers and sisters, all under ten. But, she added, her heart was with him: she was looking forward to the day when she would be free from her family obligations.

"Poor girl," Magno Rubio commented sadly.

And that was all he said, nothing more. So we kept on writing to her. Sometimes we sent her money when she asked for it, sometimes we sent clothes for her brothers and sisters. Magno Rubio never complained. Not one word of protest. The plight of the girl in Arkansas made him more industrious and frugal. He even cut down his expenses on chewing tobacco, which made him look like a Moro juramentado[1] about to go berserk among Christians so he could go to heaven an honored heather. And of course he was back to his rags.

He worked and worked. He worked like a carabao[2] but lived like a dog. Then the pea season was over. We had a rest for a week, before we started planting celery and carrots. Then the lettuce season came. We thinned and irrigated the seedlings. So the months passed, the seasons came and went. And a year passed by uneventfully, sadly, for Magno Rubio.

A stream of letters flowed from Arkansas to California. Clarabelle was still supporting her little brothers and sisters. And poor Magno Rubio, he didn't suspect anything wrong. He was still looking forward to her coming to California.

"Will you wait?" This was her constant plea in every letter.

---

1. Muslim fanatic
2. water buffalo

"I'll wait," Magno Rubio said to himself.

And he waited. It was now two years and a half since he first contacted her through Claro. Then the third year passed, and he still waited. What sustains a man to have such patience? What quality of soul does he possess to have so much faith in something he has never seen?

I don't know. But Magno Rubio had the patience and the faith. Where most men would have given up long ago, he kept on beyond belief and all reason.

"I'll wait," he said every day.

Magno Rubio. Filipino boy. Four-foot six inches tall. Dark as a coconut. Head small on a body like a turtle. Picking tomatoes on a California hillside for twenty-five cents an hour. In love with a girl he had never seen. A girl five-foot eleven inches tall. One hundred ninety-five pounds of flesh and bones on bare feet. Filipino boy. In love with a girl twice his size sideward and upward, Claro said...

"What are you giving Clarabelle for Christmas, Magno?" I asked him.

He grinned like a goat. He was carrying a big bundle under one arm. "I'm giving her a radio," he said. "A combination radio-phonograph. It costs me nearly two hundred dollars."

"That's good, Magno."

"Let's send it right away, Nick."

We did. And we waited in vain for her letter. Then Christmas day came.

We were all in the bunkhouse. The foreman and two others were playing poker in a corner of the kitchen. Claro was drinking wine at the dining table. Magno Rubio was oiling his hair near a window, where he had propped up a broken mirror. He was grinning like a monkey. He was in love.

"So Clarabelle will know I'm clean tonight," he explained.

"It doesn't make any difference to her," I said. "She's too far away to appreciate your cleanliness."

He stopped combing his oily black hair and turned to me. "We'll tell her about it the next letter, Nick."

"Sure, Magno."

"You see, Nick. I'm clean in my soul, thinking of her."

I stopped playing solitaire. I studied his monkey face, and somehow felt that a pure soul was hidden by his flat nose and fish-eyes. I glanced over at Claro. He was getting drunk. Saliva was dripping down the corners of his twisted mouth. His eyes were popping red, like frozen tomatoes.

"Don't you have a girl, Nick?" Magno Rubio suddenly asked me.

I turned my face away from Claro and looked at Magno. "No," I said.

"You should have. You are a college man."

"Education has nothing to do with love."

"You really don't have a girl anywhere in the wide world?"

I shook my head vigorously.

"If I were you I would write to all the pretty girls. There must be a girl somewhere for you, Nick."

"I don't think so, Magno."

"How come pretty girls fall for an uneducated guy like me, huh?"

"You tell me, Magno."

"Now take Clarabelle. Why didn't she fall for you, Nick?"

"You found her first."

"If you found her first and I horned in, would she still fall for me?"

"I guess so, Magno."

He laughed like a horse. Claro banged on the table with both fists and leaped to his feet.

"Listen, you peon!" He pointed a finger at Magno. "What are you laughing about?"

"He's happy, Claro," I said. "He has a girl, that's why he's happy."

"I got Clarabelle," Magno said.

"Clarabelle, my eye!" Claro screamed.

"What do you mean by that foolishness?" Magno asked. He put the comb in his shirt pocket and advanced toward Claro. "Will you clarify your statement?"

"You mean to tell me that a girl like Clarabelle loves a donkey like you?"

"What's wrong with me?"

"What's wrong with me?" Claro imitated him. "Don't you know, peasant?"

Magno advanced closer to his adversary. I stopped playing solitaire.

"Don't you know that you look like a monkey?" Claro continued his tirade. His voice was becoming hysterical, his eyes redder, and his mouth was foaming. "Don't you know that besides being a peasant you are also illiterate! Girls like Clarabelle don't fall for your kind, illiterate peasant!"

"You are also a peasant."

"An educated peasant! There, monkey-faced dog peasant!"

"What's the difference?"

"What's the difference?" Claro imitated him again.

"I don't care what you say. Clarabelle loves me."

"Prove it, dog eater!"

Calmly Magno produced his old wallet. He threw a lock of hair on the table.

"Here's the absolute proof. She sent it to me. It's from her own head."

"You think you are the only man with a lock of hair from Clarabelle?" Claro also produced a lock of hair and flung it upon the table. "There, monkey! That's the real proof. And it's not from her head, either!"

Magno Rubio was astonished. He leaned over the two locks of hair, examining one and then the other. Then the two of them were leaning over the table, examining the two locks of hair in all their minutiae, as though they were looking down the magnificent lens of a microscope. And they were growing suspicious of each other, their heads bent close together, their eyes popping like over-riped guavas. But, finally, Magno Rubio calmed down. He didn't want any violence. His soul was clean and beautiful.

"Your lock of hair doesn't prove anything," he told Claro. Carefully he put Clarabelle's faded snapshot on the table. "But this proves something definite," he added.

Claro sneered. He flung a snapshot beside Magno's face down and said, "Proof, my ass! This is the irrefutable proof! Look for yourself, pig!"

Magno Rubio reached for the snapshot. Claro snatched it away. I had a quick glance of it. I hoped Magno wouldn't see it, because it was the picture of a pretty girl, quite young and proportionately shaped. But he was aroused.

"Let me see!" he demanded.

"Go to hell!" Claro shouted.

The coconut head sunk into the turtle body. The fish-eyes shone. The flat black nose flared. The ugly mouth snarled. Then the gorilla legs leaped. Then they were rolling on the floor. Then Magno Rubio was on top of Claro, beating his face into pulp with his whirlwind fists.

I jumped to my feet. I grabbed Magno Rubio's hands. But he was strong. He was like a mad dog. I looked toward the poker players.

"You guys!" I called. "Help me!"

They looked in our direction for a minute, then continued their game. I changed my tactics on the mad dog. I squeezed his neck and kept on squeezing until he released Claro. He gasped for air, while Claro scrambled to his feet and dashed outside. I went back to my game of solitaire.

Magno Rubio walked straight to a wall. He began beating it with his fists, weeping at the same time. He kept beating the wall until his fists began to bleed. Then he sank exhausted in a corner of the kitchen, while Claro shouted obscenities from the porch.

Magno Rubio. Filipino boy. Four-foot six inches tall. Dark as a coconut. Head small like a turtle. Magno Rubio. Cutting celery for twenty-five cents an hour. In love with a girl in the mountains of Arkansas. Filipino boy. In love with a girl he had never seen. A girl twice his size sideward and upward, Claro said ...

"Have you heard from Clarabelle, Magno?" I asked him one day.

"No."

"We should write to her."

He looked at me. His serrated tongue darted out of the black pit of his mouth. Then he yawned, and the orifice at the root of his tongue revealed its yellowish membrane.

"It's no use, Nick," he said finally. "Claro fouled up everything."

"I don't think so," I consoled him. "Besides he's gone."

"He's a louse."

"How do you know?"

"He's been writing to her."

"Well, the best man wins, Magno. And you are the best man."

"Do you think so?"

"Don't you?"

He sighed. "We'll write to her tonight."

"Are you sure you didn't get a letter from her since—?"

He did not let me finish. "I have, Nick," he confessed. "Ten letters in all. I didn't want to show them to you. The letters are in my room."

"Why didn't you let me know?"

"I thought Clarabelle—"

"Of course you were wrong, Magno," I finished it for him.

"Will you read them tonight, Nick? And write a letter for me?"

"Sure, Magno."

We were packing lettuce in the shade. It was May again and the crop was good. It was now three years and four months since he had first written to her. I read all of Clarabelle's letters in translation to him. They were arranged chronologically; he had stacked them in an empty cigar box as they arrived. Clarabelle's plea of love became more fervent in every letter, for it seemed that her responsibilities were diminishing. Magno Rubio nodded his head. A genuine smile decorated his black face. When we came to the last letter, I couldn't believe its message. But it was true. Clarabelle was coming to California. She was already on the way.

"When did you get this letter?" I asked him.

"This morning."

"Clarabelle is on the way."

His dull fish-eyes shone for the first time. "Did she say she's coming to marry me?"

"That's what she says, Magno. Did you save enough money for this emergency?"

"I've fifty dollars."

"That's not enough."

"But I thought—"

"You'll have to get out of the state to get married, you know."

"Can't we get married in town?"

"You can't marry here, Magno," I explained. "You can't marry in the whole state of California. You must go to New Mexico or Washington. These are the nearest states where you can get married. And you'll need at lease two hundred dollars for the whole affair."

"I didn't know it would cost that much to get married."

"It's only the beginning, Magno."

"You mean there are other expenses?"

"Well, later."

Dreams of glory misted his eyes. "I know what you mean, Nick."

"I know you."

"I'll borrow some more from the foreman."

"You are mortgaging your whole future," I told him.

"It's worth it, Nick." Dreams of glory crossed his face again. "When is she arriving?"

"Saturday around noon, the letter says. Today is Thursday. You've barely two days to prepare. You are supposed to meet her at the bus station."

"Will you come with me, Nick?"

"Sure, Magno."

He licked his thick lips and turned away from me. "Will you lend me a hundred, Nick?"

"I'm very sorry, Magno."

"I understand. I'll go to the foreman … "

"I'm sure he'll help you."

"Do you think she wrote to Claro?"

"I don't know."

"I will kill him."

We were loading the crates of lettuce in the waiting trucks when a telegram came for Magno Rubio. It was from Clarabelle. She was arriving in town sooner than she had expected, at five o'clock Friday afternoon. And it was already Friday noon. He had only four hours to prepare, and we had five more trucks to load. He was stunned for a moment. Then he started throwing the loaded crates into the trucks, working like two men. I followed him, hoping we would finish the job before the momentous hour arrived.

We did. We rushed to the bunkhouse and took a quick shower, changed our clothes, borrowed the pickup from the foreman and drove into town.

Clarabelle was waiting in the bus station. I knew her right away. I had seen the snapshot in Claro's wallet. He didn't recognize her. He was expecting a girl five-foot eleven inches tall, one hundred ninety-five pounds of flesh and bones on bare feet. I pulled his arm. I propelled him toward her.

"Clarabelle?" I greeted her.

"Yes," she said. "Are you Claro?"

Magno Rubio winced.

"No," I said.

"I wonder why he didn't meet me. Are you his brother?"

"Claro is gone," I told her. "Claro has no brother. My name is Nick."

"Glad to meet you, Nick. Where did he go?"

"Alaska."

"Why did he go there of all places?"

"He's working in the fish canneries."

"He didn't tell me about it. Will he be gone long?"

"He left suddenly, Clarabelle. He'll probably be gone for several months. Maybe longer. I can't tell."

She looked like a prospector who had reached the promised hill in vain. The hill was there all right, but the gold—

"What a way to treat a lady," she complained.

I grabbed Magno's arm. "This is Magno Rubio, Clarabelle."

Her blue eyes flickered. The promised hill of gold reappeared. The rose mouth unfolded sweetly. The dying prospector murmured a prayer: the vein of gold was not a mirage after all.

"Yes, yes!" She grabbed his hand. "How are you, Magno?"

He blushed. He muttered something. She turned to me for help.

"May I speak to him for a minute?" she asked me.

I nodded my head. They went to a corner. I walked to the restaurant and ordered a cup of coffee. Then I saw him motioning to me. I left my cup and went to him.

"She's trying to tell me something, Nick," he said. "But I can't understand her. Will you help me?"

I followed him in silence. "What is it, Clarabelle?" I asked her.

"It's difficult for me to make him understand," she explained. "This is what I like you to tell him: I must check in a hotel before we talk things over. He understands the marriage part of our conversation. But I need some rest. Explain it to him, Nick."

I explained it to him in our dialect.

"Tell him," Clarabelle added, "that I need some expense money."

I told him.

"And tell him that I sold our engagement ring. Tell him that I need another ring."

"He can't do it today, Clarabelle," I said. "The banks are closed now."

She looked at the big clock on the wall. "Tomorrow will be okay."

I told him. He gave her fifty dollars.

"Now that everything is arranged properly," Clarabelle said, "let's look for a hotel."

He carried her small suitcase. We walked a block and found a hotel. I followed her to the desk, while he sat in a chair near the door. She signed her name on the registry and turned to me.

"Too bad you are not interested," she said in a low tone of voice. "I like you, Nick."

I shook my head.

"I suppose not," she said. "Will you come with him tomorrow?"

"I will, Clarabelle."

She threw a kiss at Magno and walked to the waiting elevator. We went out of the lobby. He was the happiest man on earth. He hopped and jumped like a little boy. He was in love.

The next day he borrowed two hundred fifty dollars from the foreman. Then we went to town again. He bought a diamond ring for one hundred dollars. I phoned Clarabelle, and she met us at the door of her hotel. He gave her the ring, and she put it on her finger. Then she kissed him. On the tip of his small flat nose.

"We'll get married tomorrow, Magno," she said.

He understood. He nodded his head.

"Have you got a car, Magno?" Her voice was like a song.

He shook his head.

"It doesn't matter," she said. "How about my expense money, Magno?"

He opened his wallet and gave her two hundred dollars. Clarabelle kissed him again. On the tip of his small flat black nose. She looked at me for a moment, trying to say something with her blue eyes. One gesture—and a life was broken forever. One word—and it could have been mended.

"You understand, Nick," she told me at last.

"Yes."

"Thanks."

"You should at least be alone with him."

"But I can't do that, Nick."

"I know."

"I'll see you both tomorrow," she said.

We left her. We rode back to our bunkhouse. Magno Rubio couldn't sleep even when midnight came. I heard him prowling restlessly in his room. He knocked at my door when daylight struck the windows.

"This is the day, Nick!" he greeted me. He was carrying a small suitcase.

"Where are you going to get married?" I asked him.

"New Mexico. It's the nearest place."

"You have enough money?"

"I borrowed some more from the foreman. I'm the luckiest man in the world!"

I followed him to the pickup. We drove into town. We parked outside Clarabelle's hotel and both went into the lobby. We went to the clerk, and I asked for Clarabelle.

"She just checked out," the clerk informed me. "Her husband came for her."

"Her husband?"

The clerk looked at me with eyes that said more than the whole words in the dictionary. Magno Rubio was beginning to understand. He pulled at my arm. We went outside in silence.

We were walking down the street when we saw Clarabelle in a car pulling out the curb. She was sitting beside a man with brown hair and thin mustache. She was laughing. He was laughing, too.

Magno Rubio watched the car pull away. He was speechless for a moment. Then he understood everything. He brushed his eyes with a finger and took my arm.

"I guess we'll start picking the tomatoes next week, Nick," he said.

"Yeah," I said.

"Well, what are we waiting for? Let's hurry back to the bunkhouse. Those guys will eat all the chicken!"

Why does everybody make it difficult for an honest man like Magno Rubio to live in the world?

Magno Rubio. Filipino boy. Four-foot six inches tall. Dark as a coconut. Head small on a body like a turtle. Magno Rubio. Picking tomatoes on a California hillside for twenty-five cents an hour. Filipino boy. In love with a girl one hundred ninety-five pounds of flesh and bones on bare feet. A girl twice his size sideward and upward, Claro said ...

Hisaye Yamamoto

(b. 1921)

Hisaye Yamamoto was born in Redondo Beach, California. In 1986, the Before Columbus Foundation awarded Yamamoto a lifetime achievement award even though she had not yet published a book. Yamamoto had published seven major short stories in a variety of magazines and anthologies in the fifties and sixties including **Martha Foley's Annual Best Short Stories, Kenyon Review, Carleton Miscellany, Partisan Review, Harper's Bazaar,** *and* **Furioso.** *The editors of* **The Big Aiiieeeee! An Anthology of Chinese American and Japanese American Literature** *(1991) note that:*

> *Her modest body of fiction is remarkable for its range and gut understanding of Japanese America. The questions and themes of Asian American life are fresh. Growing up with foreign-born parents, mixing with white and nonwhite races, racial discrimination, growing old, the question of dual personality—all were explored.... Technically and stylistically, hers is among the most highly developed of Asian American writing.... In her work we see how language adapts to new speakers, new experience, and becomes new language.*

"Las Vegas Charley" (1961) is a journey through the history of Japanese America. Along that path the main character, Kazuyuki Matsumoto, loses touch with his community, his family, and ultimately his name and identity.

Las Vegas Charley

There are very few Japanese residing in Las Vegas proper, that glittering city which represents, probably, the ultimate rebellion against the Puritan origins of this singular country. A few Japanese families farm on the outskirts, but I can't imagine what they grow there in that arid land where, as far as the eye can see from a Greyhound bus (and a Scenicruiser it was, at that), there are only sand, bare mountains, sagebrush, and more sand. Sometimes the families come into town for shopping; sometimes they come for a feast of Chinese food, because the Japanese regard Chinese cuisine as the height of gourmandism, to be partaken of on special occasions, as after a wedding or a funeral.

But there are a handful of Japanese who live in the city itself, and they do so because they cannot tear themselves away. They are victims of Las Vegas fever, that practically incurable disease. And while they usually make their living as waiters or dishwashers, their principal occupation, day after hopeful day, is to try their luck at feeding those insatiable mechanical monsters which swallow up large coins as though they were mere Necco wafers[1], or at blotting out on those small rectangular slips of paper imprinted with Chinese characters the few black words which may justify their whole existence.

The old Japanese whom everyone knew as Charley (he did not mind being called that—it was as good a name as any and certainly easier to pronounce than Kazuyuki Matsumoto) was a dishwasher in a Chinese restaurant. His employer, a most prosperous man named Dick Chew, owned several cafes in the city, staffed by white waitresses and by relatives he had somehow arranged—his money was a sharp pair of scissors that snipped rapidly through tangles of red tape—to bring over from China. Mr. Chew dwelt with his wife and children in a fabulous stucco house which was a showplace (even the mayor had come to the housewarming). He left most of the business in the hands of relatives and went on many vacations. One year he had even gone as far as England, to see London and the charms of the English countryside.

As for Charley, he worked ten hours a night in five-hour shifts. He slept a few hours during the day in a dormitory with the Chinese kitchen employees; the rest of his free time was spent in places called the Boulder Club, the California Club, the Pioneer Club, or some such name meant to evoke the derring-do of the Old West. He belonged to the local culinary union, so his wages were quite satisfactory. His needs were few; sometimes he bought a new shirt or a set of underwear. But it never failed: at the end of each month he was quite penniless.

Not that life was bleak for Charley, not at all. Each day was exciting, fraught with the promise of sudden wealth. Why, one Japanese man who claimed to be eighty-five years old had won $25,000 on a keno[2] ticket! And he had been there only a day or two on a short holiday from Los Angeles. The Oriental octogenarian's beaming face (Charley decided the man had lied about his age; he looked to be more his own age—62 or so) had been pictured on the front page of the *Las Vegas Sun*, and Charley had saved the whole newspaper to take out and study now and then in envy and hope.

And all the waitresses were nice to Charley, not only because Charley was a conscientious dishwasher (better than those sloppy Chinese, they confided), but because he was usually good for the loan of a few dollars when their luck had been bad. The bartender was also very good to him. When he came off shift at six o'clock in the morning, tired to the bone, there was always waiting for him a free jigger or two of whiskey, which would ease his body and warm his spirit, reminding him sometimes of the small glass of *sake* he had been wont to sip with an appetizer of pickled greens just before supper, after a day's toil out in the fields. (But it seemed as though it had

1.   candy about the size of a quarter
2.   lottery ticket

been another man and not himself, who had once had a farm in Santa Maria, California, and a young wife to share his work and his bed.)

Then there had been the somewhat fearful time when the Army had conducted those atom bomb tests in the Nevada desert. Everyone had talked about it. The whole town had been shaken by intermittent earthquakes, each accompanied by a weird flash of light that hovered over the whole town for a ghastly instant. It was during this time that Charley had been disconcerted by a tipsy soldier, who, after their first encounter, had searched out Charley time and again. Although Charley's command of pidgin English was not sufficient to take in every meaning of the soldier's message, he had understood that the man was most unhappy over having been chosen to push the button that had dropped the atomic bomb over Hiroshima.

Indeed, once, tears streaming down his cheeks, the soldier had grabbed Charley by the shoulders and apologized for the heinous thing he had done to Charley's people. Then he had turned back to his drink, pounded the counter with one tight fist, and muttered, "But it was them or us, you understand, it was them or us!"

Charley had not said a word then. What was there to say? He could have said he was not from Hiroshima but from Kumamoto[3], that province whose natives are described as among the most amiable in all Japan unless aroused, and then they are considered the most dangerous. He could have said that the people of Kumamoto-*ken* had always regarded the people of Hiroshima-*ken* as being rather too parsimonious. But his English was not up to imparting such small talk and he doubted, too, that information of this kind would have been of much interest to such a deeply troubled man.

So Charley was doubly relieved when the Army finally went away. The soldier had revived a couple of memories which Charley had pushed far back in his mind. There had been that time, just after the war, when he had been a janitor in Los Angeles' Little Tokyo and he had been walking down the sidewalk just minding his own business. This white man had come out of nowhere, suddenly shoved Charley against a wall, and placed an open penknife against his stomach. "Are you Japanese or Chinese?" the man had demanded, and Charley had seen than that the man, middle-aged, red-faced, had been drinking. Charley had not said a word. What was there to say at such a startling time? "If you're Chinese, that's okay, but if you're Japanese . . . !" The man had moved the point of the penknife a little closer to Charley's stomach. Charley had remained silent, tense against the brick wall of the building. Then, after a few moments, possibly because he obtained no satisfaction, no argument, the man had closed his penknife and gone unsteadily on his way.

---

3.   cities in Japan

There had been a similar incident not long after, but Charley had talked his way out of that one. Charley had just gotten off the streetcar when he bumped into a Mexican man about his own age. This man, who had also reeked of liquor, had grabbed his arm tightly and cursed him. "My boy, my Angel, he die in the war! You Japs keel him! Only nineteen years old and you Japs keel him! I'm going to keel you!" But somehow a Mexican had not been as intimidating as a white man; hadn't he hired Mexicans once upon a time, been their boss each summer when he and his wife had needed help with the harvesting of vegetables?

"Mexicans, Japanese, long time good friends," Charley had answered. "My boy die in the war, too. In Italy. I no hate Germans. No use."

Wonderingly, the Mexican had released his grip on Charley's arm. "Oh, yeah?" he had asked, tilting his head.

The magic word had come to Charley's tongue. "Verdad," he had said. "Verdad." So this man, too, had turned away and gone, staggering a bit from side to side.

It was not long after that that Charley, dismissed from his janitorial duties for spending too much time in the pool hall down in the basement, had been sent by the Japanese employment agency to Las Vegas, where dishwashers were in great demand.

It was like Paradise: the heavy silver dollars that were as common as pennies; the daily anticipation of getting rich overnight; the rejoicing when a fellow worker had a streak of luck and shared his good fortune with one and all, buying presents all around (the suitcase under Charley's bed became full of expensive neckties which were never used), and treating everyone to the drink of his choice.

It was a far cry from Tomochi-machi, that small village of his birth in the thirtieth year of the reign of the Emperor Meiji. The place had been known in those days as Hara-machi, meaning wilderness, and it had been a lonely backwoods in a sector called Aza-Kashiwagawa or Oakstream. Above his father's tiny house had risen the peaks of Azameyama and Karamata-dake; beyond that mountains higher still. Below was Midori-kawa, Emerald Lake, where abounded the troutlike fish called *ayu*. The mountains about were thick with trees, the larger of them pine and redwood, and he had as a small boy been regularly sent to bring down bundles of wood.

He still wore a deep purple scar on his leg from those days and there was a bitterness he could not help when he remembered why. A nail had lodged deep in his leg, too deep to remove; the leg had swollen to a frightening size and finally the nail had burst out with the pus. He could not forget that when he was in agony from the pain and unable to walk, his mother (that good, quiet woman) had asked, "Will you bring down one more load of wood from the mountain?"

He had attended school for two or three years, but he was not much for studying so he had hired out as a baby sitter, going about his chores with some damp baby strapped to his back. Older, he had worked on farms.

When he was twenty, he had ridden the *basha*, the horsedrawn carriage, to the town of Kumamoto, from thence taken the train to Nagasaki where he had boarded the Shunryo-Maru as a steerage passenger bound for America, that far land where, it was said, people had green hair and red eyes and where the streets were paved with gold.

In Santa Maria friends who had preceded him there from his village had helped him lease a small farm (Japanese were not allowed to buy property, they told him—it was part of something called a Gentleman's Agreement[4] between Japan and the United States). A couple of years later, his picture bride, Haru, had joined him and she had been a joy as refreshing as the meaning of her name (Spring), hard-working, docile, eager to attend to his least wants. Within the first year she had presented him with a boy-child, whom they had named Isamu, because he was the first.

What New Year celebrations they had held in this new land! Preparations had begun about Christmastime with relatives and friends gathering for the day-long making of rice cakes. Pounds and pounds of a special glutinous rice, soaked overnight in earthen vats, would be steamed in square wooden boxes, two or three piled one atop the other, over an outside fire. The men would all tie handkerchiefs or towels about their heads to absorb the sweat, then commence to clean out the huge wooden mortar, the tree trunk with a basin carved out at the top. One box of the steaming rice would be dumped into the basin; then the rhythmic pounding of the rice would begin, the men grunting exaggeratedly as they wielded the long-handled wooden mallets. Usually two men at a time would work on the rice, while one woman stood by with a pan of cold water. It was the woman's job to quickly dab water at the rice dough so it would not stick to the mortar or mallets, while the men did not once pause in their steady, alternate pounding.

The rest of the aproned women would be waiting at a long table spread with befloured newspapers and when the rice had become a soft lump of hot dough, it was thrown onto the table where each woman would wring off a handful to pat into shape before placing it on a floured wooden tray. Some of the cakes would be plain, some filled with a sweet mealy jam made of an interminable boiling together of tiny, maroon Indian beans and sugar. There were not only white cakes; there were pink ones, made so during the pounding with a touch of vegetable coloring; green ones, made so during the steaming with the addition of dried seaweed; and yellow ones, which were green ones dusted with orangeish bean flour.

But the main purpose of the work was to make the larger unsweetened cakes, which in tiers two or three high (one tier for each member of the family, topped with

---

4. Gentleman's Agreement of 1908 restricted the emigration of Japanese laborers to the United States.

choice tangerines with the leafy stems left on) decorated the *hotoke-sama*, the miniature temple representing the Buddha which occupies a special corner in every Buddhist household. On New Year's morning the cakes, reverently placed, would be joined by miniature bowls of rice and miniature cups of *sake*.

Sometimes enough *mochi*[5] was made to last almost throughout the whole year, either preserved in water periodically changed or cut into strips and dried. The sweet cakes would be eaten early, toasted on an asbestos pad over the tin winter stove (when done, the dark filling would burst out in a bubble); the soaked would be boiled and eaten plain with soy sauce or sugared bean flour, or made into dumplings with meat and vegetables. The dried flinty strips would be fried in deep oil until they became crisp, puffy confections which were sprinkled with sugar.

How rosy the men had grown during the cake-making, not only from their exertions but from frequently repairing to the house for a taste of fresh *mochi* and a sip of *sake*. There would be impromptu singing above the sound of the slapping mallets; women chasing men with threatening, floury hands; and continuous shouted jokes with earthy references more often than not.

Then, on New Year's Eve, Haru would prepare the last meal of the year, to be eaten just before midnight. This was *soba*, the very thin, grey, brown-flecked noodles served with *tororo*, the slippery brown sauce of grated raw taro yams. At the stroke of midnight, Kazuyuki Matsumoto (he was not Charley then) went outside with his shotgun and used up several shells to bid appropriate farewell to the passing year.

On New Year's morning, dressed in brand-new clothing, Kazuyuki and Haru would, following tradition, eat that first breakfast of the New Year: the thick soup of fresh *mochi* dumplings, vegetables, tender strips of dried cuttlefish. It was also necessary to take from tiny cups token sips of hot mulled *sake*, poured from a small porcelain decanter shaped like a rosebud vase.

Then it was open house everywhere for almost the whole week and it was an insult not to accept token sips of hot *sake* at each house visited. Sometimes Kazuyuki Matsumoto was so polite that when they somehow arrived home, in that old topless Ford, Haru had to unlace his shoes, undress him, and tuck him in bed.

And the ritual was the same with each friend seen for the first time in the year, each solemn, prescribed greeting accompanied by deep, deep bows:

"*Akema-shite omedeto gozai-masu.*" (The old year has ended and the new begun—congratulations!)

"*Sakunen wa iro-iro o-sewa ni nari-mashite, arigato gozai-masu.*" (Thank you for the many favors of the past year.)

"*Konnen mo onegai itashi-masu.*" (Again this year, I give myself unto your care.)

---

5. pounded rice cakes

What a mountain of food Haru had prepared on New Year's Eve, cooking till almost morning: bamboo shoots, stalks of pale green bog rhubarb, both taken from cans with Japanese labels; red and white fish galantines, fish rolls with burdock root centers, both of these delicacies purchased ready-made from the Japanese market; fried shrimp; fried chicken; thin slices of raw fish; gelatinous red and white agar-agar[6] cakes, tasting faintly of peppermint; sweet Indian-bean cakes; dried herring roe soaked in soy sauce; vinegared rice rolls covered with thin sheets of dried seaweed and containing in the center thin strips of fried egg, canned eel, long strings of dried gourd, mushrooms, carrots, and burdock root—neatly sliced; triangles of fried bean curd filled with vinegared rice and chopped vegetables; sliced lotus root stems, which when bitten would stretch shimmering, cobwebby filaments from the piece in your mouth to the remnant between your chopsticks. The centerpiece was usually a huge red lobster, all appendages intact, or a red-gold sea bream, resting on a bed of parsley on the largest and best platter in the house.

But that had been long, long ago. The young Japanese, the *Nisei*, were so Americanized now. While most of them still liked to eat their boiled rice, raw fish, and pickled vegetables, they usually spent New Year's Eve in some nightclub. Charley knew this because many of them came to Las Vegas from as far away as San Francisco and Los Angeles to inaugurate the New Year.

Then, abruptly, Haru, giving birth to the second boy, had died. He had been a huge baby, almost ten pounds, and the midwife said Haru, teeth clenched, had held with all her might to the metal bed rods behind her head; and at long last, when the infant gargantua had emerged, she had asked, "Boy or girl?" The midwife had said, "It's a boy, a giant of a boy!" And Haru, answering, "Good ...," had closed her eyes and died.

Kazuyuki Matsumoto had sent this two small sons over to a cousin of Haru's, but this woman with five older children of her own had eventually, embarrassedly, confessed that her husband was complaining that the additional burden was too much, that the babies did not allow her enough time in the fields. So Kazuyuki had taken his sons to Japan, to Tomochimachi, where his own mother had reluctantly accepted them.

Returning to California, Kazuyuki had stopped farming on his own and worked for friends for twenty cents an hour with room and board. Frugal, he sent most of his wages to Japan, where at the favorable rate of exchange his mother and father had

---

6. a gelatin or jelly-like substance made of certain seaweeds

been able to build a larger house and otherwise raise their standard of living as well as their prestige in the sector.

For several years Kazuyuki had kept to this unvaried but rewarding way of life. Friends had shaken their heads over his truly self-sacrificing ways; he was admired as an exceptional fellow.

But Kazuyuki, living in bunkhouses with the other seasonal workers who were usually bachelors, gradually came to love the game of *hanafuda*, flower cards, which relaxed him of evenings, giving him a more immediate pleasure to look forward to than taking a hot bath and going to bed. So the money orders to Japan became fewer and farther between before they had finally stopped. By the time Kazuyuki had wandered the length of California, picking grapes in Fresno, peaches in Stockton, strawberries in Watsonville, flowers in San Fernando, cantaloupe in the Imperial Valley, always ending his day and filling his Saturdays off with the shuffling and dealing of flower cards.

His mother had written once in a while in her unpunctuated *katakana*, unacknowledged (he was not one for writing letters) messages which nevertheless moved him to the core, saying that his sons were fine and bright, but that both she and his father were getting older and that they would like to see him once more before they died. When was he coming to visit them? Finally, his father had died during the New Year holidays; they found him drunk, lying helplessly there on the steep path home after visiting friends in the village below. Since this had become a common event, they had merely carried him home and put him to bed. But this, as it happened, was the sleep from which he never awoke.

Learning of this news, Kazuyuki had secretly wept. Like father, like son, the saying went, and it was true, it was true. He was as worthless, as *tsumara-nai*,[7] as his father had in the end become.

The shock had the effect of reforming him; he gave up flower cards and within a couple of diligent years had saved enough money to send for his boys. The wages had risen to fifty cents per hour with room and board; the rate of exchange had become even more favorable, so his few hundred American dollars had amounted to a considerable pile of yen.

With his sons by his side to assist him, he leased again a small farm, this time in Orange County, but somehow things did not go well. They tried things like tomatoes and Italian squash. The vegetables flourished, but it seemed that since the man called Rusuberuto[8] had been elected President of the United States, there had come into

7. good-for-nothing
8. Japanese American English for Roosevelt

being a system called prorating in which one had to go into town and get coupons which limited the number of boxes one could pick and sent to market. This was intended to keep the prices up, to help the farmer. The smaller the farm, the fewer the coupons it was allotted, so it was a struggle. They lived on tomato soup and sliced Italian squash fried in batter—this was quite tasty with soy sauce—and, of course, boiled rice, although the cost of a hundred-pound sack of Blue Rose had become amazing. During the winter the fare was usually the thick yellow soup made by adding water to soy bean paste, and pickled vegetables.

At first, too, the relationship with his sons had been a source of distress. They had expected wondrous things of America, not this drudgery, this poverty. Alien, too, to their father, they had done his bidding as though he were some lord and master who expected them to wash his feet. This had annoyed him and he had treated them sternly, too sternly. And both of them had been resentful of the fact that their contemporaries here, the *Nisei*, looked down upon them as *Kibei*,[9] for lacking English, as though there were rice hulls sticking to their hair.

As he had come to know them better, however, he saw that the two were as different as grey and white. Isamu, now nineteen, was quick to pick up colloquial English, eager to learn how to drive the old pick-up truck, fascinated with the American movies which now and then they were able to afford and his father perceived that he was ambitious, perhaps too ambitious, restless for the day when he could own a shining automobile and go on his way. Noriyuki, two years younger, was more like Haru, quiet, amiable, content to listen to the Japanese popular songs which he played over and over on the Victrola (he sang a nice baritone himself as he worked out in the fields). And he spoke nostalgically of his grandmother, the blue-green coolness of Midori-kawa, the green loveliness of the fields of rape and barley in the spring.

Then, after only a little more than a year together, had come the incredible war, and the trio, along with all other Japanese on the West Coast, had been notified that they would be sent to concentration camps. How uneasy they had been in those days with government men coming in unannounced on three occasions to inspect the small wooden house for evidence of sabotage. In their panic they had burned all their Japanese magazines and records, hidden the *hotoke-sama*,[10] buried the *judo*[11] outfits and the *happi*[12] coats the boys had brought with them from Japan. They had had to

---

9. Japanese American born in America but raised in Japan
10. items related to Buddha
11. martial arts coats
12. traditional Japanese coats

turn in their little Kodak (it had never been retrieved), lest they be tempted to photograph American military installations and transmit them secretly to Japan.

But the Arizona concentration camp, once they became accustomed to the heat and dust and mud storms, was not too unbearable. In fact Noriyuki, with his repertoire of current Japanese songs, became quite popular with even the *Nisei* girls and he was in great demand for the amateur talent shows which helped illuminate that drab incarceration. Kazuyuki Matsumoto settled for a job as cook in one of the mess halls; Isamu immediately got a job driving one of the covered surplus Army trucks which brought supplies to these mess halls; and Noriyuki went to work with the men and women who were making adobe bricks for the school buildings which the government planned to build amidst the black tar-papered barracks.

One day a white officer, accompanied by a *Nisei* in uniform, came to recruit soldiers for the United States Army and Isamu was among the few who unhesitatingly volunteered. He was sent to Mississippi where an all-Japanese group from Hawaii and the mainland was being given basic training and his regular letters to his father and brother indicated that he was, despite some reservations, satisfied with his decision. Once he was able to come on a furlough and they saw that he was a new man, all (visible) trace of boy gone, with a certain burliness, a self-confidence that was willing to take on all comers. Then, after a silence, came small envelopes called V-Mail, which gave no indication of his whereabouts. Finally, he was able to tell them that he was in Italy and he sent them sepia postcards of the ancient ruins of Rome. Almost on the heels of this packet, the telegram had come informing them of the death in action of Pfc. Isamu Matsumoto; a later letter from his sergeant had filled in the details—it had occurred near a town called Grosseto; it had been an 88-millimeter shell; death had been (if it would comfort) instantaneous.

Kazuyuki Matsumoto continued to cook in the mess hall and Noriyuki went on making adobe bricks. After the school buildings were completed—they turned out quite nicely—Noriyuki decided to attend classes in them. As he was intelligent and it was mostly a matter of translating his solid Japanese schooling into English, he skipped rapidly from one grade to the next, and although he never lost the accent which marked him as a *Kibei*, he was graduated from the camp high school with honors.

By this time, Kazuyuki Matsumoto was on the road that would lead, inexorably, to Las Vegas. At first, in that all-Japanese milieu, he had taken courage and tried courting a *Nisei* spinster who worked as a waitress in the same mess hall. Once he had even dared to take her a gift of a bag of apples, bought at the camp canteen; but the woman already had her eye on a fellow waiter several years her junior. She refused the apples and proceeded to ensnare the younger man with a desperation which he was simply not equipped to combat. After this rejection Kazuyuki Matsumoto had returned to his passion for flower cards. What else was there to do? He had tried passing the time, as some of the other men did, by making polished canes of mesquite and ironwood, by carving and enameling little birds and fish to be used as brooches, but he was not truly cut out for such artistic therapy. Flower cards were what beguiled—that occasional unbeatable combination of the four cards: the pink cherry blossoms in full, festive bloom; the black pines with the stork standing in between; the white moon rising in a red sky over the black hill; and the red-and-black crest symbolizing the paulownia tree in flower.

Then had come the day of decision. The government announced that all Japanese wanting to return to Japan (with their American-born children) would be sent to another camp[13] in northern California to await the sailing of the Swedish *Gripsholm*. The removal was also mandatory for all young men of draft age who did not wish to serve in the United States Army and chose to renounce their American citizenship. Kazuyuki Matsumoto, busy with the cooking and absorbed in flower cards, was not too surprised when Noriyuki decided in favor of Japan. At least there would not be another son dead in Europe; the boy would be a comfort to his grandmother in her old age. As for himself, he would be quite content to remain in this camp the rest of his life—free food, free housing, friends, flower cards; what more could life offer? It was true that he had partially lost his hearing in one ear from standing by those hot stoves on days of unbearable heat, but that was a small complaint. The camp hospital had provided free treatment, free medicines, free cotton balls to stuff in his bad ear. Kazuyuki Matsumoto was far from agreeing with one angry man who had one day, annoyed with a severe dust storm, shouted "America is going to pay for every bit of this suffering! Taking away my farm and sending me to this hell! Japan will win the war and then we'll see who puts who where!"

So Noriyuki was among those departing for Tule Lake, where, for a time, he thoroughly enjoyed the pro-Japanese atmosphere, the freedom of shouting a *banzai*[14] or two whenever he felt like it. Then, despite himself, he kept remembering a *Nisei* girl in that Arizona camp he thought he had been glad to leave behind. She had wept a little when he left. He recalled the habit she had of saying something amusing and then sticking out her tongue to lick a corner of her lip. He began to dream of her almost nightly. Once, he wired together and enameled with delicate colors a fragile corsage, fashioned of those tiny white seashells which one could harvest by the basketful in that region. This he sent on to her with a tender message. One morning his dormitory mates teased him, saying he had cried out in his sleep, clear as a bell, "Alice, Alice, don't leave me!" In English, too, they said. So, one day, Noriyuki, as Isamu had before him, volunteered for service in the Army of the United States. He spent most of his hitch in Colorado as an instructor in the Japanese language and

---

13. Tule Lake was the northern California camp for Japanese wishing to depart for Japan.
14. hurrah

ended up as a technical sergeant. Alice joined him there and they were married in Denver one fine day in June.

Since the war had ended in the meantime, Noriyuki and Alice went to live in Los Angeles where most of their camp friends had already settled and Kazuyuki Matsumoto, already in Las Vegas, already Charley, received a monthly long-distance call from them, usually about six in the morning, because, as they said, they wanted to make sure he was still alive and kicking.

Noriyuki was doing well as an assistant in the office of a landscape architect; Alice had first a baby girl, then another. Each birth was announced to Charley by telephone and while he rejoiced, he was also made to feel worthless because he was financially unable to send even a token gift of felicitations.

But he would make up for it, he knew. One day his time would come and he would return in triumph to Los Angeles, laden with gifts for Noriyuki (a wristwatch, probably), for Alice (she might like an ornate necklace, such as he had seen some of these rich women wear), and an armload of toys for the babies.

But Charley began having trouble with his teeth and he decided to take a short leave of absence in order to obtain the services of a good Japanese dentist in Los Angeles. He had to stay with Noriyuki and his family, and they, with no room for a houseguest, allowed him the use of the couch in the front room which could be converted into a bed at night. Charley, paid at the end of each month, had brought some money with him, so at first the reunion went quite well. After his visits to the dentist who decided to remove first all the upper teeth, then all the lower, and then to fit him with plates, he remembered to bring back a gift box of either the rice-cakes and bean confections of all shapes and colors known as *manju*, or of *o-sushi*, containing a miscellany of vinegared rice rolls and squares. He bought a musical jack-in-the-box for the older child and a multi-colored rubber ball for the baby. After a while the dentist asked for a hundred dollars as part payment and Charley gave it to him, although this was about all he had left, except for the return bus ticket to Las Vegas.

About the middle of his month in Los Angeles Charley felt unwelcome, but there was no help for it. The dentist was not through with him. He could hear from the sofa bed the almost nightly reproaches, sometimes accompanied with weeping, that Noriyuki had to listen to. Since his hearing was not too good, he could not make out all that Alice said, but it seemed there was the problem of his napping on the couch and thus preventing her from having friends over during the day, of his turning on the television (and so loud) just when she wanted the children to take their nap, and just how long did that father of his intend to stay? Forever?

Charley was crushed; it had never been his intention to hurt anyone, never once during his lifetime. The dentist, however, took his time; a month was up before he finally got around to inserting both plates and he still wanted Charley to return for three appointments in order to insure the proper fit. But Charley ignored him and returned to Las Vegas, posthaste, to free Noriyuki and Alice from their burden.

Some days before he left, Alice, who was not at heart unkind, but irritable from the daily care of two active youngsters and the requirement of having to prepare three separate meals (one for the babies, one for herself and husband, and a bland, soft diet for toothless Charley) had a heart-to-heart talk with her father-in-law. Noriyuki, patient, easygoing, had never mentioned the sorrows of his wife.

In halting Japanese, interspersed with the simplest English she could think of, Alice begged Charley to mend his ways.

"You're not getting any younger," she told him. "What of the future, when you're unable to work any longer? You're making a good salary; if you saved most of it, you wouldn't have to worry about who would take care of you in your old age. This *bakuchi* (gambling) is getting you nowhere. Why, you still owe the dentist two hundred dollars!"

Charley was ashamed. Every word she spoke was the truth. "You have been so good to me," he said, "when I have been so *tsumara-nai*. I know I have been a lot of trouble to you."

There and then they made a pact. Charley would send Alice at least a hundred dollars a month; she would put in the bank for him. When he retired at sixty-five, he would be a man of substance. With his Social Security he could visit Japan and see his mother again before she died. He might even stay on in Japan; at the rate of exchange, which was now about three thousand yen for ten American dollars, he could lead a most comfortable, even luxurious life.

But once in Las Vegas again, Charley could not keep to the pact. His compulsion was more than he could deny; and Noriyuki, dunned by the dentist, felt obliged to pay the two hundred dollars which Charley owed. Alice was furious.

Then Charley's mother died, and Charley was filled with grief and guilt. Those letters pleading for one more visit from her only son, her only child, of whom she had been so proud; those letters which he had not once answered. But he would somehow atone. When he struck it rich, he would go to Japan and buy a fine headstone for the spot under which her urn was buried. He would buy chrysanthemums (she had loved chrysanthemums) by the dozens to decorate the monument. It would make a lovely sight, to make the villagers sit up and take notice.

Charley's new teeth, handsome as they were (the waitresses were admiring, saying they made him look ten years younger), were troublesome, too. Much too loose, they did not allow the consumption of solids. He had to subsist on rice smothered with gravy, soft-boiled eggs, soups. But at least he did not have to give up that morning pickup that the bartender still remembered him with. That whiskey was a marvel, warming his insides (especially welcome on chilly winter mornings), giving him a glow that made him surer than ever that one day he too would hit the jackpot of jackpots.

But Charley's health began to fail. His feet would swell and sometimes he had to lean against the sink for support in order to wash the endless platters, plates, dishes, saucers, cups, glasses, knives, forks, spoons, pots, and pans. Once, twice, he got so dizzy climbing the stairs to the dormitory that he almost blacked out and, hearing him cry out, his Chinese roommates had to carry him the rest of the way to his bed.

One day Mr. Chew, coming to inspect, looked at Charley and said with some concern, "What's the matter? You look bad." And Charley admitted that he had not been feeling up to snuff of late.

Mr. Chew then insisted that he go home to his son in Los Angeles for a short rest. That was what he probably needed.

By that time Charley was glad for the advise. He was so tired, so tired. One of the waitresses called Noriyuki on the telephone and asked him to come after his father. Charley was pretty sick, she said; he could probably use a good vacation.

So Noriyuki in his gleaming station wagon, which was only partly paid for, sped to Las Vegas to fetch his father. Charley slept on and off during most of the long trip back.

The young Japanese doctor in Los Angeles shook his head when Charley listed his symptoms. Charley thought it was his stomach; there was a sharp pain there sometimes right between the ribs.

The young Japanese doctor said to Noriyuki, "When as *Issei* starts complaining about his stomach, it's usually pretty serious." He meant there was the possibility of cancer. For some reason, possibly because of the eating of raw fish, Japanese are more prone to stomach cancer than other races.

But the pain in Charley's stomach turned out to be an ulcer. That was not too bad. As for the swollen feet, that was probably and indication of hepatitis, serious but curable in time. Then, in the process of studying the routine X-rays, the doctor came upon a dismaying discovery. There was definite evidence of advanced cirrhosis of the liver.

"Cirrhosis of the liver?" said Noriyuki. "Doesn't that come from drinking? My father gambled, but he didn't drink. He's no drunkard."

"Usually it comes from drinking. Your father says he did drink some whiskey every day. And if his loose plates kept him from eating a good diet, that could do it, that could do it."

So Charley went to stay at the Japanese Hospital, where the excess fluid in his abdomen could be drained periodically. He was put on a low-sodium diet and the dietitian was in a quandary. A salt-free diet for a man who could not eat solids; there was very little she could plan for him, hardly any variety.

Subsequent X-rays showed up some dark spots on the lungs. The young Japanese doctor shook his head again.

"It's hopeless," he said to Noriyuki. "That means cancer of the liver, spreading to the lungs. He doesn't have much time left."

Noriyuki told Alice, who, relieved that the culinary union had provided for insurance which would take care of the hospital bills, tried to console him. "Who can understand these things?" she said. "Look at your mother—dead at twenty-four, with so much to live for . . . "

Biting her lips, she stopped. She had said the wrong thing. Noriyuki, all his life under his surface serenity, had known guilt that his birth had been the cause of his mother's death.

Thus Charley died, leaving a son, a daughter-in-law, two grandchildren. Towards the end his mind had wandered, because the medication for the cirrhosis had drained him of potassium and the pills prescribed to make up the lack had not sufficed. There was a huge stack of sympathy cards from Las Vegas, from the kitchen employees, the waitresses, the cashier, the sweet, elderly lady-bookkeeper who had always helped Charley file his income tax statements, a cab driver, and a few others who had come to accept Charley as part of the Las Vegas scene. They even chipped in to wire him an enormous floral offering.

The young Japanese doctor would not take his fee (the union insurance had not provided for his services). "The worst mistake I made in my life was becoming a doctor," he confided to Noriyuki. "Life is hell, nothing but hell."

"But you help people when they need help the most," Noriyuki tried to tell him. "What could be more satisfying than that?"

"Yeah, and you see people die right in front of you and there isn't a damn thing you can do about it! Well, at least your father had a good time—he drank, he gambled, he smoked. I don't do any of those things; all I do is work, work, work. At least he enjoyed himself while he was alive."

And Noriyuki—who, without one sour word, had lived through a succession of conflicting emotions about his father—hate for rejecting him as a child; disgust and exasperation over that weak moral fiber; embarrassment when people asked what his father did for a living; and finally, something akin to compassion, when he came to understand that his father was not an evil man, but only an inadequate one with the most shining intentions, only one man among so many who lived from day to day as best as they could, limited, restricted, by the meager gifts Fate or God had doled out to them—could not quite agree.

Diana Chang

(b.1934)

Diana Chang was born in New York City to a Eurasian mother and a Chinese father.
Diana Chang writes,

> *My father was real Chinese, born and raised in China. He had a classical Chinese*
> *education, and then attended and graduated from Tsinghua University in Peking*
> *(as Beijing was called then). An architect, he earned his degree in architecture at*
> *Columbia University. My mother, on the other hand, was Eurasian, born and*
> *raised in the United States.*

At the age of only eight months, her mother took her to China where they lived in Peking,
Nanking, and Shanghai until the end of World War II when they returned to America. She
graduated from Barnard College in 1949. Chang is generally regarded as the first
American-born Chinese American to publish a novel. Her **Frontiers of Love** *(first printed*
in 1956 and reissued by the University of Washington Press in 1994) set in the European
compounds of Shanghai is a classic story of a search for identity and a conflict of culture.
Chang is the author of five other novels: **A Woman of Thirty** *(1959),* **A Passion for Life**
(1961), **The Only Game in Town** *(1963),* **Eye to Eye** *(1974),* **A Perfect Love** *(1978), and*
three volumes of poetry: **The Horizon Is Definitely Speaking** *(1982),* **What Matisse Is**
After *(1984), and* **Earth Water Light** *(1991). Her fiction and poetry have appeared in*
numerous literary magazines and she is a recipient of several awards including a Fulbright
Fellowship and John Hay Whitney Fellowship. She is also an accomplished painter whose
work has been in many one-person shows as well as included in several private collections.
She lives and works in New York.

In "Falling Free," Kiki, the first-person narrator, ponders the last part of her life, issues of
identity, and love. She looks for the reaffirmation of all that she loved in life including her
Eurasian grandson and the reclamation of a long-lost love.

Falling Free

Let it go, let it go. This is peace. I am what I am now, one with this house I
spend my hours in—its lines which travel past corners my only distances. My worn
chair reflected in the window is ghosted before my time. Such whiteness I face from
wall to wall. White is the color of mourning where Ying has gone, the awesome color
which is absence, is purity, is outward-boundness, a flight of the pale body into pitch
blackness.

Our son-in-law looks tribal or like a gypsy with green eyes shaded by thick straight
lashes. He's part Welsh, part Portuguese. Ying, my husband, said, "I'm of two minds
regarding miscegenation. You think it's a simple matter? I'm a liberal, however, a
liberal," he repeated, his foot tapping.

"Mimi," I said, "is of one mind." She wanted that gypsy like assistant professor, and he desired her, our fine-boned daughter.

I'm almost color blind now. At any rate, green and blue I find hard to distinguish in the evening. The world in shrinking imploded into out grandchild's face and body. I can't take my eyes off him. I lean too close, I'm sure, absorbing his features, their mixed aspects, raceless or twice bred, as they slip into combinations surprising and new.

Let it go. I'm of my years airing themselves in my breath. I should not have written Timothy. I passed commensense over to him to employ—which he'll do. He shall. He won't get in touch with me.

How long is it that I've been the sensible one? If we count it from when we met—decades, only decades. By writing Timothy, Ying's colleague, I handed over commonsense. All I want is aloneness now, the choreography of meals, the pruning of plants, a walk to the corner, the easement of lying in bed, my form stretched out before me to look down at, as though I've already left it behind.

I *will* Timothy not to call. Anyway, I won't let him leave Boston.

All of us are Chinese some of the time, I say. But I'm not certain what I mean. Other times, I'm a Calvinist, familiar with dimity and yokes. My favorite summer dress is Danish, my gold ring Greek, my face cream French, my daydreams I can't place. For someone so unsure of who I am, from time to time I have such definite statements to make. My thought are reckless, braver than Ying's. Yet, for decades, I ignored Timothy, ignored even the thoughts I refused to think. *That* is Chinese.

The phone rings. It has a cutting edge. I look at it. One. Two. Three. I once had a cat who stared at phones when they rang. Now I stare, too. Four. It stops, leaving the house emptier. Fragrances have leaned against me. There's so much speech in silent things.

For a long time, I was young. Spaces happen now which I can't fill. I'm often away from myself. The past tense can bury me like a landslide. The past tense is the most populated country of the countries I've lived in. Friends have gone. Mimi, our daughter, has died. There was no one for Ying to stay in the States for, except me.

He writes twice a month. He sounds more and more Chinese. It's life which will divorce me. It'll leave me behind, receding.

Timothy.

It's too late. His names's just a reflex. I no longer secrete longing. I'm beached; and the moon's a dead pebble. My dry hands seek my dry cheek. My clocks move but return to the same hour twice a day, on time. I'm noticing in new, dry-eyed ways. As for my age, I'll never catch up with Ying's, which puts me ahead like daylight saving.

I'm months and months younger, enough months to count as years, and I always rubbed it in. "You're getting on!" I declared thirty years ago. "It's too bad!"

Ying said in St. Croix, "Compared to these people you look like an eleven-year-old."

I was forty-seven and he fifty-three then and, made self-conscious, I tugged at my bikini. "It's all that butter and sides of beef and hard liquor they stow away," I said. "And have stowed away since Druid times. They can't help it, you know."

They. Americans were they. German tourists, Swedish ones. But so were Chinese. "Look," Ying said, "they have to catch up with technology." He was worrying over mainland China. "They're of nowhere."

"From nowhere," I corrected him.

"With all its ills," he went on, "they can't bypass industrialization. Mao will learn the hard way, mark my words."

Ying's part of that "they" now. I'm now from nowhere, no longer part of a "we." Interesting. I'm only I, I am. I still am, however. So far and meanwhile. Till I leave even me.

Timothy's last name is Ayres. Scottish. I'll explain to him I was having one of my lapses when I wrote that letter.

I try not to think of China because its fate hurts so. The other side of everywhere, of everyone, living and unlived, forced to try to catch up with—to keep pace with imperfections of driven, self-searching barbarians.

I have to save my eyes. But what for? I don't watch television any more and don't miss it. My desk, my sofa, the refrigerator, the radio are islands in a sea of floor. I take beads on distances before embarking toward the letters, cushions, eggs, music—the other soul in this house.

Impossible lamp. I turned you off at four this morning. Full of yourself, you snap back on! There's a break in the shrubbery which is lined up with an aisle between a neighbor's trees. Through it, dawn rises like water filling a bathtub.

I'm to soak myself because of the insistence in my thigh and back. Perhaps camel's humps are trying to grow out of me, repositories of memory which won't lie down, go away. My hands seek out past days to knead, to work out their ache.

When I was in the hospital, I heard him say, "No heroic measures." I believe Dr. Walsh was talking to my grandson. "At her age, you understand." And then the two lads at the foot of my bed traveled away on platforms until I could no longer hear them.

When Dr. Walsh reappeared suddenly, I scrabbled at the sheets, swung my legs, moved toward him. It was as though my skirts were tied at the bottom.

"Mrs. Kuo! You do my heart good," he declared, plunging toward me.

"Nothing's wrong with mine," I said. "I'm strong. Don't think I'm on my last legs."

He carried me, put me back to bed as though, as though I were the child. Determination returned to me. Like the lamp, I snapped back on. And you see, I'm here at home again, the two of me—the me and the you. It comes of talking to oneself; however, which one of us would stop me? We laugh together. You tell me who's to stop us. I've never been freer. I think anything I like, do as I please. I'm as single as I was at nine, a sweet age. My mind is clear and could shine.

I stare at the telephone. One; two; three? Yes, four; five. It rings on, disappoints me. Bitter, yet I am also relieved.

Probably my neighbor, a strong woman, across the street and half a block down. She's short of cash, so helps out with storm windows, mowing, raking.

I'm looking at albums she took down from the attic for me, my nose a couple of inches from faces. "See," I say to you, "that was when Timothy arrived in a convertible, his scarf looped around his neck." Timothy, our guest, was Ying's colleague, both of them involved with Venus scrutinized from Yerkes Observatory, tracking gases and speeding light. They dealt with infinity, seemed to wonder at nothing. My physicist husband, Ying, was sure of me, while Timothy, married often, waited.

If only I knew I could stay in touch with myself forever.

The camera is a gun shooting down moments. I take in small people, tiny views I don't remember from where: outside Athens, on a French canal? Is that lake Swiss or in Hangchow, the honeymoon city, the sheen of one sky continuing into the next?

I expel exasperation. I will not have it. Buds, nodes, appear on my knuckles, rosaries to tell. You and I laugh. It's the beads have things to tell, not I. My neck feels yoked by an influence I'm to serve. Mimi, our daughter, was swayed by a rare disease of the blood when she was thirty-three, four months and seven days. Winston, our grandson, Ying and I brought up mostly, though his gypsy-like father would claim otherwise.

Simply because it rings, must I answer it? It yelps, so willful. You see, you're withdrawing, I point out to myself. But this is peace! I'm what I am now. My ledges, plants, cant of roof upraised. I'll leave through the skylight, God sucking me upward through his straw. I rather like that thought, I must say, vain, as usual. He'll vacuum me up, aspirate me. For once, I'll be his aspiration, momentarily in the light and years of galaxies. Ying could never get used to my most natural thoughts. After fifty-five years here, he had to go all the way to China to get away from me. That's my next to final thought about him. There's always more to think, have no fear. The life of radioactivity is forever. The life of death is everlasting. I've been married over fifty years, years made contingent by Ying's need to go home.

I'm sorry I wrote that letter. I simply won't answer the phone for a week. I'm content, after all.

He stepped out of the convertible, rather tall; I remember being nonplussed, as though his height put me in a quandary. Sitting, Timothy folded into another man. As he approached us, Ying standing next to me, the scarf around his neck slipped out of its loop. He picked it up and, as Ying introduced us, Timothy flung it over my head like a skipping rope, flicking one end through the other. The fringe, though almost weightless, prickled. We smiled at one another slowly, as if remembering, though we'd never met before.

"It's yours," Timothy talking, I recognized, to fill stopped time I knew we both heard. "It suits you. Besides, Ying, I forgot to bring a present. You know me. So this is your pearl of the Orient."

"For Pete's sake, come in," Ying answered, taking Tim's arm. Ying was American that day. "You're full of baloney, come what may." Sometimes he sounded like a Rotarian, but a xerox of one, though he didn't know it then or now.

"Leave May out of it," Tim retorted, referring to his wife who was suing him for the first of what turned out to be their two divorces. That day we were only writing our stories or reading one another's, while now our lives have become knowledge of endings. I feel I know nothing; yet I also know volumes to be remaindered. One comes to the end of mysteries generating themselves; to the end of wanting. It's a thought. Yes. I'll leave off everything except this containment, this management of myself in my home.

I wound it around my neck twice so it wouldn't slip off. It's silk is the color of moonlight on a pond, a blond presence, the color of sheen.

Friends call; visit; take me for rides. Miriam across the street goes marketing with me. There 're plenty of people left. More than enough.

I'm the center. I stand in the middle which, according to the Chinese,, is the fifth direction. Ying who often sounded like a Rotarian when it suited him here, is now Peking man, imagine. I'm the center, a Chinese direction. He needn't think I'm so American yet!

In a section of plate glass the length of a building, I saw a woman hurrying along. Her knees raised themselves to climb but the sidewalk was level. Her stepping was hurried, stiff, floating. I gasped; she, too. "That's you!" I said to me. I—who used to move like a dress hung on a hanger loose in the wind.

The woman's hair was as silver as anyone's here. That's why I didn't grasp who she was. So, finally, she resembled the rest, weathered silver like any Caucasian. Hers was a new gait, a new identity. At the corner, she and I put hands out for support on rear fenders of cars. "You're me," I said to her. "You're me," she said back. What I saw mirrored before me was also everything behind me.

Polarity, space, time. Ying and I reflected on such matters. "You, of course, in your way," he never neglected to add, which in the long run never did match his.

"You must remember you have lapses," Dr. Walsh said in his grown-up manner. "You mustn't go out any more without a companion. And I forbid you to drive."

The mind is punishing the body, denying it in exactly the way I would. The mind simply absents itself, rehearsing for the eviction of evictions. And the tenement lets in the sky even below the stairs. I sometimes feel like mesh dissolving into light. I almost died in the crash, which was my fault.

So busy; busy; so busy. In this house, I put out my palms to stroke the flanks of time. At last I have time. It lies at my feet like rugs; hangs in mid-air unsupported. By staring down time, I still it. I need no one—finally!

So busy, busy, busy! I was interviewed; won awards for my designs. I turned out costumes for *Kismets, Kings and I's,* and Rattigans, too. Ying Y. Kuo, the young physicist, was backstage when a relative of his was in *The King and I.* He picked me up off the floor when a bolt hit me out of the blue. It was heavy metallic fabric and knocked the breath out of me, so I didn't notice that he fell in love on the spot. "I was the one hit," he told me, laughing abruptly, astonished.

"Really?"

"Definitely."

He saw and he loved. "I was the one hit," he said many times, astonished.

"You felt hit?" I asked.

"Definitely."

Timothy said, "Admit to it. Just admit to it and I'll leave you alone."

I never admitted to it. I never said to him, "I saw and loved." Timothy admitted to it all, over the years, during which he married two or three or however many times. He signed notes slipped into my hand at parties, at a lunch or two: "Perpetually, comma, perpetually, Tim."

I said to him, "Sure. You'll always be perpetually Timothy Ayres."

"You're a coward," he said.

"I'm married. I've a daughter. I love Ying Y. Kuo, who happens to be my husband."

"All three are true," he answered. "But something more is also true."

"You're just another star-gazer," I told him. Ludicrous. Transcendent. Intrepid; wild with themselves, with grace. Shamelessness a part of their genius.

The Chinese are matter-of-fact. Didactic. Categorical. Yes. There are ways to be; and they know those ways. They do. These Westerners. What keeps them together,

I wonder? So selfish, so soulful. I'm a canal with locks. Timothy the open sea, his stole of silk streaming on the wind of the cosmos. Women threw him out of their beds; he abandoned ship and struck out alone, not once, not twice. I stayed happy with Ying, together we weathered Mimi's illness and death. I saw that that was the meaning of marriage. Any Chinese would agree. I even agree with myself.

For decades I longed. It was like a disease of the blood, which took Mimi away. Heart and womb, the one over the other, waited. I laughed at myself. At Palo Alto, Ying was promoted over him. It was a sign from outer space.

Timothy left Palo Alto. We lost track of him for three years. He sent cards with no return address from Paris, Buenos Aires, Baltimore. A book came out. For a season he was famous in celestial circles. I took that as a sign, too. He belonged now to his success. Thank my lucky stars.

This house is in a state of sleep. The porch snores softly. I wake into its dream daily.

The phone rings four, five, six times. I'm disappointed when it doesn't ring; disappointed when it rings too often. On the first ring, I jumped to turn off the alarm. But you're awake. It's not the clock. I'm awake like a cat or a dog, unknowing. Is that armchair wondering where Ying's gone? "China, China!" I cry out. "He's gone to a different condition, you fool," I tell the head rest. "Make no mistake. The Chinese *can* go home again." But it's given me a turn, I can tell you.

Winston, his Eurasian brow furrowed, his exasperation unconcealed, said, "I thought Chinese women were cooperative." My grandson didn't use the words, "docile," "passive." He knows better than that. " Why the hell can't you see you should be in a home? With people. You'll be taken care of. Don't you want to be safe, happy? Grandpa had no business splitting—at his age. At yours. And he was always grinding the Chinese ax of propriety. How would this look! How would that look! As though anyone's wasting a glance. You want to know what it is? It's unseemly—his favorite word. A disgrace. Abandoning you. I'm getting you into a home, I don't care what."

I banged my fist on his arm. "I like it here. This *is* my home. As he said, what would I be doing in Peking. I don't blame Gramps one bit."

"Gramps," Winston repeated. "This bi-cultural, sitting on the cusp, oh, so Westernized, mixed up family! And it isn't Peking. It's Beijing, and if we don't practice, we'll never catch onto this new spelling. Tell me straight—is it Chinese to abandon your wife when she's as old as the century?"

"Here they abandon earlier. You're the one bringing up this ethnic stuff. You true blue Chinese-American Eurasian. I used to think I belonged nowhere. But not so. I belong everywhere, anywhere, even on Maple Lane in Westchester. And I'm only seventy-nine. Try to get my age straight."

He guffawed in the agony of a twenty-seven-year-old and stopped himself in time from slapping my back. He could have broken me in two, which may be my natural condition, come to think of it.

"Winston," I said to him, "I stopped thinking in Chinese when I was just about your age. Chinese is another syndrome. But what would you know about it." I leaned too close, intrigued with his features.

"Suppose you fall and can't get to the phone."

"I'm not saying you're wrong. But Gramps is right, too. He's being Chinese. You know how they are about family. Hopeless cases."

"You're something else," Winston said. His body movements are like James Dean's or Alan Ladd's, but though his hair is brown he has Shantung[1] bones. I remember the day he arrived in America—purplish-red and kicking out of Mimi at Doctor's Hospital, the mayor oblivious a couple of blocks away of still another Oriental who'd slipped over a border. I laugh. How Chinese of me to claim him as Chinese when he's half Caucasian.

I'm at the border. This grayness may not be dusk, but a dawning. Remember that, I order myself, the thought already gone.

Mimi died on an operating table twenty years ago. How old would she be now? While I remained her horizon, she would have been becoming my past ages. My son-in-law remarried so he's no longer my son-in-law. So he, too, left. Or am I confused? No, Lewis moved back to Indianapolis. Winston, some sort of junior curator, is with a museum in Los Angeles. He makes appearances and vanishes as though I rub whatever makes genies come and go.

He wants me in an old-age home. Without a daughter how can I know my age? Since Mimi died, I've felt ageless. Periodically, Winston gives up on me. I annoy young people more and more.

The phone. I count: one, two, three, four and so forth. It's beautiful to be alone here on the sofa. I shall not answer the phone all day; I will not. This is enough. Once a week my neighbor takes me marketing. She describes new ways of making jello. I marvel at her kindness. We have supper out, my treat, and feel girlish about it. Friends take me to the movies once, twice a month, and I sit down front. What more do I want? The window sills are strands, the bush outside the kitchen is all I need of parks, and as for flowers, my thickened knuckles smart with feverish buds. I put my hand before my face, press against time's haunch. Time has volume here.

---

1.   northern province in China

Before departing, Ying said, "I'm thinking of you alone here. Though the financial arrangements are secure, more than secure. Winston's a man now, too, and will look out for you."

"From California," I didn't put in, for there are telephones in this country. It's not the Australian outback, unconscious next to insomniac cities.

I said instead, "I want you to stay, but . . ." I reassured him, "you must go. I do understand."

"I am Chinese," he said.

"No need to say," I said in Chinese, as if losing my bearings.

He said, "A man must die in his native land."

"You talk," I declared, "as if winding up a speech at a banquet." My remark was of the sort which always derailed his trend of thought. Not that my comment was so American, but that his rock bottom mode is Chinese, and he feels defined by the use of maxims.

I continued, "Die! All this talk about dying! You're only eighty-two." We didn't smile. That was three years ago when the detente was well-established, and his brother who had been imprisoned in a windowless closet under the stairs of a school building by seventeen-year-old Red Guards, asked him to visit. And to stay. By letter, he'd instructed them to ask him, I didn't let on I knew. His letter had said, "It will be easier on my wife, if you and Erjieh demand that I return. Suddenly, I'm overwhelmingly homesick, a sign, perhaps, that my time is short."

"You won't be able to adjust," he said to me. "You're too advanced in years, even if you *are* appropriately younger than I, and too used to comforts, luxuries. Where do you suppose you can get sauna treatments? Is you arthritis getting any better? How can I ask you to make such sacrifices at your age? I can't be so unreasonable, can I?"

Enough. Enough. In one breath, he asked so many questions.

He had another one. "They'll find you so foreign, don't you agree?"

I've taught myself to need no one. Long since, long since. The moon's no longer pulling at my blood. Long since.

"My native land," he said. "Fatherland." Words, phrases turned in the manner of a cadenza, the mind braking the way an ice skater does after a flourish, making himself into an exclamation point. "It's a proper goal, a fitting conclusion to my life, my career. I can bring something to China, too, as a physicist emeritus, above politics, beyond self-interest."

I remembered myself, a girl, riding through China, provinces slipping through the loop of the train.

Timothy's convertible waited outside. We proceeded indoors to our living room. Or was that when we had our first apartment in even earlier days? A tree grew through our second-floor deck. Was my hair long then, heavy as liquid coal, glinting maroon in the sunlight, or was it cropped short again? The first time its bob made me the talk of Shanghai, when I was fourteen, and here, too, a little later. My father, a magistrate educated in France, was weak in my hands, so I was told by those who found me spoiled, oh spoiled rotten. But I wasn't ruined then. It's now that I am, that things could be described as spoiled. Timothy was spoiled, too, leading directly to his being single today after three wives. Two did die of natural causes, it's perfectly true, one of them May—just before their third time together. He's irresistible, to hear everyone tell it, though I've never been fooled. I'm not Chinese for nothing. But he is also intelligent and far-sighted, focused on the horizon when most of us don't look past sills.

The four of us were at the Princeton Club. Ying was greeting someone half a room away.

Timothy was looking at him, while he said to me, "Have you ever heard me? Answer me!"

I told him, "I'm all ears, all ears, but no heart." I felt nothing at all for him, for his second wife coming down the hall from fixing her hair. Tall and singleminded about being his wife, she was perfect for him, as Ying'd been the one to observe.

Through his teeth, Timothy repeated, "Remember how I feel."

I did; I do. I remember how we felt.

"Leave me alone!" I cried. Like a mirage in the Gobi desert in August, his wife shimmered toward us ... a trick of my eyes, I suppose.

"I never will," he said, angrier at himself than at me.

"You want to wreck my life. I hate you."

"Never."

As a last resort, I said, "I am *Chinese.*"

"And cruel," he retorted, the patient one.

But he was cruel, too, his presence a hardship.

"You're so foreign!" I exclaimed, in disgust or in despair?

Oh, the phone. I count. I turn away, go to the front door, open it. It's rained. The lawn is Ireland, the flagstones like ancient Chinese mirrors before glass came into being. Freshness rushes into the house like a young athlete, wholesome, muscular. Knocked back, I lean against the door. The athlete reaches the bedroom, bounds up the stairs I no longer use. I then step back with extraneous motions and close out the glare, the universal air. What was I doing just now? Mail falls out of my hand. That's it, I'd picked up the mail left on the doormat, a special concession of the postwoman to save me a trip down the driveway in bad weather. I bend in stages, pick up all of it a second time and, hand on hip, straighten up inch by inch to go to the desk.

No letters from anyone I know this time. Most are away. Migratory. I've lived out a century of refugees, and tourists. I, too, am waiting for exit papers. I laugh at myself laughing. In the hospital they gave me quarts of someone's blood, lymph and elixirs of values not my own. Perhaps her name is Jane Smith. The tree I crashed into should have shared my semi-private room, hooked up to plant foods. Poor traumatized being, it doesn't climb aboard planes, leave and write me love's rationalizations. I'm sorry I hurt you, tree. Thank you for stopping me half dead in my tracks. I might have crashed into anti-matter instead.

"These Americans," Ying has said. "Those Chinese." I, too, have uttered these and those words. We would have been rendered speechless otherwise. Ying said, "Timothy doesn't marry for good. We Chinese are taught to love once, deeply and faithfully."

"Divorce isn't easy for anyone, including them," I put in. "That he remarries the same girl makes him nice, don't you think?"

"You always generalize from too little."

He was right and for all his star-gazing was more down to earth.

"We marry as much for the sake of the institution as for ourselves," I said, surprising myself. "We serve the institution. They marry for the sake of one another and of themselves."

"Another aspect of individualism again."

"Why don't you say what you think?"

"Selfishness," he said. "Shamelessness, too. They don't care what anyone thinks."

"I'm so glad you'll never divorce me," I said.

"I have no reason to."

He was right. I gave him no reason to go home. And we're not divorced. It's Timothy who ended up with no one. Serves him right. It's Timothy who's alone.

And I.

We Chinese are rational. It's good to know, to bank on.

At the supermarket yesterday, I said to Miriam, "These people look familiar."

"She misunderstood. "Uhn-uh ... your eyes," she said. "Hold onto me."

Americans look familiar now. After all, I did go to college here. My name was Kiki Lee before it became Kiki Kuo. Kiki Kuo. People calling me have sounded like crickets all these years, all because my father studied at the Sorbonne, and thought Kiki sounded Chinese. After Ying dies, will he still be Chinese? I feel neither Chinese nor not Chinese. I feel incredulous, living here on Maple Lane.

It Timothy Ayres who's making me carry on like this. You see, if you marry your own kind you don't have to engage in so much realizing.

I have some tea. I neaten up the counters. It's ten-thirty. I take off my silk crepe robe, designed for a production of the *Mikado*. I dress well all of the time now, no longer saving things for better occasions. I throw the robe to a chair. It slips off, but I leave it. The sleeve is snagged in several places by the chair's unrepaired arm. I will never wear out my clothes accumulated over the years. I keep three diamond rings on my left hand at all times, and wear seven bracelets and five fine gold chains. Other things are in the safe deposit for Winston's future wife. I will love her sight unseen. I love her already, whoever she may be.

The phone. One, two, three; yes, of course, four, and so on. I suppose I'll have to call my neighbor so she doesn't worry. I don't need anyone! I wash my neck and arms gingerly as if water were scarce. I don't take off the bracelets and necklaces. I put on my lacy nightgown, plait my hair, perfume my shoulders. It's a bit macabre, I agree.

I ease myself into bed, pull the comforter up to my chin. Ah. It's good to lie down. I feel capable, lying down, the way young people feel standing and ready to go.

In sleep I am ready to go. It's only a longer lapse in my day. I don't sleep so much as I swoon, aware of time passing and refusing to pass, of time hanging like curtains of snow. White is the color of mourning in China. In the dark I stare down time, as though I could win against it. I fall asleep, I suppose. I dream of a white face at the whitening window.

The ring jangles through me. I am fully awake. Two. Three rings. Then silence. Only three rings! My eyes widen. I am robbed clean of any thoughts to think. I begin to count slowly, as I told Timothy I would … and fifty-five, and fifty-six, and fifty-seven and fifty-eight and fifty-nine. Sixty. The phone begins to ring again. I am breathing with my lips parted. My mouth is dry, but my mind is a fair day on a plateau.

My letter had said, precisely, "If you are still there for me, phone me from Boston. I'm not what I used to be, so ring three times. Then hang up and, a minute later, ring again. That way I'll have time to get to the phone."

Lying on my side, I reach out. My thin braid is caught under my back. I jerk at it. I pick up the receiver.

"What an hour to call," I declare. "You're so inconsiderate!"

In such a rush, he doesn't hear me, he says what he has to say, "I've been in the hospital—nothing serious. Just got your letter last night." He sounds as if he's been running. "How are you?"

Leaning on an elbow, I take in his voice.

"I wanted to wake you up," he says, and hears himself. A pause. "Finally."

I laugh, throw back my head and lie flat listening.

"I'm not in great shape," he says. "I hope you're good and rickety, too."

"Worse than that."

He sighs. "Wasted."

"You threw yourself away on too many women."

"Wasted *years*." Voices don't change any. He sounds the way he did at the beginning.

"I've been playing dead," I say. Where do the words come from? I didn't know I'd been playing dead. "I thought it'd be easier. Isn't that turned around though?"

"Did you worry I wouldn't call?"

"No, not at all." I remember he said I was cruel. "Yes," I say.

And so we continue. What was once so hard is now so easy. We're beyond differences, situations, exempt at our age from most things, even regret. And he's agreeing to everything. That he rent an apartment nearby for now. That we take each day as it comes, staring down time together.

Fragments of conversations we've had, the scarf the color of moonlight, postcards from Brussels and Baltimore, I possess in this montage, time not a corridor but a meadow surrounding a center, a maypole rippling with ribbons. I can blossom; I can attract bees.

I'm a woman in a lacy gown, making my own way. I shall put up my silver hair for an old man to take down.

"I'm well past longing," I say into the phone, stretching an arm above my head. I've summoned him, haven't I, to the task of our prevailing?

Lonny Kaneko

(b.1939)

Lonny Kaneko is a sansei, *a third-generation Japanese American poet, playwright, and short story writer born in Seattle, Washington. His chapbook of poems called* **Coming Home fromCamp** *(1988), is a reflection of his family's experiences during and after their internment at Minidoka, the Japanese American concentration camp in Idaho. He has written two plays with Amy Sanbo, one of which,* **Lady Is Dying** *won the Henry Broderick Playwright Prize at the Pacific Northwest Writers Conference in 1977.* **Lady Is Dying** *was performed at the Asian American Theatre Workshop in 1977. His writing has won other awards including a fellowship from the National Endowment for the Arts. He lives in Vashon Island, Washington, and teaches writing at Highline Community College.*

The following story is set in the Minidoka camp and is told from the point of view of a young boy. The story focuses on the issue of proving one's loyalty in the midst of America's great betrayal of American citizens of Japanese ancestry. At any other point in American history, the boys would simply have been involved in a boyhood prank, but within the context of Minidoka, the story explores a widening generation gap between the young second-generation nisei *and their parent's generation, the first-generation* issei, *and the difficult and frustrating act of not only proving one's loyalty but defining it to the country that should have never doubted its own citizens.*

Nobody's Hero

Nobody was happy. I mean nobody. But my folks and everybody's folks, the ji-chans and ba-chans[1], all walked around pretending there was nothing wrong. If you looked, you knew nothing was right. There wasn't room for all the families moving in. They were sleeping outside under eaves and under the stars until the rains started, when they moved into the mess halls and rec rooms.

So this night it was raining again. We thought Seattle had rain, but Seattle never had rain like this. This Idaho rain never stopped and made lakes where they put our homes, so when we walked out of the house, the mud reached up and sucked our ankles. We couldn't even get to the latrines without planning how to wade through the stuff. In fact, the old folks were betting that even the outhouses could end up overflowing. What a stink that would be.

Everybody pretended that out of this Idaho mud would rise a generation of good citizens. They would have been smarter to expect a nation of frogs. At night the folks whispered in Japanese. It meant something serious was going on, and we knew there was nothing they could do. Fact was, everyone just sat around. It rained so hard, nobody went out unless it was an outhouse emergency.

---

1.   grandfathers and grandmothers

So that was how Hiroshi planned for us to talk. Nobody would be out in the rain, and the outhouse was the only dry place we could meet. I was sitting in the outhouse ignoring Mom's warning about getting piles sitting on the throne.

When Hiroshi arrived, he knocked three quick times against the side of the outhouse.

"The throne is busy," I said.

"Hemorrhoids," he replied.

That was our code—a word Jackson's brother had brought home from college. I opened the door, and Hiroshi stepped in. I would have stood but I already had the seat, and there wasn't room to switch, so he had to stand.

"I heard we're gonna get real toilets soon," he said. "They're laying the pipe for running water now."

I thought that would be a great idea and hoped for heat, too.

"Well, say something," he said. "Afraid to open your mouth? Afraid you'll get this bad smell in your mouth?" He chuckled. "I'm right. You don't want to talk because you don't want to swallow what you smell." He laughed, then said, "Listen, tonight we knock over the canteen, get us some smokes and turn into heroes."

"Hiroshi, you're crazy. For all you know Mrs. Watanabe could be sitting next door getting ready to call the coppers on you."

"You interested or chicken?" asked Hiroshi.

"It ain't right. It just ain't right," I said.

"Sure it is. Sure it is. See, you gotta understand that what we're doing has purpose to it."

Hiroshi's mind was fast. I could just hear his brain grinding out reasons. And I could see myself getting in trouble.

"You know why we're here in Idaho?" he growled.

"We'll get caught. I just know we will." I didn't want to whine, but I was.

"Answer me. You, your mother, your sister—why are they here?"

I didn't like the way things were going. "Old man Tsugu says they put us here to keep us safe," my words stumbled.

"As if those guns in the blockhouses are keeping crazy mobs of Americans out," Hiroshi laughed. "There's only sagebrush out there. At night it's coyotes howling—maybe the coyotes are angry at us." He laughed even harder but he wasn't really laughing.

My stomach was swirling. I felt that I needed the outhouse for more than a secluded meeting place, but Hiroshi wasn't going to leave me any privacy.

"Jackson's brother wants to join the army and become a hero. But they won't let him. He's tore up inside cause he wants to fight out there. But, see, he should be fighting here. Nobody's fighting here. That's what we're going to do. We're going to be camp heroes cause we're going to make life miserable for those WRA[2] guys. If they're gonna put us in here, they're gonna have to live with us."

Now this was crazy talk. Nobody in my family ever talked like this. In fact, my father was in Internal Security, drove around in a car, had a badge and a night stick, just in case. But Hiroshi, he wasn't happy being penned up in camp and decided he was going to be a hero.

"Jackson's gonna meet us here, and Itchy's gonna get us into the store, Now, you listen, Mas. If you wanna be part and parcel, you can, but if you get caught, there's no squealing. If your father catches us, you pretend he's Tojo[3] or that fascist Musclelini[4] trying to make you squeal, and you swear that you're not going to squeal for any reason, or me and Jackson will be giving you Indian burns everywhere."

If that sounded like a threat, it was. It was to get me to agree. I asked for some time alone instead cause my stomach was swirling with fear.

Hiroshi laughed in my face and then pushed open the door with such force that it caught an umbrella someone was holding and sent it reeling into the mud. At first I knew we'd been caught, then I saw it was Jackson, who had been standing too close to the door. The door had shoved him backward, and he bent forward to retrieve a soggy umbrella.

Jackson looked stupid with the umbrella, but he wasn't all wet the way I got just walking to the latrine.

"Look what you did to my mother's umbrella. It's the only umbrella in camp, and you two smashed it to hell."

Hiroshi was speechless for once, and I couldn't help laughing seeing the three bent spokes that just turned the bent cloth of the umbrella in opposite directions when he tried to straighten them.

Hiroshi tossed the umbrella at Jackson and glared at me. "You'll pay," he said, "just wait," and stalked off.

"Wait," I said, and took off after him. "Count me in." Now that I think about it, his walking off like that was probably what hooked me.

"Look," he said, "they depend on the store."

"Our folks do, yeah."

"No," Hiroshi said. "It's for us, so that we stay contented, and the old guys get cigarettes and candy, and someone's gonna buy rice and make o-sake[5] and they are gonna look the other way, so that everyone stays content." He kicked at a puddle, and mud flew before his shoe.

2. War Relocation Authority
3. Prime Minister Hideki Tojo
4. Benito Mussolini, Italy's Facist leader during World War II
5. rice wine

It was never smart to disagree when Hiroshi was serious. I agreed.

"So we mess it up, be sure that no one can get stuff out of it."

"That's crazy. We're gonna get caught, I just know it."

"It doesn't matter. Nobody else is doing anything. Not my mom, not your pop. If we can screw something up, we'll be doing good and still get some smokes."

"Well, you can count me out," I said.

"Look," said Hiroshi, "remember when Mitch and Toru ganged up on you and took your canteen money?"

He always brought that up to make me feel like I owed him some special favor.

"Well, Mitch and Toru, they're gonna rob the Canteen store tonight."

"Aw c'mon, they're not that stupid."

"The Kid, he heard them bragging about it."

"So? What are we going to do? Catch them at it and make them pay?"

"No, rob the store ourselves and let them hang for it." Hiroshi was always planning. "Yeah, and then their names'll be in the *Irrigator*, and everyone will know what creeps they are."

"How you gonna do that?"

"Simple. We rob it and let the coppers know they'll be back to get more stuff."

"Did you tell Itchy?"

"Yeah, he's waiting for us now."

So he had the perfect plan where we pull off the job and two creeps would get the blame. Hiroshi knew how to get in the Canteen. It was like two regular living spaces—one was the shop and the other was the storage. Hiroshi's plan was to take the ladder that was stored behind the Canteen and climb up along the end of the barrack, where the air vent was. He figured in less than 10 minutes, he could get it loose and crawl in above the ceiling. The second room in the barrack contained the trap door to the attic crawl space, and Hiroshi would crawl over to the trap door and let himself into the store room. Getting out was simpler. We'd load up and be out the front door.

When we got to the store, the rain was still coming down. In the spotlight, the rain looked almost solid, like a flag blowing in the wind. Hiroshi stopped under the roof of the rec building. There was someone leaning against the end of the canteen.

After a moment, Hiroshi pulled us together. "If you're in the army and fighting the Japs, and they pick you up and make you a prisoner of war in Mongolia or China, you can't break down and cry. And if you're in Europe and the Germans come shooting after you, you can't get up and run, you gotta sit in your fox hole and fire back. And if they capture you, you remember who you are and who they are and you don't break. Remember you're doing this for your folks. For your mother and your father. Don't bring shame on them."

We heard what Hiroshi had to say, and then we headed across the field. As we got nearer I could see the ladder leaning against the barrack and Itchy hiding around the corner. Jackson had a crowbar and a hammer, and the two of them went up and began working on the vent. It didn't take long because I don't think anybody pounded the slats in very hard when they built the place. Itchy and Jackson disappeared into the dark hole.

In a few minutes, Jackson opened the door, and we poured in. It was dark inside, but there was enough light from the porch that we could see large boxes full of cigarettes in the corner. I planned to take a couple of cartons of my old man's favorite brand—we all were going to, but they had a brand I never heard of. So we grabbed a few and hit the candy bars. We loaded up our pockets, when we should have come in with a suitcase or something big and sturdy to help carry our loot.

As I was getting my pockets full of Mars bars and Butterfingers, I heard Itchy whisper "Help!" When I turned I saw him juggling a huge bottle of pickles in slow motion. It seemed to wait on one palm and balance there before it began to topple to the other side, away from him and although he tried to get around it, it seemed to roll across his arms, and before Itchy could do anything else, it flipped over and onto the floor with a huge crack that sounded like a cannon or bazooka.

We were ready to run—but Hiroshi shushed us and we listened. All we could hear was the steady rain. And then, I started with a snicker that rolled into a laugh that started Itchy laughing too. It must have been just plain relief that flooded through us, because we all began to laugh, I mean, just howl. We were laughing because here we were loaded down with candy bars and cigarettes, and scared stiff. There was nothing funny, of course, but there was a large king sized bottle of pickles—I don't know what Itchy was doing with that bottle, or why he'd even think of carrying it out the door. After all who would want a three gallon jar of sour pickles anyway? But there we were with the pickle juice spreading across the floor, and Itchy with his pants stained by the fluid as well.

I put my hand in the flour bin and threw a handful at Itchy, where it caught his face and dusted his shirt. Itchy didn't take too well to that, and he looked for the rice barrel but found the bean barrel instead. A handful of beans was going to be painful, so I ducked, still laughing, but Hiroshi caught me and pushed me against the wall.

"Knock it off. This isn't kid stuff we're doing. It's like Jackson's brother wanting to join the war. This is our part—you understand? And we leave this place clean, guys. Clean. This was going to be a quiet job, remember? If it's a mess, Toru and Mitch will know something's wrong, and we don't want the coppers to think there's more than just them that messed this place up."

I forgot Mitch and Toru were due anytime.

So, like Hiroshi said, I swept up the floor and cleaned up the beans and the flour. Itchy still had flour on his face but the rain would wash that off, and then we were both on the floor wiping up the pickle juice. When we finished, the dark clean area of the floor where we had cleaned pickle juice looked like a target's dark bull's eye, surrounded by all the dust and sand that had blown through the tar paper walls the weeks before the rain began. So we swept and mopped the whole floor until we were sweating and the pickle stain was barely visible in the porch light.

The room looked pretty good, when Hiroshi said, "Pour the rest of the pickle juice in the rice barrel, the flour barrel and that bean barrel."

We looked at him like he was crazy.

"Do it," he said. "Now." In a minute he looked at his watch. "Time's up, boys. Let's move out."

Those words made me think of the army, of the movie whose title I'd forgotten from two weekends ago. Made me think of Jackson's brother wanting to ship out for boot camp. In fact I felt that way. Like a soldier behind enemy lines, doing something brave for my country, but I couldn't figure out why it was brave or how it was good for my country. I didn't have long to figure, anyway, because as I walked out the front door behind Hiroshi, Itchy closed the Canteen door behind me, and Hiroshi whispered let's run for it. And we did. We ran along the side of the barracks away from our block and circled away and back toward the latrine area. Nobody seemed to be following us.

When we got to the outhouse, I was out of breath and shaking. Hiroshi said, "Hide the stuff. Don't carry it on you."

"Where?" said Itchy.

Hiroshi pointed to the back of the outhouse. Itchy and I stuffed cigarettes and candy bars up under the tar paper hoping they wouldn't slip out and fall into the stink. But I kept some of the candy, and Jackson, I know, had his pockets full.

As we came splashing around the outhouse, I heard a voice say, "Okay, boys, don't move."

At first I thought it was Toru—his voice had changed and was low like this one, but it wasn't. It was someone in a uniform—part of Internal Security Patrol. I got set to run, when I saw there were three of them and they had their nightsticks out.

"Oh, Jesus," I heard Itchy say behind me. There we were with evidence in our pockets.

Security pulled us over to Hiroshi.

"Stand still, boys." The tall one came up behind us and patted us down. He found the Mars bar that Itchy had saved and my Butterfingers.

"Look, Sam," he said to the other cop. "A pack of cigarettes."

He'd found Jackson's pack. When he patted Hiroshi down, Hiroshi's pockets were empty. Nothing. That surprised me, because I was sure he didn't have time to empty his pockets.

"We didn't do nothing, sir," said Jackson, the rain starting to stream down his face. He had left the umbrella back at the Canteen, but nobody remembered.

"We caught these friends of yours with their pockets full. That's what we got on you. Thieves. Your folks will have hell to pay for what you've done."

"I told you," said Hiroshi, "we didn't do nothing. We were just here at the latrine. Came out here to share our candy. Can't stand being at home with all those little kids whining. So here, we can stand in the rain and have our candy."

"You smoke, boy?" The tall cop was tossing the cigarettes in the air and catching them in his left hand. I had never seen him before but the other two were familiar.

"Someone's been breaking into the canteen. We figure it had to be you three. There's nobody else out here, and we've got the evidence, now, don't we?"

"Oh, look, sir," Hiroshi was fixing himself a good story, I could tell, "sure we stole the stuff."

I couldn't believe what I just heard, but Hiroshi had everyone's attention. Itchy was biting his lip and starting to scratch at his ears. Jackson's hands were clenched into fists. But the coppers began to relax.

"I've been issued a key to the front door of the Canteen, and we just walked right in," said Hiroshi, a quiet smile on his face.

The tall cop gripped Hiroshi by the collar, and Hiroshi, his feet dangling in the air, tried to wave the cop back with his hands.

"From our parents, sir," he finished. "Those are my old man's cigarettes, see? And Itchy and Mas, they got candy from me because it was my birthday, and everyone was giving me so much candy for my birthday that it was making me sick."

"Look, son," said the cop, "we got the goods. Five Butterfingers, three Mars bars, two packs of cigarettes, a deck of playing cards, and a box of matches."

"We know it was you who's been breaking and entering. Now, just tell us names of your other gang members and how many times you been in."

"None," said Hiroshi. "None." Hiroshi glared at us, as if we were the ones who were going to break down, but Hiroshi was the one the cop was talking to. Jeez, I could tell the cop was going to make Hiroshi an example for us, and I felt cold deep in my bones, like it was raining inside of me. I was getting nervous, but I couldn't stop imagining my pop saying the same things to Hiroshi, putting him against the wall and making him sweat. I felt a little proud then, but Hiroshi was making himself like steel. Later, someone would say that steel turns to rust if it's left in the rain too long.

"Look, you little creep," he said, "we're going to publish your name in the paper and everyone will know what a delinquent you are. And your mother will be embarrassed, so embarrassed that she won't show her face in the dining hall. And your brother fighting out there for the United States of America, he'll hear about this and wonder why his little brother has become a traitor."

"There ain't no army good enough for my brother," said Hiroshi.

Without warning, the cop's hand swung from his hip directly across Hiroshi's face with a crack that sounded like a twenty-two.

Hiroshi staggered back, and his face twisted and his eyes rolled and maybe there were tears in his eyes but there was too much rain to tell for sure. Hiroshi took his time before he spoke, and when he did, his voice was stiff and had an edge to it.

"Nobody has a brother in the United States Army because they think we're traitors. We are innocent. There's nothing more to say."

"Well," roared the cop, "someone's been breaking into the canteen the last several weeks. We're going to get you and your buddies to confess even if we have to throw you in jail."

Words stuck in my throat. I didn't know what to say, but I was sure that I had to say something to keep them from taking us down to the station. I didn't think my pop would let me get hit the way Hiroshi just got hit, but then if my pop were around, he might hit me himself if he knew what I had just done. I didn't have to follow Hiroshi's lead, but I had. Itchy always wanted to be where Hiroshi was and do what Hiroshi said, but Hiroshi was in so much trouble right now, he had no way of getting himself out of it. And he couldn't help us, that was for sure. I had to admire him because he refused to cry or beg for mercy, but Itchy and Jackson were about to fall apart. So was I, but I nudged Itchy so that he looked me in the eye. And in that moment I knew that he'd be all right, but I could smell the pickle juice on Itchy's clothes. He smelled like he'd peed on himself. I moved in front of Itchy hoping that the cops wouldn't smell him.

The tall cop was still going on about what our names in the paper would do to our parents when he noticed me.

"You. You're Tom's kid aren't you?"

He had recognized me. I knew for sure that the rest of my life was going to be spent in jail. I could see my own father turning the key in the lock.

I nodded and waited for the cop to handcuff me, but he grabbed Hiroshi by the back of his jacket and twisted his arm. Just when I thought Hiroshi had had enough the cop stopped for no reason, the same way the rain will stop in the middle of a heavy downpour and the sky will open up to a ray of sunshine. The questions and the insinuations stopped. The cop took our names and told us to get the hell out of there.

Hiroshi looked at the cop and said, "What time is it, sir?"

"Time for your butt to be warming your sheets, son."

"Yes, sir, but if you don't mind, would you tell me if it's after nine! My parents went to the movie at the recreation hall tonight, and I'll meet them when the movie gets out."

The cop checked his watch again.

"It's almost 9: 30." The cops got back in their car, and as they were about to drive off, Hiroshi stepped up to the window. "It wasn't us, sir, but I heard the ones responsible were planning to be there tonight."

We got out of there as fast as we could. I couldn't believe that we had gotten free.

All the next week, Hiroshi was a hero at school. All the guys had heard. Itchy had told the Kid, who told everyone else about our run-in with the law and about destroying the barrels of rice and flour and beans to let the WRA know that we would not kowtow[6] to them. All the guys knew that Hiroshi had held his ground, laughed at Security and hadn't broken. After all, we had our cigarettes and candy bars as proof. Janey Kubo and Millie Ito were fluttering around Hiroshi as if he were their hero too, and Kimi, who was a senior, started calling him "her Hero." She walked with him when he headed home, but he ignored all of them, like Wade Bond ignored all those girls on the wagon train, talked to them as if they tumble weed or sage brush. Pretty soon, Hiroshi was everyone's hero. The name stuck. And rubbed off on us too. Kimi kind of rubbed her hands through my hair one afternoon, and I blushed and turned away when what I wanted to do was just the opposite, but I felt just like a little kid.

By the end of the week the rain had passed, the sun was drying the land, and Hiroshi was sitting behind the outhouse, smoking the last cigarette from one of the packs we had stolen. He was reading an *Irrigator* when I found him.

He was mumbling about ping pong and about how he could beat the guys who played at the rec hall. Ping pong tourneys filled the back page of the paper every week. But Hiroshi, like most everyone else, could hardly wait until spring. There was already talk about getting together a couple of leagues and having a camp world series. The older guys were tossing the casaba[7] around but you could only find one game a night around the camp because most of the guys had a lot of trouble putting the ball through the hoop. Ping pong, on the other hand, was easy, Hiroshi said, if you had self-control. You get tight and you choke, but if you stay relaxed, everything comes out just fine. Just fine. Nobody ever worried about getting hit by a ping pong ball.

When he opened the paper, Hiroshi was quiet. He was quiet a long time.

"Hey, Hiroshi, what's the matter, huh?"

He looked at me, then put his hand over his face. The newspaper dangled in his right hand. I reached over to see what had disturbed him so much.

The headline read: "Canteen Thieves Confess." The story told about Internal Security catching three adolescents redhanded. The thieves, frightened and guilty,

---

6. bow
7. casaba melon, but in this slang, for basketball

begged forgiveness, tearfully signed confessions, and gave the names of two other young men who were later apprehended. The case, the newspaper reported, was closed. The paper reported that the losses totaled less than $50, including several cartons of cigarettes, twelve pairs of sunglasses, a deck of playing cards, a box of matches, 30 pipes, a tin of tobacco and some cigars. Clearly the work of bored children. The names of the thieves were being kept confidential because of their ages.

Hirosh stood up and pounded on the outhouse wall. "Shit," he said. Then he shouted, "Liars! Goddam liars."

I could already hear the laughter at school. Nobody had talked. Nobody had cried, but we were fools and not heroes. The newspaper had seen to that. What we had done was the work of bored children. A prank. And I knew the girls would point at Hiroshi behind his back, laugh and call him "Hero." Their All-American Hero.

With a burst of energy Hiroshi leaned against the outhouse and started to alternately push and release and push and release his weight against the building until it began to rock unsteadily at its northeast corner. I could feel his anger, like the heat from the earth, it filled me, and I joined with him, my added weight providing just enough momentum to topple the outhouse to its side leaving its dark pit yawing before us, its odor filling our senses and the atmosphere.

Even there in the brilliant October sunlight, the world seemed dead. If someone had told me that spring would find the camp surrounded by fields of potatoes, sugar beets, beans, corn, and melons, I would have called that person crazy. For that autumn day, the world had come to jolting stop and began to rot.

Hiroshi looked at me. Calmly and quietly, he said, "I've got another idea. You know those fire hydrants they're hooking up all up and down the camp?"

I didn't want to hear what he had to say. I just put my fingers in my ears and said, "I don't want to be no hero."

Bharati Mukherjee

(b. 1940)

Bharati Mukherjee was born in Calcutta and has lived in Toronto and Montreal. She received a master's degree in English and ancient Indian culture from the universities of Calcutta and Baroda. In 1961 she came to America to attend the University of Iowa, where she received a master of fine arts degree and a doctorate in English. She became an American citizen in 1988.

*She is the author of five books of fiction—**The Tiger's Daughter** (1971), **Wife** (1975), **Darkness** (1985), **The Middleman and Other Stories**, (1988), and two novels, **Jasmine** (1989) and **The Holder of the World** (1993). Mukherjee has also published two works of nonfiction with her husband, Clark Blaise, called **Days and Nights in Calcutta** (1977) and **The Sorrow and Terror** (1987).*

*The following story, "The Management of Grief," is taken from **The Middleman and Other Stories**, which won the National Book Critics Circle Award in 1989. Based on the actual 1985 terrorist bombing of an Air India flight, "The Management of Grief" explores the cultural gap between a Canadian social worker and Shaila Bhave, the thirty-six-year-old fictional narrator of the story who has been assigned to help the social worker handle grieving Indo-Canadian immigrants who have lost relatives in the bombing.*

The Management of Grief

A woman I don't know is boiling tea the Indian way in my kitchen. There are a lot of women I don't know in my kitchen, whispering, and moving tactfully. They open doors, rummage through the pantry, and try not to ask me where things are kept. They remind me of when my sons were small, on Mother's Day or when Vikram and I were tired, and they would make big, sloppy omelets. I would lie in bed pretending I didn't hear them.

Dr. Sharma, the treasurer of the Indo-Canada Society, pulls me into the hallway. He wants to know if I am worried about money. His wife, who has just come up from the basement with a tray of empty cups and glasses, scolds him. "Don't bother Mrs. Bhave with mundane details." She looks so monstrously pregnant her baby must be days overdue. I tell her she shouldn't be carrying heavy things. "Shaila," she says, smiling, "this is the fifth." Then she grabs a teenager by his shirttails. He slips his Walkman off his head. He has to be one of her four children, they have the same doomed and dented foreheads. "What's the official word now?" she demands. The boy slips the headphones back on. "They're acting evasive, Ma. They're saying it could be an accident or a terrorist bomb."

All morning, the boys have been muttering, Sikh[1] Bomb, Sikh Bomb. The men, not using the word, bow their heads in agreement. Mrs. Sharma touches her forehead at such a word. At least they've stopped talking about space debris and Russian lasers.

Two radios are going in the dining room. They are tuned to different stations. Someone must have brought the radios down from my boys' bedrooms. I haven't gone into their rooms since Kusum came running across the front lawn in her bathrobe. She looked so funny, I was laughing when I opened the door.

The big TV in the den is being whizzed through American networks and cable channels.

"Damn!" some man swears bitterly. "How can these preachers carry on like nothing's happened?" I want to tell him we're not that important. You look at the audience, and at the preacher in his blue robe with his beautiful white hair, the potted palm trees under a blue sky, and you know they care about nothing.

The phone rings and rings. Dr. Sharma's taken charge. "We're with her," he keeps saying. "Yes, yes, the doctor has given calming pills. Yes, yes, pills are having necessary effect." I wonder if pills alone explain this calm. Not peace, just a deadening quiet. I was always controlled, but never repressed. Sound can reach me, but my body is tensed, ready to scream. I hear their voices all around me. I hear my boys and Vikram cry, "Mommy, Shaila!" and their screams insulate me, like headphones.

The woman boiling water tells her story again and again. "I got the news first. My cousin called from Halifax before six a.m., can you imagine? He'd gotten up for prayers and his son was studying for medical exams and he heard on a rock channel that something had happened to a plane. They said first it had disappeared from the radar, like a giant eraser just reached out. His father called me, so I said to him, what do you mean, "something bad"? You mean a hijacking? And he said, *behn*[2], there is no confirmation of anything yet, but check with your neighbors because a lot of them must be on that plane. So I called poor Kusum straightaway. I knew Kusum's husband and daughter were booked to go yesterday."

Kusum lives across the street from me. She and Satish had moved in less than a month ago. They said they needed a bigger place. All these people, the Sharmas and friends from the Indo-Canada Society had been there for the housewarming. Satish and Kusum made homemade tandoori[3] on their big gas grill and even the white neighbors piled their plates high with that luridly red, charred, juicy chicken. Their younger daughter had danced, and even our boys had broken away from the Stanley Cup telecast to put in a reluctant appearance. Everyone took pictures for their albums

---

1. A religion developed from the fifteenth century teachings of Guru Nanak in the Punjab region of India. Some Sikhs mounted a militant separatist movement in the 1980s.
2. sister
3. marinated and barbecued meat, traditionally prepared in a clay oven

and for the community newspapers—another of our families had made it big in Toronto—and now I wonder how many of those happy faces are gone. "Why does God give us so much if all along He intends to take it away?" Kusum asks me.

I nod. We sit on carpeted stairs, holding hands like children. "I never once told him that I loved him," I say. I was too much the well brought up woman. I was so well brought up I never felt comfortable calling my husband by his first name.

"It's all right," Kusum says. "He knew. My husband knew. They felt it. Modern young girls have to say it because what they feel is fake."

Kusum's daughter, Pam, runs in with an overnight case. Pam's in her McDonald's uniform. "Mummy! You have to get dressed!" Panic makes her cranky. "A reporter's on his way here."

"Why?"

"You want to talk to him in your bathrobe?" She starts to brush her mother's long hair. She's the daughter who's always in trouble. She dates Canadian boys and hangs out in the mall, shopping for tight sweaters. The younger one, the goody-goody one according to Pam, the one with a voice so sweet that when she sang *bhajans*[4] for Ethiopian relief even a frugal man like my husband wrote out a hundred dollar check, *she* was on that plane. *She* was going to spend July and August with grandparents because Pam wouldn't go. Pam said she'd rather waitress at McDonalds.

"If it's a choice between Bombay and Wonderland, I'm picking Wonderland," she'd said.

"Leave me alone," Kusum yells. "You know what I want to do? If I didn't have to look after you now, I'd hang myself."

Pam's young face goes blotchy with pain. "Thanks," she says, "don't let me stop you."

"Hush," pregnant Mrs. Sharma scolds Pam. "Leave your mother alone. Mr. Sharma will tackle the reporters and fill out the forms. He'll say what has to be said."

Pam stands her ground. "You think I don't know what Mummy's thinking? *Why ever?* that's what. That's sick! Mummy wishes my little sister were alive and I were dead.

Kusum's hand in mine is trembly hot. We continue to sit on the stairs.

She calls before she arrives, wondering if there's anything I need. Her name is Judith Templeton and she's an appointee of the provincial government. "Multiculturalism?" I ask, and she says, "partially," but that her mandate is bigger. "I've been told you knew many of the people on the flight," she says. "Perhaps if you'd agree to help us reach the others ... ?"

---

4. devotional songs

She gives me time at least to put on tea water and pick up the mess in the front room. I have a few *samosas*[5] from Kusum's housewarming that I could fry up, but then I think, why prolong this visit?

Judith Templeton is much younger than she sounded. She wears a blue suit with a white blouse and a polka dot tie. Her blond hair is cut short, her only jewelry is pearl drop earrings. Her briefcase is new and expensive looking, a gleaming cordovan leather. She sits with it across her lap. When she looks out the front windows onto the street, her contact lenses seem to float in front of her light blue eyes.

"What sort of help do you want from me?" I ask. She has refused the tea, out of politeness, but I insist, along with some slightly stale biscuits.

"I have no experience," she admits. "That is, I have an MSW and I've worked in liaison with accident victims, but I mean I have no experience with a tragedy of this scale—"

"Who could?" I ask.

"—and with the complications of culture, language, and customs. Someone mentioned that Mrs. Bhave is a pillar—because you've taken it more calmly."

At this, perhaps, I frown, for she reaches forward, almost to take my hand. "I hope you understand my meaning, Mrs. Bhave. There are hundreds of people in Metro directly affected, like you, and some of them speak no English. There are some widows who've never handled money or gone on a bus, and there are old parents who still haven't eaten or gone outside their bedrooms. Some houses and apartments have been looted. Some wives are still hysterical. Some husbands are in shock and profound depression. We want to help, but our hands are tied in so many ways. We have to distribute money to some people, and there are legal documents—these things can be done. We have interpreters, but we don't always have the human touch, or maybe the right human touch. We don't want to make mistakes, Mrs. Bhave, and that's why we'd like to ask you to help us."

"More mistakes, you mean," I say.

"Police matters are not in my hands," she answers.

"Nothing I can do will make any difference," I say. "We must all grieve in our own way."

"But you are coping very well. All the people said, Mrs. Bhave is the strongest person of all. Perhaps if the others could see you, talk with you, it would help them."

"By the standards of the people you call hysterical, I am behaving very oddly and very badly, Miss Templeton." I want to say to her, *I wish I could scream, starve, walk into Lake Ontario, jump from a bridge*. "They would not see me as a model. I do not see myself as a model."

---

5.   deep-fried spicy snacks

I am a freak. No one who has ever known me would think of me reacting this way. This terrible calm will not go away.

She asks me if she may call again, after I get back from a long trip that we all must make. "Of course," I say. "Feel free to call, anytime."

Four days later, I find Kusum squatting on a rock overlooking a bay in Ireland. It isn't a big rock, but it juts sharply out over water. This is as close as we'll ever get to them. June breezes balloon out her sari and unpin her knee-length hair. She has the bewildered look of a sea creature whom the tides have stranded.

It's been one hundred hours since Kusum came stumbling and screaming across my lawn. Waiting around the hospital, we've heard many stories. The police, the diplomats, they tell us things thinking that we're strong, that knowledge is helpful to the grieving, and maybe it is. Some, I know, prefer ignorance, or their own versions. The plane broke into two, they say. Unconsciousness was instantaneous. No one suffered. My boys must have just finished their breakfasts. They loved eating on planes, they loved the smallness of plates, knives, and forks. Last year they saved the airline salt and pepper shakers. Half an hour more and they would have made it to Heathrow.

Kusum says that we can't escape our fate. She says that all those people—our husbands, my boys, her girl with the nightingale voice, all those Hindus, Christians, Sikhs, Muslims, Parsis, and atheists on that plane—were fated to die together off this beautiful bay. She learned this from a swami in Toronto.

I have my Valium.

Six of us "relatives"—two widows and four widowers—choose to spend the day today by the waters instead of sitting in a hospital room and scanning photographs of the dead. That's what they call us now: relatives. I've looked through twenty-seven photos in two days. They're very kind to us, the Irish are very understanding. Sometimes understanding means freeing a tourist bus for this trip to the bay, so we can pretend to spy our loved ones through the glassiness of waves or in sunspeckled cloud shapes.

I could die here, too, and be content.

"What is that, out there?" She's standing and flapping her hands and for a moment I see a head shape bobbing in the waves. She's standing in the water, I, on the boulder. The tide is low, and a round, black, head-sized rock has just risen from the waves. She returns, her sari end dripping and ruined and her face is a twisted remnant of hope, the way mine was a hundred hours ago, still laughing but inwardly knowing that nothing but the ultimate tragedy could bring two women together at six o'clock on a Sunday morning. I watch her face sag into blankness.

"That water felt warm, Shaila," she says at length.

"You can't," I say. "We have to wait for our turn to come."

I haven't eaten in four days, haven't brushed my teeth.

"I know," she says. "I tell myself I have no right to grieve. They are in a better place than we are. My swami says I should be thrilled for them. My swami says depression is a sign of our selfishness."

Maybe I'm selfish. Selfishly I break away from Kusum and run, sandals slapping against stones, to the water's edge. What if my boys aren't lying pinned under the debris? What if they aren't stuck a mile below that innocent blue chop? What if, given the strong currents....

Now I've ruined my sari, one of my best. Kusum has joined me, knee-deep in water that feels to me like a swimming pool. I could settle in the water, and my husband would take my hand and the boys would slap water in my face just to see me scream.

"Do you remember what good swimmers my boys were, Kusum?"

"I saw the medals," she says.

One of the widowers, Dr. Ranganathan from Montreal, walks out to us, carrying his shoes in one hand. He's an electrical engineer. Someone at the hotel mentioned his work is famous around the world, something about the place where physics and electricity come together. He has lost a huge family, something indescribable. "With some luck," Dr. Ranganathan suggests to me, "a good swimmer could make it safely to some island. It is quite possible that there may be many, many microscopic islets scattered around."

"You're not just saying that?" I tell Dr. Ranganathan about Vinod, my elder son. Last year he took diving as well.

"It's a parent's duty to hope," he says. "It is foolish to rule out possibilities that have not been tested. I myself have not surrendered hope."

Kusum is sobbing once again. "Dear lady," he says, laying his free hand on her arm, and she calms down.

"Vinod is how old?" he asks me. He's very careful, as we all are. *Is*, not was.

"Fourteen. Yesterday he was fourteen. His father and uncle were going to take him down to the Taj[6] and give him a big birthday party. I couldn't go with them because I couldn't get two weeks off from my stupid job in June." I process bills for a travel agent. June is a big travel month.

Dr. Ranganathan whips the pockets of his suit jacket inside out. Squashed roses, in darkening shades of pink, float on the water. He tore the roses off creepers in somebody's garden. He didn't ask anyone if he could pluck the roses, but now there's been an article about it in the local papers. When you see an Indian person, it says, please give him or her flowers.

"A strong youth of fourteen," he says, "can very likely pull to safety a younger one."

---

6.   the name of a local restaurant that refers to the Taj Mahal in Agra, India

My sons, though four years apart, were very close. Vinod wouldn't let Mithun drown. *Electrical engineering*, I think, foolishly perhaps: this man knows important secrets of the universe, things closed to me. Relief spins me lightheaded. No wonder my boys' photographs haven't turned up in the gallery of photos of the recovered dead. "Such pretty roses," I say.

"My wife loved pink roses. Every Friday I had to bring a bunch home. I used to say, why? After twenty odd years of marriage you're still needing proof positive of my love?" He has identified his wife and three of his children. Then others from Montreal, the lucky ones, intact families with no survivors. He chuckles as he wades back to shore. Then he swings around to ask me a question. "Mrs. Bhave, you are wanting to throw in some roses for your loved ones? I have two big ones left."

But I have other things to float: Vinod's pocket calculator; a half-painted model B-52 for my Mithun. They'd want them on their island. And for my husband? For him I let fall into the calm, glassy waters a poem I wrote in the hospital yesterday. Finally he'll know my feelings for him.

"Don't tumble, the rocks are slippery," Dr. Ranganathan cautions. He holds out a hand for me to grab.

Then it's time to get back on the bus, time to rush back to our waiting posts on hospital benches.

Kusum is one of the lucky ones. The lucky ones flew here, identified in multiplicate their loved ones, then will fly to India with the bodies for proper ceremonies. Satish is one of the few males who surfaced. The photos of faces we saw on the walls in an office at Heathrow and here in the hospital are mostly of women. Women have more body fat, a nun said to me matter-of-factly. They float better.

Today I was stopped by a young sailor on the street. He had loaded bodies, he'd gone into the water when—he checks my face for signs of strength—when the sharks were first spotted. I don't blush, and he breaks down. "It's all right," I say. "Thank you." I had heard about the sharks from Dr. Ranganathan. In his orderly mind, science brings understanding, it holds no terror. It is the shark's duty. For every deer there is a hunter, for every fish a fisherman.

The Irish are not shy; they rush to me and give me hugs and some are crying. I cannot imagine reactions like that on the streets of Toronto. Just strangers, and I am touched. Some carry flowers with them and give them to any Indian they see.

After lunch, a policeman I have gotten to know quite well catches hold of me. He says he thinks he has a match for Vinod. I explain what a good swimmer Vinod is.

"You want me with you when you look at photos?" Dr. Ranganathan walks ahead of me into the picture gallery. In these matters, he is a scientist, and I am grateful. It is a new perspective. "They have performed miracles," he says. "We are indebted to them."

The first day or two the policemen showed us relatives only one picture at a time; now they're in a hurry, they're eager to lay out the possibles, and even the probables.

The face on the photo is of a boy much like Vinod; the same intelligent eyes, the same thick brows dipping into a V. But this boy's features, even his cheeks, are puffier, wider, mushier.

"No." My gaze is pulled by other pictures. There are five other boys who look like Vinod.

The nun assigned to console me rubs the first picture with a fingertip. "When they've been in the water for a while, love, they look a little heavier." The bones under the skin are broken, they said on the first day—try to adjust your memories. It's important.

"It's not him. I'm his mother. I'd know."

"I know this one!" Dr. Ranganathan cries out suddenly from the back of the gallery. "And this one!" I think he senses that I don't want to find my boys. "They are the Kutty brothers. They were also from Montreal." I don't mean to be crying. On the contrary, I am ecstatic. My suitcase in the hotel is packed heavy with dry clothes for my boys.

The policeman starts to cry. "I am so sorry, I am so sorry, ma'am. I really thought we had a match."

With the nun ahead of us and the policeman behind, we, the unlucky ones without our children's bodies, file out of the makeshift gallery.

From Ireland most of us go on to India. Kusum and I take the same direct flight to Bombay, so I can help her clear customs quickly. But we have to argue with a man in uniform. He has large boils on his face. The boils swell and glow with sweat as we argue with him. He wants Kusum to wait in line and he refuses to take authority because his boss is on a tea break. But Kusum won't let her coffins out of sight, and I shan't desert her though I know that my parents, elderly and diabetic, must be waiting in a stuffy car in a scorching lot.

"You bastard!" I scream at the man with the popping boils. Other passengers press closer. "You think we're smuggling contraband in those coffins!"

Once upon a time we were well brought up women; we were dutiful wives who kept our heads veiled, our voices shy and sweet.

In India, I become, once again, an only child of rich, ailing parents. Old friends of the family come to pay their respects. Some are Sikh, and inwardly, involuntarily, I cringe. My parents are progressive people; they do not blame communities for a few individuals.

In Canada it is a different story now.

"Stay longer," my mother pleads. "Canada is a cold place. Why would you want to be all by yourself?" I stay.

Three months pass. Then another.

"Vikram wouldn't have wanted you to give up things!" they protest. They call my husband by the name he was born with. In Toronto he'd changed to Vik so the men he worked with at his office would find his name as easy as Rod or Chris. "You know, the dead aren't cut off from us!"

My grandmother, the spoiled daughter of a rich *zamindar*,[7] shaved her head with rusty razor blades when she was widowed at sixteen. My grandfather died of childhood diabetes when he was nineteen, and she saw herself as the harbinger of bad luck. My mother grew up without parents, raised indifferently by an uncle, while her true mother slept in a hut behind the main estate house and took her food with the servants. She grew up a rationalist. My parents abhor mindless mortification.

The zamindar's daughter kept stubborn faith in Vedic rituals;[8] my parents rebelled. I am trapped between two modes of knowledge. At thirty-six, I am too old to start over and too young to give up. Like my husband's spirit, I flutter between worlds.

Courting aphasia, we travel. We travel with our phalanx of servants and poor relatives. To hill stations and to beach resorts. We play contract bridge in dusty gymkhana clubs. We ride stubby ponies up crumbly mountain trails. At tea dances, we let ourselves be twirled twice round the ballroom. We hit the holy spots we hadn't made time for before. In Varanasi, Kalighat, Rishikesh, Hardwar,[9] astrologers and palmists seek me out and for a fee offer me cosmic consolations.

Already the widowers among us are being shown new bride candidates. They cannot resist the call of custom, the authority of their parents and older brothers. They must marry; it is the duty of a man to look after a wife. The new wives will be young widows with children, destitute but of good family. They will make loving wives, but the men will shun them. I've had calls from the men over crackling Indian telephone lines. "Save me," they say, these substantial, educated, successful men of forty. "My parents are arranging a marriage for me." In a month they will have buried one family and returned to Canada with a new bride and partial family.

---

7.   big landowner
8.   rituals from the earliest Sanskrit texts of Brahmanical Hinduism
9.   various sites of Hindu pilgrimage, all in north India

I am comparatively lucky. No one here thinks of arranging a husband for an unlucky widow.

Then, on the third day of the sixth month into this odyssey, in an abandoned temple in a tiny Himalayan village, as I make my offering of flowers and sweetmeats to the god of a tribe of animists, my husband descends to me. He is squatting next to a scrawny *sadhu*[10] in moth-eaten robes. Vikram wears the vanilla suit he wore the last time I hugged him. The *sadhu* tosses petals on a butter-fed flame, reciting Sanskrit mantras and sweeps his face of flies. My husband takes my hands in his.

You're beautiful, he starts. Then, *What are you doing here?*

Shall I stay? I ask. He only smiles, but already the image is fading. *You must finish alone what we started together.* No seaweed wreathes his mouth. He speaks too fast just as he used to when we were an envied family in our pink split-level. He is gone.

In the windowless altar room, smoky with joss sticks and clarified butter lamps, a sweaty hand gropes for my blouse. I do not shriek. The *sadhu* arranges his robe. The lamps hiss and sputter out.

When we come out of the temple, my mother says, "Did you feel something weird in there?"

My mother has no patience with ghosts, prophetic dreams, holy men, and cults.

"No," I lie. "Nothing."

But she knows that she's lost me. She knows that in days I shall be leaving.

Kusum's put her house up for sale. She wants to live in an ashram in Hardwar. Moving to Hardwar was her swami's idea. Her swami runs two ashrams, the one in Hardwar and another here in Toronto.

"Don't run away," I tell her.

"I'm not running away," she says. "I'm pursuing inner peace. You think you or that Ranganathan fellow are better off?"

Pam's left for California. She wants to do some modeling, she says. She says when she comes into her share of the insurance money she'll open a yoga-cum-aerobics studio in Hollywood. She sends me postcards so naughty I daren't leave them on the coffee table. Her mother has withdrawn from her and the world.

The rest of us don't lose touch, that's the point. Talk is all we have, says Dr. Ranganathan, who has also resisted his relatives and returned to Montreal and to his job, alone. He says, whom better to talk with than other relatives? We've been melted down and recast as a new tribe.

He calls me twice a week from Montreal. Every Wednesday night and every Saturday afternoon. He is changing jobs, going to Ottawa. But Ottawa is over a hundred

---

10. a Hindu religious mendicant or holy man

miles away, and he is forced to drive two hundred and twenty miles a day. He can't bring himself to sell his house. The house is a temple, he says; the king-sized bed in the master bedroom is a shrine. He sleeps on a folding cot. A devotee.

There are still some hysterical relatives. Judith Templeton's list of those needing help and those who've "accepted" is in nearly perfect balance. Acceptance means you speak of your family in the past tense and you make active plans for moving ahead with your life. There are courses at Seneca and Ryerson we could be taking. Her gleaming leather briefcase is full of college catalogues and lists of cultural societies that need our help. She has done impressive work, I tell her.

"In the textbooks on grief management," she replies—I am her confidante, I realize, one of the few whose grief has not sprung bizarre obsessions—"there are stages to pass through: rejection, depression, acceptance, reconstruction." She has compiled a chart and finds that six months after the tragedy, none of us still reject reality, but only a handful are reconstructing. "Depressed Acceptance" is the plateau we've reached. Remarriage is a major step in reconstruction (though she's a little surprised, even shocked, over *how* quickly some of the men have taken on new families). Selling one's house and changing jobs and cities is healthy.

How do I tell Judith Templeton that my family surrounds me, and that like creatures in epics, they've changed shapes? She sees me as calm and accepting but worries that I have no job, no career. My closest friends are worse off than I. I cannot tell her my days, even my nights, are thrilling.

She asks me to help with families she can't reach at all. An elderly couple in Agincourt whose sons were killed just weeks after they had brought their parents over from a village in Punjab. From their names, I know that are Sikh. Judith Templeton and a translator have visited them twice with offers of money for air fare to Ireland, with bank forms, power-of-attorney forms, but they have refused to sign, or to leave their tiny apartment. Their sons' money is frozen in the bank. Their sons' investment apartments have been trashed by tenants, the furnishings sold off. The parents fear that anything they sign or any money they receive will end the company's or the country's obligations to them. They fear they are selling their sons for two airline tickets to a place they've never seen.

The high-rise apartment is a tower of Indians and West Indians, with a sprinkling of Orientals. The nearest bus stop kiosk is lined with women in saris. Boys practice cricket in the parking lot. Inside the building, even I wince a bit from the ferocity of onion fumes, the distinctive and immediate Indianness of frying *ghee*,[11] but Judith Templeton maintains a steady flow of information. These poor old people are in imminent danger of losing their place and all their services.

---

11. clarified butter

I say to her, "They are Sikh. They will not open up to a Hindu woman." And what I want to add is, as much as I try not to, I stiffen now at the sight of beards and turbans. I remember a time when we all trusted each other in this new country, it was only the new country we worried about.

The two rooms are dark and stuffy. The lights are off, and an oil lamp sputters on the coffee table. The bent old lady has let us in, and her husband is wrapping a white turban over his oiled, hip-length hair. She immediately goes to the kitchen, and I hear the most familiar sound of an Indian home, tap water hitting and filling a teapot.

They have not paid their utility bills, out of fear and the inability to write a check. The telephone is gone; electricity and gas and water are soon to follow. They have told Judith their sons will provide. They are good boys, and they have always earned and looked after their parents.

We converse a bit in Hindi. They do not ask about the crash and I wonder if I should bring it up. If they think I am here merely as a translator, then they may feel insulted. There are thousands of Punjabi-speakers, Sikhs, in Toronto to do a better job. And so I say to the old lady, "I too have lost my sons, and my husband, in the crash."

Her eyes immediately fill with tears. The man mutters a few words which sound like a blessing. "God provides and God takes away," he says.

I want to say, but only men destroy and give back nothing. "My boys and my husband are not coming back," I say. "We have to understand that."

Now the old woman responds. "But who is to say? Man alone does not decide these things." To this her husband adds his agreement.

Judith asks about the bank papers, the release forms. With a stroke of the pen, they will have a provincial trustee to pay their bills, invest their money, send them a monthly pension.

"Do you know this woman?" I ask them.

The man raises his hand from the table, turns it over and seems to regard each finger separately before he answers. "This young lady is always coming here, we make tea for her and she leaves papers for us to sign." His eyes scan a pile of papers in the corner of the room. "Soon we will be out of tea, then will she go away?"

The old lady adds, "I have asked my neighbors and no one else gets *angrezi*[12] visitors. What have we done?"

"It's her job," I try to explain. "The government is worried. Soon you will have no place to stay, no lights, no gas, no water."

"Government will get its money. Tell her not to worry, we are honorable people."

I try to explain the government wishes to give money, not take. He raises his hand. "Let them take," he says. "We are accustomed to that. That is no problem."

---

12. Hindi word for English

"We are strong people," says the wife. "Tell her that."

"Who needs all this machinery?" demands the husband. "It is unhealthy, the bright lights, the cold air on a hot day, the cold food, the four gas rings. God will provide, not government."

"When our boys return," the mother says. Her husband sucks his teeth. "Enough talk," he says.

Judith breaks in. "Have you convinced them?" The snaps on her cordovan briefcase go off like firecrackers in that quiet apartment. She lays the sheaf of legal papers on the coffee table. "If they can't write their names, an X will do—I've told them that."

Now the old lady has shuffled to the kitchen and soon emerges with a pot of tea and two cups. "I think my bladder will go first on a job like this," Judith says to me, smiling. "If only there was some way of reaching them. Please thank her for the tea. Tell her she's very kind."

I nod in Judith's direction and tell them in Hindi, "She thanks you for the tea. She thinks you are being very hospitable but she doesn't have the slightest idea what it means."

I want to say, humor her. I want to say, my boys and my husband are with me too, more than ever. I look in the old man's eyes and I can read his stubborn, peasant's message: *I have protected this woman as best I can. She is the only person I have left. Give to me or take from me what you will, but I will not sign for it. I will not pretend that I accept.*

In the car, Judith says, "You see what I'm up against? I'm sure they're lovely people, but their stubbornness and ignorance are driving me crazy. They think signing a paper is signing their sons' death warrants, don't they?"

I am looking out the window. I want to say, *In our culture, it is a parent's duty to hope.*

"Now Shaila, this next woman is a real mess. She cries day and night, and she refuses all medical help. We may have to—"

"—Let me out at the subway," I say.

"I beg your pardon?" I can feel those blue eyes staring at me.

It would not be like her to disobey. She merely disapproves, and slows at a corner to let me out. Her voice is plaintive. "Is there anything I said? Anything I did?"

I could answer her suddenly in a dozen ways, but I choose not to. "Shaila? Let's talk about it," I hear, then slam the door.

A wife and mother begins her new life in a new country, and that life is cut short. Yet her husband tells her: Complete what we have started. We, who stayed out of politics and came halfway around the world to avoid religious and political feuding have been the first in the New World to die from it. I no longer know what we started, nor how to complete it. I write letters to the editors of local papers and to members of Parliament. Now at least they admit it was a bomb. One MP answers back, with sympathy, but with a challenge. You want to make a difference? Work on a campaign. Work on mine. Politicize the Indian voter.

My husband's old lawyer helps me set up a trust. Vikram was a saver and a careful investor. He had saved the boys' boarding school and college fees. I sell the pink house at four times what we paid for it and take a small apartment downtown. I am looking for a charity to support.

We are deep in the Toronto winter, gray skies, icy pavements. I stay indoors, watching television. I have tried to assess my situation, how best to live my life, to complete what we began so many years ago. Kusum has written me from Hardwar that her life is now serene. She has seen Satish and has heard her daughter sing again. Kusum was on a pilgrimage, passing through a village when she heard a young girl's voice, singing one of her daughter's favorite *bhajans*. She followed the music through the squalor of a Himalayan village, to a hut where a young girl, an exact replica of her daughter, was fanning coals under the kitchen fire. When she appeared, the girl cried out, "Ma!" and ran away. What did I think of that?

I think I can only envy her.

Pam didn't make it to California, but writes me from Vancouver. She works in a department store, giving make-up hints to Indian and Oriental girls. Dr. Ranganathan has given up his commute, given up his house and job, and accepted an academic position in Texas where no one knows his story and he has vowed not to tell it. He calls me now once a week.

I wait, I listen, and I pray, but Vikram has not returned to me. The voices and the shapes and the nights filled with visions ended abruptly several weeks ago.

I take it as a sign.

One rare, beautiful, sunny day last week, returning from a small errand on Yonge Street, I was walking through the park from the subway to my apartment. I live equidistant from the Ontario Houses of Parliament and the University of Toronto. The day was not cold, but something in the bare trees caught my attention. I looked up from the gravel, into the branches and the clear blue sky beyond. I thought I heard the rustling of larger forms, and I waited a moment for voices. Nothing.

"What?" I asked.

Then as I stood in the path looking north to Queen's Park and west to the university, I heard the voices of my family one last time. *Your time has come,* they said. *Go, be brave.*

I do not know where this voyage I have begun will end. I do not know which direction I will take. I dropped the package on a park bench and started walking.

Jeffery Paul Chan

(b. 1942)

Jeffery Paul Chan was born in Stockton, California. As a professor of Asian American Studies at San Francisco State University, one of the oldest Asian American studies programs in the country, Chan was the first professor to teach a class on Asian American literature. His pioneering efforts to reclaim Asian American literary history led him to coedit with Frank Chin, Lawson Inada, and Shawn Wong **Aiiieeeee! An Anthology of Asian American Writing** *(1974), considered by many to be the first anthology of Asian American literature. In 1991, Chan and the other coeditors published a sequel to the first anthology called* **The Big Aiiieeeee! An Anthology of Chinese American and Japanese American Literature**. *Chan is the author of numerous short stories and essays as well as a play called* **Bunny Hop**, *which was produced by the East/West Players in Los Angeles. He is presently at work on a novel.*

"Sing Song Plain Song" is a story set in the San Francisco Chinatown of the seventies. Chan's exploration of Chinese American dialect and repartee locates the reader's ear to understanding the community as a community of American-born Chinese, perhaps the last generation of American-born Chinese to live in Chinatown before that generation died and were replaced by a newer immigrant generation.

Sing Song Plain Song

Just when a pattern of existence seems to resolve itself, my view of all this world is circumscribed by a new order (reality begging some imitation), and life heaves forward to collide with the responsibilities of old dreams where, once, I heard the cry of a million starving children in Asia bundled together in a schoolyard and pressed tightly against a cyclone fence, mouths agape. They wore black quilted uniforms that reached down to their ankles with wide sleeves they used for handkerchiefs, dabbing at their flat brown noses. I saw them as a mosaic, a puzzlework of fingers and faces reaching toward me through the squares of wire, and as they crowded forward they burst like sandbags over my forehead, where I then imagined by dreams began. A feeling of helplessness lay over me. I was a care package on the quay of some Far Eastern harbor dutifully waiting to be unloaded onto the naked back of Hedy Lamar posing as the chief of an unscrupulous band of thieves. I was afraid she would stain me with the sweat of all Asia. I was enough rice to feed a family of sixteen. I included enough farm tools and seed to harvest ten acres of rutabaga and a letter to Maryknoll Central[1] itemizing my contents in three dialects with a word of encouragement to those who might use me to advantage. It seemed improbable that Miss Lamar would be satisfied with me, but I had the dubious pleasure of watching as she consumed me,

---

1. Catholic school

plow and seed, her lips stretching wide and rubbery, her jaw crushing the pastel geography of China.

At the time, Mr. Truman was still President of the United States of America, although a straw poll taken in our third grade class picked Mr. Dewey to be the next President. (Any confusion about the results of our classroom poll must rest on the vagaries of the California election laws, circa 1948.) The results of our election naturally had nothing to do with the actual re-election of Mr. Truman. But I liked to believe that my mistake was due, in the main, to a friend of mine named Hoover.

I see him in his salt and pepper corduroys and brown cardigan sweater, insisting Mr. Dewey had invented the Red Cross and the March of Dimes. In the afternoons, Hoover attended a parochial school around the corner on Powell Street because his mother did not allow him to wander the streets unattended like the rest of us. If we favored his opinion because he was able to bring his superior education to bear on questions of national magnitude, we went so far as to curry his authority because he was able to supply our most valuable commodity, trading cards depicting baseball players, fighter planes and Catholic saints. One I especially liked was the crucifixion of Saint Sebastian, a simple white scarf around his middle, his body bent with the weight of several arrows embedded in his chest and one passing straight through his neck. That one, and the B-25 Mitchell bomber I still keep in a bureau drawer marked "miscellaneous."

Whenever Hoover emptied his pockets, it was a buyer's market. We would all gather round pulling at our pockets and bargaining with tennis balls or marbles or anything Hoover might deem valuable. It was during one of these trading sessions that Hoover began extolling the virtues of Mr. Dewey. We were anxious to expedite our trades and still retain an atmosphere of good fellowship and cooperation, so we agreed to vote for Mr. Dewey. In return, Hoover agreed that all his trading cards became the property of our association, with himself as banker. Unfortunately, when Mr. Dewey won the election, our bloc gave a victorious shout, and Hoover in his enthusiasm threw all the trading cards up in the air. They were immediately confiscated, and Hoover was thanked in front of the whole class for his gift to the poor war orphans in Asia by our teacher, who then rang for Mr. Reily, the janitor, to show that she meant business.

We all set upon Hoover during the next recess and beat him unmercifully. And it was Mr. Reily who broke up the fighting, knocking at our shins with his broom and reminding us that we had only recently won the war to end all wars. He was a very sarcastic person. His face was long and knobby with a chin shaped like the knuckle of a closed fist which he brushed along his shoulder, shrugging while lecturing to us about fighting in the schoolyard. When he threatened to tell the teacher what we had been up to, we promised to leave Hoover alone and, pleased with this conciliation, he showed us the scar on his leg that made him limp and told us about his experiences with shrapnel, bullets and, of course, the war.

The effect of all this story-telling was ruined when Mr. Reily turned to go, and I saw Hoover's trading cards in his back pocket. It was one thing to see our cards sent to Asia. It was quite another matter trusting Mr. Reily. However, the others, including Hoover, agreed we had gotten off lightly. We could very well imagine the punishment we would have received if the teacher knew we'd conspired to vote for Mr. Dewey after all she said about the privacy of the vote. I suppose each of us wondered whether we would have voted for Mr. Dewey if the trading cards had not been at issue. I, for one, clung unreasonably to my suspicions of Mr. Reily, and that evening as I fell asleep I knew I was sorely tempted to steal the trading cards back.

I woke up in darkness. With a start I reached my hands out to locate something familiar and knocked against a door. It fell open, and I was engulfed in the sweet, corrosive smell of green cleaning compound and ammonia. I had fallen asleep in a broom closet, and although the room was dark, enough light came from the windows for me to distinguish the shadowy outline of Mr. Reily's soap pail with its wringer for his mops. I was in my own classroom.

Stepping from the closet, I turned towards where the door should have been. Hoover's trading cards meant nothing to me now. I was afraid. As I stumbled and groped along the silent stretch of blank wall, I was struck with the terrible thought of making my way down the dark hallway to the front door, then down the steps and across the empty schoolyard. My hands struck the doorknob, but before I could turn it, the knob was snatched from my trembling grip and the door swung open. With tears streaming down my face and a horrible wail of fear that I hoped would reach out and touch the heart of some generous and brave passerby, I leapt backwards and fell cowering to the floor, illuminated in a pie-wedge of light.

Above the sound of my own terror I heard the rude laughter of Mr. Reily, joined by several other voices, and when I opened my eyes, I saw him standing in the doorway, a sweet golden light flickering behind him, a sparkling shower of candlefire that filled the hall with dancing shadows. He was standing with several men dressed in coveralls and wielding brushes and brooms with red and yellow crêpe paper twisted in the bristles. With a happy snort of discovery he reached me in a series of rolling strides that were, on reflection, an exaggeration of his usual daytime shuffle through the boys' bathrooms, that peculiar gait he had as he pushed his huge broom a quarter inch at a time through the schoolyard during the recess. He swept me up and onto his shoulders. Then we marched down the hall, his companions joining in behind, shouting cadence with their brushes waving over their heads, throwing smart salutes as we passed each classroom. As the last two men fell into line, they beat a smart tattoo on the walls and floors with cans of cleanser.

From my vantage point high on Mr. Reily's shoulders, I could see well past the clutter of mops and garbage cans and folding chairs stacked against the walls to a huge dining table laden with half-pint containers of milk. There was as well an arrangement of crustless sandwiches and, as a centerpiece, a large kettle filled with waxed paper bags of cookies and hard candy. Beside silver platters of raw vegetables and exotic fruit, I saw Hoover's trading cards strewn across the table in no apparent order.

The little room became congested with our noise as we filed into the tiny space and took seats. Mr. Reily caught his sleeve on the leg of a folding chair in his effort to offer me a place at the table. Rather than take me from his shoulders, he ripped his sleeve away and all of us laughed as he bowed, setting the chair down with a crash and waving his ragged sleeve like a flag. When we had all been seated and I was busy with a quarter of a jam sandwich, Mr. Reily stood up and winked, wrinkling his face and bringing his thick eyebrows together as he polished his chin furiously against his shoulder. Everyone fell silent, and in a loud voice he asked me, "Why did the moron throw his alarm clock out the window?"

Once he had laid this ancient rubric before the assembled group, he could hardly contain himself and he sputtered with delight. He slapped himself across the mouth several times with considerable violence and finally pulled his shirt over his head so as not to hint unfairly. The entire company followed suit, and I found myself slightly intimidated, looking on as they laughed and hiccoughed and jerked under their shirts, sticking their tongues out and pushing noses and fingers through their buttonholes.

Shy in the company of these rough-humored men, I nevertheless answered the riddle, then watched amazed as they all, in one breath, fell back against their chairs with such force that they teetered dangerously. A few began to spin on one leg of their chairs, and then fell backwards to the floor. As the rest of the group rocked recklessly back and forth, Mr. Reily popped out from beneath his shirt and rewarded me with a pomegranate.

Now I must confess that it was the very first pomegranate I had ever seen. It was surprisingly light, and at first I thought it was a poor cork-like imitation of an apple. I was familiar enough with bananas in cereal, and seedless grapes and peaches were always a part of the bag lunch I carried to school every day. I was tempted to test it with my teeth, but I had been taught to share. So I put it on the table and in a loud voice asked if anyone would like a bite of my prize.

Even before the words had left my mouth I knew that my offer had been a mistake. The entire company hunched ominously over the table as Mr. Reily thanked me in a baited whisper and set the fruit in the middle of the table. I knew the mood had suddenly changed, and I prayed that the whole thing was a dream, for the atmosphere in the room had become very ugly. A large mallet appeared in Mr. Reily's hand, square and wooden, with small warts running across its surface. He stood up in his chair and with an anguished cry smashed the pomegranate squarely, sending little red seeds squirting in all directions.

As if it were a signal, the men leapt onto the table and began picking up the tiny seeds and eating them, several of them swooping across the table with such force that they landed on the floor, one on top of the other. An argument began, at first between Mr. Reily and a friend over one seed hanging between them, but the argument grew wider as the seeds became more scarce. As the general uproar reached sufficient force to send me flying for cover, I saw Mr. Reily strike one of the other men on the head with his mallet, which had become an enormous club, forged, it seemed, from a single piece of iron, still red-hot. And as he struck I knew, even before he finished his swing, that he had innocently crushed another pomegranate, and I knew that he would end by striking everyone on the head and that everyone would become pomegranates. Thus reassured, I joined the heaving, struggling crowd on the table, beneath which now appeared a flood of tiny red seeds, which I ate, relishing their sharp acid flavor.

I can rest now. All my family surrounds me, and I am wrapped tightly in a baby bunting made from red silk delicately embroidered with mountain scenes reminiscent of dynastic tapestries. I am covered with tangerine peel and watermelon seeds. Auntie smooths the swatch of brown, almost red hair softly plaited across the tiny scap where sutures will eventually close out the noise and crush of hands that reach out to count my fingers and toes, that gently touch my poor ears so lamentably crushed against the sides of my head. She fingers the lobes of loose tissue slowly recurling against her gentle examination. We celebrate my nativity.

After school, I spend afternoons with poor Mah, taking the Eastern view from her window and never once in her company suspected the grey Bay waters were not the ocean, that the lights were not the port city of some distant quay, but Oakland. The war ended and the streets of Chinatown filled with men in uniform: They wore cyanotic rayon shirts with liana vines and open collars, white slacks and heavy black shoes, and were fragrant with the steady perfume of joss sticks[2] burning from iron balconies of the family associations. Only then did I swagger beyond the neighborhood in their company, beyond the broad red silk ribbons figured with calligraphy, the death-white butcher paper spread over the pavements weighed down with flower pots, women tending the family pyres. I looked across the asphalt and concrete frontier to the distant glitter of the city that sprang up tall buildings and tall people. I discovered the wind at the corner of Grant Avenue and Bush Street when I felt the rush of one-

---

2. incense

way traffic streaming past, raising my hair, bringing tears to my eyes. At last, I knew it. There was a world beyond the boundaries of my neighborhood, and I cross the boulevard with a crowd of tourists. I was an orphan set free in a mob of returned missionaries and English teachers. I was adorable. I wanted to take my clothes off, roll on the warm sidewalks and pee on myself, snap at their cuffs, chase balls, unwind a mile of fuzzy yarn, lisping sweet songs of poor butterfly.

My dead mother caught me posing with a tour group from Minneapolis. I was draped in a fox fur stole resting in the arms of a heavy-set domino champion mugging for the camera, drugged as I was by the soporific aroma of lilac sachet. My cheeks smeared with lipstick, I reach out for yet another warm embrace when Mah caught me by the hair and swung me to the sidewalk.

I could have lost my hearing the way she wrung my ears. I lost a shoe as she dragged me by the sleeves of my varsity jacket to Portsmouth Square and down the stairwell to the subterranean toilets where, in the grey waters, she baptised me, scrubbing lipstick, perfume, the touch of fur away in a litany of images too Chinese for me to make sense of.

I emerged with Kleenex lint in my hair and the smell of spit. She tied a souvenir silk scarf under my jaw and over my head tightening my glasses against my skull so they wouldn't shake loose. My eyeballs flattened against the lens. I couldn't blink. She had invented contact lenses again.

She pulled me through the streets as night came, the buzzing blue-red neon fire of sundown in Chinatown, and I saw my father emerge from a doorway set below the sidewalk; I saw Grandmah throwing the garbage away in the park; I saw dead fish dance in a current of apple cider gas welling up blue smoke lit by the light of restaurant kitchens that faced the alley.

"Go home, you dead ghost, you nightmare, you know-nothing," she intoned, sending me up the stairs.

But she died, and soon after Bah[3] negotiated another marriage. Her name was Rosie, but I called her Mah, too. We grow middle-aged together. We eat together, and she says, "If you had your own sister, you wouldn't be so mean." Rosie glanced away. She didn't want me to think she'd been thinking about me so obviously, especially on Stockton Street where everybody was shopping and listened to your business.

"I'm not mean, Mah."

"Well, not mean. You know, you're too cynical. Your mama, she had your sister but she died before she was born. Henry asked the doctor what happened. Doctor said it was a girl, and you know, Henry didn't care so much, then."

---

3.   father

Babah[4] is eighty-seven, almost blind. He doesn't hear as well as he used to hear everything that is said about him, and Rosie doesn't mind talking about him now, especially to me. How come you live so long, Bah?

Live longer than Communist in China, longer than Chairman Mao,[5] Hah!

"Where do you want to eat, Mah?"

"You are mean to him."

"He wants to fight in Franco's[6] army, Mah."

"What Franco?"

"He's been to Hong Kong twice and Tapei once. When he's dead we'll cash in his bone insurance and buy his spirit Chinese anonymity in the New Territories[7] if he wants."

"He doesn't want to die yet." But she smiled anyway, matching the ceremonial with the absurd. "He's afraid of your mother."

"What for?"

"See, you are mean." Rosie had collected some lipstick on her bridgework and worked with some tissue and her reflection in a jewelry shop window to remove it. She smiled her grinding teeth smile for my benefit. "What are you doing for your hair? Nothing, I bet. You should brush it every day. Bah has all of his hair."

"Mah was bald, Mah."

"You funny. I'm glad I'm not your real mother. You too funny-looking." Rosie hid her red smile behind one coy shoulder. She took my arm and laughed.

"No. You not funny-looking." She gaily lied. "You make yourself look funny. If your hair wasn't so long, it wouldn't fall out so fast."

"My face is oily, too. I get that from you."

"I gave you my brains. Probably too much. Anyway, you should have my legs. If you had my legs, you'd be taller."

"Come on, let's eat at Jackson." Rosie's favorite Monday night dinner with her slightly overweight stepson. May is behind the cash register. "Hi, May-May."

"Hi, Rosie. How you tonight?"

Rose once arranged a dinner that paired May and me together at a bowling night in Daly City. Younger than my father's second wife by a few years, divorced, her two children live in Sacramento with a married sister. May would not marry me if I were my father's age. She told me so when I mentioned the word "motel." "Hello, May."

"Hello yourself. You all dressed up tonight."

---

4. father
5. Mao Tse-tung, Chairman, People's Republic of China (1893–1976)
6. Francisco Franco, Spanish Dictator (1892–1972)
7. part of Hong Kong

"I'm taking Mah to a dirty movie."

"I'm not surprised."

"You wanna come along? Hot date."

She ignored me.

"Hey, I saw your boy friend on the bus today."

"Yeah? Who's my boyfriend?"

"Fatso."

"Who says dat?"

"He does."

"You are a nightmare."

Mah was already flirting with the waiter, a smooth-faced Hong Kong type, toothpick for the corner of his mouth, fine, high bones figuring his face. She found something in his eyes, some reflection of his youth. They leered at one another discussing the *wo choy*[8] menu for substitutions. Pretty boy's dessert.

Mah is a woman who appreciates youth, having been the child bride of my father, a very old man who bribed her release from a Catholic convent in Hong Kong after the war when fathers in Chinatown saw the Reds overrun by Chiang Kai-Shek[9] in a cloud of confettied war bonds. When Mah turned twenty Bah was sixty-two.

"Chicken feet. You like chicken feet, son? What about fish?"

I never take part in these negotiations.

"You bring an order of sweet and sour pork for my boy, too."

It's for me, a little in-joke. I can smell the Tiger Balm in his hair. He looks like your brother, your older brother, he says to her. I'm staring down his throat, American-born aphasia that lets me understand, but frame no intelligible response in any language this asshole understands. Eat shit, buddy. Drink piss. I count to ten.

"No, no. He's my son. He just graduated from law school. He'll be a lawyer if he can pass the test."

He snorts. School boy. Chinese reverence for education.

I do look old, soft. There I am in the mirror that runs the length of the counter trade, a few old men, a white boy in G.I.[10] Field coat, long hair, grabbing cheap chow, eating better than he ever did wherever he came from. These days, Chinatown is filled with young white boys in their fatigues, thirty-six hours from Bin Hoa,[11] discharge papers and severance pay stuck in their pockets. They must think of Chinatown as R and R. There must be a tour bus from the Presidio[12] straight to Chinatown. I see his

---

8.   special fixed menu
9.   General of the Nationlist Army in China
10.   Government Issue
11.   Vietnam
12.   Army base in San Francisco

eyes, pupils the size of tomato seeds, coffee and a smear of tapioca on a thick saucer in front of him. Derelict's dinner.

Rosie balled a limp fan of Kleenex she's pulled from her purse and polished her plate. "A'bah said you're working for the mayor's office for practice."

"Part-time. I'm on the committee to argue for better public toilet facilities in Chinatown."

"Just like March Fong?"

"No. She wanted free toilets. We want more toilets."

"How come? Chinatown has lots of toilets. You can just go to the restaurant."

"You go to the restaurant."

"Maybe you're right."

Better public toilet facilities in the Chinatown area, a place to pee. Where Mr. Commissioner, can you take a dump in Chinatown without going underground, into the dank well of the municipal garage, or the fly-spray cellars of the restaurants. The side of a building? I've seen deodorant tablets melt in warm urinals, Your Honor.

"Good soup. Drink some. You won't get so many pimples." She made it sound good, her teeth clicked against the porcelain bowl.

"You just graduated from law school and you're thirty-five already." She peered near-sightedly at the plate of chicken feet and slipped toe bones into her soup spoon.

"It's too late for you to get rich, now, you know. You better be mayor or something."

"Mayor of Chinatown, Mah?"

"You can't. Your Bah is too old."

The waiter delivered steamed rice under my nose and steamed my glasses. I made a great show of cleaning them, collecting a stack of paper napkins.

"You better get married to somebody rich."

"May-May?"

"Ha. She told me. How come a motel? You should have asked her to your apartment. How come you didn't do that? She's not rich."

The fish arrested conversation. She spooned juice over the fish, then cut a line with her chopsticks along the spine, then removed its cheek, putting it in my rice bowl with a bouquet of parsley. "It's good for your hair."

It smelled good, but I wasn't hungry. I was afraid to go to the bathroom. Or that I might have to. The vet at the counter folded a thick sheaf of papers that he drew from his belt. He had lined twenty-dollar bills along the counter as if he wanted to play Concentration. The manager noticed in his booth by the front door and set his poem aside.

"No trouble, no trouble," he said, stumbling against the counter stools, terrified.

A twenty filled with tapioca and twisted like a won ton sailed over my head. "Incoming!" He choked off a full cry as pretty boy and some friends from the kitchen, gleaming silk blue jackets and full linen white duffs, sensed the lunatic in the restaurant. Mah focused on her fish, as they hustled him downstairs where the bathrooms and the pay phones were.

Take him outside. I have to go. So did Rosie. We went out the door with May while the sounds of flesh on flesh and customers fleeing the restaurant drew a small crowd on the sidewalk. The manager yelled down the stairwell to bring the lunatic up the stairs. Probably, it was his constant mention of the word "lunatic" that brought people to the door. Perhaps it was someone they knew.

We toiled up Washington Street shopping. Mah wanted to buy dental floss. There was a drugstore that stayed open late and Mah thought the service was worth the climb. She climbed steadily, depressed because she hadn't finished dinner, but she brightened at a pastry shop that was closed when she saw one sad-looking doughnut on an otherwise bare rack. "I forgot to tell you something." That was impossible. "Your Bah wants you to visit a widow for him."

That was utterly impossible. Bah was senile. "Sure."

"Mrs. Lee, in Yuba City."

"Is she rich?"

"Her husband had a policy with the burial association. He's been dead for three years. His bones are going back to China, and Bah wants you to collect them. You, a lawyer and all that in case there's legal trouble."

"Why would there be any problem?"

"I don't know. Bah didn't tell me, you know. He said the association would pay your fee and expenses because it's a very old policy. They don't do that too much anymore. He paid twenty dollars when he came, but the association is honoring his claim at their own loss. Good advertising for the new cemetery. It's important to them, and it's business for you."

Business and a rich widow. What the hell.

A pleasant fireplace piled with dry scrub for kindling and wrist-thick scrap from some farmer's pruning was the only source of light, a stove for heat and a tall platform bed standing in the center of the room promised little warmth. A grey sheet covered the bed, reaching all the way to the floor, and when Mrs. Lee ducked under one corner to find tea, I could see shelves and drawers gleaming with oil on finished wood and brass fixtures. The rest of the room was weathered boards stuck with nails where hung brooms, a heavy rubber raincoat, some clothes or at least a canvas clothes bag.

"I have some poor tea here someplace if de' mouses didn't get it."

"This is where Mr. Lee ... ?"

"Yep. He walked here every day to make sure some kids wouldn't get in and wreck stuff like at de temple. Da Hindu fella who owns the property found him by the fireplace. He must have passed away like a rock because part of his arm got burnt up in de fire. The rest of him was okay. He was very old, you know."

"A Hindu fellow owns this house?"

"Yes. Lessee. A Gee *bok* use to own de farm and he let the Association build this place for de old bachelors who didn't have no place to stay. But dat was a long time ago. History, you know, before my time. Anyway, Mr. Singh's father bought it, but he gave us a lease on the ground in back and the building. Nobody can live here now. You can see de charnel house, mebbe like a mortuary. You know Cathay Mortuary in San Francisco? Just like dat, only the old men could live here too when they didn't have no famblies."

The air was thick with the smell of winter fields. We'd walked the mile from the highway crossing puddles of steaming straw in the orchards that fed the tule fog where the sun couldn't reach in the deep gullies that led to the shack. There was a dead walnut tree just outside the door, a tangle of dead leaves stuck in the ground like a broom struck by lightning, and a rusty spigot where she drew water.

We had met at her office, Lily Lee's Land Investments and Farm Properties. She had the punctual and informal air of the business woman, some jewelry, a pencil on a long chain that rested on her lap. She stepped from behind her desk in Cuban heels, flannel grey skirt cut at her knees. "You Rosie's son, huh?"

"Stepson."

"Yeah, sure. I know about you. You guys are almost de same age. Did you pass your test to be a lawyer yet? Maybe I shouldn't ask. I know about you already."

People who command intimacy have their way with me.

"You call me Lily 'cause I'm like your sister. Rosie and me are real good friends."

"Lily, may I use your bathroom?"

"Sure, of course, it's a long drive."

I hate tea. I avoid drinking it whenever I can. Tea and a long drive in the car attacks my thyroid balance. But Lily seemed to think tea important enough to boil water on the wood stove. I was laughing when she lit it with her butane lighter, but I understood when the wood chips gave off a thick stench of sandalwood.

"Don't you laugh. There are real dead ghosts here."

"The ghosts would be more amused by your cigarette lighter."

"Why."

"You don't smoke. At least I haven't seen you smoke."

"I smoke sometimes. You want to see me smoke?"

As we bantered and gossiped in this fashion I began to associate the damp chill in the air with a nameless resignation, our situation here in this charnel house, that I would try finally to sleep with Lily and counting the liabilities—there was no plumbing—I would succeed. She folded her arms across her breasts, gripping the raised border of her sweater trying to feed more wood into the fire. What would follow would be chilly and messy. If I could not stay the night, I would drive back without fresh underwear. Maybe she would marry me. That way, I could use her bathtub.

I was torn by success. "I hope you don't believe in ghosts." Believe in me.

"No—yes. Rose tole me she saw one once at your house before she moved out."

"That was probably my father."

"You shouldn't say that. Lee is buried just outside there and he was a good friend to your father. I'm his wife so I could be offended when you talk like that."

"Lily." Cutting the crap.

"What."

What, indeed. I always have trouble with this part. First, smiling, then I set the cold tea down. I take her arm. She looks down at my pants. "Do you think the bed is warm?"

I asked hopefully.

"No," she whispered. "My husband will see," without much conviction.

"Let him."

I take her in my arms.

"I tell you a secret. He liked to watch me." She did not look up, but I let her feel the shudder that passed through me.

As nasty a puddle of rain ditch slime as I can imagine, the quicksilver spoor of banana slugs, rank amphibian chill and the stillness creeps over me. I hear my voice, all the breath of me vaporizing the cool evening just past my lips, a flume of white cloud, sex music, the rustle of field mice in the closet. No dream. No words, just my cautious breathing, afraid of stepping in something in the dark out there behind the shack.

"It's here, can you see it?"

The field is a black carpet. Lily stood beneath a clutch of young oak trees pointing to a raised mound covered with chicken wire and staked at the corners.

"That's him."

Mr. Lee, I presumed.

"When we buried him here we had flowers covering the whole grave. Mr. Singh planted them right between the wires and we spelled out his name with white carnations. That was nice. People from the associations came out to pay their respects the whole year, and one man won a lot of money during the New Year's gambling. They said Charlie Lee's grave was luckier than catching the ring for Bomb Day.[13] It's

---

13. February 2nd, Chinese holiday celebrated in Marysville, California

because Charlie was respected for paying attention to Chinese traditions. The last man to die in the death house, pretty good for him."

We embraced.

"Lucky for you, too, huh?" Lily stepped on my foot and I could feel it sink into the mud.

"Let's go up to Sacramento tonight, Lily. I can get somebody to dig him up on Monday."

"Dig him up? Why do you want to dig him up. He's dead here."

"Oh." Bless Rosie and bless Charlie Lee in his grave. "Rosie sent me up here to collect his bones so they could be buried in China."

"That's funny old Rosie. They used to do that, you know. Even my father in China, they put his bones in a big pot. But they don't do that now. Besides, who would he know in China now? He's born here, you know, right outside Yuba City. He was a very famous person in town. Everybody knew him."

"I guess Rosie was just playing Cupid."

"Sure. Aren't you glad?"

"Very glad, darling."

"Besides . . . "

"Yes?"

"I don't think the Association would let you move him now. He's a good luck charm for the gamblers. They buy flowers to put on his grave, you know. They have to buy the flowers at the temple, or grave food sometimes. I told you one guy won a lot of money, more than five thousand dollars, you know. Chinese are very superstitious, but they're right about his grave."

"Lucky us," I said.

"Yes. Let's drive to Sacramento."

We drove to Sacramento in her new Buick station wagon, and she accepted my proposal to be married if I passed my test to be a lawyer. Meanwhile, I continued to see Rosie for dinner on Mondays until the other night.

Rosie sat by the cash register talking with May and looking at the new goldfish the owner bought.

"Congratulations, Henry. Rosie says you're in love." She snapped the light on and began netting brine shrimp into the aquarium. Crazy May, the goldfish, popeyed, fed on mites and cilia, wiggling in that unhinged way it had of grabbing at bubbles of air just at the surface of the water, its spine bent like a hairpin, eyes floating in the halo of cataract white and its thick scales around the head warped like old shingles. When the light went on, she saw herself all over the walls and everything I feel must be appallingly empty for surely there is no difference between seeing and feeling here, this goldfish shivering with indigestible delight, choking and gagging in a cloud of good eats, a neon jewel.

"Thank you, May-May. I am very happy."

Rosie sits distracted by the fish. Pretty boy was absent tonight with no explanations. She follows the eye of some hard guys into the noisy pitch of the restaurant, crowding their heels, snubbing their fierce glares. She has me for the while, her ugly duckling. No crazy white boys here, just the oil smell and smoke from the kitchen and the waiters slapping plates and bowls on the table, strewing chopsticks.

"Take me home, Henry. I have to go."

"Good night, Henry. Invite me to the wedding." May laughs. I let her hold her silence up Pacific Street to the Projects and we climbed the outside stairs and headed down the hall to the elevator. The elevator is dark, the shattered bulb hangs from its wires. We usually take the stairs but we are ready to burst. I almost wet my pants smelling the warm piss welling from the cool, machine-oil darkness. We are ruined by permissive immigration. The children, the drunks, everyone finds the elevator to piss in. The floor is covered with urine.

I spread newspapers on the floor for Mah and me to stand on, and I pushed the button to close the door. The elevator started up, then stopped abruptly.

The trap door above us opened and a muffled voice said, "Put your hands where I can see them. Give me your money."

"Don't stop here, I have to go to the bathroom, you stupid." Rosie barked back.

And I remember now that I saw by the light of a passing window as we traveled upwards that the thief's hand held a pearl-handled derringer, essentially decorative, but I could see that it was cocked. At that distance, I felt sure he could shoot me in the eye with little difficulty.

I put my wrist watch and wallet on the newspaper as we reached the fourth floor. The doors parted, and I stepped out onto the cement balcony and walked a few paces before turning around. But I heard Rosie exclaim as the doors drew tight, and the elevator continued to the next floor, "I'm old enough to be your mother."

I hoped and prayed that Rosie's disappearance with our robber was an observance of Mother Country deception in the pursuit of passion. I did recognize his voice.

Janice Mirikitani

(b. 1942)

Asian American poets and writers coming of age in the late sixties and early seventies gravitated spiritually and politically toward the work of one third generation Japanese American sansei poet—Janice Mirikitani. She was and still is such an influence that many Asian American wrtiers simply refer to her by her first name—it seemed to make her words and her role more of a place or a destination rather than a person. Janice's poetry is all-inclusive and uncompromising in its ability to act as a tool to fight racism, sexism, injustice, war, and poverty across racial boundaries, across continents, and across class differences. And where Janice worked, Glide Foundation of San Francisco, Glide Memorial Methodist Church—was in itself a center, a staging ground, a stronghold, and the high ground from which words might be hurled in order to heal or simply to speak the truth. The Glide Foundation has an arts program and provides an extensive outreach as well as services to the poor and homeless of San Francisco. In 1981, Janice was elected president of the Glide Foundation.

George Leong, editor of Mirikitani's first book of poetry, wrote,

> From the eye of racist relocation fever which came about and plagued America during World War II, Janice Mirikitani grew/bloomed/fought as a desert flower behind barbed wire. She grew with that pain, of what it all represented; from multinational corporations to war from Korea to Vietnam to Latin America to Africa to Hunter's Point and Chinatown.

Janice Mirikitani, who took on the history of all people in her poetry, was herself incarcerated as a child in a Japanese American concentration camp in Rohwer, Arkansas, during World War II. She has published three collections of poetry: **Awake in the River** (1978), **Shedding Silence** (1987), and **We the Dangerous** (1995). Many Asian American writers can trace their first published poem or story or their first public reading to a publication or an event that Janice Mirikitani directed or organized. She has served as editorial director, editor, or coeditor of several anthology projects including **AION** (1971), **Third World Women** (1972), **Time to Greez! Incantations from the Third World** (1975), **Ayumi: A Japanese American Anthology** (1980), **Making Waves: An Anthology of Writings by and about Asian American Women** (1989), **I Have Something to Say about This Big Trouble: Children of the Tenderloin Speak Out** (1989), and **Watch Out, We're Talking: Speaking Out about Incest and Abuse** (1993).

"Spoils of War" is excerpted from Janice Mirikitani's first collection of poetry and prose, **Awake in the River.** The story focuses on all wars against Asian people and how one woman challenges the racial and gender stereotyping, haunting genocide, and oppression of the memory of war.

Spoils of War

She could barely breathe, the desire was so heavy, like the weight of a wave, wafting her around in a vast sea. He was very blond, very blue and very sure of himself. Their lovemaking was wet, heaving. His weight on her pressed her deep into a place she thought she had dreamed about a long time ago.

The grasses grew high during the early spring. Lupins, deep purple, swung by the wind like a wave of dancers. The smell was so sweet, she thought she could pluck and eat. The color deep like pools in sleeves of stored kimonoes. She wove the full stems into a wreath. "Don't wear live flowers, or there will be death in the family," her mother warned.

She would slip them into the throat of her grandmother's lap, as she rocked in her silent timelessness. Grandma, always rocking, as if to nurse memories of another place. The family all vied and competed for her—she was magic, glowing from her quiet secret of peace. When grandma died, she felt a deep guilt.

The men were a silent, commanding presence . . . wordless except for spurts of hostility and occasional glowing threats of violence. Perhaps because of the inflexible will of these men, bound tightly within, giving nothing of their deep selves for the women to nurture, that the women had little to reflect themselves. The cycle perpetuated was isolation/surface blank mirrors/ unspoken seethings.

What she knew best was the steady, controlled progression to survive, like the turning of a slow wheel.

She longed for the intensity of verbal presence . . . but he tried to maneuver her into the bed. His impatient need, the words to get more, get more.

The distance he created after it was over drove her to perform strange soundings: turmoil, dependency, exotic addictions. She didn't even know how she did it, turning on her side, weeping. Telling him of the deep hurt he would inflict. And he would appease, weakly.

What he represented . . . a power only they possessed . . . that they could turn minds into libraries, laboratories, brick buildings, bombs. Somewhere in the back of her being, she was awed. They could demolish an entire people and no one questioned their supreme authority to do so. The people, whom she knew in her mind, and had been able to feel the edges of their reality through grandparents, were somehow mystically related to sea creatures. She saw how when they became dangerous, they were destroyed. But still, Japan was just a name. Like "parent." Like "camps." During World War II, over

119,000 Americans of Japanese ancestry were unjustly incarcerated in the most barren and desolate areas of the United States. Like "Issei, Nisei, Sansei, Yonsei."[1]

Birth by Fire.

"Burn it," Yuki said, eyes flowing like spigots. Hard wet eyes, determined to see the red silk wrapping the emblem, the dense character filled, folded scrolls for the last time. Destroy by fire. "So they don't find any trace of home here. Burn it." The fire lept and swallowed paper, silk, even porcelain. Flames yellowed as the last strand melted. That day, only the sounds of fire's final licking, the dying, sucked the densely quiet room. Yuki's womb still draining hot afterbirth.

Bundles, knotted tightly, quickly, some left behind, heavy like the bodies lifting them to the truck taking them to the depot. Signs, posted on the door, flapped like an obscene wing, waving farewell: "Instructions to all persons of Japanese ancestry pursuant to the provisions of Civilian Exclusion Order No. 33, dated April 22, 1942, all persons of Japanese ancestry both alien and non alien will be evacuated … "[2]

Yuki, her bundles, boarded the train, infant in arms. Sachiko, her eight year old niece, trailed behind her, pulling her coat, a tag like those used to mark luggage, tied around her neck. Eyes cold, lips pressed as the infant writhed in hunger, tightly screaming, Yuki sat. "Burn it," she whispered as the train steamed to start. Sachiko, Okasan,[3] Otosan,[4] limply rocked like the bundles in the motion of the train. Silent weeping whispered to the rhythm of its wheels. Sachiko was gagging.

She flopped properly when Gerald fucked her, pressing her deep within herself, until she was transformed into that which his weight would define. She didn't think she cared about climax, only that he thought she had it. She was caught somewhere between the spoken complaint and the need to be opaque. Others had told her and Gerald repeated: you are not inadequate because of anything the others say, but because you are. You make it so, inherently.

Yuki watched out the window. Another time, though time blurred like the trees, hills, specks of animals the train left behind. California to Tule Lake. Tule Lake to Chicago. Chicago to California.

---

1. Issei are the first generation of Japanese who emigrated to the United States, nisei are the second generation (born in America), sansei are the third generation, and yonsei are the fourth generation.
2. Quote taken from Evacuation Poster issued by General J.L. DeWitt, Aprill 22, 1942
3. Mother
4. Father

Her child, now five, crumpled next to her, bag over her mouth, gagging steadily from motion sickness all the way from Illinois to Utah. Her new husband slept across from her, mouth open in his snoring. He was no comfort. Already in their short time of marriage he began to change, now openly cruel to the child. She was dazed at his apparent hatred toward it. Because it was ugly—"Look, those eyes, puffed up folds. Teeth rolling out."

She felt the desert in her bones. And it frightened her so she clung to him to hide the dread, the darkening yawn of emptiness. She thought it would be better if they moved to California. It would be alright now since the war was over for a few years. They wouldn't be so cruel to them, as memory and hatred grew dimmer. He would be able to feel freer, perhaps his pride less hurt on the farm, relatively independent. It's better to owe her parents than be owned by a company, they rationalized.

How long ago, this same feeling. The train, and this desolation. This child, an infant in my arms. Sachiko next to me, gagging. Swallow the vomit. There are so many people. Shame on shame. Sickness, the smell, the red swollen faces from so much crying. Rigid resignation. Trees fading, wind and sand blowing. Sage scattered like skeletons. Clouds like ghosts mocking in the dry, dry, heat.

She didn't have the strength to be sympathetic anymore. The child would mercifully sleep for several hours, wake up gagging over her mother's skirt. How much more can she get up? No food for days. She was getting so weak, flopping like a cloth over her mother's lap. They both hung in the motion of the train, speeding through the endless flats of salt.

How familiar, my skin feeling the airless wind. The smell of vomit all around me. Then the barracks spiking the ground. Wondering what the crime. My infant, wet, weak from the journey. Rash breaking from her face. A rush to the crudely constructed toilets. Guards looking through us. And the stalless places. Strangers looking on my crouching nakedness. Red humiliation cloaking me. The smell of naked piss.

Don't you think it wrong to be so pompous? Cold? Critical? Keeping me isolated? Weakened by guilt. Her feeble attempts to define herself were unheard, perhaps because they were mouthed with little resolve. The weakness was reinforced somehow by the ever opening of her thighs, the hungry tight closing around him as he pressed her deeply into the bed.

As long as she could remember, she did not exist. There was a physical body, thin legs and arms, small torso, flat hips, and a face that changed as often as the reactions to it. There was a thing they did praise ... the length and shape of her thighs. Otherwise, she was flat, faceless.

She remembered the childhood make believe names she and her friend, Junko, adopted when their families lived in adjoining apartments in the tenement on lower south side Chicago. She hated her own name. And they would dream together of escape from endless clotheslines, the taunting boys whose haircuts were shaped like bowls. Her mother, the fair skinned, untouchable, "beautiful one" was a shadow to her, who cried in anger when she'd tantrum for attention. Yuki floated in and of her daughter's life with many suitors. The handsome Haru brought flowers until they got married. He would even woo the daughter.

She could understand why any man would court her mother. Yuki seemed created to have a man take care of the delicate, snow like beauty. After their marriage, Haru brought them west to the farm, where her mother worked like a man.

She imagined Yuki was only happy when she was in bed with Haru. She complained a lot otherwise. In the early evening, sometimes she'd see a happy glaze over her mother's eyes. Those times, late night, she'd be awakened by the suppressed moan, the whispers of Haru: "Yuki, kimochi eh."[5] The tender calm of those moments, hearing the closeness of bodies, she would feel the strange stir in herself, where the thighs met, and she'd be ashamed of the wet and toss herself to sleep.

Yuki would catch Haru staring at the young girl's developing body, fuller busted, elongated, articulate.

When the daughter first bled, frightened, ashamed, Yuki told her it was because she was thinking too much about forbidden things, and she must not let any man kiss her or she would become pregnant. Her schoolmates laughed at her for weeks when she repeated that horror to them.

The perimeters of her being were defined by the growing shape of her flesh. Use it well, she was told and she would know happiness.

When Gerald fondled her, his hands were oppressive, too present, but his eyes were someplace else. Not seeing, but watching as she groaned in the right tone, closed her eyes in feigned ecstacy. He kneaded her breasts as if they could rise, as she heaved herself up. He would bring himself to release and leave her to shower.

---

5.   translation: "Yuki, feels good."

She would try to talk to him of Spinoza, Augustine and British law, but it bored her, and he could conduct monologues for hours. "Politics is simply a transient reflection of society's mood ... frivolous, predictable, shallow. Without immutable law, humans would be reduced to irrational barbarians. War, for example, is a logical manifestation of the irrational nature of man. And for man, all is fair in war." She wished he would hold her again.

The train became a part of her. It breathed for her. Whatever it felt, Yuki felt. The belly of her child, heaving. The belly of the train rancid. California was a dream. A place/blurred with the smell of vomit, as she had boarded the other train to another desert place.

Sachiko gagging. Sachiko of the ready smile, quick to comfort, sensitive to the other's hurt, making infants laugh with her laughter, lifting even Ojichan[6] from his gloom, with antics commanding joy.

Guardtowers held young men, barely men. Rifled. Helmets hiding their eyes. They were there a long time.

One day, Ojichan went to the barbed fence, looking for pieces of wood to carve, forgetting the forbidden closeness to the gate. When he stooped to grasp the wood, the boy in the tower abruptly drew his rifle. Yuki gasped. Sachiko suddenly slid to him, laughter loud. Pulled him from the fence. "You will make me a fine Daruma[7] from that." Ojichan, smiling, not noticing the soldier's frightened aim, led back to life by Sachiko. Yuki wanted to cry like an infant, her own in her arms, squirming for her breastmilk.

"Immutable law ... " the consequences of law are unquestionable. Debateable, but unquestionable," Gerald droned. "One can question the morality of warfare, especially nuclear, but one cannot deny that the dropping of the A-bomb in Japan ended the war unconditionally ... they surrendered. And isn't that the bottom line? to win, regardless."

"They had made peace overtures before the bomb was dropped, I read ... " she interjected. "But war doesn't justify any country being used as America's laboratory ... "

"Atrocity is inconsequential. People forget," he huffed. "My Lai is also called an atrocity, but in the context of the situation, is a means to an end. Besides, in World War II, we would have had to share the spoils of war with Russian if we didn't drop ... " His face swelled with a smile.

---

6. affectionate term for grandfather
7. wooden carved statute that rights itself

"The spoils of war ... " she began to weep.

"You're too emotional. Each event has a matching mark in history ... there is nothing new under the sun ... "

Then there is no hope for me, she thought.

Words like a wall, keeping her out, locking her in. Words choking her in the face of something so wrong. Empty space between the space of letters in her head. Win. Profit. Human life inconsequential. They would surrender. All is fair in war ... Do the people know what the generals weave?

Gerald ceased fire for the night. Lifting her to the demilitarized zone. Pulled the bedcover. She, drowning in a wave of sheets, surrendering to dark sleep:

The road shimmered across farmlands in the heat.

Three families managed the farms, and expanded little by little, though they were poor and had to start over on their land after the war.

Everyone was irritable today because of the heat wave, unrelenting, windless.

All the children wanted to play across the road where the creek ran, the cool relief of that shaded place, willows hanging like they'd been there forever. Even they drooped more.

The children loved to catch tadpoles in the spring, and in the heavy summer months, when the frogs were everywhere, they caught them in jars, fed them dragonflies.

The water was a magic place where fantasies became real. The stream carrying her to the sea, where she played like a mermaid, singing in the sun, traveling continents, speaking strange tongues, scaling new mountains, plunging new depths, dancing in the holiness of music.

Today, with the heat stabbing their skin, the children begged to go to their creek. Her cousin, dark eyed, blossom lipped Sachiko, thin, quick, short straight bangs whipping as she ran, was scolded for her impatience. She was older and at age 14 always led the others. Today she laughed with her head thrown back as she danced on the pebbles leading to the creek

The road was a freeway to another large town, and traffic was always too fast. They were cautioned frequently.

Sachiko broke from the younger cousins, eager to get to the cool shade. The screaming of brakes pierced the dense heat. Everyone ran, suddenly chilled, hoping it was a chicken, a dog or another small animal they often saw split by the tires of speeding cars. The children were stopped near the open gate to the road. All the adults ran down the road quite a ways where the car had veered crazily and stopped.

Afterward, Yuki, tears choking, told them Sachiko had been thrown so far it took them a few minutes to find her. Her thin legs, like the stalks of grass jutting from the ground on the side of the road.

"We should have taken it." Haru almost shouted.

Startled, Yuki looked up slowly, her red eyes burning with more than grief. "$200.00?" she almost hissed. "We'll see," Haru said. "We'll see what the courts do for a hakujin[8] and what they do for us." His jaw was working tightly, as he rushed out of the room.

She thought she would suffocate in the room full with the women's sobs, their grief shrouding the walls. Death was a stranger to her then.

She sat up in the darkness. Gerald grunted softly and stirred, turned on his side. Her skin prickled as she felt the terrible emptiness of air on her arms. "Without the law, humans would be reduced ... "

Attorney Magnusen said they should not sue. Costly, lengthy for an accident. Settle out of court.

Incense circling over Sachiko's coffin. Silent lines of mourners. Chants and white paper over flowers. Sachiko looked older lying there. She reached out a hand to stroke the pale cheek. Suddenly she was very afraid.

The family got nothing from the man who said he was not drunk when his car hit the kid. She came from nowhere he had said, like a chicken flying across the road.

Law, mutable by the makers.

The days of her life flew on. She was panicking because she would soon finish her degree. Somehow she couldn't face the end of this phase of her life. The institution kept her snug in its rigidity, its walls promising to keep everything the same until she could find the strength to move on, tomorrow. There were practical problems like money. And she was bored with the menial jobs. Maybe she could use the sociology. Gerald encouraged her to get a Ph.D. The relationship certainly had no feeling of progression, but it was one she would rather kill than break or change.

---

8. white person

The world he wanted to keep her in was sufficiently isolated and protective of his values ... brick on brick, the tomb was still attractive.

She went for an interview for a part-time summer position at the Community Counseling Service. The black man who sat behind his disarrayed desk was muscular, animated, his flesh shining as he talked and smiled. She was aware of the look he gave her as their conversation coursed through many subjects, and she wanted to draw closer. When he asked her to dinner, she lowered her eyes, a technique she had learned. Busy tonight or anytime? Wanting to keep him near, but not too near, she looked at her hands.

His eyes flashed, and her blood sang with fear, excitement, dread. It depends ... she started.

"On whether you get this job or not?" he interrupted. Her mouth was open, caught. "You intellectual broads are all the same. Same game, same line, same pose." The sinking feeling of losing herself again ... it had something to do with guilt.

Her uncle offered her a walk through the field. It was dark. She had stayed at her grandmother's too long. She welcomed the offer. In the hot night, toads were thick on the dust dry stretch where the corn had been cut. She dreaded stepping on them. Obscene croaks. He held the flashlight so she could see the toads parting the path, his free arm on her shoulders. Flashlight clicked off. The ground silently leaping around her. Thoughts of escape. No courage to step through the toads. Nervous laugh. Feeble shove. Darkness like toads, swallows wandering insects.

After bathing, she approached Yuki, still shaken and asked why her uncle would want to touch her in that way. Her mother rose up with a surprising rage ... " What did you do ... " "he wouldn't do that unless ... " Her young body quivered in a strange abstract guilt, not understanding but certain her mother spoke with a knowledge that came from some experience of her own. Blushing, she tried to protest, but her mother was lost to her. Her rage turned cold, as the child shivered in the wake of accusations.

Woman. Victim? Violator? Perpetrator? The conspiracy.

"Don't you have it turned around," She began to protest.

His face grew darker: "You use your body like your mind. A lot of pages of books that you can quote, memorized. You can't even field a hit. You probably have some steps you've memorized for a *meaningful relationship,* so you don't have to fuck. Really fuck. You have *intercourse.* All up there. You won't cop to your responsibility ... "

"Who do you think ...

"You come in here for a job, lead the game, spout sociological garbage and pretend it ain't happening." His eyes burned with an anger she knew nothing about. It frightened her. But she couldn't leave. Something made her stay, and they talked. They talked.

He stood up, over her, pulled her up from the chair, gently, and held her for some moments.

Fingers burning. Flesh searing. His warmth reaching. He was honest and it touched a deep need she did not know she had. Her life built on mistrust and fear. His directness attracting/repelling her. She felt herself fade again, not able to keep her presence in his embrace. The flame he built in her she washed with denial. When he pulled her face to his, she turned away, the old vacuum creeping into her belly.

Suddenly, he pulled her hair back. Whispered protests. Small fists whipping, pushing. He humped over her, containing movement. His mouth opened. Loud laugh. He fully clothed. Laughing as he released her, she struggled with the clothing, choking crimson, weak with humiliation. He was still laughing … " Better go Home … " as she vanished.

Yuki, Haru stood like flames before the yawning black square of Sachiko's grave. They flickered in the sunset, shoulders firm as if to hold back final statements. She stood between them, feeling their pillar strength. She quieted at Haru's iron set face.

Going home from the cemetery, Haru spoke gently to Yuki, "Sorry I asked you to take the money." That was one of the few times she ever heard "sorry" from him.

"We'll fight, Yuki. Magnusen isn't the only attorney around. Too bad Yas isn't in California. He'd show that judge something." Uncle Yas, Haru's brother who finished first in law school and had opened his own office in Chicago.

Haru's voice rose in controlled fury, addressing something beyond Yuki. "We can't give up. Too much too long."

Yuki was sobbing, wet words streaming … " How much suffering."

"What good does that do? Suffering forever. What matters is how you bear it when it happens. We won't be broken. Besides. It never stopped when we were quiet."

She had not hear such a clear, focused fire. The car seared the road, spinning through Haru's hurt, crushing the brush that blew across his path. She knew she mustn't speak. It is that pride when violated that flares and threatens everything around it. And she thrilled in the beauty of its strength.

They fought. The new lawyer was indifferent, they said, and he didn't push for anything. But they fought. Each day, Haru would wear a hated tie and his best jacket; Yuki would put on her suit, and they'd go with Sachiko's parents to the court. Each day, they returned. Drained, firm lipped. Haru holding all of them tightly in his determination.

She would catch Yuki looking at him, her face open, admiring. Yuki knew he was set to get what he wanted. Even though their weariness told them the case was lost, she felt Haru steadily fight even those who had given up, to win the suit against the man he called murderer.

Case dismissed.

Haru spoke no more of it. But hurt glistened from him like a tree wearing rain.

Don't forget from where you have come. Don't desert dignity to endure. Don't abandon the struggle to shape your own soul.

The sound of his laugh burning in her being. Something she knew she did. The collusion with the game. And she was left faceless. He had stripped her of even her body ... the only means of her definition. He exposed, lay bare, revealed fully, and finally rejected the empty shell. The deceptions upon which she had built her life.

Refusal to take responsibility. Making herself victim was the punishment. Self fulfilling destruction. She walked for a long time into the evening not knowing the direction.

Visions of famine
like trees
burned from a fist of flame
I wander from village
to village
asking stalks of people
who stare with eyes
hollow from too much light.
Where is home?
Silence follows me
like the clouds.
Answer please.
The ground rises
with a terrible swell
of smells from bodies
buried in her.

She found herself by the beach. The water thundering in her. The rage of foam spat on her face as she thought again, again, of the man today, the erection on her chest as she lay on the floor, pinned like an insect who had come too close to the flame.

> *Arashi*   Storm wind
> *fuku*[9]   blows
>   ocean waves outstretched
>   clutching for the moon.

Her mind tossed, something in her ribs searing. Foam like fingers reaching for her thighs. Seaweed spread like strands of a dying woman. Flame growing. She had not cried like this before. Water streaming from her shoulders.

> *Ame*   Rain Rain
> *Ame furu*[10]   dressing the flame
>   in strands of
>   silver

She shivered and ran to the rain cleaned streetlights. She wanted to curl up in the safe, predictable place of Gerald's weight. At least it was something she could touch ... turmoil follows, everywhere.

That night, as he held her in the foam of sheets, T.V. blasting, she looked into the mouth of night and saw the electronic vision clearly before her. Between gasps of the fucking. T.V. droning.

> Nixon, nose skiing to the corners of his jaws, fingering long stems of microphones, pumping with fists for emphasis ... "It is necessary to escalate penetration into enemy harbors. These communists stop at nothing ... spread like maggots in a democracy clean world ... "

She longed to draw him closer, closer ... as if driven to experience the depths of torture. She cast away her own body, plummeting the emptiness, scaling the strange new pain.

> "Of course Lt. Calley was acting in the line of duty ... necessary to show we mean business."

Gerald stroking her flesh.

> "Napalm is a success ... their surrender imminent ... "

---

9. storm wind blows
10. the rain falls

mounting her again, pressing breath from her.

"My fellow americans ... the spoils of war ... "

as he entered/grinding deep within her

"We'll bomb them to the peace table ... "

releasing without thought to her reaching

electronic eyes following the pumping bodies, sweat popping, "victory at all cost ... "

The sick feeling spread to her arms, as she clawed his shoulders to dismount. This was not desire. Her shape changed/defined by the slit she needed filled.

> *Umi*   *Ocean*
> *Kagami*[11]   *mirror of the night*
>   *show me nothing.*
>   *Everything.*

Gerald took her to a dinner party given by friends. "Very influential with the bar association." Chic, glib, society's elite. Stiff discomfort for her. Gerald smiling a lot. Indifferent conversations on war, politicians, My lai, cuisine. Voices raised in consternation, intense, angry voices on the injustice toward ducks ... victims of oil. Angry indignation about whales and jap whalers.

> *Kujira*   *whales sounding*
> *ochite*[12]   *where did the fish hide*
>   *when the water*
>   *filled with death's light*

They say the worst way to go is by drowning. Slow. Except for unforeseen attacks, where weeks, years after the mushroom cloud people vomited up their life.

She remembered the helpless flock of chickens, scattered by the slightest sound. Her heart felt like that, flying across the road in the path of crushing tires. Not able to take flight, splattered on dead asphalt.

The scavengers feasted.

1941 newsflashes. Boycott Japan. "The question was how we should maneuver Japan into firing the first shot without allowing too much danger to ourselves ... we have provoked war ... " stated the secretary of war.

---

11. ocean (is a) mirror
12. whales sound (dive)

Flame in her fueling. All is fair in war. Flame rising. Bone burning. Mushroom clouds flashing.

"We do live from the ocean," laughed Mr. Hashimoto. His gentle laugh warming his customers when he came with his truck. All the Japanese American farmers called it the "ark" because it connected them to each other. He delivered foodstuffs from Japan they couldn't buy anywhere in the predominantly white nearby towns.

Octopus, dried shrimp, kamabuko,[13] unagi,[14] real rice, fresh tofu[15]–everything they craved for their diets he carried to them in his "ark." The woman, all the children, even sometimes Haru, would run out to greet Hashimoto[16]–san, rejoicing in his Wednesday visits.

They would not only get their essential food supplies, but the latest news about the Yamaguchi's new baby, the crop failure of the Shimizu's, the illness of Mrs. Arai, the big catch of trout by Mr. Asaki. Mr. Hashimoto would be an hour or so late sometimes because he would be so busy conveying good wishes, get wells, and good lucks exchanged between the farmer families in the vast area he covered with his truck.

Yuki said, "He's such a good man," when they couldn't pay up their bills some weeks, and he would cheerfully whisper, "next time."

When Hashimoto–san became ill, his color paled, his smile dimmed. They would give him gifts, home remedies, tell him to slow down. Still he came every week, knowing they could not get their food from home ...

She thought she would never forget Mr. Hashimoto's smile, and the fish smells from his wonderful ark.

Provoke war, tramping to the rhythm of her footsteps. The scattered plates of food thrown at the shocked dinner party still sticking on her shoes. She couldn't remember the words spuming from her at the doughfaced gathering, but she knew she wouldn't be seeing him/them again.

> *Action is the name*
> *for hope.*

---

13. fish cake
14. eel
15. soy bean curd
16. affectionate term for Mr. Hashimoto

She had walked very far. The street lights in the fog were an eery runaway. dangerous for flight. Ready for flight. Her face burned into shape. Her nameless face tingling in the fog, mixed with salt.

> *Gold flesh shouts*
> *remember me.*
> *Colors were so vivid*
> *in her other eye.*
> *Crimson walls and live*
> *flowers jumping from*
> *her mother's throat*
> *barbed wire crowning her hair.*
> *Little by little*
> *she remembers the shadow*
> *of herself*
> *dancing in the presence*
> *of flowers,*
> *grandmother,*
> *and the language of the sea.*
> *Yuki, nodding,*
> *as blood*
> *flows from her forehead*
> *waving goodbye,*
> *my nameless child.*
> *Wear live flowers*
> *in your hair—you will die.*
> *Live again*
> *in a new time*
> *and send me*
> *back yourself.*

The cold, like the hate she felt for herself, retreated from her blood. Pumping another song. She wished she could talk to Haru, just once, and let him know what she let herself remember.

She called Haru, "Papa." Always came in after dark from the work ... his weariness like a coat he slowly shed as Yuki brought him hot tea. He had beautiful arms, lean, taut. Long arms that lifted heavy sacks of grain. She thought he must be very strong, because he carried them without straining, carefully, like a body.

Those sacks of grain. Like gold. No. Food for life. She would have to go to the stockroom, and sweep up any that had spilled, carefully like coins. No. Food for life.

The man with the red, beefy face, with the stomach shaped like a pear, would come every week to collect the bill for the grain. He'd stand around, eyes shifting at Yuki's behind, until Papa came out; then he'd laugh, holding out his hand.

Papa never shook his hand. She never told him how proud that made her.

She had heard that when a child is about to be born, the family hangs blue fish to insure the birth of sons. She wondered how blue the fish before her birth.

Water reaching
foam spraying
the shape of men
or our race/emerging
without fins.
Where have you been?
Looking to a faceless mirror
I have hated you
father, turning away from me.
My need for your love
so deep
you, out of reach
like this sea
that circles the world
to the place that is home.
Gold skinned men
firm lipped men
black eyed, silent
men—touch me.
Turning, turning
from myself
I could not see you—
dust covered hands
pain wracked pride
sweat tracked backs
muscles popping from the weight.
Dignity is to be unbroken

I did not hear your strength unspoken,
Love deep/hurt deeper,
we destroy
before we change.
Love spreads like the shoreline
crumbles everything
even the great rocks
of hate we sculpt.

Wave on wave, the ocean stretched for her, linking her to a place she would slowly remember ... "better go home ... "

Home was changed. New. Yuki, Haru standing like strong trees in a yellow sunrise.

She, no longer faceless. Barefaced. The ocean raged, but she was not the helpless vessel tossed. She was the foam.

Tthe ocean's hem
       dancing in the sanctity
       of its sound,
       circling full
       around.

In the deep cave of night she called, contrapuntal to the water's cry, My Name is Hatsuko.

Never be faceless
and silent
when you are near
the shore that
is your own strange song.

Jessica Hagedorn

(b. 1949)

Born and raised in the Philippines, Jessica Hagedorn arrived in San Francisco in 1962 and credits her education to the San Francisco literary scene in the early seventies. In her book **Danger and Beauty** *(1993), a compilation of her early books* **Dangerous Music** *(1975) and* **Pet Food and Tropical Apparitions** *(1981) and other writings, she describes the scene as*

> *Defiant, naive, and passionate, we are sprouting up all over the Bay Area—artists of color who write, perform, and collaborate with each other, borders be damned. We are* muralistas, *filmmakers, musicians, dancers, painters, printmakers, small press publishers, playwrights, poets, and more poets.... San Francisco seems to be more a city of poets and musicians than anything else. Rock 'n' roll, R&B, the funk mystique of Oakland, the abstract seduction of jazz, and the glorious rants and chants of* loup garous, *gypsies, sympathetic cowboys, and water buffalo shamans.*

Her novel **Dogeaters** *(1990) was nominated for a National Book Award. Set in the Philippines, it is a surrealistic postcolonial neo-passion play about the religious and colonial occupation of the Filipino self, mind, and cultural spirit. Hagedorn called the novel "a love letter to my motherland: a fact and a fiction borne of rage, shame, pride ... and most certainly, desire."*

While Hagedorn explores the religious and colonial occupation of the Filipino "self" in **Dogeaters***, the following story, "The Blossoming of Bongbong"(1975) explores the occupation of Filipinos by the American dream of wealth and opportunity, and their ultimate disillusionment, and America's betrayal.*

The Blossoming of Bongbong

Antonio Gargazulio-Duarte, also fondly known as Bongbong to family and friends, had been in America for less than two years and was going mad. He didn't know it, of course, having left the country of his birth, the Philippines for the very reason that his sanity was at stake. He often told his friend, the Painter Frisquito, "I can no longer tolerate contradiction. This country's full of contradiction. I have to leave before I go crazy."

His friend Frisquito would only laugh. His laugh was eerie because it was soundless when he laughed, his body would shake—and his face, which was already grotesque, would distort—but no sound would emit from him.

People were afraid of Frisquito. They bought his paintings, but they stayed away from him. Especially, when he was high. Frisquito loved to get high. He had taken acid more than fifty times, and he was only twenty-six years old. He had once lived in New York, where people were used to his grotesque face, and ignored him. Frisquito had a face that resembled a retarded child: eyes slanted, huge forehead, droopy mouth, and pale, luminous skin. Bongbong once said to him, "You have skin like the surface of the moon." Frisquito's skull was also unusually large, which put people off, especially women. Frisquito learned to do without women or men. "My paintings are masturbatory," he once said to the wife of the president of the Philippines. She never blinked an eye, later buying three of his largest murals. She was often referred to as a "trend-setter."

Frisquito told Bongbong, "There's nothing wrong with being crazy. The thing to do is to get comfortable with it."

Not only had Frisquito taken acid more than fifty times, he had also taken peyote and cocaine and heroin at a rate that doctors often said would normally kill a man. "But I'm like a bull," he would say, "nothing can really hurt me, except the creator of the universe."

At which point he would smile.

Bongbong finally left Manila on a plane for San Francisco. He was deathly afraid. He wore an olive green velvet jacket, and dark velvet pants, with a long scarf thrown casually around his scrawny neck. Frisquito saw him off to the airport. "You look like a faggot," he said to Bongbong, who was once named best-dressed young VIP in Manila. Bongbong felt ridiculously out of place and took two downers so he could sleep during the long ride to America. He arrived, constipated and haggard, and was met by his sister and brother-in-law, Carmen and Pochoy Guevara. "You look terrible," his sister said. She was embarrassed to be seen with him. Secretly she feared he was homosexual, especially since he was such good friends with Frisquito.

Bongbong had moved in with his sister and brother-in-law, who lived in a plush apartment on Twin Peaks. His brother-in-law Pochoy, who had graduated as a computer programmer from Heald's Business College, worked for the Bank of America. His sister Carmen, who was rather beautiful in a bland, colorless kind of way, had enrolled in an Elizabeth Arden beauty course, and had hopes of being a fashion model.

"Or maybe I could go into merchandising," she would say, in the afternoons when she wouldn't go to class. She would sit in her stainless-steel, carpeted electric kitchen. She drank cup after cup of instant Yuban coffee, and changed her nailpolish every three days.

"You should wear navy blue on your nails," Bongbong said to her one of those afternoons, when she was removing her polish with Cutex lemon-scented polish remover. "It would look wonderful with your sallow complexion." Sallow was a word Bongbong had learned from Frisquito.

Sallow? What does that mean?" Carmen never knew if her brother was insulting or complimenting her.

"It means pale and unhealthy," Bongbong said. "Anyway, it's in style now. I've seen lots of girls wearing it."

He wrote Frisquito a letter:

"Dear Frisquito,
Everyone is a liar. My sister is the biggest one of them all. I am a liar. I lie to myself every second of the day. I look in the mirror and I don't know what's there. My sister hates me. I hate her. She is inhuman. But then, she doesn't know how to be human. She thinks I'm inhuman. I am surrounded by androids. Do you know what that is? I'm glad I never took acid.
I wish I was a movie star.

Love,
Bongbong."

The apartment had two bedrooms. Pochoy had bought a leather couch and a Magnavox record player on credit. He owned the largest and most complete collection of Johnny Mathis records. At night Bongbong would lay awake and listen to their silent fucking in the next room, and wonder if Carmen was enjoying herself. Sometimes they would fuck to "Misty."

Carmen didn't cook too often, and Pochoy had a gluttonous appetite. Since he didn't believe in men cooking, they would often order Chinese food or pizzas to be delivered. Once in a while Bongbong would try to fix a meal, but he was never talented in that direction. Frisquito had taught him how to cook two dishes: fried chicken & spaghetti.

"Dear Frisquito,
I can't seem to find a job. I have no skills, and no college degree. Carmen thinks I should apply at Heald's Business College and go into computer programming. The idea makes me sick. I am twenty-six years old and no good at anything. Yesterday I considered getting a job as a busboy in a restaurant, but Carmen was horrified. She was certain everyone in Manila would hear about it, (which they will) and she swears she'll kill herself out of shame. Not a bad idea, but I am not a murderer. If I went back to Manila I could be a movie star.

Love,
Bongbong."

Bongbong stood in the middle of a Market street intersection slowly going mad. He imagined streetcars melting and running him over, grounding his flesh and bones into one hideous, bloody mess. He saw the scurrying Chinese women, no more than four feet tall, run amok and beat him to death with their shopping bags, which were filled to the brim with slippery, silver-scaled fish.

He watched a lot of television. His eyes became bloodshot. He began to read—anything from best-sellers to plays to political science to poetry. A lot of it he didn't quite understand, but the names and events fascinated him. He would often visit bookshops just to get out of the apartment. He chose books at random, sometimes for their titles or the color of their bookjackets. His favorite before he went crazy was "Vibration Cooking" by Verta Mae Grosvenor. He even tried out some of Verta Mae's recipes, when he was in better moods on the days when Carmen and Pochoy were away. He had found Verta Mae's book for seventy-five cents in a used bookstore which he frequented.

"What is this?" Carmen asked, staring at the bookcover, which featured Verta Mae in her colorful African motif outfit.

"That, my dear, is a cookbook," Bongbong answered, snatching the book out of her hands, now decorated in Max Factor's "Regency Red."

On the bus going home there was a young girl sitting behind Bongbong wearing a Catholic school uniform and carrying several books her pale, luminous arms, which reminded him of the surface of the moon. When the bus came to a stop she walked quietly to the front and before getting off she turned, very slowly and deliberately, and stared deep into Bongbong's eyes. "You will get what you deserve," she said.

One time when Bongbong was feeling particularly lonely he went to a bar on Union street where young men and women stand around and drink weak Irish coffees. The bar was sometimes jokingly known as the "meat factory." The young men were usually executives, or trying to look like executives. They wore their hair slightly long, with rather tacky muttonchop whiskers and they all smoked dope. The women were usually chic or terribly hip. Either way they eyed each other coolly an all wore platform shoes.

A drink was sent to Bongbong from the other end of the bar by a twenty-eight year old sometime actress and boutique salesgirl named Charmaine. She was from Nicaragua, and quite stunning, with frizzy brown hair and the biggest ass Bongbong had ever seen.

"What're you having?" she asked, grinning. Her lips were moist and glossy, and the fertile crescent was tattooed in miniature on her left cheek.

Bongbong, needless to say, was silent for a moment. Ladies like Charmaine were uncommon in Manila. "Gimlet," he murmured, embarrassed because he disliked the idea of being hustled.

Charmaine had a habit of tossing her head back, so that her frizzy curl bounced, as if she was always secretly dancing. "Awright," she said turning to the bartender, "bring the gentleman a gimlet." She giggled turning to look full at Bongbong. "I'm Charmaine. What's your name?"

Bongbong blushed. "Antonio," he said, "but I go by my nickname." He dreaded her next question, but braced himself for it, feeling the familiar nausea rising within him. Once Frisquito had told him that witches and other types of human beings only had power over you if they knew your name. Since that time Bongbong always hesitated when anyone asked him for his name, especially women. "Women are more prone to occult powers than men," Frisquito warned. "It comes natural to them."

Charmaine was smiling now. "Oh, yeah? Whatisit?"

"Bongbong."

The bartender handed hint the gimlet, and Charmaine shrugged. "That's a funky name, man. You Chicano?"

Bongbong was offended. He wanted to say, No, I'm Ethiopian, or Moroccan, or Nepalese, what the fuck do you care … Silently he drank his gimlet. Then he decided, the nausea subsiding, that Charmaine wasn't malicious, and left the bar with her shortly after.

Charmaine showed him the boutique where she worked, which was next door to the bar. Bongbong stared at the platform shoes in the display window as if he were seeing them for the first time. Their glittering colors and whimsical designs intrigued him. Charmaine watched his face curiously as he stood with his face pressed against the glass like a small child, Then she took his arm and let him to her VW.

She lived in a large flat in the Fillmore district with another sometime actress and boutique salesgirl named Colelia. They had six cats, and the place smelled like a combination of catpiss and incense.

Colelia thought she was from Honey Patch, South Carolina, but she wasn't sure. "I'm all mixed up" she said. Sometimes she thought she was a geechee.[1] She was the only person Bongbong knew who had ever read "Vibration Cooking." She had even met Verta Mae at a party in New York.

Bongbong spent the night in Charmaine's bed, but he couldn't bring himself to even touch her. She was amused, and asked him if he was gay. At first he didn't understand the term. English sometimes escaped him, and certain colloquialisms, like "gay," never made sense. He finally shook his head and mumbled no. Charmaine told him she didn't really mind. Then she asked him to go down on her.

"Dear Frisquito:
I enrolled at Heald's College today so that Carmen would shut up. I plan on leaving the house every morning and pretending I'm going to school. That way no one will bother me. I think I may come back to Manila soon, but somehow I feel I'm being trapped into staying here. I don't understand anything. Everyone is an artist, but I don't

---

1.   a black person from Ogeechee River area in Georgia

see them doing anything. Which is what I don't understand … but one good thing is I am becoming a good cook.

Enclosed is a copy of 'Vibration Cooking' by Verta Mae.

Love,
B."

Sometimes Bongbong would open the refrigerator door and oranges would fly out at him. He was fascinated by eggs, and would often say to his sister, "We're eating the sunset," or "We're eating embryos." Or he would frown and say, "I never did like chickens."

He began riding streetcars and buses from one end of the city to the other, often going into trances and reliving the nightmare of the streetcar melting and running him over. Always the Chinese women would appear, beating him to death with silver-scaled fish, or eggs.

Bongbong saw Charmaine almost every day for a month. His parents sent him an allowance, thinking he was in school. This allowance he spent lavishly on her. He bought her all the dazzling platform shoes her heart desired. He took her to fancy nightclubs so she could dance and wiggle her magnificent ass to his delight. She loved Sly Stone and Willie Colon, so he bought her all their records. They ate curry and spice cake every night of the week (sometimes alternating with yogurt pie and gumbo) and Charmaine put on ten pounds.

He never fucked her. Sometimes he went down on her, which she liked even better. She had replaced books and television in his life. He thought he was saved.

One afternoon while he was waiting for Charmaine in the bar where they had met, Bongbong had a vision. A young woman entered the bar, wearing a turban on her head made of torn rags. Her hair was braided and stood out from her scalp like branches on a young tree. Her skin was so black she was almost blue.

Around her extremely firm breasts she wore an old yellow crocheted doily, tied loosely. Her long black skirt was slit up the front all the way to her crotch, and underneath she wore torn black lace tights, and shocking pink suede boots, laced all the way up to her knees. She carried a small basket as a handbag, and she was smoking Eve cigarettes elegantly, as if she were a dowager empress.

She sat next to Bongbong and gazed at him coolly and deliberately. People in the bar turned their heads and stared at her, some of them laughing. She asked Bongbong for a match. He lit her cigarette. His hands were trembling. She smiled, and he saw several of her teeth were missing. After she smoked her cigarette, she left the bar.

Another day while Bongbong was walking in the Tenderloin, he had another vision. A young woman offered to fuck him for a mere twenty-five dollars. He hesitated, looking at her. She had shoulder-length, greasy blond hair. She had several teeth missing too, and what other teeth she had left were rotten. Her eyes, which were a dull brown, were heavily painted with midnight-blue mascara. She wore a short red skirt, a tight little sweater, and her black sheer tights had runs and snags all over them. Bongbong noticed that she bad on expensive silver platform shoes that were sold in Charmaine's boutique.

He asked her name.

Her voice was as dull as her eyes. "Sandra," she replied.

He suddenly felt bold in her presence. "How old are you?"

"Nineteen. How old are you, honey?" She leered at him, then saw the blank look on his face and all the contempt washed out of her. He took her to a restaurant where they served watery hamburgers and watery coffee. He asked her if she had a pimp.

"Yup. And I been busted ten times. I been a hooker since I was thirteen, and my parents are more dead than alive. Anything else you wanna know?"

Her full name was Sandra Broussard. He told her she was beautiful. She laughed. She said her pimp would kill her if she ever left the business. She showed him her scars. "He cut my face once, with a razor," she said.

He felt useless. He went back to the apartment and Carmen was waiting for him. "We've decided you should move out of this place as soon as possible," she said. "I'm pregnant, and I want to redecorate your room for the baby. I'm going to paint your room pink."

He went into the bathroom and stared at the bottles of perfume near the sink, the underarm deodorant, the foot deodorant, the cinnamon-flavored mouthwash, and the vaginal spray. They used Colgate brand toothpaste. Dove soap. Zee toilet paper. A Snoopy poster hung behind the toilet. It filled him with despair.

Bongbong moved into Charmaine's flat shortly after. He brought his velvet suit and his books. Colelia reacted strangely at first. She had been Charmaine's lover for sometime, and felt Bongbong would be an intrusion. But all he did was read his books and watch television. He slept on a mattress in the living room. He hardly even spoke to Charmaine anymore. Sometimes they would come home from work in the evenings and find Bongbong in the kitchen, preparing Verta Mae's "Kalalou Noisy LeSec" or her "Codfish with Green Sauce" for all of them. Colelia realized he wasn't a threat to her love life at all. Life became peaceful for her and Charmaine.

During the long afternoons when Colelia and Charmaine were gone and the cats were gone and the only thing Bongbong could sense was the smell of piss from the catbox, he would put on his velvet suit and take long walks in the Tenderloin, trying to find Sandra Broussard. He thought he saw her once, inside a bar, but when he went in he found it was a mistake The woman turned out to be much older, and when she turned to smile at him, he noticed she wore the hand of Fatima[2] on a silver chain around her neck.

When he really thought about it, in his more lucid moments, he realized he didn't even remember what she really looked like anyone. Dullness was all he could conjure of her presence. Her fatigue and resignation

Charmaine, on the other hand, was bright, beautiful, and selfish. She was queen of the house and most activity revolved around her. Colelia always came home from work with a gift for Charmaine, which they both referred to as "prizes." Sometimes they were valuable, like jade rings or amethyst stones for Charmaine's pierced nose, or silly—like an old Walt Disney cup with Donald Duck painted on it.

Bongbong found the two women charming and often said so when he was in a talkative mood. "You are full of charm and your lives will be full of success," he would say to them, as they sat in their antique Chinese robes, painting each other's faces.

"You sound like a fortune cookie," Charmaine would say, glaring a little.

He would be silent at her outbursts, which naturally made her more furious. "I wish you'd tell me how much you want me," she would demand, ignoring her female lover's presence in the room.

Sometimes Charmaine would watch Bongbong as he read his book and she would get evil with him out of boredom. She was easily distracted and therefore was easily bored, especially when she wasn't the center of attention. This was often the case when Colelia was at work and it was Charmaine's day off.

Bongbong said to her, "Once you were a witch but you misused your powers. Now you resent me because I remind you of those past days."

Charmaine circled Bongbong as he sat in the living room immersed in "Green Mansions" by W.H. Hudson. He had found the hardback novel for one dollar in another secondhand-bookshop called Memory Lane.

"I'm going to take my clothes off, Bongbong," Charmaine would tease.

"What're you going to do about it?" Bongbong would look up at her, puzzled. Then she would put her hands on her enormous hips. "Men like them most of all because of my ass, Bongbong ... they can't really get next to me. Most of them have no style ... but you have a sort of style—"

By this time she often removed her skirt. "I don't wear panties," she said, so whenever I want, Colelia can feel me up." Bongbong tried to ignore her. He vas getting skilled in self-hypnosis, and whenever external disturbances would occur, he would stare off into the distance and block them slowly from his mind.

The more skilled he became in his powers, the more furious Charmaine would get with him. One time she actually wrenched the book from his hands and threw it out the window. Then she lay on the couch in front of him and spread her legs. "You know what I've got, Bongbong? Uterina Furor ... that's what my mother used to say ... Nuns get it all the time. Like a fire in the womb."

---

2. a symbol of feminine curiosity

To make her smile Bongbong would kiss her between her legs, and then Colelia would come home and pay more attention to Charmaine and Bongbong would cook more of Verta Mae's recipes, such as "Stuffed Heart Honky Style" (one of Charmaine's favorites) and everything would be all right.

Charmaine's destructive words focused on Bongbong twice a month, and got worse when the moon was full. "You're in a time of perennial menstruation," Bongbong told her solemnly, after one of her fits.

One morning while they were having breakfast together, Colelia accused Charmaine of being in love with Bongbong. "Why I don't know—" Colelia said. "He's so funny-looking and weird. You're just into such an ego trip you want what you can't have."

Charmaine giggled. "You're forever analyzing me! Don't I love you enough?"

"It's not that."

"Well, then—why bring him up? You never understood him from the very beginning," Charmaine said. "Or why I even brought him here in the first place. I must confess—I don't quite know why I brought him home myself. Somehow, I knew he wasn't going to fuck me ... I really didn't want a fuck though. It was more like I wanted him around to teach me something about myself ... Something like that, anyway."

Colelia looked away. "That's vague enough."

"Are you really jealous of him?" Charmaine asked.

Colelia finally shook her head. "Not in that way ... But maybe because I didn't understand him, or the two of you together—I am jealous. I guess because I feel left out of his mystique.

Charmaine embraced her, and the two of them wept.

Bongbong's visions and revelations were becoming more frequent. A Chinese woman with a blonde wig and a map of the world on her legs. A black man with three breasts. A cat turning doorknobs. A tortoise crawling out of a sewer on the sidewalk, and junkies making soup out of him. Frisquito assassinating the president of the Philippines who happens to he his wife in drag who happens to be a concert pianist's mother ... The visions were endless, circular, and always moving.

> "Dear Frisquito:
> Yesterday a friend of Charmaine's named Ra brought a record over by a man named John Coltrane. Ra tells me that Mr. Coltrane died not too long ago, I believe when we were just out of high school. Ra decided that I could keep the record, which is called 'Meditations', I believe it is the title of one of your paintings.

Every morning I plan on waking up to this man's music. It keeps my face from disintegrating. You once said your whole being had disintegrated long ago, and that you had the power to pick up the pieces from time to time, when it was necessary — such as the time you gave an exhibit of your works, for the benefit of the First Lady. I think there may be some hope left for me.

Yesterday I cooked Verta Mae's 'Uptight Ragout' in your honor.

Love
B."

Bongbong now referred to himself as "B". He could not stand to speak in long sentences, and tried to live and speak as minimally as possible. Charmaine worried about him, especially when he would go on one of his rampages and cook delicious gumbo dinners for herself and Colelia, and not eat with them.

"But B," she protested, "I never see you eat anymore."

One time he said, "Maybe I eat a saxophone."

He loved the word saxophone.

His parents stopped sending money, since Carmen wrote them that he had never attended one day of school at Heald's Business College. His father wrote him and warned him never to set foot in the Philippines again, or he would have him executed for the crime of deception and subversion to one's parents a new law put into practice in the current dictator's regime.

Bongbong decided to visit Carmen. She was almost six months pregnant, and very ugly. Her face had broken out in rashes and pimples, and her whole body was swollen. Her once shimmering black hair was now dry and brittle, and she had cut it short. Her nails were painted a pale pink, like the bedroom that had once been his. He stared at her for a long time, as they sat in the kitchen in silence. She finally suggested that he see the baby's room.

She had decorated the room with more Snoopy posters, and mobiles with wooden angels hung from the ceiling. A pink baby bed stood in the center of the room, which was heavily scented with floral spray.

"It's awful," Bongbong said.

"Oh, you're always insulting everything!" his sister screamed, shoving him out the door. She shut the door behind her, as if guarding a sacred temple, and looked at him, shaking with rage. "You make everything evil. Are you on drugs? I think you're insane," she said. "Leave this house before I call the police." She hated him because he made her feel ashamed in his presence, but she couldn't understand why.

Frisquito, who never answered any of his letters, sent him a check for a considerable amount of money. A postcard later arrived with the note "Don't worry" scratched across it, and Frisquito's valuable signature below the message. Bongbong who now wore his velvet suit everyday, went to a pawnshop and bought a soprano saxophone.

In the mornings he would study with Ra, who taught him circular breathing. He never did understand chords and scales, but he could hear what Ra was trying to teach him and he surprised everyone in the house with the eerie sounds he was making out of his new instrument. Charmaine told Colelia that she thought Bongbong was going to be all right, because Bongbong had at last found his "thing."

Which was wrong, because Bongbong's music only increased his natural visionary powers. He confessed to Ra that he could actually see the notes in the air, much like he could see the wind. Ra would study him and smile, not saying anything.

Bongbong would watch Charmaine at the kitchen table eating breakfast, and when she would look up at him, she would suddenly turn into his mother, with Minnie Mouse ears and long, exaggerated Minnie Mouse eyelashes, which glittered and threw off sparks, when she blinked. This would frighten him sometimes, because he would forget who Charmaine was. As long as he could remember who everyone was, he would feel a surge of relief. But these moments were becoming more and more confusing, and it was getting harder and harder for him to remember everyone's names, including his own.

Colelia decided that Bongbong was a "paranoid schizophrenic" and that she and Charmaine should move out, for their own safety. "One of these days well come home from work and find all our kittykats with their throats slit," she said. She refused to eat any more of Bongbong's cooking, for fear he would poison her. "He doesn't like women basically. That's the root of his problem," she told Charmaine. "I mean, the guy doesn't even jack-off! How unnatural can he be? Remember Emil Kemper!"

"Remember Emil Kemper" became the motto of the household. Emil Kemper was a young madman in Santa Cruz, California who murdered his grandmother when he was something like thirteen years old, murdered his mother later on after he was released from the loony bin, cut her head off, and murdered about a million other female hitchhikers.

Charmaine sympathized with Bongbong, but she wasn't sure about him either. Only Ra vouched for his sanity. "Sure the cat is crazy," he said, "but he'll never hurt any of you."

Bongbong practiced the saxophone everyday, and seemed to survive on a diet of water and air. Charmaine came home from the boutique one night and brought him two pairs of jeans and two t-shirts. One t-shirt had glittery blue and silver thread woven into it, and Bongbong saw the shirt become a cloud floating above his narrow bed. "Well," Charmaine said, trying to sound casual as she watched Bongbong drift off dreamily, "Aren't you going to try it on? Do you like it? I seriously think you should have your velvet suit dry-cleaned, before it falls apart."

Bongbong touched the cloud. "Oh, how beautiful," he said.

He never wore the shirt. He hung it above his bed like a canopy, where he could study it at night. His ceiling became a galaxy. To appease Charmaine, (he was very sensitive to her feelings, and loved her in his own way) he wore the other shirt and sent his velvet suit to the cleaners.

Frisquito sent him more money the next month, and Bongbong bought a telescope.

"Dear Frisquito,
As you know I am only five feet and two inches tall? Without my platform shoes, of course. Why do people like to look—like cripples? Yesterday I saw a fat young woman wearing platform shoes that made her feet look like boats. Her dress was too short on her fat body and you could see her cellulite wobbling in her forest green pantyhose. Cellulite is the new fad in America. Some Frenchwoman discovered it and is urging everyone to feel for it in their skin. Its sort of like crepe-paper tissue that happens when you put on too much weight. I told the fat young woman she was beautiful, and she told me to fuck off. She was very angry, and I realized there are a lot of angry people around me. Except in the house I live in, which is why I've stayed so long.
The Coltrane record is warped from having been left in the sun. I am writing a song about it in my head.
With my telescope I can see everyone, and they don't have to see me.

Love,
B."

Bongbong often brought the telescope up to the roof of their building and watched the people on the streets below. Then at night he would. watch the stars in the sky and try and figure out different constellations. Charmaine took him to the planetarium for his birthday, and the watched a show on Chinese astronomy called "The Emperor of the Heavens," narrated by a man called Alvin. Bongbong was moved to tears. "I love you," he told Charmaine, as they laid back in their seats and watched the heavens.

But he had forgotten that she was Charmaine Lopez, and that she lived with him. He thought she was Sandra Broussard, or the blue lady with the rag turban on her head. "When the show was over he asked her to marry him."

He didn't say another word until they reached the flat. He cooked Verta Mae's "Jamaican Curried Goat" for birthday dinner and Colelia gave him a cake which had a sugar coated model airplane on it. Bongbong removed the airplane and hung it next to the canopy above his bed.

After dinner he asked Charmaine if she would sleep with him. She didn't have the heart to refuse, and kissing Colelia on her forehead, followed Bongbong into his room. The next morning Charmaine told Colelia they should both move out.

"Was he a freak? I mean, did he hurt you?" Colelia asked.

Charmaine shook her head. "No. But I don't want to live around him anymore. It may be best if we left today."

They packed their clothes and rounded up their cats and left in Charmaine's VW, leaving Bongbong with a note on the kitchen table.

> "We will send for the rest of our things. Forgive us.
> CC."

Bongbong awoke from a beautiful dream, in which he had learned how to fly. Everything in the dream had an airy quality. He floated and glided through the atmosphere, and went swimming in the clouds, which turned out to he his glittery blue sweater. Charmaine Lopez and her dancing girls did the rumba in the heavens, which was guarded by smiling Chinese Deities. Alvin from the planetarium sang "Stardust" for him as he flew by. He was happy. He could play his saxophone forever. Then he saw Frisquito flying far away, waving to him. He tried and tried, but he couldn't get any closer to him. Frisquito became smaller and smaller, then vanished, and when Bongbong opened his eyes, he found Charmaine gone.

He decided to stay in the flat, and left the other rooms just as they were. Even Ra stopped coming to visit, so Bongbong had to teach himself about the saxophone. There were brief moments when he found that the powers of levitation were within him, so while he would practice the saxophone he would also practice levitating.

> "Frisquito,
> Just two things. The power of flight has been in me all along. All I needed was to want it bad enough.
> Another is something someone once said to me. Never is forever, she said.
>
> Love."

He didn't sign his name or his initial, because he had finally forgotten who he was.

Darrell H. Y. Lum

(b. 1950)

Literary scholar Stephen H. Sumida, author of **And the View from the Shore: Literary Traditions of Hawaii** (1991) describes Darrell H.Y. Lum as "a master of local symbols, especially his use of pidgin and creole vernaculars." Born in Honolulu, his two collections of short stories—**Sun: Short Stories and Drama** (1979) and **Pass on, No Pass Back!** (1990)—are remarkable stories mostly narrated in pidgin and faithful to the oral storytelling tradition in Hawai'i called "talk story." Sumida goes on to note that:

> Stories like Lum's are chock full of allusions to fads, significant uses of things, places, words, and activities known only to a child growing up in the particular times and places the stories are set; and they are characterized by references to much else that appears transitory. It is precisely this transience, however, that when skillfully treated implies the idyll's truth: "small keed time" is short and runs quickly away on its bare feet. At the same time, the pidgin used in some of the idylls is a powerful symbol of the past and a lost childhood.... In Hawaii still, outside the workplace, pidgin generally unites local generations and the various ethnic groups like the food heaped in generous, multicultural array on everyone's paper plate at a community potluck dinner in Hawaii.

In a 1989 issue of **Manoa: A Pacific Journal of International Writing**, Lum writes of his own stories:

> So the stories here may not have that confrontational edge or be quite so trendy or pegged so easily into a theoretical hole. The characters may seem more circumspect because we've learned—we might be related; and you don't 'talk stink' about family. Listen carefully to the story our character's telling, pay attention to the silences. The guys who say only a little, often say the most. He might wind way around the back alleys and side streets to get where he wants to go. Kinda like getting around the congestion in Waikiki. He'll get there eventually (probably late), but he'll get there.

Sumida writes that in Lum's short story "Beer Can Hat" from **Pass on, No Pass Back!**

> Junior [the narrator] himself plays two roles in the story: he is the child as swain, and yet he is also the supposedly more knowing one, in his relationship with his retarded partner [Bobo]. Bobo, then, is doubly the simple folk of the pastoral: he is perpetual child (we know he is older than Junior but do not know his age); and even to a younger child, his best friend, Bobo is perpetually simple-minded, though sometimes suspiciously smart.... Out of this weave of characterizations, roles, and values comes a violent incident that tests Junior's and Bobo's relationship.

Primo Doesn't Take Back Bottles Anymore

"Four cases, that's one dollar and seventy-six cents, Rosa." Harry of Receiving Bottle Empties wrote up the ticket for Rosa and made change from the register. Rosa K. dropped his load of empty Primo bottles on the counter and figured out his profit. If he walked home he could save a quarter busfare. Rosa used to list his occupation as "construction laborer" whenever he got picked up by some rookie cop for being a "suspicious person" rummaging through garbage cans. But now that he only collected empties to turn in at the brewery, he figured himself to be a "collector." It was forty cents a case, even more for the bigger bottles.

"Tanks eh, I see you," Rosa said and shuffled out of the brewery, the money carefully folded into his handkerchief and jammed into his front pocket. He hoped that Harry wouldn't check the last case until he left. It was short three bottles. The three unbroken ones he should have gotten if that old lady hadn't caught him.

Harry checked the cases and smiled as he filled the empty slots in Rosa's last case with some extra bottles he always saved for Rosa. He remembered the first time Rosa had come in all shabby and ragged, a pair of tattered jeans buttoned underneath his pot belly and a silken aloha shirt with hula girls and Diamond Head and "Honolulu-Paradise" written all over it.

"Sorry man, read the sign, can't refund any amount less than three dollars. Come back when you have seven cases," Harry had said.

"Look Bruddah, I no can carry all dis back home, I nevah know about the rules. C'mon give a guy a break. As means I no mo' busfare home."

"Okay, look I'll cash in your three cases now and add 'em to the next guy's load. But just this once. My boss finds out and I'm in trouble, you understand?"

Rosa had smiled and had given him a little thumb and pinkie wave. "Thanks eh," he had said. Since then Rosa had been coming in every week with his pickings in his arms, catching the bus to the brewery and walking home to save the quarter.

Sometimes he brought something for Harry, some seaweed, a small bass, a little opihi[1] in a smelly shopping bag along with his empties.

We used to have kick haole[2] ass day in school. One time this one kid, little ass buggah with one big mouth, his fahdah was one manager of someplace or something, he went come inside the bathroom, cocky and smart mouth, went

---

1. fish
2. white

push Willy so I went kick the shit out of him. Nothing on the face so no can see the marks, just in the balls. The little shit started cry. He say, "I going tell my father ... I going tell my father ... " So I tole him, "Look boo, you tell your fahdah and you going get somemore." Yeah, we used to think we was big stuff. Go smoke in front the teacher for see what she do. She no can do nothing. One time she call my muddah though, and my fahdah beat me up bad. He tell I gotta get one education, I nevah go school for one week. The social worker had to take me hospital. Willy, he just one mahu. The kids used to tease me that my bruddah one tilly[3], but I take care of them. Willy, he wanna be one mahu, he be one mahu, as okay. One time Willy and his frens go make one mahu day in school, come all dress up. Whooo, make the girls jealous.

Rosa peered through his dark glasses out at the large metal garbage bin of the apartment building. He had to squint because the flimsy lenses did little to cut the glare. He had found them outside the theatre about two months ago when there was a 3-D movie. It was good a pair with plastic frames and looked like regular sunglasses except for the small print at the top of the frame which said, "For 3-D Panavision only. Do not use as sunglasses." The garbage bins looked a funny shade of white, the glasses cancelling the green paint of the metal. Large bins rarely held empties because only places like business offices and schools used them. But this was an apartment building and it was sure to have at least a case or two of empties. If someone asked him he could always say that he lost something in the bin. Rosa figured that apartment building garbage was surely anybody's. No one could tell whose garbage was whose. His search yielded a case of Miller, two six-packs of Schlitz, and only one six-pack of Primo. "Fucking haoles only drink shit," he muttered and stuffed the Primos into his shopping bag.

I used to think all the haoles look at me funny so I kick their asses and they still look at me funny. I wasn't that bad though. When I make "search take" on one guy, I everytime give 'em back busfare. Bumbye they gotta call their fahdah for come pick them up after school.

The entry on the police record said, "Assault and Battery, Petty Theft, Item—Bottles, empty, six dozen; Bottles, unopened, approximately one dozen; Location—Jay's Bar and Grill, suspect apprehended boarding Municipal bus (Aala Park) 10:55 P.M., owner James Nakayama reported prowler in back of premises, scuffle ensued; Damage—Two dozen empty bottles, broken, one dozen unopened Primo brand beer, approximate cost $3.50; Previous Record—Rosario Kamahele, A & B, Central Intermediate School, enrolled student, grade 9, 17 years old, charged as adult on request of school authorities and referred to Department of Social Services; Present

---

3.   silly

Occupation—Unemployed laborer." The sergeant at the desk had said that he was an unemployed laborer when Rosa was brought in and booked. The lady at the welfare office had also told him that after he got kicked out of the ninth grade of his third and final school. He was just a kid then, a smart ass kid who beat up on anybody who didn't pay protection money. He was the bull of the school and ruler of the second floor lavatory. Some haole kid had told his father and the judge had sent him away to the Boy's Home for three months. When he got out he joined the union and was a laborer. He almost became a carpenter's apprentice when he and half the crew got laid off. That was when he started collecting bottles. For awhile the money from empties was all he had to live on until the welfare came.

> *After I come out of the Home, the judge tell me I join the army or go work, 'cause I too old for go back ninth grade. The judge he say I can go night school with older people so I no beat up people no more and then he assign me one social worker, one haole lady, Miss Pate, for check up on me. I tell Miss Pate that I like live with Willy, that I gotta take care Willy. She say I no can, that mahus, that home-saxtuals like live with their own kind. I tell her, "... but that my bruddah." She tell I gotta get one healthy family relationship and atta- tude. So Miss Pate she find me one place with one Portagee[4] family and man, they thought I was one servant. Rosa do this, Rosa do that or we going tell the social worker for cut your check down. So one time I get fed up and I say, "Shove it," and I split.*

The sticky smell of stale beer at the brewery always made Rosa thirst for a "tall, cool one." A dollar seventy-six was enough for a six-pack and still leave extra for busfare. Almazon, the Filipino bookie expected his ten bucks today. Almazon sold everything from lucky number chances to a "social worker home," a place where guys like Rosa could claim legal residence in a respectable home for the social worker's visits. Ten bucks a month to Almazon kept the family quiet.

> *The one time that I was scared for beef one haole after school was with this six-foot guy from California. He was in the smart class. I went tell one of my guys for let him know I wanted for see him, to tell him who was the big shit around Central. He was one show off too, that guy. He had driver's permit and drove one car to school everyday. The day I was supposed to beef 'em I went skip class and went send Willy for steal some booze for me. Willy come back with Mama's bourbon inside one empty jelly bottle. Willy say the guys was talking that the haole's fahdah was a Marine. I tell, "So what," and drink the liquor down real fast and started for punch the wall of the lav for practice. The wall*

---

4.   Portuguese

was hollow cement tiles and the pipes inside 'em went make one "tonk" everytime I punch the wall. I thought of all the haoles in the whole world and I went punch the wall somemore. Willy, he come scared and say something about Mama and I say to him, "Fucking mahu!" and Willy come real quiet. Ass the first time I call Willy that and he come real quiet. That make me more piss off and I punch the wall somemore until my hand it start for bleed and I no can feel no sore but I still punch the wall and then the teacher come and tell me for stop and I no can stop and my hand it keep making one fist and keep going and then I cry and Willy, he cry too, but Willy cry easy. I no cry, I no supposed to cry, but I cry. And then the teacher he take me to the dispensary and I try punch the nurse and get blood on top her nurse dress ... They say that the haole was looking for me after school for beef me and I wasn't there ...

Rosa got off the bus with a stinking paper sack and one case of empties under his arm. He had spent most of the week picking opihi from the rocks at low tide and only had had enough time to collect one case of empties. But he had a mayonnaise jar of opihi to give to Harry.

Workmen were painting over the old red brick of the brewery when Rosa shuffled up with his load. The "Receiving Bottle Empties" sign was painted over and the old smells were replaced by those of fresh paint and turpentine. Harry had acted brusquely last week and had mumbled something about bums who trade in bottles below minimum refund amount and get employees in trouble and new management and aluminum cans but Rosa had just smiled and walked out quickly because his cases were short again.

One of the painters noticed his empties and said, "Eh man, you can't bring back empties anymore. The new man doesn't want them. Ought to just throw them away."

Rosa felt an old rage and the tight clenching of his fists, the punching feeling. He turned to the painter and said, "Why you paint over the sign, why you no want my bottles, why you do that, I bring something for Harry today, and you do that, where Harry my fren', Harry my fren' he no do that ... "

The painter shook his head and said, "Not me fella, why don't you talk to the boss." He turned and left. Rosa walked around in little circles, clenching and unclenching his fists, finally stopping before the blanked-out sign. A brush and paint can sat on the ground before him. Rosa grabbed the brush and in several quick motions wrote "F-O-C-K" on the sign. The paint was the same color as the sign but the work was visible as the sun glistened off the dripping letters. Rosa crossed the street and sat at the bus stop watching his word dry in the afternoon heat. The painter never came back and the word disappeared as the sun dried the glistenings and the streaks melted away.

O. Wini Terada

(b. ?)

Stephen Sumida, in his book **And the View from the Shore: Literary Traditions of Hawai'i** *(1991), writes that a number of contemporary writers*

> *have turned to the childhood idyll as the mode of expressing and examining the experience of being 'local'.... These writers have, in some respects, broken from or altered literary conventions that do not fit their sense of Hawai'i or of themselves; they are engaged in discovering something fresh and honest to say about everyday life.*

Among contemporary writers the inclusion of the oral tradition of pidgin English as a written form is but one example of their altering literary conventions.

O. Wini Terada, a teacher at Honoka'a High School and Elementary school on the Hamakua coast, is one of a great number of writers from Hawai'i involved in this discovery. First published in **Bamboo Ridge: The Hawaii Writers' Quarterly** *in December 1979, Terada's coming-of-age story "Intermediate School Hapai" orchestrates perfect "school" English, pidgin English, and Japanese American English. While the story is written for the page it begs to be read aloud because of the oral tradition of Hawaiian pidgin.*

Terada is a member of Ho'okahe Wai Ho'oulu 'Aina (let the land flourish), an organization dedicated to the growth of Hawaiian language and culture in the context of traditional Hawaiian agriculture. He states that "writing, like teaching, is an instrument for social change. I want to help us preserve and revitalize what were and are the strengths of Hawai'i."

"Intermediate School Hapai" is a tender and funny account of an older brother watching over the welfare of his younger sister, Val, who thinks she might be pregnant (hapai). Terada is a master of weaving several kinds of language in and out of his story. In a scene at a local carnival Vince, the older brother, must translate between the Japanese woman who is running a ring-toss game and Val. Vince's Japanese is part English, made-up Japanese, Hawaiian pidgin English, and hip street attitude. This section is especially meant to be read aloud. If the reader doesn't understand the meaning of the words, that meaning may reveal itself to be English even though the words appear visually on the page to be Japanese. Direct literal translations in this story can simply confuse the reader. For example, Vince calls the ring-toss booth a "manju booth." Manju is a steamed bun filled with sweet bean paste, but obviously the booth doesn't sell manju. The use of the term by Vince is a measure of his attitude toward the Japanese booth, as in the way he describes the woman running the booth as having a "mochi-dango face," the literal translation being something like pounded rice cake dumpling face.

Intermediate School Hapai

just the other night
Val a junior at UH
me four years older than her and cruising

I was tuning up my car the other night when my sister Val came up to me and asked, "Eh, Vince. You get some dope or what?" Just like that, out and out, with no beating around the bushes. "Eh Vince. You get some dope or what?" Usually, when you talk to your brother or sister, you just make conversation and you talk-story about really useless stuff like "Eh, your turn for wash the dishes tonight," or "What you doing?" or "You went play around with my guitar or what?" The other night, not Val. She just came up to me while I was tuning up my car and she asked, "Eh, Vince. You get some dope or what?" What a little punk.

I was trying to get the distributor gear lined up with the camshaft gear. Real pain in the ass business. Especially for one GTO—Pontiac, that's why—the distributor stay way in the back of the motor. I was lying on the fender, holding the Accel dualpoint distributor, the one Duki got for me free so no can complain, trying to keep the two sets of points at top-dead-center open, while trying to match the two angle-cut gears. Then she asked me that. I gave her a stink side-eye and kept on with my business. She was probably only joking anyway, and I wasn't going to let her pull my leg.

"Vince!" She insisted, "You get some dope or what? I asked you one question." She was still standing there at the front of my '64 Goat, obviously determined to get some kind of answer from me.

I figured too-bad-for-you and shook my head while I kept on with the distributor.

"Come on, Vince. You get. I know. Just the other night you bought one O-Z[1] from Duki for 90 cents."

I gave her a meaner stink-eye, looking straight at her this time. And I went back to work.

"Vince, no make stink. Come on." She was still standing there at the front of my car, leaning against the nose of the Goat.

Apparently she wasn't satisfied with the subtleties of non-verbal communication. Goddam it. I put the distributor down on the aluminum intake manifold and slithered backwards off the fender. I hopped to my feet and looked at her.

She was going out tonight. She was dressed, maybe not to "kill," but she was set at least on "stun." Tight, dressy jeans and a silkie top that wasn't too shiny in a semi-aloha print theme. Looking good. A white loose-mesh sweater was draped over her shoulder and this thin clutch purse was tucked under her armpit. The purse was supposed to be rabbit fur, but the poor skinned rabbit must have either been scrawny or just given a grunt crewcut.

Once I told her, "Eh, that's not rabbit skin, Val. Look more like cow fur."

She looked at her purse and then at me, saying, "Doubt it. Cow fur! Who ever heard of cow fur!"

---

1. ounce

So I told her, "What you think—cows stay bolo-head[2] or what? You and me, we went go Lani-Moo Farm down Kahukuside when we was small kids. We both went go pet Lani-Moo and her baby cow ... "

"'Baby cow!' Try 'calf!'"

She probably still thinks it's rabbit. She was standing at the front of my car, waiting for an answer. She was barefoot.

"Val, honey. It you are going out, I think more better if you wear rubber slipper[3] at least. How you figure? I was talking sassy."

"Ne[4], later. I going back inside the house."

"Howz about the grease all over the ground?"

"Grease!" She looked down at the garage floor, stepping carefully backwards.

"Ne, I just kidding. Fool you, eh? So what you like again?"

"Eh! You think you wise, one eh, Mr. Speed-Racer with the pseudo-fast car that no can catch up to Z-28!" She was teasing me. I was sure about that when she started singing the chorus from the theme song of the old "Speed-Racer" cartoon. "Go, Speed-Racer! Go, Speed-Racer! Go, Speed-Racer, go-o!"

"Funny, funny, funny. You ever thought about getting one job as one knee-slapping comedian? And what's this about some plug Z-28?"

"Oh, yo! No make, Vince! Duki told me about the time you got dusted by the red '68 Camaro!"

"Duki? Fuck that shet! I gave the guy in the Camaro one chance and the bugga took advantage of my kind generosity. Never mind that. You went ask me something or what?"

She was singing again, "Go, Speed-Racer. Go, Speed-Racer ... "

"Okay. If you going make like that ... " I started to lean over the fender again.

"Ne-ne-ne-ne-ne! You no can take one joke or what? Shi, what a sourpuss."

I stood back up. "So what you like then!"

"Gee, no need get all piss-off."

"Okay, okay, okay. I not. What!"

"I just wanted to know if you had some dope."

"Ye, I get. So what?"

"I can have couple J's or what?"

"Magic word?"

"Shet."

"Oh! Sorry, you lose. That is definitely *not* the magic word."

---

2. bald head
3. coris
4. then

"May I *please* have a few J's[5] then, Vince-sir?"

"For what?"

"I was going clean out my ears with them."

"Well, it that case, why you no try the Q-tips in the bathroom? Mo' better."

"Come on, Vince."

I looked at her. Who does this junior-in-college child think she is? To ask her big brother for some rolled-up sweet cannabis buds? She's still yet four years younger than me!

"Ye, okay. Stay in my guitar case. You know where."

"Eh, thanks, ye, Vince." Val smiled. She has such a pretty smile with these cute tiny dimples. Her eyes sparkled in the glare from the trouble-light dangling from the raised hood of my car, and she kind of skipped off to the kitchen door.

I called her, "Eh, Val!"

"Ha?" She turned before the kitchen door. Ye, she had her eyelashes on. I told her how many times before, "No need!"—her real eyelashes were long and thick enough—but she still always wears those things when she goes out anyway.

Her hair is black touched with brown. I told her once that it was "almost 'ehu"[6] and she said, "I doubt!" And her hair isn't the dried-out brown of peroxide or lemon juice or sun scorch. I have the same kind of hair but not as thick. Her hair is full and curling with soft waves, but it's not severe enough to be kinky or Brillo pad. She had it cut to just below her shoulders and it curled at her forehead, away from the sides of her face. She was always worried about the frizzies when she hardly had any.

"Ha?" She asked again from the kitchen door.

"Ah, nothing," I told her.

She gave me her "how bizarre!" look and turned back to the door. Val has a nice figure—she takes care of her body. She's almost slender but not skinny like a bony baby Bambi-deer. "Try fawn,'" she would probably tell me. Ye, ye. She opened the kitchen door and went inside the house.

Val's four years younger than me. She's a junior at UH, easing into an English degree, the same thing I was going to go into. But I quit UH, for a little while at least. I'm working at Times now—I got hired after I got turned down three time—the McCully branch, the ones across from Washington Intermediate and Zippy's. I figure I'll go back to UH maybe next year—I'm doing okay, I guess. At least I have a full-time job. My friend Duki doesn't even have a job and he's older than me. I'm doing okay.

Inside the house, Mom called, "Val! No forget, your turn to wash the dishes tonight. And did anybody feed the dog?"

---

5. joints, marijuana
6. red

Val answered from my bedroom, "Mommy! Not my turn tonight! I washed 'em last night. Vince's turn now. And I thing the dog was fed already.

Mom said, "I hope so."

I was going to protest this laying-on of the chores on top of me, but I figured, Whatevers. BD's. Val, what a liar. And Taro wasn't fed yet. I could see him from the garage. The old shaggy poi[7] dog was sticking his head out of his doghouse, looking sad and starving. One paw was resting in his empty food dish, his way of hinting to us about feeding him. No worry, I going feed you. If Val was to feed Taro when she was in a rush, all she would give him would be the dry dog food, not the Kal Kan.

"Eh, Vince. You get some dope or what?" Just 'cause she's a junior at UH, she thinks she's pro-Joe grown-up mature. Tsa! She's still yet four years younger than me! She still has all her stuffed animals like the chubby snow-white bear with the red nose. She still goes to sleep with her Winnie-the-Pooh bear, the one I gave her for Christmas when she was in tenth grade.

> five years ago
> Val in ninth grade
> me at UH

Back then even, she thought she was so grown-up. When she was in ninth grade at Kawananakoa Intermediate, she was going out with this senior guy from 'Iolani.[8] Well, not really going out with. It was more like hanging around with—they weren't going steady or anything like that. I remembered the guy from high school—he was one grade below me at 'Iolani. I guess that's how she met him, through me in the school.

Was the summer after her ninth grade. She was all excited about going to Roosevelt come fall. Big duduz, ye? I had finished a harsh first year at UH-Manoa. Now it was in the summer, after most of the high-school graduation parties were pau.[9] The guy from 'Iolani was taking her around to all the parties and sometimes he would bring her home real late at night, if not early in the morning. Mommy and Daddy, they were concerned about the late night hours of their baby girl. I told them, "Ah, let her. Stay graduation party time, that's why. Only for little while, going be. Plus the guy taking her around, he's okay. He just graduated. I know him—he's a good guy." The guy was really laters, but I said that just so that they could let Val go out. Val had begged me to talk to Mommy and Daddy. Reluctantly, they let her stay out late, since

---

7. implied meaning here is "old Hawaian rural dog," but poi is actually cooked toro root thinned with water
8. a private school
9. finished

it would only be for a little while, being graduation party time, and since big brother seemed to know what he was talking about.

That summer, after the graduation parties were pretty much pau, I was moping around the house early one Saturday morning, thinking of what to do. School was pau for me and no way was I going to go to summer-school session. I had been turned down by Times Supermarkets and about five other places and I wasn't in the mood for going job-hunting again.

The sun wasn't high enough in the sky to make the morning hot. A tradewind easing down Pauoa Valley rustled the leaves of the mango tree in our yard. The weak drying leaves dropped off the tree's branches and scattered themselves in the yard, around the rose bushes along the back stone wall, onto the green onion and string bean patch in the corner, into the garage.

That afternoon I was going to go to Al's house to help him pull the motor out of his '66 Chevy. But I had nothing to do in the morning. I turned on the TV and clicked through all the channels couple times. I looked out the parlor window at the old gingerbread-type house across the street. The old haole[10] man was sitting in his fat padded recliner in his living room, staring blankly out the window. At me. "Fucken senile old shet," I mumbled, giving the old man a stink-eye. The old man slowly leaned forward, got out of his chair, and shuffled off to another room.

I walked to Val's room. I knocked softly at the closed door. I turned the doorknob and pushed the door open a little. I looked into her room.

The midmorning sun was shining through the yellow curtains on the windows facing the front yard. Val's stuffed animals on the shelf above the head of her bed were all leaning back or lying down, taking in some of that sun. Rhinos, dogs, cats, elephants, and even turtles. A monkey hung from the end of the shelf, practicing for a starring role in some upcoming Tarzan movie. In the middle of that row of upholstered beasts sat the chubby snow-white bear with the red nose that I had won for Val at the Hongwanji carnival long time ago, small-kid time.

> twelve years ago
> Val in second grade
> me in sixth grade

I was in the sixth grade, she was in second. I remember I had to stay with her at the Hongwanji carnival 'cause Mommy and Daddy said so. I walked with her, holding her hand, as we played all the games the carnival had.

---

10. white man

"We get some more scrip,[11] Vince?"

"Of course. We get plenty. What you like play?"

We played all the games. We rode most of the rides too. Except for the Round-up, 'cause we saw this guy get off the ride and puke his guts out. How sick. We saw my friend Duki who snickered at us.

I said, "What!"

He said, "Look the tilly holding hands with the baby girl."

Duki was razzing, but Val was my sister. I gave him a "how bizarre!" look and I led Val away to the Giant Ring Toss game.

"Play that one for me again, Vince!"

"Why you no like play?"

" 'Cause I not tall enough for throw the ring over the animals, that's why."

"Oh. Okay." I elbowed our way through the crowd, to the front of the booth, and nodded to the fat middle-aged Japanese lady with the mochi[12]-dango[13] face who was tending the booth. "Eh, lady. Excuse me, I like three rings, please."

"Nandeska?" She smiled a mochi smile.

I had to fumble into my pidgin Japanese. "Ah, boku, mitsu that kind man-marui rings suki des. Chodai. Onegai. I think."

"Ah! Guru boi, ne! Anta no Nihongo wa tot'temo joozu des, ne! Guru boi!" She wiped her hands on her white cotton apron. She patted my arm.

I forced a smile and mumbled under my breath, "Ye, ye. Howz about the rings, obasan?"

"Hai, hai." She heard! "Mitsu wa jyuu-go mai scrip narimas yo!" She held out three rings.

"Ha?" I gave Val a side-eye and whispered to her, "What she said?" Val shrugged. I looked back at the lady. "What? I mean, nani?"

She smiled mochi. "Ara, ara. An'nani joozu ja nai, ne! Hai, 'Mitsu' wa 'three' des. You like three ringuz, ne? Boy-san?" Ye, Ye. I know what "mitsu" means. "To, 'jyuu-go mai' wa 'fifteen scrip' des. You give me, ne?"

Oh I knew that all along. This was such a jiu-fut game anyway. So cheapskate, five scrip got you only one ring. More worse, three scrip could get you one ride on the Ferris Wheel. But this manju[14] booth had all the good prizes—the giant stuffed animals that were thick and fluffy, with none of them having any eyes missing. I gave the lady fifteen scrip and she smiled, handing me three almost basketball-size wooden hoops.

"Here, Val. Go try one." I gave her a hoop.

---

11. script, tickets
12. pounded rice cakes
13. dumpling
14. steamed bun filled with sweet bean paste

"Well. Okay. But you gotta go first."

She took a hoop and stood to one side to let the pro do his thing. I leaned forward carefully and softly tossed the hoop towards a monstrous fluorescent orange walrus. The hoop floated down and snagged an upholstered walrus tusk. No good—shet.

"Almost though." Val was trying to be encouraging. I leaned forward again, this time putting my weight on the knee-high wooden beam around the edge of the booth. I aimed for the fat Filipino pig—it was purple—next to the walrus. Again I softly tossed the hoop. Again I missed. I caught the pig's curlicue tail.

"Oh, shet. Your turn, Val."

"Okay."

She didn't even aim. She didn't even take her time. She tossed the hoop overhand even. She was aiming for a chubby snow-white bear with a red nose. It was *all* the way on the other side of the booth. She just threw the hoop at it. No wonder she missed. The hoop didn't even go above the bear. Instead, it hit the bear on it's pon-pon.[15]

"Aw." Val was disappointed. But that's the way it goes.

"Hai, hai." The smiling Japanese lady again. "Too bad, ne, kawa-i gyoru! Here, I give mo-shtotsu chance!" The lady was smiling dango as she held out one more hoop in her mochi hand for Val.

Val looked at me and I nodded at her to go take it. She took it from the lady and mumbled, "Thank you."

"Nihongo[16] de? Nani yuu ka?"

"Ah, arigatoo."[17] Very good, Val. I knew you knew that one.

"Here, Vince. You throw for me. Aim for that bear I was going for." She handed me the hoop. The fat lady managed to frown while she was smiling. Apparently, I wasn't kawa-i enough for her.

I was figuring what a junk game anyway. Juice, in other words. Disgruntled, I just threw the hoop away in the direction of the bear.

You got 'em! You got 'em!" Val was so happy. I was so surprised.

"Talent," I told Val.

The fat lady got off her dango ass and took the white bear off the square base around which the hoop I had just thrown nestled snug. She handed the big stuffed animal to Val, not to me, all the while smiling mochi at Val and frowning kogegohan at me.

So I told her, "Thanks, eh, Babasan!"

When we walked away, Val hugged me and the chubby snow-white bear with the red nose. I grinned and said, "Only talent."

---

15. stomach
16. Japanese
17. thank you

She said. "No act. You just lucky," and she took my hand and we went looking for our parents.

> seven years later, back to five years ago
> Val in ninth grade
> me at UH

That same chubby snow-white bear with the red nose was still on the shelf in Val's room seven years later. She had been taking care of it—its smooth white fur wasn't even dusty.

Val was wrapped up in her blanket, the thin quilted futon that Obaachan[18] had sewn for her long time ago. She was lying on her side, curled up, facing towards me at her door.

"Hui! Val!" I just wanted to bother her.

She groaned and moved under her blanket. She lifted up an edge of the blanket and squinted out at me. Her eyes were red and puffy. She had been crying. She dropped the edge of the blanket back down and turned over to face the wall.

I looked behind me to make sure Mommy and Daddy weren't around. I walked into her room, closing the door behind me. Stepping over her summer school books, I sat on the edge of her bed and touched her shoulder.

"Eh, Val. You okay or what?"

"Leave me alone."

"Val-baby. Something the matter?"

"Leave me alone, Vince."

"You sure?"

"Vince. Come on." She wasn't mad. She just wanted to be left alone for now.

So I tucked the blanket in around her and left her in her room, closing the door again. I went into the kitchen and looked out the window at Taro. Mommy walked in from their bedroom.

She said, "You look like you looking for something to do."

"Not really." I wasn't looking forward to doing *chores*.

"How about cleaning out the garage?"

"Mommy!"

"I think that's a good idea. Most of the junk is yours anyway." She walked away.

I walked out the kitchen door and scratched the matted fur on Taro's back on my way to the garage. There were some car parts in the back of the garage. Greasy. I looked over the sheets of plywood leaning on a side-wall of the garage. Ah, righteous!

---

18. grandmother

My old paipo board! The one I used to use when I was in intermediate school. Heavy duty! This was a beauty. I had carved this out of three-quarter inch marine plywood. Most everybody else's paipo boards were just flat pieces of plywood with rounded edges. Mine was *contoured*, with no flats anywhere. It was carved, planed, and sanded smooth. It was a bust-ass job. But it turned out beautiful. It was maybe three feet tall and a little less than two feet wide. It was still beautiful. I hadn't used it since intermediate school time. The seven coats of marine varnish still gleamed with the dark brown wood grain showing through. Dings had been filled with linseed oil putty and revarnished.

I got this brilliant inspiration to paint a design on the top. I went into the storeroom and got some sheets of number one-fifty and four-hundred sandpaper. With the one-fifty I roughed an area of the top's varnish in the center of the board. I smoothed the sandpaper scratches out with the four-hundred paper. I got a small can of appliance-white paint and medium pointed brush. I imagined the design: a Hawaiian petroglyph of a guy throwing net. I pried open the can of paint with a screwdriver and I started painting. I figured—if look ugly, look ugly.

It looked ugly. Besides, Daddy once told me that the ancient Hawaiians didn't know how to throw net in the old times of petroglyphs. *Of course, Hawaiians would say that they taught the Japanese how.* Daddy said the art was introduced by some crazy Japanese fisherman immigrant who had decided to bring his throw net along with him to Hawaii, to the sugar plantations. Think—what good would a throw net be when you had to katchi-ken and hole-hole all day long?

I pounded the lid back on the paint can, rinsed the brush in some old paint thinner, and put everything away. I leaned the board against the back of the garage to let the ugly design dry. It looked stupid.

"Vince."

"What!" I was thrown off. It was Val. "Oh, You scared me, baby-girl. Good morning, Val." She had just gotten up. She was still in her sleep clothes—her red play shorts and the oversize 1973 'Iolani Carnival t-shirt I had given her last year. Her hair was a mess. She was looking down at the ground. She had on Daddy's bust-up leather zoris.[19] Something was heavy on her mind.

She just stood there next to me, looking down at her toes sticking out of the zori straps. The quiet red nail polish she had brushed on her toes about two weeks before was showing its age—dulling and chipping. She rubbed at the nail polish on one big toe with the front of the zori on her other foot. The hard nail polish became scratched—thin flat-white lines on the fading red gloss. She bent down, licked her thumb, and glided spit on the scratched nail polish on that big toe. The wet glistened

---

19. rubber slippers

over the shallow scratches, over the dulling red. The wet gloss of spit temporarily rejuvenated the old nail polish, making it look freshly brushed on. Like an illusion of nice and new all over again. I sat down next to her and put a hand softly on her shoulder.

"Hey, Val. How's everything?"

She was quiet, still intent on inspection of her big toe's nail polish.

"Val."

"Ah ... " She looked at me. Her eyes were still red and puffy. "Everything's cool. Pretty much."

"Well, that's nice." I wasn't going to press the issue.

"Vince." She hesitated, and continued. "Except, you see ... " She was looking at her big toe. One tear splashed on it.

"Vince." She was whispering. "I scared."

"How come?"

" 'Cause I think maybe I might be hapai."[20] She was talking so soft I could barely hear her.

But I heard her. I stifled this "What!" that I felt forced to say. 'Cause I heard her. I managed a weak "Oh." She was still bent down on her ankles, looking at her toes. They were wet with her tears. I stood up and pulled her up too.

"Come, Val. We go take one walk, to the park maybe. We no can let Mommy and Daddy see you all sad like this."

"But look the way I ... "

"Ye, ye. 'Look the way I dressed!' I knew you was going say that. Big duduz. Let's go take a walk, Val."

We walked down the driveway. I had my arm around her shoulders.

Mommy called to us from in the house, "Eh! Where you two kids going?"

I shouted back without turning around, "Ah, we just going to the park, look around little while. We come back."

"Everything okay?"

"Ye, ye. No worry."

We turned onto Pauoa Road and walked towards the park. Val wasn't crying or anything anymore.

She told me softly, "Was your friend, ye, but wasn't his fault, see, we got drunk at one graduation party at this hotel, and, we was feeling good, you know, and, you know, we went into the bedroom, and ... "

"Ye, I know. You no need tell me about it."

"I missed my period, two weeks already. You mad?"

---

20. pregnant

"No. Why should I be mad? No can help, so no use come huhu.[21] You went go see one doctor?"

"No."

"Well, you gotta go see one doctor. He can give you one pregnancy test."

"But I missed my period."

"Ye, but this way we can make sure. You know, if yes or no, stay for reals."

"Okay. Vince, no tell Mommy and Daddy."

I looked at her. She was pleading with me. "No worry, Val."

We walked to the park.

"Tell you what, Val. Duki's Uncle Sei, he one doctor. And he's cool. I know him. He not going tell nobody."

"Not even Mommy and Daddy?"

"Course not."

"Not even Duki?"

"*Course* not!"

"Okay."

We sat underneath a monkeypod tree.

"Vince, what if I for real hapai? Pregnant."

"You no can have one baby, no way."

"Ye, I know."

"Uncle Sei can fix that up. Abortion."

"Abortion? Scary, eh?"

"Ne, safe. Easy. He do 'em, and you stay in his office overnight, and then pau."

"Ye? How you know all this?"

"Duki's cousin Lei . . . "

"Lei? Ne! Lei?"

"Ye. She had. Duki told me."

"How Duki went find out if Uncle Sei so cool and quiet?"

" 'Cause Lei told Duki. They close, that's why."

"Oh."

We sat under the tree for little while and then we walked back home. Val was okay. I was surprised—I didn't know my baby sister was this strong.

I called up Uncle Sei that afternoon. He said to bring Val in to his office Sunday morning so he could take urine and blood samples for the hapai test. He was real cool about it.

When I left to go to Al's house to help him fix car, Val was washing clothes. I came back home after sunset. Mommy said that Val had gone out. She went out with

---

21. angry

that guy, the one who ... I didn't understand. I was tired and all greasy from working on the car. I took a bath, ate dinner, and sacked out.

I woke up when I heard Val and the guy come home little before midnight. They came inside the house and Val turned the TV on soft. I didn't want to eavesdrop but I could hear them talking.

The guy was all sad about something. I think he was starting to sniffle. What a tilly. I heard him ask Val, "You sure you don't want to see me anymore?"

Val's voice was soft. "Yes."

"Why?"

"I just think would be better for you and me." Val wasn't going to comfort the nakimiso. Good.

"Oh." The tilly was sniffling. Shi, what a crybaby. More worse, he's only one year younger than me. I should slap his head for what he did to Val. Tell the muff off, Val!

The tilly squeaked, "Val. I was wondering. I don't want to worry you, but, you know, from that time, I was wondering if you could be pregnant or what?" The tilly kept on sniffling.

Goddam it. This was becoming unbearable, especially to a samūrai like me. Chiksho! Aksame yo! Ukininam! What a sensitive performance. Give the silly-willy a Tony award. What a crybaby and a half! I wanted to run into the living room and scream the tilly. Just for scare the shets out of him.

I wanted to scream out with all my might:

Fuck, no cry. What crying going accomplish? What a dumb-shet panty! You supposed to flip out. You supposed to go pupule[22]-kitchigai-mento.[23] You supposed to get this blank look in your face as you think, think hard!

Hapai? pregnant? hara ga futoku nat'ta? remember something about that from Health class? one late period? period—menustration, menstruation. ovals, ovaltine, ovulation and uterine linings. blood, not blood, that's the menstrual FLOW. rags, tampax, kotex, modess—every month of so like the full MOON. rag-out 'cause of puberty. rag-in, rag-out, ovaries and fallopian TUBES. uterus and cervix and vagina. you cunt and clit. water retention and uncomfortability. that bloated feeling, hymens and hairy lips. if I was back in Health class, I'd stand up and scream the teacher, "WHATS IT ALL ABOUT, BRA!"

But this is not Health class. and the big deal is not about where the shi shi puka stay. no, not the scrotum bags and the testes balls—nuts and vas deferens. no, not kohes and bilots and botos and uleules. no, not the bone. no, not the anatomy of the

_____

22. crazy
23. mental

genitalia, no, not the horrors of VD. this no stay one wet DREAM when you wake up sticky tomorrow morning. when you wake up, the girl still stay hapai. it's too late to "rap" about the problems of contraception and responsible parenthood with one of the good fun counselors. it's way too late for anything, kids.

Fuck, this not Health class anymore. no ways. nobody's giggling-snickering-cracking futs and dirty jokes in the back row with friends. no, everything's pretty serious now. pretty fucken serious.

Nobody paid any attention in Health class. everybody figured they knew all about the shet. they all heard about it before. you know—balling, fucking, blowing, finger banging and K-Y jelly and rubbers and foams that taste gross. you know, the dick-cock, the two nuts-balls, the cunt, the clit. fucken ding-ding and ching-ching. big fucken shet. all the dirty pictures, all the positions all the moves.

Fuck that! You crybaby! Fuck that!

But I stayed in bed, lying still. Screaming never helps the situation. I listened. Val let the crybaby sniffle a little bit more. I could tell she wasn't even patting his shoulder. She was probably sitting at the other end of the sofa. That's the way it ends, pal. The sofa springs squeaked as she stood up.

She told him, "It's time for you to go now. And no worry about me. I not pregnant." She's not? Since when? Ha?

She clicked the TV off and pulled him up from the sofa. She opened the front door for him. He put on his shoes. He got no goodbye-goodnight kiss. He stopped sniffling as he walked to his car.

Val locked the front door shut. On her way to her room, she stopped at my bedroom door. She pushed the door open and whispered to me in the dark, "What time tomorrow morning?"

"Nine."

"I thought you was sleeping, big ears." She shut the door. She was teasing me again.

Next morning I drove Val to Uncle Sei's office. He took urine and blood samples from her with no lectures. He knew me, so he figured he knew her. Val and me, we ate lunch at Rainbows'. We drove to Diamond Head Road and watched the surfers from the cliffs. I called Uncle Sei up before we left for home. The tests were negative. Val wasn't hapai. That Christmas, I gave her the Winnie-the-Pooh bear.

five years later, back to just the other night
Val's a junior at UH
me four years older than her and cruising

The kitchen door opened and Val skipped back out of the house.

"Eh, dreamer! What you doing?" she called out to me.

"Ha?" I was leaning against the fender of my car. I hadn't gone back to fixing the distributor. I was doing nothing, just daydreaming. She slipped on her cork-and-leather sandals and walked up to me.

"I found 'em in the guitar case. I took two. Thanks."

"Nihongo de?"

"Arigatoo!"

"Who you going out with tonight?"

"Carol."

"Movies?"

"Ye."

Carol's car drove up into our driveway. Taro barked lethargically—he was old and hungry. Carol beeped her horn at us. I nodded at her. Val turned to go.

"Eh, Val. Try come."

"What?" She walked to my side and I kissed her on her cheek. She said, "Oh, yo! What was that for?"

"Nothing much."

"Gee, I hope you never mess up my make-up."

"What?"

"Ne! Just kidding."

"Go already. Carol stay waiting."

"Bye then, Vince." And she kissed me on my cheek and walked to Carol's car.

"Bye, Val."

In the car, Carol asked Val, "What was that all about?"

"I don't know. He was fixing his distributor. He's always a little bit stony. Maybe too much mosquito punk[24] when he work on his car outside at night."

"For real." Carol drove off with Val.

I left the car as is and washed up. I fed Taro some dry dog food. I went into the house and, in passing her room, I saw the chubby snow-white bear with the red nose on the shelf and the Winnie-the-Pooh bear on her bed. I washed the dishes that night.

---

24. smoke to keep mosquitos away

R. A. Sasaki

(b. 1952)

*R. A. Sasaki is a sansei (third-generation) Japanese American from San Francisco. She is a graduate of the University of California at Berkeley and San Francisco State University. Her fiction won the 1983 American Japanese National Literary Award and has appeared in several anthologies and literary journals. Her collection of short stories, **The Loom and Other Stories**, was published in 1991. Her stories explore numerous issues, such as the coming-of-age of a young girl, a tragic death in the family, and cultural conflicts between and within generations. In one story, a nisei, or second-generation Japanese American character, is described in one of the stories as*

> *wearing two faces of a second-generation child born of immigrant parents. The two faces never met; there was no common thread running through both worlds. The duality was unplanned and untaught.*

The nine stories in her collection weave together stories of three generations of Japanese Americans and in the process each generation is given a unique voice. These stories are not tales of acculturation and assimilation but, rather, reclaiming history and self-determination. The story that follows, "First Love," is from this collection.

First Love

It was William Chin who started the rumor. He had been crossing California Street on a Saturday afternoon in December when he was almost struck down by two people on a Suzuki motorcycle. As if it weren't enough to feel the brush of death on the sleeve of his blue parka, a split second before the demon passed, he had looked up and caught sight of two faces he never would have expected to see on the same motorcycle—one of which he wouldn't have expected to see on a motorcycle at all. No one would have imagined these two faces exchanging words, or thought of them in the same thought even; yet there they were, together not only in physical space, but in their expressions of fiendish abandon as they whizzed by him. He was so shaken, first by his nearness to death, then by seeing an F.O.B.[1] hood like Hideyuki "George" Sakamoto in the company of a nice girl like Joanne Terasaki, that it was a full five minutes before he realized, still standing in amazement on the corner of California and Fourth, that Joanne had been driving.

When William Chin's story got around, there was a general sense of outrage among the senior class of Andrew Jackson High—the boys, because an upstart newcomer like George Sakamoto had done what they were too shy to do (that is, he

---

1. Fresh Off the Boat

had gotten Joanne to like him), and the girls, because George Sakamoto was definitely cool and Joanne Terasaki, as Marsha Aquino objected with utter contempt, "doesn't even like to dance." Joanne's friends remained loyal and insisted that Jo would come to her senses by graduation. George's motorcycle cronies were less generous. "Dude's fuckin' crazy," was their cryptic consensus. Opinions differed as to which of the two lovers had completely lost their minds; however, it was unanimously held that the pairing was unsuitable.

And indeed, the two were from different worlds.

Hideyuki Sakamoto ("George" was his American name) was Japanese, a conviction that eight years, or half his life, in the States had failed to shake. He had transferred into Jackson High's senior class that year from wherever it was that F.O.B.s (immigrants fresh off the boat) transferred from; and though perhaps in his case the "fresh" no longer applied, the fact that he had come off the boat at one time or another was unmistakable. It lingered—rather, persisted—in his speech, which was ungrammatical and heavily accented, and punctuated by a mixture of exclamations commonly used on Kyushu Island[2] and in the Fillmore District.[3]

An F.O.B. at Jackson High could follow one of two routes: he could be quietly good at science or mathematics, or he could be a juvenile delinquent. Both options condemned him to invisibility. George hated math. His sympathies tended much more toward the latter option; however, he was not satisfied to be relegated to that category either. One thing was certain, and that was that George wanted no part of invisibility. As soon as his part-time job at Nakamura Hardware in Japantown[4] afforded him the opportunity, he went out and acquired a second-hand Suzuki chopper (most hoods dreamed of owning a Harley, but George was Japanese and proud of it). He acquired threads which, when worn on his tall, wiry frame, had the effect—whether from admiration, derision, or sheer astonishment—of turning all heads, male and female alike. He had, in a short span of time, established a reputation as a "swinger." So when William Chin's story got around about George Sakamoto letting Joanne Terasaki drive his bike, the unanimous reaction among the girls who thought of themselves as swingers was voiced by Marsha Aquino: "God dog, what a waste."

Joanne Terasaki, or "Jo," as she preferred to be called, was, in popular opinion, a "brain." Although her parents were living in Japantown when she was born, soon afterwards her grandparents had died and the family moved out to "the Avenues." Jo was a product of the middle-class, ethnically mixed Richmond District. She had an air of breeding that came from three generations of city living, one college-educated

---

2. Japanese island
3. black neighborhood in San Francisco
4. Japanese business section in San Francisco

parent, and a simple belief in the illusion so carefully nurtured by her parents' generation, who had been through the war, that she was absolutely Mainstream. No one, however, would have thought of her in conjunction with the word "swing," unless it was the playground variety. Indeed, there was a childlike quality about her, a kind of functional stupidity that was surprising in a girl so intelligent in other respects. She moved slowly, as if her mind were always elsewhere, a habit that boys found mysterious and alluring at first, then exasperating. Teachers found it exasperating as well, even slightly insulting, as she earned A's in their classes almost as an afterthought. Her attention was like a dim but powerful beacon, slowly sweeping out to sea for—what? Occasionally it would light briefly on the world at hand, and Jo would be quick, sharp, formidable. Then it would turn out to faraway places again. Perhaps she was unable to reconcile the world around her, the world of Jackson High, with the fictional worlds where her love of reading took her. In her mind, she was Scarlett O'Hara, Lizzy Bennet, Ari Ben Canaan. Who would not be disoriented to find oneself at one moment fleeing the Yankees through a burning Atlanta, and the next moment struggling across the finish line in girls' P.E.? Tart repartee with Mr. Darcy was far more satisfying than the tongue-tied and painful exchanges with boys that occurred in real life. Rebuffed boys thought Jo a snob, a heartless bitch. The world of Andrew Jackson High was beneath her, that was it—a passing annoyance to be endured until she went out into the wider world and entered her true element. It must be on this wider world, this future glory, that her vision was so inexorably fixed.

Or perhaps it was fixed on a point just across San Francisco Bay, on the imposing campanile of the Berkeley campus of the University of California. She had always known she would go there, ever since, as a child, she had often gone to her mother's dresser and surreptitiously opened the top drawer to take out the fuzzy little golden bear bearing the inscription in blue letters, "CAL." It was one of the few "heirlooms" that her mother had salvaged from the wartime relocation. She had taken it with her to internment camp in the Utah desert, an ineffectual but treasured symbol of a shattered life. The government could take away her rights, her father's business, her home, but they could never take away the fact that she was U.C. Berkeley, Class of '39. Jo would have that, too. People often said of Jo that she was a girl who was going places; and they didn't mean on the back (or front) of George Sakamoto's bike.

Only love or drama could bring together two people cast in such disparate roles. When auditions began for the play that was traditionally put on by the senior class before graduation, Jo, tired of being typecast as a brain, tried out for the part most alien to her image—that of the brazen hussy who flings herself at the hero in vain. For a brief moment she stood before her fellow classmates and sang her way out of the cramped cage that their imaginations had fashioned for her. The moment was indeed brief. Marsha Aquino got the part.

"You have to admit, Jo," said William Chin apologetically, "Marsha's a natural." And Jo agreed, somewhat maliciously, that Marsha was.

George, for his part, went for the lead. It was unheard of for a hood (and an F.O.B., at that) to aspire to the stage, much less the leading part. So thoroughly did George's aspect contradict conventional expectations of what a male lead should be, that the effect was quite comic. His goodnatured lack of inhibition so charmed his audience that they almost overlooked the fact that his lines had been unintelligible. At the last moment, a voice of reason prevailed, and George was relegated to a nonspeaking part as one of six princes in a dream ballet, choreographed by Jo's friend Ava.

And so the two worlds converged.

"Grace," Ava was saying. "And—flair." She was putting the dream princes and princesses through their paces. "This is a ballet."

The dancers shuffled about self-consciously. After hours of work the princes and princesses, trained exclusively in soul, were managing to approximate a cross between a square dance and a track-and-field event.

"You've got to put more energy into it, or something," Jo, who was a princess, observed critically as a sheepish William Chin and Ed Bakowsky leaped halfheartedly across the floor.

"Like this, man!" George yelled suddenly, covering the stage in three athletic leaps. He landed crookedly on one knee, arms flung wide, whooping in exhilaration. There was an embarrassed silence.

"Yeah," Jo said. "Like that."

"Who is that?" she asked Ava after the rehearsal.

"I don't know," Ava said, "but what a body."

"That's George Sakamoto," said Marsha Aquino, who knew about everyone. "He's bad."

Jo, unfamiliar with the current slang, took her literally.

"Well, he seems all right to me. If it wasn't for him, our dream ballet would look more like 'The Funeral March.' Is he new?"

"He transferred from St. Francis," Marsha said. "That's where all the F.O.B.s go."

Jo had always had a vague awareness of Japanese people as being unattractively shy and rather hideously proper. Nothing could have been further from this image than George. Jo and her friends, most of whom were of Asian descent, were stunned by him, as a group of domesticated elephants born and bred in a zoo might have been upon meeting their wild African counterpart for the first time. George was a revelation to Jo, who, on the subject of ethnic identity, had always numbered among the ranks of the sublimely oblivious.

George, meanwhile, was already laying his strategy. He was not called "*Sukebe* Sakamoto" by his friends for nothing.

"This chick is the door-hanger type," he told his friend Doug. "You gotta move real slow."

"Yeah," Doug said. "Too slow for you."

"You watch, sucker."

He called her one weekend and invited her and Ava to go bowling with him and Doug. Jo was struck dumb on the telephone.

"Ha-ro, is Jo there?"

"This is Jo."

"Hey, man. This is George."

"Who?"

"George, man. Sakamoto."

"Oh." Then she added shyly, "Hi."

The idea of bowling was revolting, but Jo could bowl for love.

She told her mother that she had a date. Her mother mentally filed through her list of acquaintances for a Sakamoto.

"Is that the Sakamoto that owns the cleaner on Fillmore?"

"I don't think so," Jo said.

"Well, if Ava's going, I guess it's all right."

When George came to pick her up, Jo introduced him to her father, who was sitting in the living room watching television.

"Ha-ro," George said, cutting a neat bow to her startled father.

"Was that guy Japanese?" her father asked later when she returned.

"Yeah," Jo said, chuckling.

There was an unspoken law of evolution which dictated that in the gradual march toward Americanization, one did not deliberately regress by associating with F.O.B.s. Jo's mother, who was second generation, had endured much criticism from her peers for "throwing away a college education" and marrying Jo's father, who had graduated from high school in Japan. Even Jo's father, while certainly not an advocate of this law, assumed that most people felt this way. George, therefore, was a shock.

On their second date, Jo and George went to see Peter O'Toole in a musical. From then on, they decided to dispense with the formalities, a decision owing only in part to the fact that the musical had been wretched. The main reason was that they were in love.

They would drive out to the beach, or to the San Bruno hills, and sit for hours, talking. In the protective shell of George's mother's car they found a world where they were not limited by labels. They could be complex, vulnerable. He told her about his boyhood in Kyushu, about the sounds that a Japanese house makes in the night. He had been afraid of ghosts. His mother had always told him ghost stories. She would make her eyes go round and utter strange sounds: *"Ka-ra ... ko-ro ... ka-ra ... ko-ro ... "*—the sound made by the wooden sandals of an approaching ghost. Japanese ghosts were different from American ghosts, he said. They didn't have feet.

"If they don't have feet," Jo asked curiously, "how could they wear sandals?"

George was dumbfounded. The contradiction had never occurred to him.

They went for motorcycle rides along the roads that wound through the Presidio,[5] at the edge of cliffs overlooking the Golden Gate. Then, chilled by the brisk winter fog, they would stop at his house in Japantown for a cup of green tea.

He lived in an old Victorian flat on the border between Japantown and the Fillmore, with his mother and grandmother and cat. His mother worked, so it was his grandmother who came from the kitchen to greet them. (But this was later. At first, George made sure that no one would be home when they went. He wanted to keep Jo a secret until he was sure of her.)

The Victorian kitchen, the green tea, all reminded Jo of her grandparents' place, which had stood just a few blocks away from George's house before it was torn down. Jo had a vague memory of her grandmother cooking fish in the kitchen. She couldn't remember her grandfather at all. The war had broken his spirit, taken his business, forced him to do day work in white people's homes, and he had died when Jo was two. After that, Jo's family moved out of Japantown, and she had not thought about the past until George's house reminded her. It was so unexpected, that the swinger, the hood, the F.O.B. George Sakamoto should awaken such memories.

But they eventually had to leave the protective spaces that sheltered their love. Then the still George of the parked car and Victorian kitchen, the "real" George, Jo wanted to believe, evolved, became the flamboyant George, in constant motion, driven to maintain an illusion that would elude the cages of other people's limited imaginations.

He took her to dances Jo had never known existed. Jo had been only to school dances, where everyone stood around too embarrassed to dance. The dances that George took her to were dark, crowded. Almost everyone was Asian. Jo knew no one. Where did all these people come from? They were the invisible ones at school, the F.O.B.s. They *dressed* (unlike Jo and her crowd, who tended toward corduroy jeans). And they danced.

George was in his element here. In his skintight striped slacks flared at the calf, black crepe shirt open to the navel, billowing sleeves and satiny white silk scarf, he shimmered like a mirage in the strobe lights that cut the darkness. Then, chameleonlike, he would appear in jeans and a white T-shirt, stocking the shelves of Nakamura Hardware. At school, George shunned the striped shirts and windbreaker jackets that his peers donned like a uniform. He wore turtleneck sweaters under corduroy blazers,

---

5.   Army base in San Francisco

starched shirts in deep colors with cuff links. When he rode his bike, he was again transformed, a wild knight in black leather.

"The dudes I ride with," George confided to Jo in the car, "see me working in the store, and they say, 'Hey, what is this man? You square a-sup'm?' Then the guys in the store, they can't believe I hang out with those suckers on bikes. 'Hey George,' they say, 'you one crazy son-of-a-bitch.' In school, man, these straight suckers can't believe it when I do good on a test. I mean, I ain't no hot shit at English, but I ain't no dumb sucker neither. 'Hey George,' they say, 'you tryin' to get into college a-sup'm?' 'Hey, why not, man?' I say. They can't take it if you just a little bit different, you know? All them dudes is like that—'cept you."

Jo was touched, and tried to be the woman of George's dreams. It was formidable endeavor. Nancy Sinatra was the woman of George's dreams. For Christmas Jo got a pair of knee-high black boots. She wore her corduroy jeans tighter in the crotch.

"Hey, George," Doug said. "How's it going' with Slow Jo?"

"None of your fuckin' business, man," George snapped.

"Oh-oh. Looks bad."

On New Year's Eve Jo discovered French kissing and thought it was "weird." She got used to it, though.

"You tell that guy," her father thundered, "that if he's gonna bring that motorcycle, he doesn't have to come around here anymore!"

"Jesus Christ!" Jo wailed, stomping out of the room. "I can't wait to get out of here!"

Then they graduated, and Jo moved to Berkeley in the spring.

The scene changed from the narrow corridors of Andrew Jackson High to the wide steps and manicured lawns of the university. George was attending a junior college in the city. He came over on weekends.

"Like good ice cream" he said. "I want to put you in the freezer so you don't melt."

"What are you talking about?"

They were sitting outside Jo's dormitory in George's car. Jo's roommate was a blonde from Colusa who had screamed the first time George walked into the room with Jo. ("Hey, what's with that chick?" George had later complained.)

"I want to save you," George said.

"From what?" Jo asked.

He tried another analogy. "It's like this guy got this fancy shirt, see? He wants to wear it when he goes out, man. He don't want to wear it every day, get it dirty. He wears an old T-shirt when he works under the car—get grease on it, no problem. It don't matter. You're like the good shirt, man."

"So who's the old T-shirt?" Jo asked, suddenly catching on.

"Hey, nobody, man. Nobody special. You're special. I want to save you."

"I don't see it that way," Jo said. "When you love someone, you want to be with them and you don't mind the grease."

"Hey, outasight, man."

So he brought her to his room.

George's room was next to the kitchen. It was actually the dining room converted into a young man's bedroom. It had the tall, narrow Victorian doors and windows, and a sliding door to the living room, which was blocked by bookshelves and a stereo. The glass-doored china cabinet, which should have housed Imari bowls, held tapes of soul music, motorcycle chains, Japanese comic books, and Brut. In Jo's grandparents' house there had been a black shrine honoring dead ancestors in the corner of the dining room. The same corner in George's room was decorated by a life-size poster of a voluptuous young woman wearing skintight leather pants and an equally skintight (but bulging) leather jacket, unzipped to the waist.

George's mother and grandmother were delighted by Jo. In their eyes she was a "nice Japanese girl," something they never thought they would see, at least in conjunction with George. George had had a string of girlfriends before Jo, which had dashed their hopes. Jo was beyond their wildest expectations. It didn't seem to matter that this "nice Japanese girl" didn't understand any Japanese; George's grandmother spoke to her anyway, and gave her the benefit of the doubt when she smiled blankly and looked to George for a translation. They were so enthusiastic that George was embarrassed, and tried to sneak Jo in and out to spare her their effusions.

They would go to his room and turn up the stereo and make love to the lush, throbbing beat of soul. At first Jo was mortified, conscious of what her parents would say, knowing that "good girls" were supposed to "wait." But in the darkness of George's room, all of that seemed very far away.

So her first experiences of love were in a darkened room filled with the ghosts of missing Japanese heirlooms; in the spaces between the soul numbers with which they tried to dispel those ghostlike shadows, sound filtered in from the neighboring kitchen: samurai music from the Japanese program on television, the ancient voice of his grandmother calling to the cat, the eternal shuffle of slippers across the kitchen floor. When his mother was home and began to worry about what they were doing in his room, he installed a lock, and when she began pounding on the door, insisting that it was getting late and that George really should take Jo home, George would call out gruffly, "Or-righ! Or-righ!"

But there was the other world, Jo's weekday world, a world of classical buildings, bookstores, coffee shops, and tear gas (for the United States had bombed Cambodia).

Jo flitted like a ghost between the two worlds so tenuously linked by a thin span of steel suspended over San Francisco Bay. She wanted to be still, and at home, but where? On quiet weekday mornings, reading in an empty courtyard with the stillness, the early morning sun, the language of Dickens, she felt her world full of promise and dreams. Then the sun rose high, people came out, and Jo and her world disappeared in a cloak of invisibility, like a ghost.

"Her English is so good," Ava's roommate remarked to Ava. "Where did she learn it?"

"From my parents," Jo said. "In school, from friends. Pretty much the same way most San Franciscans learn it, I guess."

Ava's roommate was from the East Coast, and had never had a conversation with an 'Oriental' before.

"She just doesn't know any better," Ava apologized later.

"Well where has that chick been all her life?" Jo fumed.

Then she would long for George, and he would come on the weekend to take her away. Locked together on George's bike, hurtling back and forth between two worlds, they found a place where they could be still and at peace.

George tried to be the man of her dreams. They went on hikes now instead of soul dances. He would appear in jeans and a work shirt, and he usually had an armload of books. He was learning to type, and took great pains over his essays for Remedial English.

But they began to feel the strain. It began to bother George that Jo made twenty-five cents an hour more at her part-time job in the student dining room than he did at the hardware store. He had been working longer. He needed the money. Jo, on the other hand, never seemed to buy anything. Just books. Although her parents could afford to send her to college, her high-school record had won her a scholarship for the first year. She lived in a dream world. She had it so easy.

He asked to borrow fifty dollars, he had to fix his car, and she lent it to him immediately. But he resented it, resented his need, resented her for having the money, for parting with it so easily. Everything, so easily. And he tortured her.

"Hey, is something wrong, man?" George asked suddenly, accusing, over the phone.

"Wrong?" Jo was surprised. "What do you mean?"

"You sound funny."

"What do you mean funny?"

"You sound real cold, man," George said. His voice was flat, dull.

"There's nothing wrong!" Jo protested, putting extra emphasis in her voice to convince him, then hating herself for doing so. "I'm fine."

"You sound real far away," George went on, listlessly.

"Hey, is something bothering *you*?"

"No," George said. "You just sound funny to me. Real cold, like you don't care." He wanted her to be sympathetic, remorseful.

And at first she was—repentant, almost hysterical. Then she became impatient. Finally, she lapsed into indifference.

"I have the day off tomorrow," George said over the phone. "Can I come?"

Jo hesitated.

"I have to go to classes," she warned.

"That's okay," he said. "I'll come with you."

There was another long pause. "Well ... we'll see," she said.

As soon as she saw him the next day, her fears were confirmed. He had gone all out. He wore a silky purple shirt open halfway to his navel, and skintight slacks that left nothing to the imagination. There was something pathetic and vulnerable about the line of his leg so thoroughly revealed by them. As they approached the campus, George pulled out a pair of dark shades and put them on.

He was like a character walking into the wrong play. He glowed defiantly among the faded jeans and work shirts of Berkeley campus.

Jo's first class was Renaissance Literature.

"If you want to do something else," she said, "I can meet you after class."

"That's okay, man," George said happily. "I want to see what they teaching you."

"It's gonna be real boring," she said.

"That's okay," he said. "I have my psych book."

"If you're going to study," Jo said carefully, "maybe you should go to the library."

"Hey," George said, "you tryin' to get rid of me?"

"No," Jo lied.

"Then let's go."

They entered the room. It was a seminar of about ten people, sitting in a circle. They joined the circle, but after a few minutes of discussion about *Lycidas*, George opened his psychology textbook and began to read.

Jo was mortified. The woman sitting on the other side of George was looking curiously, out of the corner eye, at the diagram of the human brain in George's book.

"Would you care to read the next stanza aloud?" the lecturer asked suddenly. "You—the gentleman with the dark glasses."

There was a horrible moment as all eyes turned to George, bent over his psychology textbook. He squirmed and sank down into his seat, as if trying to become invisible.

"I think he's just visiting," the woman next to George volunteered. "I'll read."

Afterwards, Jo was brutal. Why had he come to the class if he was going to be so rude? Why hadn't he sat off in the corner, if he was going to study? Or better yet, gone to the library as she had suggested? Didn't he know how inappropriate his behavior was? Didn't he care if they thought that Japanese people were boors? Didn't he know? Didn't he care?

No, he didn't know. He was oblivious. It was the source of his confidence, and that was what she had loved him for.

And so the curtain fell on their little drama, after a predictable denouement—agreeing that they would date others, then a tearful good-bye one dark night in his car, parked outside her apartment. Jo had always thought it somewhat disturbing when characters who had been left dead on the set in the last act, commanding considerable emotion by their demise, should suddenly spring to life not a minute later, smiling and bowing, and looking as unaffected by tragedy as it is possible to look. She therefore hoped she would not run into George, who would most certainly be smiling and bowing and oblivious to tragedy. She needn't have worried. Their paths had never been likely to cross.

Jo was making plans to study in New York when she heard through the grapevine that George was planning a trip to Europe. He went that summer, and when he returned, he brought her parents a gift. Jo's parents, who had had enough complaints about George when Jo was seeing him, were touched, and when Christmas came around Jo's mother, in true Japanese fashion, prepared a gift for George to return his kindness. Jo, of course, was expected to deliver it.

She had had no contact with him since they had broken up. His family was still living in Japantown, but the old Victorian was soon going to be torn down for urban renewal, and they were planning to move out to the Avenues, the Richmond District where Jo's parents lived.

As Jo's dad drove her to George's house, Jo hoped he wouldn't be home, hoped she could just leave the gift with his mother. She was thankful that she was with her father, who had a habit of gunning the engine as he sat waiting in the car for deliveries to be made, and was therefore the ideal person with whom to make a quick getaway.

George's grandmother opened the door. When she saw who it was, her face changed and she cried out with pleasure. Jo was completely unprepared for the look of happiness and hope on her face.

"Jo-chan!"[6] George's grandmother cried; then, half-turning, she called out Jo's name twice more, as if summoning the household to her arrival.

Jo was stunned.

"This is for George," she said, thrusting the gift at George's grandmother, almost throwing it at her in her haste. "Merry Christmas."

She turned and fled down those stairs for the last time, away from the doomed Victorian and the old Japanese woman who stood in the doorway still, calling her name.

---

6. abbreviated Japanese version of Joanne

Sylvia Watanabe

(b. 1952)

Sylvia Watanabe was born on the island of Maui in Hawai'i. Her collection of stories **Talking to the Dead** *(1992) won the Josephine Miles Award from the Oakland, California, chapter of PEN. She has also received a 1991 O. Henry Award, a Japanese American Citizens League National Literary Award, and a fellowship from the National Endowment for the Arts. Watanabe coedited with Carol Bruchac two anthologies of Asian American writing—***Home to Stay: Asian American Women's Fiction (1990)** *and* **Into the Fire: Asian American Traditions in the Making (1995).**

The central issue in "A Spell of Kona Weather," a story from her collection **Talking to the Dead***, focuses on the intensity of* place *and the urgency to define oneself against the seemingly overpowering presence of Hawai'i and family. One sister, Lulu, fights both the very real currents in the ocean and the currents of tradition in an effort to define her identity.*

A Spell of Kona Weather

For a couple of months after my sister Lulu ran Henry Hanabusa's '49 DeSoto into the tree at the bottom of Dead Man's Slide, she had to go to Doc McAllister's once a week to get the glass picked out of her face. Every Saturday morning, after she came home from the hospital, I walked her to his surgery in the big white house across the road, and then stood with my eyes shut, squeezing her hand, as he picked the slivers out with a pair of pointed stainless steel tweezers.

The accident had happened in April, the night she found out that Henry's son Jimmy had been killed in Vietnam. Jimmy and she had been going together since their senior year in high school, and his mother had always had about as much use for Lulu as our grandmother had for him. At any rate, Lulu didn't get the news of his death till nearly a week later when she overheard a couple of customers gossiping during her shift at Grandmother's store. That night, after she'd finished work, she stole over to the Hanabusa house and hot-wired Jimmy's father's DeSoto. She told me later that she and Jimmy had spent almost every minute of his last R and R[1] working on that damn thing, and according to her calculations of time put in, it was more hers than anyone else's. After she got it started, she drove to the top of Dead Man's Slide, turned off the ignition, and let out the brake. For a couple of seconds, she said, she had the highest high she'd ever had.

On the day when Lulu's bandages came off, Grandmother locked up the grocery and accompanied us to Doc's for the first and last time. Dressed all in black, with her black-dyed hair pulled tightly into a bun, she looked like she was going to someone's

---

1. rest and relaxation

funeral. When my sister emerged from the examining room, the old lady took in the damage with that measuring gaze of hers. Lulu had never been a beauty, but she had had a kind of vividness that almost made you think she was—with her brown skin, and black hair, and large dark eyes. Now, much of her face was still badly bruised. There were small gashes all over her cheeks and lips, and a row of stitches extended along one side of her jaw to her chin.

"Lucky nothing was broken. Just give it time," Doc said, putting the bandages aside and gently smoothing Lulu's rumpled hair, still as long and glossy as ever—so strangely untouched.

Grandmother got to her feet, then said, "There's nothing to be done. It's too broken to fix."

With that assessment, she abandoned years of trying to put my sister right. Once, when I asked the old lady exactly what she thought was wrong with Lulu, she'd said, "If you were a perfect stranger, would you ever guess that that girl was a granddaughter of mine?" I have always considered it my bad luck that no one could mistake me for anything else. Lulu gets her looks from our father, on the Amalu side of the family. I take after the tight-lipped, narrow-eyed Koyamas. When we were going to school, Lulu was called fast, and it wasn't for her brain. I was a plodder who got good grades. She is "wild" like our mama was. My middle name is Caution.

The one advantage I ever got from all this was that Grandmother left me alone the whole time she was sending my sister off to learn kimono wearing, or tea pouring, or pigeon-toed walking at the deportment classes sponsored by the Buddhist Mission's Ladies Auxiliary. If this reform program worked, Grandmother had believed, she could eventually hook Lulu up with some Nice Young Man, like Clyde Sakamoto, who had recently inherited his father's hardware business, or Mrs. Kobayashi's cousin's friend's son who was opening a dermatology practice in the resort town nearby. According to Grandmother's standards, Jimmy did not qualify as a Nice Young Man. He belonged to another category called Bad Influences. I never had anything against him, though. It seemed Lulu had found something in him that she'd always been looking for.

Before Lulu met Jimmy, she used to drive me crazy with her talk about finding our mama. Sometimes, when she got fed up with Grandmother's meddling, she'd do more than talk, she'd run away, then Grandmother would call in the authorities to haul her back. Once, to teach Lulu a lesson, the old lady even had her put in the Girl's Detention Home over at the county seat. For a while, all that stopped when my sister was with Jimmy.

Personally, I can't say I ever understood Lulu's obsession with Mama, especially since I can't remember a thing. Papa died when I was just a few years old, and our mother took off for California not long after. As the old saying goes, out of sight, out of mind; that's pretty much how it's been with me.

Lulu is only two years older than I am and can't claim much more of a memory. Still, while we were growing up, she tried to convince me that grief had driven Mama away, and that she'd send for us once she was feeling herself again. But when our mother went off, she left everything, except the five thousand dollars from our father's insurance policy, behind with our grandmother—a sure sign, I'd decided when I was old enough to figure things out, that she'd never intended to return. Besides, if someone ups and leaves for sixteen years and you don't hear anything from them except an occasional store-bought greeting with no return address, you figure they're trying to tell you something, and it isn't Dying to See You, Please Come Soon. For the last five years or so, we haven't heard a single word.

With Jimmy's death and then the accident, I was afraid that the old craziness would start up again. But Lulu seemed to have left all that behind. After her visits to Doc's had ended, and her face had started returning to normal, she began going for long swims out in the bay. Though she hadn't gotten her old looks back, she wasn't exactly at a loss. Several times, I saw her with a white guy. I saw him running after her on the sand, catching her, brushing back her hair with his hands. You could tell by the way he moved that he was older than the surfers who usually hang out at the beach, and there was something familiar about him, though I'd never gotten close enough to find out what.

Then, a couple of weeks ago, Lulu asked me to go with her. There's almost nothing I hate worse than ocean swimming—with the sting of salt in your eyes and the live feel of the water. But I know that Lulu knows that about me, so I make it a point never to refuse her invitations. That day, I followed her into the surf where it broke high up on the beach and swirled around our legs, pulling us deeper and deeper until the ocean bottom suddenly dropped off into nothing. Beneath the surface, I felt the current pulling at me, and fear tightened my chest. We swam out to the raft about a hundred yards from shore and stayed there talking awhile before turning back.

She told me about the man I'd seen her with. "It isn't like it was with Jimmy," she said. "But after his divorce, we'll move to the West Coast, and maybe I can even get one of those plastic surgeons there to fix my face."

I said, "You mean he's *married*? How do you know he's going to leave his wife?"

"I just know," she answered, and smiled dreamily.

"But did he actually come out and say so?" I demanded.

She snapped, "Not in so many words. You've got to read between the lines." She sat up and put her legs in the water. "Annie, do you know what your problem is? You've got no imagination."

"And maybe you have too much of one," I said. But she was already swimming back toward shore.

After that day, she didn't bring up the subject again, though I continued to go with her on her swims. Each time we swam farther and farther, until one afternoon we reached the buoy at the center of the bay. The currents were stronger there, and ran deeper, and if you fitted yourself into the wrong channel by mistake, if you went out between tides, you could be swept into the open sea. As I stroked out toward the buoy, I fought down the voice in my head screaming to turn back.

Then, a couple of days ago, she did not turn around. I stopped and clung to the buoy as it bobbed up and down, and I watched her moving, strong and smooth, away from me. When I could hardly see her anymore, I turned and headed for the beach, now more afraid of the ocean than of Lulu.

She took a long time swimming back, and stumbled out of the surf, nearly falling. When she saw me watching her, she broke into a run. She gasped, "Annie, you chicken. I turned to look for you, and you weren't there."

As she sat catching her breath, I asked, "You been seeing that guy?"

Lulu laughed. "Sure have. He's crazy about me." She looked out over the water. "But not crazy enough to ditch his wife."

Around us, in the gathering dark, the afternoon had turned to lead. The sky and the sea had become the same dull shade of gray, and you couldn't tell where one began and the other ended.

"So, aren't you going to say, 'I told you so'?" she finally said. I looked down and began digging at the sand with a stick. She tossed back her hair. "Who needs him anyway?" She gave me a sly, triumphant look. "This morning I got a letter from Mama. She's moved to Oregon, and she wants me to join her."

I began to protest, but I looked at her face just then and stopped. Instead, I said, "What are you going to do for a plane ticket?"

She gave me a pitying look. "Poor Annie," she said. "Always the businesswoman."

Yesterday morning, when Lulu was supposed to be working at the store, she emptied the cash register. Grandmother put Sheriff Kanoi on her, and he found her a few hours later, full of vodka and 7-Up, at the La Hula Rhumba Bar and Grill. After he'd brought her back and I'd put her to bed upstairs, the old lady and I sat outside on the front steps with sodas.

Grandmother swallowed the last of her root beer and set down the bottle. "If that girl doesn't get hold of herself, she's going to end up in a crazy house, just like your mama."

When she said that, she caught me off balance the way she and Lulu are always so good at; and, for a second, I couldn't believe I'd heard what I did. "What're you talking about?" I finally said. "Mama's in Oregon."

She stood and started up the steps. "That's just another of your sister's stories."

I knew it was, but I wasn't admitting anything. "What about California?" I cried. "She sent us birthday cards. That wasn't a story."

Grandmother turned back toward me, then said, "No, she was in California all right. Still is. But what do you suppose she's been doing there? She went nuts after your father died; that man had such a hold on her, I never understood it." She sighed. "From what I've heard, they shot her brain full of electricity a few years back, and she hasn't done much letter writing since."

I was so stunned at first, I couldn't move. Then I threw my soda at her. She ducked as it went past, and the bottle crashed against the wall and broke, spewing root beer across the porch.

Grandmother stepped around the puddles of soda and broken glass. "You be sure and clean up that mess," she called over her shoulder as she pushed open the door to the grocery and went inside.

Upstairs, the screen door slammed, and there was the sound of footsteps on the stairs. I knew that Lulu must have heard.

"Lulu!" I called as she headed down the road to the beach. "Where're you headed?" She began walking even faster in the direction of the water. I could see the old lady at the back of the store, closing up the register, but I didn't say anything, and took off after my sister.

When I got to the beach, it was deserted, and the tide was going out. "Lulu!" I shouted again, but she ignored me. I was still feeling tired from the previous day's swim, and shouting only used up breath.

The sand pulled at my legs. My chest burned. I stumbled and nearly fell, but I was gaining on her. She was so close—just ahead, at the edge of the water. Oh, please, I thought, please let me reach her before we have to start swimming. The waves fanned out across the sand, pulling at my ankles. Lulu was about ten feet away. Then, suddenly, she seemed to drop off the edge of the world. I saw her head bobbing above the water, and I knew I had to go in too. I waded in, feeling sand under my feet, and sand, and sand, then nothing. The ocean was unbearably alive around me, the pull of the current strong. I swam toward Lulu, closed on her, reached, and missed. The movement disrupted the rhythm of our strokes. We flailed around for a little, trying to pick it up again.

"Go back," she gasped. I reached for her, and she repeated, "Go back."

I reached a third time and got her. She struggled. We both went under. She stopped fighting. We were almost at the raft; then we were there. We pulled ourselves onto it and lay, panting, with our heads on our arms. For a long time we were too spent to talk. When we'd recovered a little, she said she'd return with me; maybe she knew I wouldn't make it if I had to pull her in.

We swam across the current to get back to shore and crawled out onto the beach. As we rested, side by side, I kept remembering how it was when we were kids—the way she'd marched straight into things, while I tagged along. "Are you sure, Lulu? Is it safe?" But I'd followed, afraid of what lay ahead—the top branch of the mango tree in the graveyard, Dead Man's Slide in the dark, the deep water out beyond the buoy—but more afraid to be left behind.

I reached over and touched her face with my fingers. I could still feel the hard lumps under her skin where the fragments of glass sometimes came poking through. She opened her eyes and smiled. "I bet I could have made it clear to the other side," she said.

During the night the wind shifted to the southeast, and the Kona[2] weather moved in. Now the wet, still air presses close, heavy with the threat of rain. My sister has stayed upstairs and slept all day. Whenever I look at my grandmother's face or hear her voice, I think of the pistols I was once in a glass cabinet at the Sakamoto Hardware, and I imagine picking one of them up in my hand, and feeling the weight of it, and slowly easing the trigger back.

"It's better if Lulu goes away for a little while," Grandmother says from across the store. Her angular shape pokes out from behind the cash register—her black dress, blacker than the shadows around her. "Doc McAllister's told me he knows a place where they will give her proper care."

You mean, like they did to Mama? I want to say. Instead, I pick up a rag and begin dusting the jars of colored puffed rice, preserved plums, and dried cuttlefish lined up on tiers across from where she's sitting. Beads of moisture drop from my forehead onto the heavy glass lids.

Grandmother finishes counting out the cash in the register, and slips it into a bank bag. "There's nothing more to be done," she says.

Upstairs, Lulu has wakened and is moving around. It is the sound I have been listening for. "You finished counting the money?" I ask, a little too loudly. The screen door bangs softly, as if a breeze is pushing at it, but there is no breeze. There is the sound of footsteps on the stairs.

Grandmother is halfway to the door, then turns. "You saw me," she says. "Do you need glasses?" The footsteps move across the drive and out into the road.

I say, "You're right. I forgot. Shall I close up now?"

"There's no need to shout." The old lady waves impatiently, muttering, "Do what you like," and lets herself out.

When she is gone, I switch off the lights and sit for a while, listening.

---

2.   on big island of Hawai'i

Fae Myenne Ng

(b. 1956)

Fae Myenne Ng was born in San Francisco. The short story reprinted here was first published in **Harper's** *in 1989 and later was added as a chapter in her first novel,* **Bone** *(1993). In* **Bone** *one almost needs to be Chinese American to know and to recognize and to appreciate the feeling, the texture, the setting, the language, the characters, the time, and the setting. The latter is San Francisco's Chinatown in the early seventies, a community still showing the vestiges of a bachelor society created in part by restrictive immigration and anti-miscegenation laws. Ng's Chinatown is a Chinese American community as much as Little Italy is an Italian American community. In other words, the children for the most part are second- or third-generation American-born Chinese—born to Chinese American parents who are either second-generation or who have been in America long enough to be considered second-generation. In spite of being in America "longtime," the presence of the Immigration and Naturalization Service and its agents interrogations remain in the immigrant generation's recent memory and caused one of Ng's characters to note, "In this country, paper is more precious than blood."*

Ng's novel features a generation of older Chinese Americans with names like Croney, Dulcie, Leon, and Chester, a generation that lived a second-class citizenship in America. Legal and social boundaries kept them working as waiters, cooks, seamstresses, and laundrymen inside of Chinatown. The American-born generation of the fifties, as represented by the novel's narrator, Leila Fu, is the lucky generation. They have more freedom than their parents—they go to college and can live outside of Chinatown. In short, as Leila notes, they have a choice because their American citizenship is a fact of birth.

> *Mah and Leon forced themselves to live through the humiliation in this country so that we could have it better. We know so little of the old country. We repeat the names of grandfathers and uncles, but they have always been strangers to us.*

Chinese American readers will see a familiar pattern and hear a voice and dialect that is truly Chinese American. Only three other novels ring this true: Louis Chu's **Eat A Bowl of Tea***, Frank Chin's* **Donald Pink***, and (perhaps stretching it a bit), British writer Timothy Mo's* **Sour Sweet***, which is set in London's Chinatown.* **Bone** *is not about the exterior of San Francisco's Chinatown, the neon lights and tourist shops, but rather an interior organic sensibility of what once was.*

Backdaire

Mah left early to get her hair electrified at Duckie's mom's. On her way out she tapped on my door. "Get up Leila!" she said. "Leon's coming home today. Clear a space in the bathroom. And vacuum! Don't forget under the couch." The door clicked shut. Like the journeys of the eight holy immortals,[1] Leon Leong's comings and goings ordered Mah's life.

Leon's work as a merchant seaman was a good thing because it kept him away for months at a time. She learned from experience; my father was a wolf. He married her quickly and just as quickly he left her. Now she thought it was better to let a man into her life slowly.

Leon Leong was her second husband, the one she married for the green card. It was no secret; even Leon knew that was why she said yes. He didn't care; he knew his card was good forever.

This voyage was special; the S.S. *Independent* docked two days in Melbourne[2] and Leon had planned to look up the father I'd never seen: Lyman Foo. This time I was as nervous as Mah was about Leon's return.

My boyfriend and I were still in bed. I listened to Mah's footsteps going down the rickety steps below our apartment window, then rolled over and hugged Mason; there was a faint metal smell in his hair. Mason is a mechanic—a really good one—foreign cars only.

"Huh?" Mason stirred. "What?"

Mason doesn't speak Chinese, so I translated. "She just gave me a list of things to do, getting-ready-for-Leon stuff." Then I whispered, "And she said not to sleep the morning away with you."

"Nah." He gave a laugh. "She likes me now. I can tell."

At first, Mah didn't like Mason staying over, so I made him leave in the middle of the night. He was working on the Karmann Ghia[3] then, and it made such a racket starting up that Mah finally gave in. She said, "Better for the neighbors to see the car in the morning and wonder, than for them to look out the window in the middle of the night and know."

The first time Mason came over, I waited for him downstairs. It was night and the street lamp on Pacific poured a sliver of light into Salmon Alley. His white car glistened, clean as the inside of a cut turnip.

There's an old, blue sign at the bottom of our steps: #2-4-6 UPDAIRE. You can't miss it, and it was the first thing Mason saw. He pointed at the sign with his chin. Then he threw his head back and laughed.

"D-A-I-R-E?" He looked at me and laughed again.

I shrugged. *So?* I thought. It was my address; it was home, where I lived.

---

1.   Eight Chinese immortals represent conditions in life—poverty, wealth, aristocracy, plebianism, age, youth, masculinity and feminity
2.   Australia
3.   a car made by Volkswagen

Mason is my first born-here boyfriend. The others were all born-theres, like me. They didn't feel comfortable outside of Chinatown; they didn't even much like doing things outside the family. Mason works in the Mission,[4] and he takes me out to eat there sometimes. He knows what to order; his last girlfriend was Mexican. Mason likes to ski and we go to Tahoe as much as we can. He doesn't care if he's the only Chinese guy on the expert runs; he knows he's good enough. What surprises me is that he never gambles. "It's too Chinesey," he says. There's that about him though; he says stuff in that half-embarrassed tone.

When we were getting to know each other, I liked that we did things on our own, so I didn't ask about his family. But then I started to wonder, didn't they care about him? Didn't he like me enough to introduce me to them?

I asked Mimi Fang, and she told me what she heard: "Real messed-up family, one sister married a white guy and another overdosed on Q's."[5]

"Hey," Mason said now, nudging me. "Looks like she's in a good mood today, maybe you could tell her, huh?"

Mason was moving into his own place in the Mission and he wanted me to move in with him. I wanted to, but I didn't know how Mah would take it.

"Maybe," I said. I didn't know how to tell her. One thing I liked about Mason: he *said* things. I mean, I thought about a lot of things, but I never actually *said* them. Out loud. I turned away from him, gave a kick under the covers to show my irritation.

"Just don't take too long, that's all," he said.

I knew why I was putting it off; I was waiting for Leon too. I expected him to bring back something from this meeting with my father—a word, a picture, an expression—something that would unlock me from Mah, this alley, Chinatown.

"I can't help it, I just feel like I owe her. It's always been just me and her."

Mason's voice was soft. "Lei, she's got Leon now."

When I was seven, Mah took me out for dim sum[6] and told me about Leon Leong.

"He'll make a suitable husband," she said. "One, he's got his papers; two, he works at sea. He'll be away a lot. It'll be just you and me. Like now. I won't have to work so hard. We can take it easy, and it'll be just like the Hong Kong days."

"*Fuun!*[7] *Fuun!* Shrimp, pork, beef!" The waitress called out the items on her cart in a bored singsong. Mah waved the waitress down and asked for a plate of shrimp and beef.

I wasn't surprised about Leon Leong. I knew Mah was looking for a husband. Jimmy Lowe, the presser at the factory, brought her breakfast sweets. There was Tex,

---

4.   Mission Street in San Francisco
5.   quualudes, tranquilizers
6.   small, usually steamed, lunch food
7.   wide rice noodles

the day manager at Silver Palace, and Stephen, with his own electronics company. After Leon, Mah liked Victor, the contractor, second best—he was a spender, but not a talker. Money is a good thing, Mah said, but so is a pretty mouth and a heady compliment.

"Why him?" I said.

"He asked me." Mah cut a piece of *fuun* with her chopsticks. "What do you think?"

I poured soy over my *fuun,* swirled it around on my plate, then put the whole sloppy piece in my mouth. I'd seen him only a few times, so I didn't know what to say. I chewed. "Well," I said, "he's kinda bald up there."

Mah laughed. "You know the saying, 'Ten bald men and nine are rich.'"

Mah and Leon were married in Reno. I was their witness. Leon's cousin Alvin was service manager at Harrah's and booked the Pink Room at a discount. Mah finished our dresses the night before. Pink lace over pink satin, a princess neckline, cap sleeves, an Empire waist, and a big satin bow in the back.

I coached Mah about the ceremony. "The man'll look up at you after saying a lot of stuff. Just say, 'I do.' And nod." But when she said it in the justice's office, her accent made it sound like a question. "I do?"

Afterwards we gambled. Mah and I played the slot machines in between watching Leon play poker. A bus from Chinatown arrived bringing some of Mah's friends from the sewing factory. They had coupons for free coffee and they invited Mah, so I walked around looking into shops. I was fingering a suede shoulder bag when Leon came up from behind.

"Do you want it?" he asked.

This is what I'd worried about all through the bus ride up here: what to call him after they married. I expected Mah to give me directions, but she didn't, and now Leon and I were alone, and I just stared at the bag.

"Let me but it," he said.

I shrugged. I drew my finger back and forth on the suede, making lines.

He handed me two twenties and nodded toward the register. "Go on." He smiled. "Pay the lady. It's a souvenir."

When we stepped out of the store, I turned and said thanks, but avoided looking at him.

"No need." He tapped my shoulder lightly almost like he was saying thanks.

The leather smell was strong. I looked at the bag and wondered if the braided straps and long suede fringe were me. Would I ever use this? Was it too American? I worried that I was wasting his money. I looked straight at him and asked, "What do I call you now?"

He shrugged. "Call me Leon … or call me L. That's what they call me on the ships."

Lyman Foo, my real father, was called many things. In the villages, he was known as the FaFa Prince—a garden stroller, a flower picker.

Mah said, "In those days, we didn't have a choice. I was young and he picked me."

Mah said he told her. "I don't need a match-maker; I don't need a pointer or a list. I could have picked you blind. You don't belong on these muddy roads, in these water-carrying villages. Come with me, let's go! To fast, fast Hong Kong."

"A few good years," Mah said, "… ate well, dressed well. There was a motorcar."

"But like a blink," Mah cried, "he lost it all, lost it fast, slapping tiles on a three-night mah-jongg run."

After that she called him Talk Big Words. He took his stories about gold and the easy life down to the docks, into the bars, the gambling dens, and whorehouses. The lame ones, the beardless boys, the gamblers—they all listened. Lyman Foo encouraged the dreamers. He was a crimp—a coolie broker.

"A few years is all I need," he promised. Australia was the new gold mountain, every coolie's dream.

I'll send for you, he said.

Mah believed; she thought the child growing in her belly was insurance.

But I wasn't a son and no tickets came in the mail.

Every spring Mah sent him my picture to remind him: *This daughter is yours, this daughter is growing.* She cut my hair, bought me a new dress, and told me to smile for him.

I've never seen him—when I say never seen, I'm thinking of the Chinese term for "seen his face." I've seen his picture and read his letters. I know him by the name he used in letters, "Your father, Foo Lyman."

As a child, I traced over his characters: *Are you my good daughter? Would you make me proud?*

Mah saved every one of his letters and studied them, turned his phrases inside out. She read them out loud and asked, "What does it sound like to you? Does he want to come back?"

I grew up waiting on the mail, too, collecting stamps; Australia was the biggest part of my collection. I held the miniature pictures in my palm: the big rock, the koalas, Queen Elizabeth. The scalloped edges pieced together the faint world he lived in, and the more I had, the more of him I felt I owned.

His money orders shrunk first in figures and then in frequency, until Mah said they were only eggs, rotten ones.

In his last letter, his message fit into one square corner. Each stroke was bold, magnified: *Leila, Don't blame me.*

Mah's eyes dimmed first from crying and then from the sweat jobs: hemming skirts, sewing collar buttons, bead-embroidering dragons and phoenixes onto wedding cheongsams.[8] She was inconsolable. She went to bed with questions: Tell me *how* to live? *How* to face life? *How* to see people? She woke with curses: Turtle! Salted Egg! Drunk-head!

Mah called long-distance to her brother in San Francisco. She held the black mouthpiece with two hands and shouted, "Ai! Ai! Aiyah!" Her cries told the whole story: the runaway husband, the child in school, the red in her face. Her heavy, heavy face. Her child's matted hair. She didn't hint, she threatened. "Death. I will jump into the harbor. Take this child, this no-good child." Her brother sent money, and in three months, we were in San Francisco.

When we arrived, the factory was sewing woolen coats. "Flipped," her brother explained. "We work the summer fabrics in the winter and the winter fabrics in the summer." All summer the fans whirled, thick with dust.

From then on, whenever anyone mentioned Lyman Foo, Mah spat out three names: Gambler. Drunk. Corpse.

Just before noon, Mah came home from Duckie's mom's smelling like the perfume section of Woolworth's. Mason and I were still having coffee.

"Nice perm, Mrs. Leong," Mason said.

"Really? My face not too round?"

"No," Mason said. "You look like Miss Chinatown."

Mah laughed. "Bad boy! Talk pretty!"

After Mason left, I helped Mah dress for Leon's welcome-home dinner. She'd made three new outfits, but now she couldn't decide which one to wear: the gabardine pantsuit, the pink wool coatdress, or the A-line dress with the lace bib. She stood on the bed and looked at herself in the wide mirror of the dresser. She turned back and forth, pressing down on the pocket flaps, pulling at the pant seams. "My body's changed, nothing fits like before," she said.

"That looks okay," I said. I was sitting on the bed and could see myself in the mirror. "You know, Mason gave me a couple of driving lessons."

"Oh yeah?" she said. "It's always good to have a skill."

"Yesterday I parked on Broadway, you know, on the steep side near Taylor," I said.

---

8.   long Chinese dress with a high collar

She frowned. "Does this look too tight?" She turned sideways, sucked in, one hand pushed down on her belly.

I went over and tugged at the seams. "Maybe just a little," I said.

"You shouldn't sleep with him so much," she said.

I looked at her but didn't say anything.

She scrunched up her nose and scowled into the mirror. "My stomach sticks out too much. I'm going to try on the dress." She climbed off the bed.

"It's not *that* bad." I smoothed the footprints out of the bedspread.

"You never know. Mason's good now, but he could change," she said.

"He's not like that." My voice sounded harsh.

"Oh." Her mouth made that round O shape that meant she was embarrassed. "Tomorrow, I'm going to start exercising," she said. She peeled the waistband over her belly.

I started at the top of her head. "You know Leon saw my father this trip," I said.

Her legs stopped moving from side to side and I saw the pink of her kneecaps. She looked up at me.

"What do you think of him, my father, now?"

"Waste of time," she muttered.

"Well," I said, looking away, "don't you ever think about him?"

"Why should I? That was so long ago." She took the dress off the hanger, bunched it up in her fists, and slipped it over her head.

I folded her pants. "Mah," I said, looking up, "I'm going to move to the Mission with Mason."

Her head slowly emerged from the folds of pink wool. She looked at me in the mirror. It was quiet for a long time. I thought, *I look like her.* The shape of the face, the single fold above the eye, the smallish round mouth. I wondered: Will I be like her? Will I marry like her?

She turned around, away from me. The unzipped dress showed her back, still straight; her skin was still smooth. I went over to zip her up, and when she turned around, I said, "Wear this, you look great."

"No Chinese there, you know," she said.

"There are some," I said.

"Why not get married?" she asked. She still wouldn't look at me.

"I'll see how it goes," I said. For a minute I expected the worst, that she'd slap me, hit me with a hanger, call me names.

"Give it a test." She nodded and then muttered, almost to herself, "Remember to have a way out."

At Tao-Tao's, we sat under Genthe's photo of two little girls walking down an alley; they're holding hands, looking back. I had other favorites: the grocer with the beckoning smile, the cobbler, the balloon peddler. We ordered enough to invite the spirits of the old-timers to join us. The food came steaming: clams with black beans, lobster, fresh sea bass, and oysters, salt-and-pepper prawns, and soft-shelled crabs. Our hands were busy, messy from cracking the shells. I let Leon eat his first bowl of rice in peace. When Mah handed him his second bowl, I refilled his tea and asked him, "What did he look like? My father. You saw him, didn't you?"

Leon put an oyster in his mouth. "Dark," he said.

"Dark? Like how?" I asked.

"Like a coolie,"[9] Mason said.

Leon looked at Mason. "Hey, you know that word?"

"Sure," Mason shrugged.

Leon grinned. "From the sun, like a dried plum."

"I thought he was some big developer," I said. "A man inside, behind a desk, you know?"

Mah muttered something as she cracked open a clamshell.

"That's people talking." Leon said.

I thought about it. "So, what'd you talk about?"

"Not much. I mentioned the situation here."

"Well?" I waited. "What exactly did you say?"

"I told him about your mah and me." Leon looked over at Mah, who was busy with a crab claw.

"Well? What did he say?" I couldn't stand it; Leon was so slow sometimes, it killed me. I wanted more. I gave my chopsticks three hard taps on the tabletop. Mah looked up, scowling.

"Easy." Mason put his hand on my leg. I sat back. He peeled a prawn and put it on my plate and I popped the whole thing into my mouth.

"What about me? Did he ask about me?"

"Sure," Leon said. "I told him that you'd finished school, stuff like that." He looked at Mah.

She gave him some fish. "Good piece," she said.

I wasn't satisfied. "How'd it end?"

"End?" He put the morsel in his mouth. "What else? Shook hands, said goodbye, long life and good luck."

---

9. Chinese worker in nineteenth century

I listened to us eating—Mah and Leon, Mason and me—the soft suck of the rice in our mouths, the click of the chopsticks against the bowls. These sounds were comfortable, and for a moment, I was tempted to fall back into the easiness of being Mah's daughter, of letting her be my whole life.

When Mah and Leon were first married, I was always surprised when he came home from his voyages. I expected him to change at sea—to come back a different man—I think I even expected him to come back as my father. But it was always Leon Leong, in his starched whites, his burnt-sugar tan, his S.S. *Independent* laundry sack full of presents. And I finally saw what Mason had been saying: Mah loved Leon.

All my things fit into the back of Mason's cousin's Volvo. The last thing I saw as Mason backed out of the alley was the old, blue sign, #2-4-6 UPDAIRE. No one's ever corrected it; somebody repaints it every year because, like the photos at Tao-Tao's, the ghosts of the old-timers hang over us, wanting us to look back, to remember.

I was reassured; I knew what I kept in my heart would last. So I wasn't worried when I turned that corner, leaving the blue sign, Salmon Alley, Mah and Leon—everything—backdaire.

Carol Roh-Spaulding

(b. 1962)

Carol Roh-Spaulding was born in 1962 in Oakland, California. Her stories explore issues of biraciality, specifically Korean Americans and Anglo-Americans in which conflicts of identity is perhaps best defined in her words as "ethnic disequilibrium." As to the tradition that work might belong to Carol Roh-Spaulding states,

> *I have a feeling that literature with themes of the mixings and mergings of bloods and cultures in America will take on greater importance, due to the sheer demographics of the coming century and to the need for ethnic paradigms that can adapt to such boundary crossings. Meanwhile, what we mean when we say "multicultural" will be continually debated and redefined.*

Her fiction has appeared in the **Beloit Fiction Journal**, **Ploughshares**, *and in the* **Pushcart Annual XVI**. *She is presently working on a doctorate in American ethnic literature at the University of Iowa.*

Waiting for Mr. Kim

When Gracie Kang's elder twin sisters reached the age of eighteen, they went down to the Alameda County Shipyards and got jobs piecing battleships together for the U.S. Navy. This was the place to find a husband in 1945, if a girl was doing her own looking. They were Americans, after all, and they were of age. Her sisters caught the bus down to the waterfront every day and brought home their paychecks every two weeks. At night, they went out with their girlfriends, meeting boys at the cinema or the drugstore, as long as it was outside of Chinatown.

Gracie's parents would never have thought it was husbands they were after. Girls didn't choose what they were given. But the end of the war distracted everybody. While Mr. Kang tried to keep up with the papers and Mrs. Kang tried to keep up with the laundry, Sung-Sook slipped away one day with a black welder enrolled in the police academy and Sung-Ohk took off with a Chinatown nightclub singer from L.A. with a sister in the movies.

Escaped. Gracie had watched from the doorway that morning as Sung-Sook pulled on her good slip in front of the vanity, lifted her hair, breathed in long and slow. Her eyes came open, she saw Gracie's reflection. "Comeer," she said, "You never say goodbye." She kissed Gracie between the eyes. Gracie had only shrugged: "See you." Then Sung-Ohk from the bathroom: "This family runs a laundry, so where's all the goddamn towels?"

When the girls didn't come home, the lipstick and rouge wiped off their faces, to fold the four o'clock sheets, she understood what was what. On the vanity in the girls' room she found a white paper bell with sugar sprinkles. In silver letters, it read:

Call Today!
Marry Today!
Your Wedding! Your Way!
Eighteen or Over?
We Won't Say Nay!
(May Borrow Veil And Bouquet)

As simple as having your hair done. Gracie sat at the vanity, thinking of the thousand spirits of the household her mother was always ticking off like a grocery list—spirit of the lamp, the clock, the ashtray. Spirit in the seat of your chair. Spirit of the stove, the closet, the broom, the shoes. Spirit of the breeze in the room, the Frigidaire. Gracie had always been willing to believe in them; she only needed something substantial to go on. Now, in her sisters' room, she felt that the spirits had been there, had moved on, to other inhabited rooms.

Those girls had escaped Thursday evenings with the old *chong-gaks*,[1] who waited effortlessly for her father to give the girls away. No more sitting, knees together, in white blouses and circle skirts, with gritted smiles. Now Gracie would sit, the only girl, while her father made chitchat with Mr. Han and Mr. Kim. Number three daughter, much younger, the dutiful one, wouldn't run away. If her mother had had the say, the girls would have given their parents grandchildren by now. But she didn't have the say, and her father smiled his pleasant, slightly anxious smile at the *chong-gaks* and never ever brought up payment.

He was the one paying now. No one got dinner that night. Pots flew, plates rattled in the cabinets, the stove rumbled in the corner, pictures slid, clanked, tinkled. "Now we'll have a nigger for a grandson and a chink for a son-in-law, Mr. Kang!" her mother shouted. She cursed Korean, but had a gift for American slurs, translating the letter found taped to the laundry boiler into the horrors of marrying for love.

Gracie and Little Gene pressed themselves against the wall, squeezed around the Frigidaire, sidled to the staircase. They sat and backed up one step at a time, away from the stabs and swishes of the broom. "Or didn't you want Korean grandchildren, Mr. Kang? You're the one who let them fall into American love. Could I help it there aren't any good *chong-gaks* around? Thought we'd pack the girls off to Hawaii where the young ones are? Ha. I'd like to see the missionaries pay for that!"

---

1. bachelors

Their father came into view below. Hurried, but with his usual dignity, he ducked and swerved as necessary. Silently, solemnly, he made for the closet, opened the door, and stepped in among the coats. The blows from first the bristled then the butted end of the broom came down upon the door.

Little Gene whispered, "I'm going outside."

"Fine," Gracie told him. "If you can make it to the door."

"Think I can't manage the window? I land in the trash bins pretty soft!"

Gracie told him, "Bring me back a cigarette, then," and he left her there. A year younger than she and not very big for thirteen he was still number one son. Gracie stuck her fingers in her mouth all the way to the knuckle, clamped down hard.

She chopped cabbage, scrubbed the bathhouses, washed and pressed and folded linen and laundry, dreaming up lives for her sisters. From their talk and their magazines, she knew how it should go. Sung-Sook stretched out by the pool in a leopard-print bathing suit with pointy bra cups and sipped colored drinks from thin glasses, leaving a pink surprise of lips at the rim. Somebody else served them, fetched them, cleaned them. Her husband shot cardboard men through the heart and came home to barbecue T-bones. Every night they held hands at the double feature. Sung-Ohk slipped into a tight Chinese-doll dress and jeweled cat-eyes, sang to smoky crowds of white people from out of town. Her lips grazed the mike as she whispered, "Thank you, kind people, thank you." In the second act, her husband, in a tux dipped her, spun her, with slant-eyed-Gene-Kelly-opium flair. As the white people craned their necks and saw that Oriental women could have good legs.

They left Gracie and her mother with all the work. At first, her father tried to help out. He locked up the barbershop at lunch, crossed the street, passed through the kitchen, and stepped into Hell, as they called it. But her mother snapped down the pants press when she saw him and from a blur of steam shouted, "Fool for love! I'm warning you to get out of here, Mr. Kang!"

She bowed her head at the market now. She had stopped going to church. Lost face, it was called. And there was the worry of it. No one knew these men who took the girls away. Maybe one was an opium dealer and the other was a pimp. Maybe those girls were in for big disappointment, even danger. Her father twisted his hands, helpless and silent in the evenings. Her mother clanked the dishes into the sink, banged the washers shut, punched the buttons with her fists, helpless, too.

It was true he was a fool for love, as far as Gracie could tell. Her mother slapped at his hands when he came up behind her at the chopping board to kiss her hair— pretty brave, considering that knife. When her mother tried to walk behind him in the street, he stopped and tried to take her hand. Gracie and her mother were always nearly missing buses because she'd say, "Go on, Mr. Kang. We're coming," and they'd stay behind as she cleaned out her purse or took forever with her coat, just to have it the way she had learned it, her husband a few paces ahead, women behind. Maybe the girls would never have gotten away if he'd been firm about marriage, strict about love.

Where her parents were from, shamans could chase out the demon spirits from dogs, cows, rooms, people. Maybe her father had had the fool chased out of him, because when Thursday came around, he sat in the good chair with the Bible open on his knees, and Gracie sat beside him, waiting. Life was going to go on without her sisters. Her life. Gracie watched her father for lingering signs of foolishness. Above the donated piano, the cuckoo in the clock popped out seven times. As always, her father looked up with a satisfied air. He loved that bird. Her mother believed there was a spirit in the wooden box. The spirit was saying it was time.

Little Gene was free in the streets with that gang of Chinese boys. She waited for her cigarette and his stories—right now, he might be breaking into the high school, popping open the Coca-Cola machine, busting up some lockers. There weren't any Jap boys left to beat up on, and they stayed away from the mostly black neighborhoods or they'd get beat up themselves. Gracie sat with her hands clasped at her knees, worrying about him, admiring him a little.

First came the tap-tap of the missionary ladies from the United Methodist Church. Their hats looked like squat bird's nests through the crushed ice window. Every Thursday, they seemed to have taken such pains with their dresses and hats and shoes, Gracie couldn't think how they had lasted in the mountain villages of Pyongyang[2] province. She had never been there herself, or been to mountains at all, but she knew there were tigers in Pyongyang.

Her father rose and assumed his visitors smile. "Everyone will be too polite to mention the girls, Gracie," he told her. That was the only thing at all he said about them to her.

The ladies stepped in, chins pecking. One bore a frosted cake, the other thrust forward a box of canned goods. American apologies. As though the girls had died, Gracie thought. Her father stiffened, but kept his smile.

"We think it's wonderful about the war," the cake lady began.

"Praise be to God that we've stopped the Japanese," the Spam lady went on. They looked at one another.

"The *Japanese* Japanese," said the second. She paused. "And we are so sorry about your country, Mr. Kang."

"But this is your country now," said the first.

Her father eased them onto more conversational subjects. They smiled, heads tilted, as Gracie pressed out "Greensleeves," "Colonial Days," "Jesus, We Greet Thee,"

---

2.   province in Northwest Korea

on the piano. And at half past the hour, they were up and on their way out, accepting jars of *kimch'i*[3] from her mother with wrinkle-nosed smiles.

The barbershop customers did not come by. Mr. Woo from the bakery and Mr. and Mrs. Lim from the Hunan restaurant stayed away. All the Chinese and Koreans knew about saving face. Except the *chong-gaks*, who knew better, surely, but arrived like clockwork anyway, a black blur and a white blur at the window. They always shuffled their feet elaborately on the doorstep before knocking, and her father used to say, "That's very Korean," to Sung-Sook and Sung-Ohk, who didn't bother to fluff their hair or straighten their blouses for the visitors. They used to moan, "Here come the old goats. Failure One and Failure Two." Her father only shushed them, saying, "Respect, daughters, respect." Gracie saw that he could have done better than that if he really expected the girls to marry these men, but after all, the girls were right. Probably her father could see that. They were failures. No families, even at their age. Little money, odd jobs, wasted lives. A week before, they had been only a couple of nuisances who brought her sticks of Beechnut gum and seemed never to fathom her sisters' hostility. They were that stupid, and now they were back. One Korean girl was as good as any other.

Gracie could actually tolerate Mr. Han. He had been clean and trim in his black suit, pressed shirt, and straight tie every Thursday evening since her sisters had turned sixteen. He was tall, hesitant man with most of his hair, surprisingly good teeth, and little wire glasses so tight over his nose that the lenses steamed up when he was nervous. Everyone knew he had preferred Sung-Ohk, whose kindest remark to him ever was that he looked exactly like the Chinese servant in a Hollywood movie. He always perched on the piano bench as though he didn't mean to stay long, and he mopped his brow when Sung-Ohk glared at him. But he never pulled Gracie onto his lap to kiss her and pat her, and he never, as the girls called it, licked with his eyes.

He left that to Mr. Kim. Mr. Kim in the same white suit, white shirt, white tie, and white shoes which had never really been white, but always the color of pale urine. His teeth were brown from too much tea and sugar and opium. This wasn't her hateful imagination. She had washed his shirts ever since she'd started working. She knew the armpit stains that spread like an infection when she tried to soak them. The hairs and smudges of ash and something like pus in his sheets. She could smell his laundry even before she saw the ticket. His breath stank, too, like herring.

Mr. Kim found everything amusing. "It's been too warm hasn't it, Mr. Kang?" he said by way of greeting. Then he chuckled, "I'm afraid our friend Mr. Han is almost done in by it."

"Yes, let me get you some iced tea," her father announced. "Mrs. Kang!"

---

3.   hot pickled cabbage and other vegetables

Mr. Kim chuckled again at his companion. "Maybe his heart is suffering. Nearly sixty, you know. Poor soul. He's got a few years on me, anyway, haven't you, old man?"

Mr. Han lowered himself on the piano bench. "Yes, it's been too warm, too much for me."

His companion laughed like one above that kind of weakness. Then he said, "And how is Miss Kang? She's looking very well. She seems to be growing."

Gracie hunched her shoulders, looked anywhere but at him.

"Yes, she's growing," her father answered carefully. "She's still a child." The men smiled at each other with a lot of teeth showing, but their eyes were watchful. "Of course, she's a little lonesome nowadays," her father continued. Mr. Kim eyed him, then he seemed to catch on and slapped his knee—good joke. Mr. Han squinted in some sort of pain.

If Mr. Kim hadn't been in America even longer than her father had, with nothing to show for it but a rented room above the barbershop, then he might have been able to say, "What about this one, Mr. Kang? Are you planning to let her get away, too?" But if he'd had something to show for his twenty or so years in America, he wouldn't be sitting in her father's house and she wouldn't be waiting to be his bride.

Then from the piano bench: "Lonesome, Miss Kang?" Everybody looked. Mr. Han blinked, startled at the attention. He quietly repeated, "Have you, too, been lonesome?" Gracie looked down at her hands. Her father was supposed to answer, let him answer. At that moment, her mother entered, head bowed over the tea tray. Gracie could hear the spirit working in the cuckoo clock.

Her father had told her once that he'd picked cotton and grapes with the Mexicans in the Salinas Valley, and it got so hot you could fry meat on the railroad ties. But that was nothing compared to the sticky summers in Pyongyang,[4] where the stench of human manure brought the bile to your throat. That was why he loved Oakland, he said, where the ocean breeze cleaned you out. It reminded him of his childhood visits to Pusan Harbor, when he'd traveled to visit his father who had been forced into service of the Japanese. And it reminded him of the day he sailed back from America for his bride.

Bright days, fresh wind. Gracie imagined the women who had waited for the husbands who had never returned. Those women lived in fear, her mother had said. They were no good to marry if the men didn't come back, or if they did return but had no property, they had no legal status in America and no prospects in Korea. Plenty of the women did away with themselves, or their families sold them as concubines. "You think I'm lying?" she told Gracie. "I waited ten years for him. People didn't believe the letters

---

4.   Southwest tip of Korea

he sent after a while. My family started talking about what to do with me, because I had other sisters waiting to marry, only I was the oldest and they had to get rid of me first!"

Gracie imagined those women, their hands tucked neatly in their bright sleeves, their smooth hair and ancient faces looking out over the water from high rooms. And she thought of Mr. Han gazing from his window out over the alley and between skyscrapers and telephone poles to his glimpse of the San Francisco Bay. Where he was, the sky was black, starless in the city. Where she was, the sun rose, a brisk, hopeful morning.

On a morning like that, Gracie took the sheets and laundry across the street and up to the rented rooms. Usually the *chong-gaks* had coffee and a bun at the bakery and then strolled around the lake, but Gracie always knocked and set the boxes down.

Mr. Han's door inched open under her knuckles. The breeze in the bright room, the sterile light of morning in there, the cord rattling at the blinds. Something invisible crept out from the slit in the door and was with her in the hall.

"Mr. Han? Just your laundry, Mr. Han." Spirits of memory—she and Little Gene climbing onto his knees, reaching into his pockets for malted milk balls or sticks of gum. "Where are *your* children?" they'd asked. "Where is your stove? Where is your sink? Where is your mirror?" Mr. Han had always smiled, as though he were only hiding things they named, could make them appear whenever he wanted.

She pushed the door open, and the spirits of memory mingled with the spirits of longing and desire. The bulb of the bare night light buzzed, like a recollection in a head full of ideas. Mr. Han lay half-on, half-off the bed. One shoe pressed firmly on the floor, as though half of him had somewhere to go. The glasses dangled from the metal bed frame. That was where his head was, pressed against the bars. His eyes were rolled back, huge and amazed, toward the window. And at his throat, a stripe of beaded red, the thin lips of flesh puckering slightly, like the edges of a rose.

Spirits scuttered along the walls, swirled upwards, twisting in their airy, familiar paths. They pressed against the ceiling. They watched her in the corner. His spirit was near, she felt, in the white field of his pillow. Or in the curtains that puffed and lifted at the sill like a girl's skirt in the wind.

Gracie squatted and peered under the bed. The gleam there was a thing she had known all of her life, a razor from the barbershop. Clean, almost no blood, like his throat. She knew it was loss of air, not loss of blood, that did it. She knew because she'd heard about it before. Two or three of the neighborhood Japs had done the same, when they found that everything they thought they owned they no longer had a right to. They'd had three days to sell what they could and go. She didn't know where. She only knew that her father had been able to buy the barbershop and the bathhouse because of it.

Wind swelled in the hall, with the spirits of car horns, telephone wires, shop signs, traffic lights, and a siren, not for him. They were present at the new death—

curious, laughing, implacable. They sucked the door shut. Gracie started. "Leaving now," she announced. "Mr. Han," she whispered to the *chong-gak*. Then she remembered he'd become part of something else, something weightless, invisible, near. She said it louder. "Mr. Han. I'm sorry for you, Mr. Han."

Mr. Kim ate with the Kangs that afternoon, after the ambulances had gone, and again in the evening. His fingers trembled. He lowered his head to the rice, unable to lift it to his mouth, scraping feebly with his chopsticks. Of the death he had one thing to say, which he couldn't stop saying: "I walked alone this morning. Why did I decide to walk alone, of all mornings?"

Mrs. Kang muttered guesses about what to do next, not about the body itself or the police inquiry or who was responsible for his room and his things, but about how best to give peace to the spirit of the *chong-gak*, who might otherwise torment the rest of their days. He didn't have a family of his own to torment. She'd prepared a plate of meat and rice and *kimch'i*, saying, "Where do I *put* this?"

Little Gene, jealous that Gracie had found the body and he hadn't offered, "How 'bout on the sill? Then he can float by whenever. Or in his room? I'll stay in there all night and watch for him." Then he patted his stomach. "Or how 'bout right here?"

"Damn," her mother went on. "I wish now I'd paid more attention to the shamans. But we stayed away from those women unless we needed them. My family was afraid I'd get the call because I was sickly and talked in my sleep, and we have particularly restless ancestors. But I didn't have it in me. Was it food every day for a month or every month for a year? What a mystery. Now we'll have spirits till we all die."

"Girls shouldn't be shamans, anyway," Little Gene announced. "Imagine Gracie chasing spirits away."

Asshole, Gracie mouthed. Little Gene flipped her off. None of the adults understood the sign.

"You don't chase them, honey," Gracie's mother said to her. "You feed them and pay them and talk to them."

"Tell *him*," Gracie answered. "He's the one who brought it up."

"Feed everyone who's here first," Little Gene suggested. Gracie flipped him off in return.

"What's that you're doing with your fingers, Gracie?" he shot back. She put her finger to her lips and pointed at her father. His eyes were closed. He kept them that way, head bowed, lips moving.

"Fine," her mother announced. "Let's do Christian, Mr. Kang. It's simpler, as far as I'm concerned."

Mr. Kim lifted his head from his rice bowl, looking very old.

Her mother eyed him sternly. "Cheaper, too."

That night Gracie lay in her bed by the open window. Where was his spirit now? In heaven, at God's side? Or restlessly feeding on *bulgogi*[5] and turnips in his room? Or somewhere else entirely, or nowhere at all? Please God or Thousand Spirits, she prayed. Let me marry for love. Please say I'm not waiting for Mr. Kim. It's fine with me if I'm a *chun-yo*[6] forever.

They held a small service at the Korean United Methodist Church. Her father stood up and said a little about the hard life of a *chong-gak* in America, the loneliness of these men, the difficulties for Oriental immigrants. Gracie felt proud of him, though he was less convincing about heaven. No one even knew for certain if Mr. Han had converted.

Mr. Kim sat in white beside Gracie. "Thy kingdom come," he murmured, "thy will be done." And he reached out and took her hand, looking straight ahead to her father. His hand was moist. She could smell him.

"And forgive us our trespasses," she prayed.

"As we forgive those who trespass against us," he continued, and he squeezed her hand with the surety of possession, though her fingers slipped in his palm.

Gracie never got to the "amen." Instead, she leaned into his side, tilted her face to his cheek, and brought her lips to his ear. "You dirty old bastard," she whispered. Then she snatched her hand back and kept her head bowed, trembling. She wished she could pray that he would die, too, if it was the only way. From the corner of her eye, she could see Mr. Kim's offended hand held open on his knee. Sweat glistened in the creases of his palm. She would never be able to look into his eyes again. For a moment, pity and disgust swept through her. Then, as the congregation stood, she said her own prayer. It went, Please oh please oh please.

Little Gene stuck his head in the laundry room. "Hey, you! Mrs. Kim!"

Gracie flung a folded pillowcase at him.

"Whew. Step out of that hellhole for a minute. I've got something to show you."

He slid a cigarette from behind his ear and they went out the alley-side steps and shared it by the trash bin. "The day they give you away, I'll have this right under your window, see? I'll even stuff it with newspapers so you'll land easy."

"Nowhere to run," Gracie told him. It was the name of a movie they'd seen.

"Isn't Hollywood someplace? Isn't Mexico someplace?"

Gracie laughed out loud. "You coming?"

"Course I am. Mama's spirit crap is getting on my nerves."

Gracie shrugged. "You're too little to run away. Why should I need help from someone as little as you?"

---

5.   barbecued beef
6.   virgin

Little Gene stood on tiptoe and sneered into her face. "Because I'm a boy." Then he grinned and exhaled smoke through his nose and the sides of his mouth.

"Dragon-breath," she called him.

"Come on, Mrs. Kim. This way." They scrambled up the steps, took the staircase to the hall, then stepped through the door that led down again to the ground floor through an unlit passage to the old opium den. It was nothing but a storage room for old washers now, a hot box with a ceiling two stories above them. It baked, winter or summer, because it shared a wall with the boiler.

They'd hid there when they were little, playing hide-and-seek or creating stories about the opium dealers and the man who was supposed to have hung himself in there. They could never figure out where he might have hung himself from since the ceiling was so high and the walls so bare. They looked up in awe. Once, Little Gene thought he'd be clever, and he shut himself in the dryer. Gracie couldn't find him for the longest time, but when she came back for a second look, the round window was steamed up and he wasn't making any noise. She pulled him out. He was grinning, eyes vacant. "You stupid dumb stupid stupid kid."

Little Gene felt for the bulb on the wall, pulled the chain. Now the old dryer was somehow on its side. There were two busted washers and a cane chair. The air was secret, heavy with dust and heat. Gracie felt along the walls for loose bricks, pulled one out, felt around inside like they used to do, looking for stray nuggets or anything else that might have been hidden and forgotten by the Chinese who had lived there before.

Little Gene got on his hands and knees. "Lookit." He eased out a brick flush with the floor. "Lookit," he said again.

Gracie crouched. He crawled back to make way for her, then pushed her head down. "Down there, in the basement."

She saw dim, natural light, blackened redwood, steam-stained. The bathhouse. "So what? I clean 'em every day of my life."

"Just wait," he said.

Then the white blade of a man's back rose into view. Little Gene's hand was a spider up and down her side. "See him, Mrs. Kim? Bet you can't wait."

The back lowered, rose, lowered again, unevenly, painfully. She saw hair slicked back in seaweed streaks, tea-colored splotches on his back, the skin damp and speckled like the belly of a fish. Little Gene's hand was a spider again at her neck. Gracie slapped at him, crouched, looked again. "What the hell's he doing? Rocking himself?"

Little Gene only giggled nervously.

The eyes of Mr. Kim stared toward the thousand spirits, his mouth hung open. Then those eyes rolled back in his head, pupil-less, white, and still. "God, is he dying?"

Gracie asked. If she moved a muscle, she would burst. "Is he dying?" she asked again. "Don't touch me," she told her brother, who was impatient with spidery hands.

Little Gene rolled his eyes. "That's all we need. He's not dying, stupid. Unless he dies every day." Life in a dim bathhouse, Gracie thought. Deaths in bright rooms.

A door slammed hard on the other side of the wall. Her mother cursed, called her name. Little Gene giggled and did the stroking motion at his crotch, then Gracie scrambled to her knees and pulled him up with her. He grabbed for the chain on the bulb. Dark. "Don't scream," he giggled.

"Gracie! Damn you!" her mother called.

Then his hands flew to her, one at her shoulder, the other, oily and sweet, cupping her open mouth.

A letter arrived the next Thursday. Sung-Sook had used her head and addressed it to the barbershop. Her father brought it up to her in the evening. Gracie was at her window, leaning out, watching the sky begin to gather color. "For 'Miss Gracie Kang,'" he read. "'Care of Mr. Park A. Kang.'" There was no return address. The paper smelled faintly like roses.

With his eyes, her father pleaded for news of them. He said, "You look like you're waiting for someone."

She shrugged. "It's Thursday." She wanted him to leave her alone until it was time to go downstairs and sit with Mr. Kim. Instead, he came to the window and looked out with her. "Where's your brother?"

"Wherever he feels like being."

He only smiled. Then he told her, "Mr. Kim has given me money. A lot of money."

She drew herself up. She couldn't look at him. "What money?"

"It's for a ticket, Gracie. He wants me to purchase him a ticket to Pusan and arrange some papers for him."

"Alone?" she asked.

"Alone."

She smiled out at the street, but asked again, "What money?"

Her father answered, "He will be happy to have a chance to tell you goodbye." And he left her at the window.

His money, she knew. Her father's. She kept still at the window. With her eyes closed, she saw farther than she had ever seen. "Did you hear that?" she said out loud, in case any spirits, celestial or domestic, were listening.

Then she carefully opened her letter. There was a piece of pale, gauzy paper, and a couple of photographs—a good thing, since the girls had stolen a bunch of family snapshots whey they left.

Dear Gracie,

I hope they let you see this. You're going to be an auntie now. Sung-Ohk's the lucky one, but me and El are really trying. For a baby, you know. That's El in his rookie uniform and I'm in my wedding dress. We're at the Forbidden City, the club in San Francisco. Louie, that's Sung-Ohk's husband, got us in free on our wedding night. The other picture is of Louie and Sung-Ohk at Newport Beach. Isn't he handsome? Like El. We all live near the beach, ten minutes by freeway.

You'd love it here, but I guess you'd love it anywhere but Oakland. How are the old creeps, anyway? Maybe they'll die before Mom and Dad give you away, ha-ha.

Be good. Don't worry. We're going to figure something out. El says you can stay with us. Sung-Ohk sends her love. I do, too.

The letter fluttered in her hand in the window. She pulled open the drawer at her bedside table, folded the paper neatly back in its creases, and set it inside. Then she took out the only thing her sisters had left behind, the sugar-sprinkled, silver-lettered, instant-ceremony marriage advertisement. Gracie breathed in deeply, as her sister had done with the hope of her new life—as, perhaps, Mr. Han had done, with the hope of his release. Somewhere near, Little Gene laughed out loud in the street. Her mother banged dinner into the oven. Her father waited below, his Bible open on his knees, to greet the missionary ladies, to say goodbye to Mr. Kim. Below, a white, slow figure stepped from a door and headed across the street. Again, she breathed in. And what she took in was her own. Not everything had a name.

T. C. Huo

(b. ?)

*"Those Years" was previously published in the **Seattle Review** (1988), under the pseudonym T. C. This story is about transitions from Laos to America, from past to present, and from generation to generation, transitions mirrored by the transition of the author's name. In the editor's search to discover the whereabouts of T. C. for publication in this anthology, another story in **Amerasia Journal** was discovered published under the name of T. C. Huo and written in roughly in the same style. T. C. explained the mystery by saying that*

> *For my American friends it's serious detective work to just keep track of my name(s). I have childhood nicknames, a Laotian/Thai name, a Chinese name (the same name, depending on the dialect you speak, undergoes a sonic transformation ...). Huo becomes "Fork" in Cantonese, TonChi becomes TonKee.*

T. C. Huo was born in Laos and emigrated to the United States fourteen years ago. He received a master of fine arts in creative writing from the University of California at Irvine.

"Those Years" is from a work-in-progress. Even though the young narrator of the story has emigrated to America he understands that his identity is rooted to the family's former home in Laos and to the ancestors buried there.

Those Years

The Mekong is a river by which a villager, probably a fisherman, on one misty morning heard a baby's cry. The king's advisers, because they discovered the baby prince at the time of his birth, had a set of thirty-two teeth lining in two rows and could already speak fluently, considered him evil, bound to incur bad luck to the kingdom. They advised the king to send the baby in exile at once.

They put the baby in a basket and sent him down the river, knowing that he would be drowned or starved to death.

Currents carried him, sleeping, tucked in a blanket. The basket flowed and flowed. By morning it was caught in a cluster of twining bodhi roots, along the river bank, where a fisherman found the baby.

The villagers revered him as a prodigy. He grew up to be a king, established a kingdom by the river, in a land where elephants roamed.

The place became known as the Kingdom of a Million Elephants, in which I was born.

Because Grandma had forbidden me to go near the river, I didn't let her know about my trip to the pier to watch the sunset with a classmate.

We sat by the steps, drowned in the sunset that dyed the river. Merchants disembarked from a barge, a dark outline against the shimmering surface of the water, like a goldfish's armor of scales. Sparrows, arguing and gossiping, flew in and out of the tamarind tree by the steps. My classmate sighed and, hands on his knees, said I should write a poem to commit the passing moment to eternity.

About two miles from the pier was a temple, where Grandmother often took me. At the back of the temple stood a statue of Buddha, about three stories high, facing the river, presiding over it.

The Buddha loomed overhead: the oblong ears with pointed lobes, the broad forehead, the red dot between the eyebrows.

Looking up at the Buddha made me dizzy: the towering features seemed alive, seemed to sense and know. For this reason, at home I often knelt in front of the pillow and prayed, "Protect us, protect our family, provide us with safety and health," and bowed three times on the pillow before going to sleep.

Looking down, I saw a steep flight of stairs arching out to the river, the brown currents rolling by. I felt dizzy and shut my eyes. On religious occasions, monks took the stairs and went down to the river to release caged clams, a gesture of releasing life, multiplying it.

I did not connect the Mekong with death even when my teacher's sister, the valedictorian, got drowned in 1975. It happened on the first day of the Water-Splashing Festival. People crossed the river to party at the small islands in its middle. The accident happened on the way back—too many people were in the boat. Other girls were saved. Except the valedictorian. She clung too hard to the young man who tried to rescue her. Rescuing other drowning girls had worn him out. But he plunged back into the river for the last one, the valedictorian. She dragged him down.

In 1976, after the emancipation, I crossed the river for the first time, on a field trip. It took the barge ten to fifteen minutes to cross. The motor churned the water. The ripples rolled. The pier looked diminished, the shore distant. I found myself in the center of a giant well.

The Mekong, in Laos, flows from the north through my hometown, Luang Prabang, to the capital, and separates Laos from Thailand. In the late seventies, people got drowned, got shot as they tried to escape to Thailand. Some were caught and sent back; some were robbed and then murdered. My classmate, the one who suggested I write a poem, swam across the river. His family in Laos didn't hear of him. No one in the refugee camp saw him. In fact no one on either side had ever seen him again. He simply disappeared.

Maybe the Pathet Lao[1] had caught him and sent him up north for a brainwash, or shot him. Who knows? More than likely he was drowned. Later on his family crossed the border. In the camp, I saw his parents and sisters, plus an absence.

I saw many absences, among them was Budhha, who presided over the Mekong and did nothing as if he did not see, did not know.

Under the pale fluorescent light in the hut, Grandmother turned away from me, looked down, and whispered, as if she were afraid that her breath would blow away the particles on the table, "Coming back? Returning? He's here." She patted my hand. "He's with us now." I had just rejoined my family in the camp.

Two praying mantes crawled slowly up the bamboo pole, the smaller one following her mother. To see them, I had to follow where Grandmother was looking when she spoke.

She talked to the praying mantes, "Coming back to see us? You want to be with us? You want to—" She took out her damp handkerchief.

The two praying mantes crawled ahead, going away slowly as if the two bundles of grief on their backs were too heavy.

Father said I needed new shoes. In a few weeks we would leave the camp for America.

We went to see Grandmother's tomb, in a temple outside the refugee camp, near downtown of Nongkhai province. In the temple yard, Father used a stick to brush away the leaves fallen in front of the tomb.

Afterwards we went downtown on foot. We stopped by a jewelry shop. From his pocket my father took out a small purse that Grandmother had put her jewelry in. From the purse he took out the pair of gold bracelets my sister wore. They must have been on her wrists when my father found her body.

"I'm comfortable in them." I peered at my toes through my sandals. "They still fit me. I need no new shoes."

But he went ahead and sold the bracelets. He then took me to a shoe shop.

I didn't want new shoes.

I had no excuse. That I had school work was not enough of a reason. My father said he scheduled the wedding on a Saturday. I had to attend it. I had no say and no choice—from the beginning I was made mute.

---

1. Laotian communists

My aunt and uncle picked me up in San Jose and drove me to San Francisco. We parked at Stanyan Street, next to Golden Gate Park. We crossed the street to the row of Victorian apartments.

Uncle rang the apartment doorbell while Auntie held the wedding gift. I stood behind them.

A woman in a pink dress, no doubt the bride's helper, opened the door. Her smile narrowed her eyes. She greeted us. "Come in, come in and have a seat."

We walked into the narrow hallway.

"Come, come this way." The woman led us into the living room.

I didn't know any of the guests there, a roomful. They spoke in Chinese, Lao, and English. I sat on the sofa and wondered where the bride was. I saw my father greeting the guests across the room. He wore a *complét*[2] and a *cravat*.[3] Where did he get the suit? He looked so different—and presentable.

He came over. "You've arrived," he said.

I nodded.

He and Uncle, the two former brothers-in-law, talked as if there were no harsh feelings between them. I didn't understand how they could act so friendly to each other. Neither looked awkward or uncomfortable.

I ate candies and studied the posters on the wall—simple decoration for a wedding—the flower patterns on the drapes, the ceiling corners, the guests' faces and clothes. I parted the drapes to glance outside: the heavy traffic in the park, the sunny sky, joggers with their walkmans.

The bride in a pink gown came over to greet the guests. I wore a smile.

She looked different than she was in the refugee camp. Whenever I dropped in to see my grandmother in the hospital, I would see her across the ward tending to her bedridden father. The morning my father wrapped Grandma in a sheet of white cloth, she was present too, standing next to the coffin. And at the funeral, I spotted her in the crowd watching the smoke rising from the crematorium.

"Good food," Auntie remarked to the bride. She told the bride she wanted to get the recipe for the Lao dish.

My uncle and aunt did not stay long. My father told me to go home with them because he had to stay with the guests. I left with Uncle.

Grandmother prompted me to go ahead and have dinner before it got cold. She didn't feel like eating, she said. Her eyes became red again.

---

2. three-piece suit
3. tie

My father stood outside the school, across from the hut. The sky had turned black and the dinner cold, yet he did not come in. He just stood there leaning against the post.

Earlier Grandma had talked to him outside the hut. I had stayed in the stilted bedroom, leaning against the bamboo wall, not daring to stir. The air was still. I heard Grandma urge my father to get married. His voice rose above hers. As his voice rose higher and higher, her sobs became harder and harder to restrain. The streaks of sunlight cast on the wall became fierce orange, then faded. Grandma had glued Thai newspapers on the walls. Mosquitoes flew around me. Grandmother came inside the hut blowing her nose with a handkerchief.

A neighbor, the French language teacher, helped Grandmother rally for marriage candidates. The teacher asked me to be nice to one of her students.

The chosen candidate was in her thirties, single and, according to herself, self-reliant.

I was polite to her, thinking that probably one day she could become my stepmother.

"I'm not thinking of marriage at the moment," she assured me. "I won't marry your father. Talk is just talk."

Her sister got caught at the Thai border and was put in prison in Bangkok.[4] The candidate needed someone who knew Thai to write to her sister. Almost every night, she stayed after her French lesson to dictate to me in Mandarin.[5] And I translated it into Thai, writing letter after letter, in the first person, asking the prisoner if she needed money, utensils, clothes, and when she would be released.

When she had no letter for me to write, the candidate stayed after class and told me about her plan to go to Canada and her progress in French and English. She talked until the light went off—the Thai administrator turning off all the light in the camp. I lighted a candle on the table and placed it between me and her. She stayed until eleven.

Grandma's illness began.

Mother frowns, her eyebrows in a knot. It stays with her. She does not talk. She has been this way in my dreams.

I look in the mirror. I want to find her. I study my gaze and see her somewhere in my eyes. I smile and see her somewhere at the corners of my lips. The eyes smile back at me. I look more and more like my mother.

When I am by myself, she is in my silence just the way I used to see her sitting by herself in her hair parlor, in silence.

---

4. city in Thailand
5. Chinese dialect

As to my sister, many times I have confused her with my half-brother in dreams. He is six now and she was about seven when she got drowned. After I wake up, I can't tell who was in my dream, whether it is my sister or my half-brother. They seem to have the same gaze and the same bright laughs, the same prance. I wish I can tell them apart: it can be either one of them. They blend.

"Who knows what happened to her?" The anthropologist friend glanced at me. "She's in the river. For all I know, her body is rotten by now, the fish having nibbled at her, pieces of her came off."

I shut my eyes. "My mother will be hungry if there's no food for her on her death anniversary."

"There's no such thing. She will not be hungry! She's dead."

"I can feel it. There has to be food—"

"You don't do the offering for her. You do it for yourself."

"No, I do it for her sake."

"No! It's the projection of the fact that you miss her. And there's no ghost. It's merely a projection, yours."

"You don't believe in spirits? Ghosts?"

"I don't like to think of my own mother as a ghost." She's not scary. She's dead but she doesn't appear as a ghost to scare her children."

"You go through the ritual yet you don't believe in it?"

"It makes me feel better."

"I'll feel better if I know for sure there's food for the dead, and they don't go hungry on their death anniversary," I said.

"If the ritual makes you feel better, then do it!"

"I haven't done any for my mother all these years."

"How about your father? Doesn't he—"

I shook my head. "He doesn't believe in it."

"See? He doesn't have the need. But you do! Let's do it this time." She asked for the date. "On that day we will perform the ritual."

"I feel phony though." I looked outside my friend's apartment window; under the overcast sky, the Bay Bridge stretching through Yerba Buena Island, toward San Francisco in the far distance. "When I kneel down to pray and bow my head, I know my mother or my grandmother does not come to the altar to take the food—since I don't see them. It sounds hypocritical to go through the ritual—but if I don't offer the incense and food, they'll be hungry. I can feel it."

"It's not for the dead, you see. It's for yourself: you do it to put your mind at ease. The hunger is your own projection." She stopped. "Did I upset you?"

Even if I become a ghost, I would rather wander than go back to my old home. Even if I cannot find a resting place, I will not go back.

Grandma had told me that my father, when he left Laos, had turned everything over (the shop, the beds, the cabinets, everything, even family photos) to his employee. Who later got married and lived in our house.

I wonder if they (the employee and his wife and their children) still live in the house, sitting on the chairs we (the living and the dead) all used to sit on, passing through the door we passed through more than a decade ago. The same parlor. The same air.

While in other parts of the house there were cobwebs and ant trails, in the hair parlor there was none. Every morning my mother swept the floor and, holding a feather duster, dusted the decliner chair, the hair dryer, the framed black-and-white enlarged photos of my sister on the wall (the room full of images of the girl's smile), and the sewing machine with which she made my sister's and my clothes. Later in the day her friends and visitors would show up for a hairdo.

I wonder if the employee's family will realize our absence. His children must have unpacked the boxes stored in the parlor, belongings that my father couldn't take along when he fled the country for Thailand. From the boxes the children uncovered my sister's framed blowups and mother's brush, combs, hair rollers, scissors. Maybe the employee's wife had taken the brush and, after using it, left it around where she pleased.

Of course, to this family, except for the employee, there are no living and no dead, as if we'd never lived in the house.

I wonder if the dead return there, their home. I wonder if the employee's children have seen the shadows or heard some noises in the parlor, some rustling at night.

I bet my father will never go back either, even if he is free to. He cannot bear to see the house. He has given up his claim: he has a wife and two children now. And they never know the dead and gone.

Robert Ji-Song Ku

(b. 1964)

Born in Korea, Robert Ji-Song Ku's family moved to Hawai'i in 1973, where he lived until he graduated from high school. He holds degrees in English from Loma Linda University, New York University, and the University of California at Los Angeles, and he is presently finishing a doctorate in English at the Graduate Center of the City University of New York.

Leda, *published in a slightly different version in 1991 in* **Amerasia Journal**, *is a story of the clash of western mythology, Asian classicism, American popular culture, filial duty, and finally Ku's explorations in colonizing and redefining Western European culture into a contemporary Asian American cultural vision instead of what has been the tradition.*

Leda

I

I have developed, over the years, a condition which irritates even the closest friends. Indeed, this condition is considered by many to be "terminal." I have lost many friends, some dear friends, not to mention a few lovers, because of this flaw, tragic or otherwise. I have come to believe that I am, in rather a salient fashion, a fictional character, and that my life (or my reality) is just another book, a *work of literature,* shall we say. For this reason, I frequently find myself doing things, saying things, and making certain choices for no reason other than that some of the most intriguing characters in books have done the same.

Arguably, some of these choices have not resulted in the healthiest of consequences. I started to smoke and drink—heavily—for example, simply because every one of Hemingway's heroes did it. For a while, I drank only vodka martinis in public because I read that James Bond drank it exclusively. When I read that Bond also smoked a particular brand of cigarettes (the Parliament brand in *Casino Royale*), I started to follow his taste in the label of tobacco. This, of course, did not necessarily mean that I was fond of Ian Fleming's books or of the character, Bond, *per se*. On the contrary, I found the entire Fleming *ouevre* rather crude and flippant, if not outright obscene. Nor did it mean that I trusted Fleming's, or for that matter, Hemingway's sense of refinement or taste. It was simply important to me that the choices I made in my life (or "in my book") contained multiple levels of referentiality to "other" works of literature, whether directly or indirectly, for better or for worse.

So, quite naturally, it was not too long before I started to develop some unorthodox ideas about women and sex. Of course, I must give credit where it is due most, to Junichiro Tanizaki, and in particular to his novella, *The Bridge of Dreams*.

II

Leda spoke Korean to me only when we made love; only when we made love did she called me by my Korean name. "Suckle on my breast," she would invite me, and I would suddenly, during those vaporous moments of passion, become Sorin for the first time since I was twelve years old. "Sorin, you beautiful, beautiful boy," Leda would whisper in her Cheju accent (even though I was five years older than she) as I circled the outlines of her nipples with my tongue. I often wondered, whenever she spoke in Korean, whenever we made love, what my mother, an aristocrat from Seoul, would say if she learned that Leda, the woman without whom I cannot live, was merely from Cheju Island.

Although I was eleven when I left Korea, I have never been to Cheju, the southernmost island of Korea, nestled between the Yellow Sea and the Sea of Japan. Before Leda was written into the book of my life, Cheju Island existed only in my imagination: where people lived in villages, instead of cities, and where women, not men, went off to sea in their boats before sunrise, returning only when the moon and the stars beckon them back to shore with a path of light to home. The men of Cheju Island, meanwhile, in a very modern (or primitive, depending on the point of view) way, would spend the day taking care of domestic duties, be it rearing the children or preparing meals for their wives who would soon return from the ocean. But most of all, I knew Cheju Island as the home of the "underwater women;" where the most beautiful women in all of Korea would dive into the jagged ocean, submerged, at times, for twenty minutes, only to surface once again, with arms full of oysters, abalones, and conchs. These women would all dress the same, all year round: black rubber wetsuits that clung tightly to their bodies, accentuating every curve and swell of their anatomy. Although they spent all day in the sun, their skin would be pale and unblemished even with a tan.

Leda, of course, spoiled this image—just a bit—when she confessed that she did not swim. "I don't even like to take baths," she said in Korean, in her Cheju accent softening my disappointment. "I prefer showers."

III

Tanizaki's novella, *The Bridge of Dreams*, is a frightening story about women, sex, and dreams. It is a tale about obsession, about the fusion of dream and reality, of life and art. But most of all, it is Tanizaki's haunting retelling of the Oedipal myth. It is a story, I would like to believe, not unlike the story of Leda, the woman from Cheju Island, and me. We met, believe it or not, for the first time in my dream, then three days later in a bookstore in New York City where we were both students— at the same university: I, a graduate student in comparative literature, she, an undergraduate in philosophy.

In my dream, I am sitting on a park bench, sipping coffee from a paper cup. It appears to be summer, perhaps August, judging from the perspiration cooling my neck and under my arms. I huddle around my coffee, as if warming myself in front of a dying campfire, and pass the cup back and forth between my hands, pretending to neutralize the teasing cold of the sun. A squirrel jumps across from one tree to another as if no human being is in sight but, in reality, (in my dream), there are too many people. Included among the too many people is Leda, the most beautiful woman in the park. She is dressed in black, in a one-piece dress that clings tight to her torso—accentuating the swells of her breasts—while flaring in folds down to her knees. Her skin is white, perhaps better described as pale, almost to the point of appearing sickly. She is wearing an unusually bitter shade of lipstick, like the color of coagulated blood. I watch her as she walks toward the fountain in the middle of the yard. The giant, foamy fingers of the geyser dwarfs her. Without fear, she walks into the giant's mouth, shudders at the caress of his ice-cold teeth and his uninhibited tongue, and vanishes into his wet embrace. It is not long before she emerges from the heart of the fountain. Cupped gingerly in both hands is a giant, piebald conch of brilliant red and blue. I walk over to her, step into the fountain, and receive her gift. She smiles at my gesture and closes her eyes, smoothing her hair back with both hands, free now of the conch, and reveals a tiny widow's peak. She points her chin, accusingly, towards the sun, and takes a deep breath. I carefully place the conch down into the water, next to our feet. I undress her and my tongue races with the sun to remove every drop of water from her body. As I take her breast into my mouth, as we embrace tighter in the middle of the fountain, she whispers in her Cheju accent, "Go to sleep, Sorin, go to sleep."

When I tell Leda of this dream I had three days before I met her for the first time at the bookstore, she does not believe me. "That is a beautiful story, Sorin," she says, as if she were speaking to a little boy hungry for her approval. I suddenly want to cry, knowing that I am but a little boy with her (although I am five years older than she) but I resist because I am happy.

IV

Leda was born on Cheju Island, in a fishing village near the city of Taejong, the southernmost city in the southernmost island of Korea. Her father, like most males in her village, worked hard maintaining a pleasant household until the day of his death. Leda does not remember him much since she was only three when he died of stomach cancer. But she tells me, although the memory off her father is vague, that she remembers, quite vividly, the view of Halla Mountain which made up the bulk of Cheju Island. "I have visions of it during the strangest moments," she would tell me. "Sometimes I see it in my dreams and sometimes I see it as a reflection on a subway window, particularly as the train enters a dark tunnel between stations." I asked her to explain what these visions were like but she would quit after a few aborted attempts. "It's impossible to describe it without using words you do not know," she would say in her Cheju accent. "I would have to use the dialect of Cheju Island to faithfully reproduce my vision of Halla." She would, more often than not, change the subject at this point by pressing my head against her bosom and promising, "Maybe someday when you are ready, Sorin. Maybe someday."

Since it was impossible for her mother to take care of both Leda and her two older sisters, she decided a year after her husband's death to move her family to the city of Ulson on the mainland of Korea. Although the reason Leda's mother gave for moving to Ulson always involved something about her distant cousin who ran a tavern there, Leda was convinced that there was something else. "It was tried several times by the village shamans to exorcise my mother of evil spirits," Leda would say. "But everyone failed. Even a famous shaman brought over from the city of Cheju failed to exorcise the demon from my mother's body."

It was Leda's theory that her mother moved her family to Ulson,[1] and finally to New York City, not to flee from the evil demons in her body, but to flee the shamans that wanted so desperately to exorcise her of bad spirits.

"My mother is a good woman," Leda would say with a heavier Cheju accent than usual. It was obvious that her Cheju accent always got heavier when she spoke about her mother. "Although she worked all day out at sea, she still suckled me when she got home, no matter how late it got, until I was almost three. It did not matter that she had no more milk." As I suckled on the breast of Leda, it, too, did not matter that I tasted no milk. There, however, was the sweet, undeniable taste of salt on her skin.

V

Although this may seem a bit far fetched, I saw Leda for the first time after the dream in a bookstore, picking up a copy of Junichiro Tanizaki's *Seven Japanese Tales*, a collection of his short stories which includes the novella, *The Bridge of Dreams*. I knew, then, that this woman, the most beautiful woman I have ever seen, was in my dreams a few nights ago. The woman in my dreams was not just any Asian woman with pale shin and long, black hair. The woman in my dream was the woman in the bookstore. I watched her as she casually flipped through the pages of the book, stopping for a moment now and then to read a sentence or two. Although I was afraid to do so, I approached her anyway, in a manner that might appear to be unplanned, and suggested to her that she read the book. "It changed my life," I whispered to her.

---

2. city in South Korea

We left the bookstore together that night, to drink coffee and smoke cigarettes at a cafe down the street, and my life changed; my life was good. It was like a dream.

She spoke her first Korean word to me that night as I cupped her breasts in my hands and pressed my lips to her open mouth. "*Mah-uhm*," she said into my mouth, the vibration of the word travelling into my body. "*Mah-uhm*." Spirit.

VI

"What is your name?"

"Shipman."

"No. What is your name?"

"Shipman Ahn."

"No. What is the name that your mother gave you?"

"Sorin. Ahn Sorin."

"Like your mother, I, too, from this moment on, will call you Sorin, my child."

"Yes."

"Here, take my nipple into your mouth. Suckle on my breast, my Sorin."

Pause

"Should I read to you, my darling?"

"Yes."

"Should I read to you from the book that changed your life?"

"Yes."

"I will translate to Korean as I read."

"Please."

"I sat down before her so close that our knees were touching, bent my head toward her, and took one of her nipples between my lips. At first it was hard for me to get any milk, but as I kept on suckling, my tongue began to recover its old skill. I was several inches taller than she was, but I leaned down and buried my face in her bosom, greedily sucking up the milk that came gushing out. "Mama," I began murmuring instinctively, in a spoiled, childish voice."

"The Bridge of Dreams."

"Yes, my Sorin."

"Please, read more."

"No, my child. It is time to sleep. Fall asleep between my breasts."

VII

While Leda suckled me by night, I toiled as a graduate student in comparative literature by day. Leda, on the other hand, was an undergraduate at the same school, majoring in philosophy. She would frequently be reading from a book on continental philosophy, the chapter on Hegel's dialectics, when I would wake up, and curl beside her in a fist with my legs wrapped around her body. I knew, as she did, that she was the worst kind of philosophy student there was. She did not understand Hegel at all. She stayed up nights thinking about Hegel, or so she claimed.

My favorite philosopher was, predictably, Nietzsche. Leda found Nietzsche (and my favorite band at the time, the Beatles) juvenile so I, too, was juvenile in Leda's eyes. Hegel, on the other hand, was a genius. The fact that she did not understand a word of him had her convinced of this. She was convinced, so passionately, of just one other thing: I would, very soon, hurt her dearly.

"No, Leda. I could never hurt you, just as I could never hurt my mother."

"Please, please do not say such a thing, Sorin. Do not make matters worse."

One day, as I was showering after we had made love, Leda opened up my bag and took out a volume of poetry by W.B. Yeats. When I came back into her bedroom, naked, she looked up suddenly from the pages of Yeats. Her eyes were filled with tears; there was a look of anguish on her face. She look at me with contempt. She then read from the book, in English, as is.

"'A sudden blow: the great wings beating still above the staggering girl, her thighs caressed by the dark webs, her nape caught in his bill, he holds her helpless breast upon breast.'"

"Leda and the Swan," I said awkwardly, referring to the title of the poem she had just read, a poem which I had marked up extensively, as students in literature were known to do. Then, not knowing what to say, "I understand that Leda is the mother of Helen and Clytemnestra."[1]

Leda, my Leda, did not say a word. She placed the book back into my bag and looked up at me.

"Do you want to meet *my* mother?"

VIII

Leda's mother was not a small woman, as I had expected. Although Leda was a full two inches taller than I was, I always pictured her mother to be petite, perhaps like my mother. I suppose I pictured all Korean mothers to be no taller, or shorter, than my mother. We met in a midtown Korean restaurant. While we waited for the food, Leda and her mother spoke quietly in Korean. Leda spoke in her usual Cheju accent but her mother spoke as my mother—a woman from Seoul—did, without any noticeable regional trace in her Korean. It occurred to me then that this was the first time I had ever heard Leda speak Korean outside of her bed. This realized, like some ridiculous dog in Pavlov's experiment, I started to get hard between my legs. I found myself staring at Leda's breasts without realizing what I was doing.

I welcomed the arrival of the food for more than one reason. I could not eat much as I had strange thoughts going through my mind. As Leda's mother told me

---

1. In Greek mythology, Zeus made love to Leda in the form of a swan and she gave birth to Helen, wife of Menelaus, and Clytemnestra, wife of Agamemnon.

about her childhood in Cheju Island, I could not help but imagine her, as a seventeen year old, squeezed into the customary black rubber wetsuit of the "underwater women," although I knew that she never worked as one. How long could *she* stay underwater, I wondered. Feeling a bit brave from my third bottle of the bad Korean beer, I asked her about the "underwater women."

"I do not know which is more beautiful," said Leda's mother. "The seductive breeze of Cheju Island or the multitudes of 'underwater women' of my village."

The "underwater women," according to Leda's mother, was a rapidly diminishing breed. She witnessed this as long as seventeen years ago when she was last there, before she moved her family to Ulson,[2] before she eventually moved to New York City. The postwar industrialization of Korea, an economic phenomenon which transformed Korea from a war-torn wasteland to the capitalist power it is today, did not fail to impact Cheju Island, even though most mainlanders still looked down at the people of Cheju Island as plebeians or steerages, if not down right primitives. The art of underwater diving, once an activity that women from the ages thirteen to even eighty found necessary and meaningful, had now become a lost tradition, much like the magic of shamans that once wandered to every corner of Korea.

After the meal, after walking Leda's mother to the parking garage a few blocks away, I said goodbye to Leda's mother, who was headed back to Long Island, where she lived with Leda's oldest sister and her husband.

On the subway, as we sat silently for several minutes, I turned to Leda and whispered into her ear, in my best imitation of the Cheju accent, "Your mother is very beautiful."

"Yes, I know," said Leda, placing a hand between my legs.

IX

Although this may sound embarrassingly trite, I believe that all things, no matter how intense, come to an end. I suppose that it is clear that I am referring to my relationship with Leda. Things between Leda and I came to an abrupt end one evening three weeks after my dream about her and eighteen days after I met her as she looked up from pages of Junichiro Tanizaki's *The Bridge of Dreams*.

It was a humid summer day in New York City. We had just returned from the park where we sat beneath a tree for several hours, I, reading an obscure literary journal and Leda attempting Hegel once again. Leda, through the duration of the day, was unusually moody. At first I thought she was, once again, fed up with her incomprehension with Hegel. Although I could not be certain of this—since I literally slept like a baby every night between Leda's bosom—I suspected that Leda had

---

2.   city in South Korea

frequent nightmares. I would like to believe that she had nightmares about her mother. It is not that I am cruel. It is just that Leda refused to answer any of my question regarding her nights, sometimes getting overly upset at my questions, just as my mother did when I asked her silly questions about her personal affairs. So, I did my best to try and piece things together myself using my powers of literary deduction.

That evening, several hours after we returned from the park with our reading materials, while I innocently played with one of her nipples, I made the fatal mistake of telling Leda my theory regarding her, her mother, her place of birth, and the reason why she was having her reoccurring nightmares

"I know, Leda," I said, "that you are having nightmares. It is not Hegel who is keeping you awake at night, as you would like to believe. It is your mother and the spirit that was in your mother in Cheju Island. I am not saying that this spirit is evil. On the contrary, this spirit is good. Very good. Like your mother. I knew this the moment I met your mother. I have, over the past three weeks, become like your son. You have nourished me with the milk from your breasts. The spirit that has been with your mother—and is now with you—is the spirit of your father. I have realized, very recently, that I am the reincarnate of your father. I knew this when I first met your mother; I knew that I had loved her very deeply long ago, just as I love you now. I am your son. Please, Leda, let me suckle from your breast."

With these words, I sought out one of her nipples, hungrily, and my tongue quickly recovered its old skills. Liquid flowed freely from her breasts. But the taste was not sweet. It was salty, like blood.

X

It has now been three months since Leda asked me to leave her life and as long since she refused to see me or to speak to me. I have never before known so much pain. I cannot imagine feeling more grief than this very moment. Perhaps I will know this kind of pain again when my mother passes away.

I am to meet Leda for lunch today. She finally gave in after I called her repeatedly. She told me over the phone that she was seeing someone else, someone she cares greatly about. I do not know why I want to see Leda so desperately, knowing that she will never come back to me. I have read Junichiro Tanizaki's novella, *The Bridge of Dreams*, many times since Leda left me. I intend, today, to give her my copy. Although it is well-worn with a lot of notes in the margins, and although she has her own copy, I feel I need to do this. I have inscribed in the book a single word: *Mah-bum*. I do not think I will ever see her again after today.

Monique Thuy-Dung Truong

(b. 1968)

Monique Thuy-Dung Truong has lived in Boiling Spring, North Carolina; Centerville, Ohio; Houston, Texas; and New Haven, Connecticut. Truong writes,

> *I like to rattle off the names of the U.S. cities that I have tried on like a dress that's always a bit over-sized. I am now in New York City in Columbia Law School quickly learning the difference between law and justice.*

She was born in Saigon, South Vietnam, in 1968. She writes, "Both the city and the country have disappeared. My memories are the only things keeping them on your maps."

Truong's short story "Kelly" is followed by autobiographical notes from the author that focus attention on issues of place and language and, in the case of the story's characters, examine how friendships "can often end or... begin at the boundaries of race, class, beauty, and the components of power and powerlessness."

Kelly

Dear Kelly—

I am writing to say you and I are still entwined in a childhood we would rather forget. A childhood we would rather let lie underneath the leaves of the white oaks that stand guard around Boiling Spring's town square.

It has been four years since I've written to remind you of our bond. Have you noticed that each of these letters has been written in the sweet and early days of spring? That's when the daffodils are in full bloom. They are yellow, blinding and looking like artificial teacups and saucers in a fabled toy set given to girls with pretty hair all tied up in ribbons. They, the daffodils not the girls, are the same ones that lived ever so precariously on the patches of green grass that was my sidewalk along the one-lane road leading to school. I write to remind us of the fat girl and the freak who were so much of you and me in that place of learning about nothing but that both tears were salty and that even together we couldn't cry a cupful of tears.

I'll tell our story from the beginning lest we forget and let all that pain slip underneath the leaves of the white oaks.

You see, I was lost because my parents were lost in a place that they had never heard of and had never planned to be. The United States, you understand, is a place marked by New York City on the Atlantic side, with a middle filled in by Chicago and The Alamo, and then Los Angeles is on the Pacific closing it all in. The United States for those who have been educated by the flicker of Hollywood is a very short book. No one in Saigon bothered to read the footnotes; they were too busy looking at the pictures. Boiling Spring, North Carolina is a footnote that I wished to God my parents had read before setting forth to this place that had not changed since the Civil War.

Kelly, that town was named for a hole in the ground encased in a gazebo chipping off coats after coats of summer whites. There was something hot and still about the gazebo, and if we both stood dead silent we could hear a single bubble gurgling to the surface. I think we saw that damn spring boil once during my four years of paying homage to the South and to its fine and hospitable families.

We, my family not you and me, were driven into town sometime in the deep of summer in 1975. You don't know this but I keep telling you that the summer of 1975 was earth shattering. It wasn't the heat that had cracked and blistered the whole of the United States of which the South is a blood red caboose.

I am afraid it was me.

Kelly, remember how Mrs. Hammerick talked about Veterans Day? How about the Day of Infamy when the Japanese bombed Pearl Harbor? Mrs. Hammerick, you know, the mayor's wife always had a sweet something surrounding her like she had spent too much time pulling taffy. She'd open her beautiful painted lips and talk all about the fighting and the glory of the good old Red, White and Blue, but Pearl Harbor stuck to her lower lip like nothing I've ever seen not even taffy. Mrs. Hammerick, with her curlicue's waxed to the side of her face, would never look at me when she said those two words, but I knew, Kelly, that she wanted to take me outside and whip my behind with that paddle with Boiling Spring Elementary School printed on it in black letters.

I don't think you ever knew the anger that lay underneath that beehive of Mrs. Hammerick. Kelly, you only knew that she liked the Beths and the Susans cause they wore pink and never bulged and buckled out of their shirt plackets. I was scared of her like no dark corners could ever scare me. You have to know that all the while she was teaching us history she was telling, with her language for the deaf, blind and dumb; she was telling all the boys in our class that I was Pearl and my last name was Harbor. They understood her like she was speaking French and their names were all Claude and Pierre. I felt it in the lower half of my stomach, and it throbbed and throbbed until I thought even you sitting three rows away could hear it.

So it was me, Kelly.

It would be so many years after I said good-bye to you, with you talking all the while about someday skating in the Olympics, that I would understand that Pearl Harbor was not just in 1941 but in 1975. Mrs. Hammerick wanted to hit me for everything in between for all the changes in her husband's town and in her little school house. I wasn't a little black girl with twisted hair and silent reserve. Mrs. Hammerick knew what to do with them, and they knew what to do with her. You see, didn't you, that I was yellow with a wardrobe of matching outfits ordered from Sears

Roebuck. Clothes that only a mother would order who had her head in books and her heart in a suitcase ready to go home. Sears Roebuck not even J.C. Penney, Kelly.

But I guess it was her books that brought you and me together. I think you and I would have had to find each other anyway, but I like to tell our story this way, you know, like it was destiny and not necessity. My mother was so beautiful when she wasn't crying or worrying. She didn't turn any heads, though, cause Gardner Webb was a true Southern Baptist college where women were white or they weren't at all. And my father, he was there hovering and running around like he was playing dodge ball with the entire campus. You and I were library kids, do you remember that? Sometimes, I feel like I'm the only one left talking and writing about us. Sometimes, I know you're wearing some pretty dark glasses hoping that I won't recognize that you were the fat girl and that I was your friend.

Reading, you know we were only looking at the pictures, from one explorer to the next, lots of Spaniards and Italians one after the other; we met at Amerigo Vespucci. You were scared, and your eyes showed it like a T.V. screen. I had only been in North Carolina for a summer, but I saw your brown eyes staring at me and I knew you thought I should be smelling up that place like I was trash on a ninety degree day. It would take me years to figure it all out. When people like you looked at me and my yellow skin, you didn't see color you saw dirt, and I was a walking pile of it confronting you between the library aisles. You know, I dropped my eyes and then pretended to look for them around my feet.

But like destiny, like it was written in a Grimm's fairy tale, your mamma and mine came to gather their daughters home. I forget, I'm always forgetting the joyous parts, how the words of greeting were exchanged. Your mamma had seen mine and extended a hand, and our friendship was sealed with a maternal handshake and a second glance.

Kelly, you were the fattest girl I had ever seen. I looked at you a third time not knowing how to stop myself. You smiled cause your mamma was smiling. And maybe, you had taken a quick sniff and smelled nothing but a nose full of Johnson & Johnson Baby Shampoo. I wanted to laugh cause you looked like that teddy bear that some lady from the church had given me. She didn't think I saw her take it out of the trash bag along with all the kitchen utensils but I did, you know. I never let it lie in my bed, and I didn't give it a name.

I liked your name.

I still use it now when I write about nice girls with brown hair and a tendency to be ten pounds overweight. That summer before school started, I'd spend hours sitting in our trailer home thinking up conversations, like the ones on T.V., with my figment friends. I'd sit on the plastic-covered kitchen chair and feel the coolness of the vinyl disappear underneath me then I'd move to the next. There were only four chairs, and sometimes they didn't get cool again quick enough to keep my pursuit for relief from the July heat going. The couch that the married couple left for my mom and dad for a fee of twenty dollars was like an oven radiating heat. It was covered in a woolly, itchy fabric of furniture meant for a den with five kids to abuse it day in and day out. When our trailer burnt down, I don't think I ever told you about the fire, I was hoping that sweaty piece of furniture had gone up in flames emitting toxic waste for miles and for days, but the thing was flame-retardant like a dragon with an ungodly protective shield.

I hated our aluminum box. Who the hell thought it would be ideal to live in a heat collecting, linear space, conducive of nothing but the electrical flames that finally charred it? Thank God, living on wheels and dying on wheels was just not written in my destiny nor yours.

I liked your house.

It had corners and hallways that turned left and right leading into spaces wide and rounded, filled with chintz and cotton-covered furniture nice and cool like indoor swimming pools. Did you know, your refrigerator was also a pool of plenty? There was the purple Kool Aid tasting like bubble gum and cream pies swirled high with Cool Whip. I'll tell you now that we are so far away no longer able to talk except through stories of the past that we once shared. I'll tell you now that I entered your house and wanted you gone so I alone could wade freely in your concentric rings of luxury.

By the time school started, my family had moved into a brick duplex off of a gravel road so you never saw my aluminum box. It was a secret I shared with you only when we became true sleep-over friends. You said only black people lived in trailer homes. I said I wasn't black as if your mamma and poppa would have let me in their house if they thought I was.

Boiling Spring, you know now don't you, is a place that had not changed since the Civil War. That means pre- not post-Civil War. The black families lived where the white families didn't. In school, Mrs. Hammerick never touched the black children not even the girls with their pretty braids sometimes three or four with ends clasped in bright plastic balls. Mrs. Hammerick hugged me once in front of my mother. Her red velveteen blazer with a gold reindeer in mid-leap protruding from its lapel covered me and made me forget to breathe for almost thirty seconds afterward. The antlers of that reindeer poked ever so menacingly into my right ear waiting for a squeeze to pierce through the cartilage. Kelly, I wanted to spit, you know, like your cat when she gets a throat full of hair balls. Mrs. Hammerick smelling like Oil of Olay and chalk said it was a pleasure to have me in her homeroom. My mother smiled and lead me away with me shaking and scared that Mrs. Hammerick was going to be my homeroom teacher again next year.

Do you remember that crazy little girl Michelle? Her name was Hammerick too, but she was so far from Mrs. Hammerick's relation that no one even thought once about the idea. Michelle lived across from me past a field bordered by patches of wood with honeysuckles and wild blackberries rambling in and out. You don't know this part yet so read carefully cause I may not write it again the next time around. Michelle with her brown hair, brown eyes and brown face was covered in a light layer of gravel, dirt and dust every day of the year. She smelled like a mattress left outside in the elements for far too long. Even you the fat girl and me the freak knew that Michelle was something that the good people of Boiling Spring didn't want to see. Her entire family, a sibling in almost every grade, disturbed an order that struck back by shunning and ignoring them into an oblivion not even you and I understood. Kelly, you think maybe the black girls knew?

Michelle had a mouth like no one I had ever heard. She said words that you knew were dirty even if you didn't know what they meant. It's all in the way she'd spit it out and then smile like we were all going down to hell with her just cause we had been in hearing reach. She'd crawl underneath the tables in reading class and scream dirty, bad, foul, absolutely bright and wonderful words at the rest of us. Mrs. Hammerick would never get down on her knees, but she'd always call in our principal. What was his name, Kelly? That man would take off his jacket, roll-up sleeves, and get down on his knees and drag Michelle out catching her hair in between his fists and her collar. You'd watch with fascination like he was catching a lion. I'd watch with horror thinking all the time about the Day of Infamy.

I liked her.

Michelle would walk through the field that separated our houses and invite me to play house with her siblings. She lived in a huge three-story house with rotting floorboards, mice, lots of ants, and no heat. If I had told you, Kelly, you would have said only black people lived in a house like that.

The most beautiful and fascinating thing in that house was the staircase and its gently curving banister. The wood was so shiny like someone had spilled cooking oil all over it. It was the softest thing in that house filled with children all crying and biting at one another. Michelle's voice was always so hoarse from trying to shut up the rest of Hammericks. Whenever I came over for a visit, her brothers and sisters would all look at me like I was going to explode but never liked I would smell like garbage. They'd watch my every movement. Kelly, I think they were watching my eyes to see if I could open them up any wider than they were already.

I don't remember when you stopped looking at me that way, but I'm sure you did. Maybe, it was at Jennifer's birthday party. You know, the one that her mamma made her invite all the girls in our homeroom to with the invitations with the balloons embossed on the cover. Jennifer must have cried so hard when she realized what that meant. Little Jennifer was going to have the fat girl and the freak at her blessed eighth birthday sleep-over eating her chocolate cake and drinking her strawberry punch.

Why did our mammas let us go? None of the black girls in our homeroom came that should have been our sign.

I never felt as much longing, it hurts even more that the sight of blooming daffodils now, as when I saw her bed with its yellow and white lace. It was a bed that Sleeping Beauty or I Dream of Genie would have slept in every night until somebody would change the canopy to a sweet shade of pink. Kelly, remember her dressing room? Jennifer didn't have a closet but a whole room filled with dresses and shoes and a painted cedar chest to sit on when her mamma pulled up her knee-socks. Jennifer and her mamma looked just like one another with hair like they were on a shampoo commercial on T.V. Lots of shine and bounce. Wasn't her mamma nice, Kelly? Remember how she sat in the kitchen and talked with us when Jennifer decided that we couldn't play in her tea party.

Kelly, that was when you stopped looking at my eyes waiting for them to do something they could never do.

Your friend,
Thuy Mai

Notes to "Dear Kelly"

How to write about the Southern United States when you are not White or Black? How to write in voice, an intonation, a rhythm that you have grown up hearing and knowing when everyone else out there expects you to write about mothers and talk-story? How to write about a place that is you but one that you have to go back, call out and claim because no one there will ever claim you as their own? These were the narrative tensions that I am trying to explore in this piece.

I have written a considerable amount of autobiographical works while here at Yale. They have mostly centered around Vietnam and my fading memories of that place and that time. I have avoided, therefore, everything that has come after especially my childhood in North Carolina. Boiling Spring was the first American town I ever called home. I have despised it, cursed it and hoped for its demise since leaving it the summer before fifth grade.

Something happened, though, when I read William Faulkner's *Absalom! Absalom!* here at Yale my freshman year. I understood that narrative climate better than Kingston's and that could be a rather revealing comment on their literary abilities but I would think rather that it was revealing comment on my psyche. For all that I hated about Boiling Spring, I have realized that it informs and forms me in ways that I have been unwilling to admit. I listen to Patsy Cline and Hank Williams and feel deep inside that I know the environment that produced their twangy melodies and their heartaches. Even if I do not really understand, I know that there is an affiliation an empathy on my part, if not theirs, that connects me with this region of the United States that did now want to see me then in 1975 nor now in 1990.

This is only the second time I have written directly of the southern United States. In this piece, I have assumed a voice with a southern twang (which I hope the reader can "hear") that I know has been lying inside me waiting for the few times I say "North Carolina" or "Boiling Spring" in every day speech. It is a twang that my mother has and that I have eradicated from my middle America and now Ivy League speech. It is there, though, every time I say "North Carolina." It is a way of speaking that I understand but have rarely chosen or been given an opportunity to use, like my sister who understands my parent's Vietnamese but never speaks it herself.

I write this piece in the form of a letter to my friend Kelly. We were best friends by circumstances of being outcasts as the piece indicates. I hope that it is clear that the society in Boiling Spring did not simply consist of an inside and an outside. The layers were built on top of one another based on differences of race, class, beauty and other components of power or powerlessness.

I hope that it is also clear why the piece took a letter form as well as its shifting languages of childhood and "adulthood." I no longer keep in touch with my friend but the thought of ever communicating with her again seems so remote that I am sure it would take the form of some enigmatic, time-standing-still language like the one I attempted to imagine and to create in the piece. It is a language that would shift back and forth from the consciousness of a twenty-one-year-old woman and the eight-year-old-girl. It is a language that would hopefully allow the contrasts between the two to become vibrantly clear in some instances and subtle and deceptive in others. I do not think we ever grow-up and leave our eight-year-old selves behind especially when it is a self so immersed in a past that is painful and difficult to resolve.

A letter allows for an anonymity and a safe distance that a phone call can not. It is also a form of communication that can not be interrupted and ended abruptly by a receiver who no longer chooses to participate in the sharing process. A letter arrives and can be thrown away but at least one communicant has already had her say and that process of release is complete. I attempt to insinuate that Kelly is a hesitant if not unwilling participant in this remembering ritual that is sent to her through the U.S. mail. I hope the reader can imagine, through the narrative ellipsis, that Kelly is no longer the fat girl but whoever is writing to her is still the freak. They share a present that differs in the same way that their past had also been different. Kelly only saw how their past had been shared in a solidarity of misfits, a displacement that in reality one girl outgrew and the other grew into.

The constant "you know" and "you see" are meant at first as conversational quirks and then gradually as ironic interjections in the flow of the writer's thoughts. Kelly had not known nor seen beyond her blinders She had not realized how her family and the other families of Boiling Spring allowed for certain differences but not for others. There is also a distinct tension between the two little girls and their storehouse of knowledge and survival instincts. Friendship can often end or, in the case of Michelle, begin at the boundaries of race, class, beauty and the components of power and powerlessness.

The piece is a forced and deliberate run-through of a past that only Kelly can let lie somewhere quiet like the gazebo in Boiling Spring, North Carolina.

POETRY

Lawson Fusao Inada

(b. 1938)

If there were such a position as poet laureate of Asian America and only fellow Asian American poets could vote, Lawson Fusao Inada would probable be elected to this post unanimously. His first book of poetry, **Before the War: Poems As They Happened** *(1971), was the first book of poetry sponsored by a major publishing company in America. Inada has been asked to be a community voice and read his work—or actually write "poems for the occasion"—at public schools, churches, parks, dedications, conferences, community festivals, pilgrimages, community agencies, and even the White House. Indeed, some of his poems are inscribed in stone on the banks of the Willamette River in Portland's Japanese American Historical Plaza.*

He wrote in his second volume of poetry, **Legends from Camp** *(1993), that*

> *One of the most gratifying things for me, as an artist, has been the development, the emergence of an* audience. *Various perceptions have changed or disappeared; various barriers have come down, brought down by demand, by downright need for access for creative, cultural expression. More and more, artist and audience are becoming one—for the greater cause of community and mutuality … I began functioning as a* community *poet—with new people, places, and publications to work with. And it's a privilege, actually, to be asked to contribute, share, collaborate, participate, and to be granted a* functional, responsible *role in society.*

A sansei (third-generation) Japanese American born in Fresno, California, Inada was interned in Japanese American concentration camps in Arkansas and Colorado during World War II. Of this experience Inada wrote,

> *Still there's a remoteness to history, and to simply know the facts is not always satisfactory. There's more to life than that. So you might say I've taken matters into my own hands … What did I find? What I expected to find: Aspects of humanity, the human condition.*

Since 1966, Inada has taught at Southern Oregon College in Ashland, Oregon, where he is a professor of English.

Legends from Camp

Prologue

It began as truth, as fact.
That is, at least the numbers, the statistics,
are there for verification:

10 camps, 7 states,

10 camps, 7 states,
120,113 residents.

Still, figures can lie: people are born, die.
And as for the names of the places themselves,
these, too, were subject to change:

Denson or Jerome, Arkansas;
Gila or Canal, Arizona;
Tule Lake or Newell, California;
Amache or Granada, Colorado.

As was the War Relocation Authority
with its mention of "camps" or "centers" for:

Assembly,
Concentration,
Detention,
Evacuation,
Internment,
Relocation—
among others.

"Among others"—that's important also. Therefore, let's not forget contractors, carpenters, plumbers, electricians and architects, sewage engineers, and all the untold thousands who provided the materials, decisions, energy, and transportation to make the camps a success, including, of course, the administrators, clerks, and families who not only swelled the population but were there to make and keep things shipshape according to D.C. directives and people deploying coffee in the various offices of the WRA,[1] overlooking, overseeing rivers, cityscapes, bays, whereas in actual camp the troops—excluding, of course, our aunts and uncles and sisters and brothers and fathers and mothers serving stateside, in the South Pacific, the European theater—pretty much had things in order; finally, there were the grandparents, who since the turn of the century, simply assumed they were living in America "among others."

---

1. War Relocation Authority, the federal agency in charge of the removal of Japanese Americans from the West Coast to relocation camps

The situation, obviously, was rather confusing.
It obviously confused simple people
who had simply assumed they were friends, neighbors,
colleagues, partners, patients, customers, students,
teachers, of, not so much "aliens" or "non-aliens,"
but likewise simple, unassuming people
who paid taxes as fellow citizens and populated
pews and desks and fields and places
of ordinary American society and commerce.

Rumors flew. Landed. What's what? Who's next?

And then, "just like that," it happened.
And then, "just like that," it was over.
Sun, moon, stars—they came, and went.

And then, and then, things happened,
and as they ended they kept happening,
and as they happened they ended
and began again, happening, happening,

until the event, the experience, the history,
slowly began to lose its memory,
gradually drifting into a kind of fiction—

a "true story based on fact,"
but nevertheless with "all the elements of fiction"—
and then, and then, sun, moon, stars,
we come, we come, to where we are:
Legend.

I. THE LEGEND OF PEARL HARBOR

"Aloha or Bust!"

We got here first!

II. THE LEGEND OF THE HUMANE SOCIETY

This is as
simple
as it gets:

In a pinch,
dispose
of your pets.

III. THE LEGEND OF PROTEST

The F.B.I. swooped in early,
taking our elders in the process—

for "subversive" that and this.

People ask: "Why didn't you protest?"
Well, you might say: "They had *hostages*."

IV. THE LEGEND OF LOST BOY

Lost Boy was not his name.

He had another name, a given name—
at another, given time and place—
but those were taken away.

The road was taken away.
The dog was taken away.
The food was taken away.
The house was taken away.

The boy was taken away—
but he was not lost.
Oh, no— he knew exactly where he was—

and if someone had asked
or needed directions,
he could have told them:

"This is the fairgrounds.
That's Ventura Avenue over there.
See those buildings? That's town!"

This place also had buildings—
but they were all black, the same.
There were no houses, no trees,
no hedges, no streets, no homes.

But, every afternoon, a big truck
came rolling down the rows.
It was full of water, cool,
and the boy would follow it, cool.
It smelled like rain,
and even made some rainbows!

So on this hot, hot day,
the boy followed and followed,
and when the truck stopped,
then sped off in the dust,
the boy didn't know where he was.

He knew, but he didn't know
which barrack was what.
And so he cried. A lot.
He looked like the truck.

Until Old Man Ikeda
found him, bawled him out.
Until Old Man Ikeda
laughed and called him
"Lost Boy."
Until Old Man Ikeda
walked him through
the rows, and rows,
the people, the people,
the crowd.

Until his mother
cried and laughed
and called him
"Lost Boy."

Until Lost Boy
thought he was found.

V. THE LEGEND OF FLYING BOY

This only happened once,
but once is enough—
so listen carefully.

There was a boy
who had nothing to do.
No toys, no nothing.
Plus, it was hot
in the empty room.

Well, the room was full
of sleeping parents
and an empty cot.

The boy was bored.
He needed something to do.
A hairpin on the floor
needed picking up.

It, too, needed
something to do—
like the wire, the socket
over there on the wall.

You know the rest
of the story—
but not the best
of the story:

the feel of power,
the empowering act
of being the air!

You had to be there.
Including the activity
that followed.

Flying Boy—
where are you?

Flying Boy—
you flew!

VI. THE LEGEND OF THE GREAT ESCAPE
The people were passive:
Even when a train paused
in the Great Plains, even
when soldiers were eating,
they didn't try to escape.

VII. THE LEGEND OF TALKS-WITH-HANDS
Actually, this was a whole,
intact family who lived
way over there at the edge
of our Arkansas camp.

Their name? I don't know.
Ask my mother—such ladies
were friends from "church camp."

Also, the family didn't just
talk with their hands.
The man made toys with his,
the woman knitted, and the boy
could fold his paper airplanes.

And, back in those days,
a smile could go a long ways

toward saying something.
And we were all ears.
Talking, and during prayers.

VIII. THE LEGEND OF THE HAKUJIN[2] WOMAN

This legend is about legendary
freedom of choice, options—

because this Hakujin woman
chose to be there.

She could have been anywhere—
New York City, Fresno, or over
with the administration.
Instead, she selected an ordinary

barracks room to share
with her husband.

IX. THE LEGEND OF COYOTE

Buddy was his name. And, yes, he was a Trickster.[3]
He claimed he wasn't even one of us.
He claimed he had some kind of "tribe" somewhere.

He claimed he "talked with spirits."
He claimed he could "see God in the stars."
He claimed the "spirits are everywhere."

He was just a kid. We were just barracks neighbors.
And the one thing Buddy did was make paper airplanes
out of any catalog page or major announcement—

and I mean to tell you, those things could fly!
Those things would go zipping off over barbed wire,
swirl by amazed soldiers in guard towers,

and, sometimes in the swamp, they didn't seem to land.

---

2.   white
3.   a type of character from Native American myths and stories

That was when another claim came in—they went
"all the way to Alaska" and also "back to the tribe."

Buddy. If I had smarts like that, I'd be an engineer.
Buddy. His dreams, his visions. He simply disappeared.

X. THE LEGEND OF THE MAGIC MARBLES

My uncle was going overseas.
He was heading to the European theater,
and we were all going to miss him.

He had been stationed by Cheyenne,[4]
and when he came to say good-bye
he brought me a little bag of marbles.

But the best one, an agate, cracked.
It just broke, like bone, like flesh—
so my uncle comforted me with this story:

"When we get home to Fresno,
I will take you into the basement
and give you my box of magic marbles.

These marbles are marbles—
so they can break and crack and chip—
but they are also magic

so they can always be fixed:
all you have to do is leave them
overnight in a can of Crisco

next day they're good as new."

Uncle. Uncle. Uncle. What happened to *you*?

XI. THE LEGEND OF SHOYU[5]

Legend had it that, even in Arkansas,

---

4.   city in Wyoming
5.   soy sauce

some people had soy sauce.
Well, not exactly *our* soy sauce,
which we were starved for,
but some related kind of dark
and definitive liquid
to flavor you through the day.

That camp was in the Delta,[6]
where the Muddy Waters lay.

Black shoyu. Black shoyu.
Let me taste the blues!

XII. THE LEGEND OF THE JEROME[7] SMOKESTACK

There is no legend.
It just stands there
in a grassy field,
the brush of swampland,
soaring up to the sky.

It's just the tallest
thing around for miles.
Pilots fly by it.

Some might say it's
a tribute, a monument,
a memorial to something.
But no, not really.

It's just a massive
stack of skills, labor,
a multitude of bricks.

And what it expressed
was exhaust, and wasted.

It's just a pile of past.

---

6. Mississippi Delta
7. city in Arkansas, relocation camp

Home of the wind, rain,
residence of bodies, nests.
I suppose it even sings.

But no, it's not legend.
It just stands, withstands.

XIII. THE LEGEND OF BAD BOY
Bad Boy wasn't his name.
And as a matter of fact,
there were a lot of them.

Bad Boy watched. He saw
soldiers shoot rats, snakes;
they even shot a dog.

Bad Boy learned. He did
what he could to insects—
whatever it took to be a Man.

XIV. THE LEGEND OF GOOD GIRL
Good Girl was good. She really was.
She never complained; she helped others.
She worked hard; she played until tired.
Good Girl, as you guessed, was Grandmother.

XV. THE LEGEND OF THE FULL MOON OVER AMACHE[8]
As it turned out,
Amache is said to have been named
for an Indian princess—

not a regular squaw—

who perished upstream,
in the draw,
of the Sand Creek Massacre.

Her bones floated down

---

8.   camp in Colorado

to where the camp was now.

The full moon?
It doesn't have anything to do
with this. It's just there,

illuminating, is all.

XVI. THE LEGEND OF AMATERASU
The Sun Goddess ruled the Plain of Heaven.
She did this for eons and eons, forever
and ever, before anyone could remember.

Amaterasu, as a Goddess, could always do
exactly as She wanted; thus, She haunted
Colorado like the myth She was, causing

wrinkles in the heat, always watching You.

XVII. THE LEGEND OF GROUCHO
Hey, come on now, let's hear it for Groucho!
Groucho was a florist by profession
and doggone best natural-born comedian.

It was said by some, with tears in their eyes,
that ol' Groucho could make a delivery to a funeral
and have everyone just a-rollin' in the aisles.

Even on the worst of bad days, he was worth a smile.

Groucho was Groucho—before, during, after.
Wherever he was, there was bound to be laughter.

And the thing is, he really wasn't all that witty.
He was actually serious, which made it really funny—

him and that broken English and the gimpy leg.
He was reserved bachelor too, a devoted son
who sent whatever he had to his mother in Japan.

Still, he had that something that tickled people
pink and red and white and blue and even had
the lizards lapping it up, basking in it, happy!

Maybe that was the magic—he was "seriously happy."
And not only legend has it, but I was there,
when a whole mess of pheasants came trekking clear
from Denver, just for Groucho and the heck of it,
and proceeded to make themselves into sukiyaki—

with the rest of us yukking and yakking it up all the while!

Ah, yes, Groucho! He brought joy out in people!
And when he finally got back home to Sacramento
and the news, he threw his flowers in the air,

toward Hiroshima[9]—and of course he died laughing!

XVIII. THE LEGEND OF SUPERMAN

Superman, being Superman,
had his headquarters out there
somewhere between Gotham City
and Battle Creek, Michigan.

Superman, being Superman,
even knew my address:

Block 6G,5C
Amache, Colorado
America

And Superman, being Superman,
sent me his Secret Code,
based on all the Planets—

---

9. a city in Japan destroyed by an atomic bomb dropped by the United States at the
end of World War II

with explicit instructions
to keep it hidden from others,
like "under a bed, a sofa,
or under stockings in a drawer."

Superman, being Superman,
didn't seem to understand.
Where could anything hide?

And, since we all spoke code
on a regular basis, day to day,

Superman, being Superman,
gathered up his Planets
and simply flew away!

XIX. THE LEGEND OF OTHER CAMPS
They were out there, all right,
but nobody knew what they were up to.
It was tough enough deciphering
what was going on right here.

Still, even barracks have ears:
so-and-so shot and killed;
so-and-so shot and lived;
infants, elders, dying of heat;
epidemics, with so little care.

It was tough enough deciphering
what was going on anywhere.

XX. THE LEGEND OF HOME
Home, too, was out there.
It had names like
Marysville, Placerville,
Watsonville, and Lodi—[10]

---

10. cities in California

and they were all big cities
or at least bigger than camp.

And they were full of trees,
and grass, with fruit
for the picking, dogs
to chase, cats to catch

on streets and roads
where Joey and Judy lived.

Imagine that!
That blue tricycle
left in the weeds somewhere!

And when you came to a fence,
you went around it!

And one of those homes
not only had a tunnel
but an overpass
that, when you went over,

revealed everything
going on forever up to
a gleaming bridge
leading into neon lights
and ice cream leaning
double-decker.

Imagine that!

XXI. THE LEGEND OF THE BLOCK 6G OBAKE[11]

I still don't mention his name in public.
And I'm sure he's long since passed on.
As a matter of fact, he may have died in camp.

---

11. ghost

He was that old. And he was also slow—
slow and loud enough to frighten
grown men out of their wits.

And all he did was go around our block
banging a stick on a garbage can lid
and chanting, droning, *"Block 6G Obake."*

He did that every evening, when the ghost
to him appeared—his personal ghost,
or whatever it was that haunted the camp.

He was punctual, persistent, specific.
And then I guess he either moved or died.
Whatever it was, we never spoke of him.

Because, the thing is, he was right.
Amache really was haunted. As it still is.
Amache was, is, are: Nightly, on television.

XXII. THE LEGEND OF BURNING THE WORLD

It got so cold in Colorado we would burn the world.
That is, the rocks, the coal, that trucks would dump in a pile.
Come on, children! Everybody! Bundle up! Let's go!
But then, in the warmth, you remembered how everything goes up
In smoke.

XXIII. THE LEGEND OF TARGETS

It got so hot in Colorado we would start to go crazy.
This included, of course, soldiers in uniform, on patrol.
So, once a week, just for relief, they went out for target practice.
We could hear them shooting hundreds of rounds, shouting like crazy.
It sounded like a New Year's celebration! Such fun is not to be missed!
So someone cut a deal, just for the kids, and we went out past the fence.
The soldiers shot, and between rounds, we dug in the dunes for bullets.
It was great fun! They would aim at us, go *"Pow!"* and we'd shout *"Missed!"*

XXIV. THE LEGEND OF BUDDHA
Buddha said we are all buddhas.

XXV. THE LEGEND OF LEAVING
Let's have one more turn
around the barracks.
Let's have one more go
down the rows, rows, rows.
Let's have one last chance
at the length of the fence—

slow, slow, slow,
dust, dust, dust
billowing behind
the emperor's caravan,
king of the walled city.

Head of State.
Head of Fence.
Head of Towers.
Head of Gate.

Length, height, weight,
corners and corrections
duly dedicated
to my dimensions
and directions.

It's early, it's late.
I'm in no hurry.
An Amache evening.
an Amache morning.
Slowly, this date
came dusty, approaching.

One more turn,
another go,
one last chance—

fast and slow—
before I go.

Who would have known.
Who would have guessed
the twists, the turn
of such events
combined in this
calligraphy of echoes
as inevitable,
as inscrutable
as nostalgia

jangling the nerves,
jangling the keys
of my own release.
Let's have one more turn
of the lock, the key.
Let's have one last look
as I leave
this morning, evening.

All my belongings
are gathered.
All my connections
are scattered.

What's over the horizon?
What's left to abandon?
What's left to administer?
Will anyone ever need
another Camp Director?

Woon Ping Chin

(b. 1945)

Woon Ping Chin was born in Malacca, Malaysia, and has lived and taught in Indonesia, Singapore, China, and the United States. She was a senior Fulbright lecturer in China and Indonesia and has taught at Drexel University, Haverford College, and Bryn Mawr College. She coauthored a book of translations of Malaysian aboriginal myths, **Tales of a Shaman** *(1985), and in 1993 published her first collection of poems,* **The Naturalization of Camellia Song**, *and the text of her performance piece entitled* **Details Cannot Body Wants**. *She is currently an associate professor of English at Swarthmore College.*

Chin's poetry is strongly rooted to an Asian imagery that speaks to her Malaysian roots. The following poems, all excerpted from **The Naturalization of Camellia Song**, *tell the story of the immigrant in America, yet the presence of the cultural symbols that can be identified as American remain just hidden under the rich imagery of Asia in the first poem, "The Naturalization of Camellia Song," and in the second poem, "In my Mother's Dream." By the last poem, "Seven Vietnamese Boys," the icons of popular American culture are not only present, but invasive and the memory of the Asian landscape fades.*

The Naturalization of Camellia Song

—for G.

One night Camellia woke to face
her face mirrored, saw the moon at foot
brilliant as a jade disc, fresh as a
Lifesaver, and succumbed to waves of *rindu*.[1]
In all her dreamings, there were traces
of the desperate years, poverty's clutter,
clatter of too many china spoons on a stone top,
a gaunt, serious man holding up
chipped glass by murky
kitchen light to scan signs of aging.
Did he see his father in those same lines,
the somber one keeping dignified
bearing as he watched his son wend way
out of the walled tribal place,
past waddling ducks, neat canals,

---

1. yearning

rowed yearcakes,[2] heaped straw, catching
last glimpse of elder with frayed
cotton apron blotting her cheek?

She heard the nameless bird's insistence,
squeezed memory's gates
for another garden's music,
when air was palm-fringed, gloriosa-heavy,
when elders sat in rowed satisfaction,
when the moon was soft as dough and edible
and all talk was in her baby tongue.

> *Sudah lama kami ada di sini.*
> *Kami telah menyembunyikan diri*
>   *dari yang ada di rumah.*
> *Kami tidak mau kembali.*
> *Kami gembira di sini dengan bidang-bidang*
>   *kecil dan pohon-pohon yang*
>   *kami jaga dengan rapi.*[3]

She was that fisherman forever rowing,
searching for the sweet commune, peachblossom
spring, learning to keep the thing she prized
and finding it to be formless.
If she had a knack for picking up
this language or that, could it have
come from being on the run,
Shaanxi to South, Rangoon to Singapore,
Malacca to Perth, Manoa to Mauritius,
Cologne to Kingston, Philadelphia to Rio?

Where would she wish her ashes scattered
if not in Ithaca, then like that Digger

---

2. large round Chinese New Year cakes made of rice-flour
3. Malay poem whose English translation is:
    We have all been here ever since.
    We have hidden from the ones back home.
    We did not want to go back.
    We are happy here with our small
        plots and tended trees.

who asked to be thrown into the compost heap
to give the squash a push?
If in hostile places or unjust times, she broke
into angry words or action, was this
the way of the warrior?

She could have been shopkeeper,
kongsi[4] mama, jungle-clearer
breaking her nails at simple clod,
Jia Por[5] tearing at tropic vine,
feeding nine mouths by sifting dirt,
halloing across the camp to the likes of
Yap Ah Loy,[6] back when the land was fierce
as tigers and intractable.

Too many miles from mother locked
in her city apartment dreaming Nu Wa's[7]
blessing borne on the sacred dolphin,
she understood how some prayed
for longevity, while others worked unceasingly
to return to an imagined place
tasting of all the things they loved at childhood.

She could hear the city's last engines riding home—
how peaceful were the pauses!
Yes, this too was home, the here and now
afforded by industry and chance, the breathing
in and out of three million lives in a packed
place built on the dreams of fellow diasporics,
all the beauties raised from digging
into earth, all that was learned
from *luodi shenggen,*[8]
hawkers and soldiers
nurses and cleaners

---

4. housekeeper of a Clan association (Chinese)
5. Hakka term for maternal grandmother
6. leader of early Chinese miners and settlers in Selanger, Malaysia
7. Chinese mythological figure associated with the moon
8. literally, enter earth, grow roots (Chinese)

prostitutes and professors
poets and drunkards
in maudlin karaoke[9] lounges
in humming flats heaped higher than pigeon
roosts, in tawdry ghetto rooms smoky
with offerings to Guanyin, Mary or Krishna,[10]
they called this island-home
home, there was little to fear
if she could just trust the ground
of her goodness, if she could just
close her eyes now and trust
the wash of sleep.

In My Mother's Dream

There is no pain needling hands swollen to young
ginger knots, there are no children fading
into the wide lands of Ah Yo Fah or Ten Ah See[1]
(here in Fui Chang, the white-
powder fellow ready to pounce)
there is no square-jawed
soo-woon[2] man bruising with his passions
and committing small acts of betrayal,
no broken wedding plates, lizard tails
sliding from condensed milkcans, no buckets
and buckets of wet torn clothes to be scrubbed
with hard Gor Si Li[3] soap, centipedes slithering
up damp walls, there are no rumors
of Japanese soldiers advancing
with gleaming hatreds and no running
for refuge to leech-deep jungles, no digging
for tapioca root, no tears when all that was hoarded
was Banana notes for a smoky bonfire,
the body does not split with pain as it evicts

---

9.   sing along to a music video
10.   Chinese Goddess of Mercy; Virgin Mary; Hindu deity
1.   Hakka pronunciation of Iowa and Tennessee
2.   polite and gentlemanly (Chinese)
3.   brand name of soap

the unwanted dead and courses its accompanying
effluents of crimson, relatives do not mock
with refusals or pitiful gifts of powdered
milk and bits of unwanted cloth, rats do not
die in secret places to spread a vast
stench or sneak up to bite toes in her sleep,
cockroaches do not fly up in a swarm, glittering
like a length of Indian sari, spiders do not piss
in her eye or babies snort with incomprehensible
agony in their palsied rage of eleven years,
the sun does not burn black spots on her face
or nourish the fire ant, there is no forced
solitude, her elders' graves are not overgrown
with lalang,[4] no dirtiness follows her home
from the cemetery, no hemp, no grass sandals
to wear and to uniformed officials speak
a language she cannot understand.
In my mother's dream it is Spring
Festival and we in crisp, new dresses
are seated round the table while joss[5]
sticks waft a late scent to her smiling face,
the chicken is boiling in its great
wide pot and pigs' feet pickle in black vinegar,
Oh her white hairs are falling one by one
and she would like to be around for just one
more Wankang[6] pageant, so don't turn off
her favorite soap though it's not Jee
Lor Leen[7] or Tam Pek Wan,[8] she likes the Young
and the Restless and has travelled
by bus to Hollywood.

---

4. Malay name for tall, grassy weed
5. incense
6. Festival of Boats by Chinese fishermen in Southeast Asia, in which offerings are
    sent out to sea to appease spirits. Held once every 10 to 20 years, rarely practiced
    today.
7. Cantonese movie star
8. a popular Cantonese actress

Seven Vietnamese Boys

crossing the road at 46th and walnut
where the 7-11 parking lot meets sunoco station
and the watutsi[1] pub meets the gothic complex
apartment's arched balconies from where sullen
cambodian men scan lines of traffic:
their skin-tight jeans and denim jackets
hightops and one tall dude's hair slashed
diagonally with orange dye, blue shadow
dolling his eyes gorgeous as Prince's
a slick overcoat falling to his shins billowing
in the wind, they waited at the spot
where someone split open john cooper's[2] head
to clean his pockets one summer night.
almost adoring i wanted to run up to ask,
when you get to where you are going
what do you do for thrills?
do your mothers sit with bare light bulbs
hanging overhead when they keep your rice
warm waiting? do your fathers watch miami vice
and drink rolling rock to unwind?
do you lie awake at night remembering the skyscraper
waves off the indian ocean, the stinging
sands of pulau bidong?[3]
when the snow melts into clumps peppered with black soot
does it bother you the way it bothers me?
does the smell of lemon grass give you a pang?
do you dream of moving to the suburbs
with cars as long as alligators
and refrigerators full of spring rolls?
are you fooled by the wasp
world of michael j. fox?
have you noticed how the sun
setting over the end of chester avenue
leaves a hue as fiery as dragons?

---

1.   name of African group of people; also sixties dancy style
2.   name of personal friend of poet
3.   island off east coast of Malaysia peninsula where Vietnamese boat people were
      quarantined

Russell Leong

(b. 1950)

Russell Leong was born and grew up in San Francisco Chinatown in the 1950s. At that time, Chinatown was an ethnic enclave squeezed by the fears of the McCarthy era and the pressures of a conservative Chinese American society to conform. During this time many Chinese American artists, entertainers, designers, and writers, could not openly express their social and political beliefs, much less a gay or lesbian lifestyle.

Russell Leong was a member of the Kearny Street Asian American Writers Workshop and attended San Francisco State University. A professional editor and accomplished writer his fiction and poetry has been published in numerous anthologies and journals. He edited **Moving the Image: Independent Asian Pacific American Media Arts** *(1991), the first book on independent Asian American filmmaking. His first collection of poetry,* **The Country of Dreams and Dust**, *was published in 1993. A graduate of UCLA's School of Film and Television with a MFA degree, Leong has produced two video documentaries,* **Morning Begins Here** *(1985) and* **Why is Preparing Fish a Political Act? The Poetry of Janice Mirikitani** *(1990).*

His first published work, **Rough Notes for Mantos** *(originally published under the pseudonym Wallace Lin in 1974 in* **Aiiieeeee! An Anthology of Asian American Writers***), is a lyrical and moving story in two parts; the first part is part love story of sexual dislocation between two men and the second part is a story of generational dislocation between father and son. According to Leong, his most recent work explores "the sensuality of the floating world now tempered by his political consciousness and Buddhist beliefs." His first collection of poetry,* **The Country of Dreams and Dust**, *was published in 1993.*

The Country of Dreams and Dust

1 DREAMS

As the son went away ·
From home, and did
So much that was wicked;
So we have gone away.*

Fragment by fragment
China bobs and sinks
below our eyes.

---

*   The italicized passages at the head of each of these sixteen poems are from the Rev.
I.M. Condit's *English and Chinese Reader* (1982), a missionary lesson book used to
convert the Chinese in the Americas and Australia to English and Christianity.
The italicized passages at the head of each of the sixteen poems, in order of appearance,
are from lessons 86, 26, 91, 30, 91, 36, 73, 69, 73, 96, 19, 29, 111, 35, and 94.

We furrow through green foam;
roofs, relatives and village relations
release themselves
from the Canton[1] delta mud.

Rising, rising, rising,
we migrants,
mosquitoes,
malcontents,
do hereby defy the Ching[2] emperor.

Boarding decrepit ships
of foreign name and dubious claim,
we scrape, beg, or borrow
silver coins, sacks of rice,
steel knives, and oranges.
Back to belly
we swear, belch and snore,
blanket steerage with stiff bodies

Under a harvest moon
we chisel surnames on wooden decks,
pick curses, and cast our fates
into the hands of Kwan Kung[3]
and Tien How—protectors
of borders and of the seas.

Indentured to dreams
we imagine America,
the soft breast of a green island
almost a mirage beyond our eyes.
To darker men who dive
like cormorants
and catch coins in their mouths,

---

1. Canton, Guangdong Province, is a region in Southern China from which many
   Chinese immigrated to the Americas, Southeast Asia, and Australia.
2. Ching, or Qing, refers to China's last dynasty (1662–1911), before the Republican
   Revolution of 1911 led by Dr. Sun Yat-sen.
3. traditional folk guardians

we pitch copper cash for pineapples
packed on dinghies around our ship.

Warm rain whitens into fog
yielding to Yerba Buena.
Our tongues unloosen
when we find ourselves
in the country of dreams and dust—
meng chen.[4]

Some scatter to sift gold dust
in the Mother Lode.[5]
Others, who linger too long
in the shifty shantytown
of tents and timbers,
are prey for missionaries
under church mandate to open dusky
souls to the holy spirit.

Stricken by faith and a November wind,
the Reverend William Speer
follows goldseekers to Calafia,[6]
casts blue eyes on the muddy bay,
anchors his faith
at the thumb of San Francisco,
thus cornering the first church
for Chinamen in the new world.

"Jesus men" arrive, one season
after another: Augustus Loomis,
duty-worn from Ningpo;
Otis Gibson; Ira Condit.[7]

---

4. Chinese buddhist terms that stand for the "dreams" and "dust" of the material
world
5. refers to the northern parts of California and Nevada in which gold could be
panned or mined
6. old name for California, originally a Negro Amazon
7. among the nineteenth-century missionaries originally sent to China and then to the
United States to convert the Chinese to Christianity

They queue up to teach heathens
how to pray
and how to pray for pagan sins.
Souls fall to missionaries
who charm their way inland
wherever Chinamen mine
minerals or track trains:
Marysville, San Leandro,
San Jose, Sacramento.
Yellow earth and brown men—
twice undermined.
As the son went away
From home
So we have gone away.

2 FIRE

The Gate is wide.
The fire is hot.
The wind is cold.
A warm fire.
That girl is lean.

Two hands carry the century
into the twentieth.
So strikes the clock,
so swings the latch key
that locks me within
the brick-roomed asylum[8]
that crowns the San Francisco hill.

In disgrace, I stand trial
for bartered women of my race.
I am told
only the Jesus white woman,
Donaldina Cameron,[9]
has the key to open heaven's gate.

---

8. Presbyterian Home for Girls, later renamed Donaldina Cameron House in San Francisco Chinatown

9. Donaldina Mackenzie Cameron (1869–1968) was a Presbyterian who rescued many Chinese women who had been sold into prostitution in San Francisco Chinatown.

Through barred windows
of the women's mission,
I see rooftops ramble to the Bay,
trace my route back to Canton,
Macao, San Francisco,[10]
through eastern and western portals
of men's carnal desires.

Crossing her breast,
clenched stick in hand
this bold woman
broke down the door to my alley cage.

She dragged me from the crib
where my sister slaves sang
and solicited for men
who bought us each night.
Donaldina Cameron
spirited off my powder and paint,
pushed my legs into percale,[11]
taught me how to pray, forgive
and forget.

Save my body
but not my soul,
which is my original creation
and does not belong to Miz Cameron
or the Mission Asylum
for Chinese Women.

Here, they teach me to fry fish
and roast chickens, clean windows
and dust floors, to sleep
on an iron bedstead alone.

---

10. ports through which Chinese immigrants passed
11. non-gloss type of cotton fabric

O dreams of escape
without end.
Mine own Chinamen
sold me out for silver
and white women traded the devil
they saw in me
for their own salvation.
How will I find my way home again?

In America, I trade one prison garb
for another—silk for muslin,
bracelets for bibles, jade for Jesus.

Spring and I dance together
in the April air,
toss and tremble,
quake and rumble.
Has my brother across the sea
come to vanquish those who sold me?

In flash, electric wires
shorten their circuits;
in tandem, cool waters
break their mains.

Fire and ashes surpass two days,
smolder three nights.
May earth open
and the quake bare Chinatown
and me for all to see
Burn this asylum to ashes.

The fire is hot
the wind is cold.

3 IRON
The world does
Not stand still,

But it turns
Round like a top.

Turn, turn, turn,
the world turns round like a top
depressing the market
turning stocks, bonds and signatures
into pulp;
prodding brokers and bankers
to jump out of iron skyscrapers.

But we ordinary folk can
fall no further.

Down at the heel, three brothers—
Germany, Italy and Japan—[12]
dust the ground on which
my sisters and I stand.

Bobbed hair, thin eyes,
butterfly lips, and teenaged hips
flow into Chinese chemises.

Riveted to the radio, we hold our breaths
as China falls to Japan:
first the North—Peiping and Tientsin.
The South—Kwangtung and Kwangsi.
Then, the middle—Amoy, Suchow,
Shanghai and Hankow.[13]

Paper flowers we fashion
from crepe paper and wire,
sell tickets to Chinatown
ricebowl parties
where Cantonese acrobats
dance and sing

---

12. three Axis countries during World War II
13. Chinese cities that fell to the Japanese invaders during the war

to send food and but bombers
for the beloved homeland
that we have never seen.

Shoulder to sleeve, we seam
six thousand flannel jackets for Chinese
soldiers at the front.

Moon and tide thread the Pacific.
Another freighter glides through
the Golden Gate,
Spyros—the Greek ship—comes
to load scrap iron for the land
of the rising sun.

From sewing factories, stores, and schools
we unfurl quick designs and hurl angry signs
"Embargo against Japan,"
"Nix Nippon."[14]

Longshoremen dare not cross
our furious sleeves;
they abandon forklifts,
vans and iron debris by the dock.
Three thousand picket the piers:
mothers soldered to daughters,
fathers steeled with sons.

Scrape of iron will against iron scrap,
against freighters with empty holds—
San Francisco, Oakland, Seattle.

Turn, turn, turn.
By turns we hold each other,
and onto our will.

---

14. U. S. Chinese strikers who supported an embargo against selling steel to Japan for
its military exploits

The world
Does not stand still.

4 CAMPHOR

What do you work at?
I am a cook.
How long have you been here
When will you go home?

I did not seek life here, it came to me
after the Second World War.

Life drifted up the tenement lightwell,
stitched of aluminum sheets,
threaded here with fish,
there with ducks,
or underwear hung out to dry.

All eyes and ears,
I attended the daily show
of my neighbors' cooking breakfast,
making love, or beating their children
behind half-drawn windowshades.

We live on the fourth floor
under a grid of T.V. antennae,
electric wires, and clotheslines
which bisect our vision.
Music spirals up
from Anna's record shop—
foxtrots out of Shanghai,
harmonies
from Hong Kong.

The mistress
of a certain businessman
lived on my floor.
I pass her door, knock,
then hide

around the hallway.
She opens the door, exhaling an air
of camphor in exile.

And if Sam below,
retired after thirty years
of frying filets at the Cliff Hotel,
decides to take a bath
or flush the toilet twice,
no water comes up to my floor.
Steam and Havana cigar smoke
flood the bathroom lightwell.
When he unplugs the tub,
the gurgling is someone dying
to clear his throat of phlegm
for a long time.

Year after year pigeons migrate
across the square of the lightwell.

How long have you been here?
When will you go home?

5 CLAN

Twenty five thousand
Miles around
The world, and eight
Thousand miles
Through the center.

Yawning, Joe McCarthy[15]
snoozed off for half an hour
between hearings.

My sister and I slip
onto the edge of the eaves,

---

15. an anti-communist politician instrumental in the Red Scare hearings and deportation of suspected communists in the fifties

blue and green rooftiles baroque
with bird droppings that
catch the bay fog.

From a Chinatown rooftop,
the clan cavorts
in the blue smoke of Ching Ming,[16]
grave-sweeping day.
Leaving their line of sight,
we bounce to the asphalt below
and break through.

Knowing that China lies
at the other end, we close our eyes,
plummet through sedimentary
layers of red and yellow
Fong Fong Brothers[17] strawberry cake.

Above us, Ba and Ma
in pinstripe suit and peter pan collar
hail us, but gaudy banners
block their sight.
St. Mary's mission[18] bells
muffle the sound of our joy
and their fury.

From the end of the eaves,
we have slipped past them
bent on entering another world.

Eight thousand miles
Through the center.

6 TET

A horse has four feet
He has a head,

---

16. traditional ancestral gravesweeping day
17. a popular Chinatown eatery and bakery, famous for its western-styled pastries
18. Cathloic mission in Chinatown

Neck, and tail.
His skin and hair are soft.
Men ride on his back.

Tet is the lunar New Year celebration,
the day the Offensive[19] began.
That day the reverend took me away
from my father and mother
who work hard and braid
my sister's black hair,
keeping her head above water,
her virginity intact.
They believed that boys like me
who fight right, play cards
and basketball
could fend for themselves.

The reverend[20]
rules his Chinatown roost,
named Donaldina Cameron House.
In his private office
he insinuates at least three kinds
of Christian love: philia, agape, eros.
But which love is which lie,
which passion is which poison?

Father,
twice as wide and whiter
than my real father incarnate,
incarcerate me in your arms.
Save me with your hands
on my chest and legs.

---

19. Tet Offensive during the Vietnam War
20. Caucasian Presbyterian minister who resigned his ordination after being accused of molesting several Chinese teenagers while he was director of youth programs for a large Chinatown religious organization. He was accused of molesting at least nineteen male teenagers under his charge in incidents that allegedly occured twenty years ago at Cameron House, according to the *San Francisco Chronicle*, 1989.

Promise not to tell
in the name of him
who died to save us all.

How doth move a missionary's hand?
Who moves inside me,
plucks ribs,
forks intestines,
enters esophagus,
takes tongue?
What is a mercenary's hand
doing here?
Where is the shame,
what's in a name?
What's this evil game?
My body tailspins
like a basketball out of court.
I cry foul.

No one hears the fear behind
the mashing of mah jong[21] tables,
sewing machines, Mekong
machetes under the moon.
Under his reverent hands
my body slips.

His skin and hair are soft.
Men ride on his back.

7 ECLIPSE

As it turns,
Every part has day
And night by turns.

As a child, a fugitive flees from me,
he who was bound to suffer

---

21. traditional Chinese table game

in the shadow of his body,
casually as a boy's or carefully as a girl's.

As a child, he plays hide
and seek behind the grave
thoughts of his mother and father.
Now you see him, now you don't.

As a child, he picks up odd things,
sticks and stones, and so discovers
how another's love or loneness
can desire or diminish him.

As a child, the one who awaits me
eclipses his own flesh,
frame for arm and form for thigh:
thus bound, and thus free.

Every part
Has day and night
By turns.

8 IDEOGRAPHS

I am teaching you.
You are taught by me
A lady taught me to speak
And read English.

Alphabetically, the Oriental School[22]
is spelled out along these lines—
a stone's throw away
from the Chinatown Mission,
for Oriental children only,
an extension of pale teachers,
protestant missionaries,
proper English.
For the record, desegregated

---

22. pre-1950 name for an elementary school in San Francisco Chinatown, later renamed
Commodore Stockton

after Rosa Parks[23] refused
to give up her seat, this school
born again, rechristened
Commodore Stockton Elementary.

Parenthetically, after American school
we skip to Chinese school
in a Christian church
where Chinese history begins
with ideographs carved on buried bones,
but ends up a blank slate.
Jesus, Chiang Kai-shek[24]
and Joe McCarthy bury the lesson
of Mao Zedong's[25] revolution.

Note: smell of hair pomade, snot,
bubble gum, and black ink of our graffiti
on wooden school desks
spell out "your mama."
No Angel Island poets here
carving curses in verses
behind foggy prison walls.

Repeat:
My name is Ah Sam.
My name is Ching Chong.
My name is Gook Go Home.
Most recent name, Vincent Chin—[26]
taken for Japanese,
beaten breathless in Detroit

23. Montgomery, Alabama, African American woman who defied racial separatist laws by
    refusing to give up her bus seat on February 1, 1955, to a white person, thereby
    sparking off the first Civil Rights sit-ins across the United States. A symbol of the
    black civil rights movement in the sixties.
24. Chiang Kai-shek (1886–1975) was a general and former president of Taiwan from
    1948–1975.
25. Mao Zedong (1893–1976) was a statesman and chairman of the Chinese Communist
    Party from the establishment of the People's Republic of China (1949) until his
    death.
26. Chinese American man who was fatally beaten with baseball bats in 1982 by white
    autoworkers in Detroit and whose case united Asian Americans politically
    throughout the United States in the eighties

mistaken in a missionary's mind
who believed that in the beginning
was his word, alone.

I am teaching you.
You are taught by me.

9 MONSOON

God made the body
Of dust. The
Soul is made of
The breath of God.

China breathes
between two atmospheres,
the southern monsoons
and the northern Gobi winds.
Nixon embraces Beijing,[27]
while below, Taipei[28]
still holds its children
close in the grip of martial law.

Between curfews
Taipei consummates itself:
Mormon missionaries[29] pedal home
on their bicycles,
polyester shirts soured by large bodies,
armpits and privates sticky
with the sweat of faith.

Like the August monsoon
of unknown origin,

---

27. During his tenure (1969–1974) as president of the United States, Richard Nixon
    went to Beijing, thereby reviving U.S.-China relations after the Cold War.
28. capital of Taiwan, an island off the coast of Fujan, China
29. members of the Mormon Church who do missionary work abroad

I search this island to seek
an Other who awaits me—
under a palmtree in a park
or in a barrio, where kept girls
in Japanese houses
and rattlesnakes in apothecary jars
vie for my happiness.
For I am twenty and footless
making my way across Asia.
Through a soda straw,
sweet milk and ice
mixed with mango and sugar cane
bribe my lips.
I slurp the concoction
down like a Mormon
who stops by a roadside stand
for a drink on his way home.

Red and yellow taxis
whisk us above the city lights
to the peaks of Yangminshan[30]
where merchants, expatriates, and
industrialists habit and cohabit.
The German businessman,
faithful to the flesh,
fondles Chinese boys,
but in a pinch a girl will do.
Angels of desire and deja vu
who float above green fronds,
our spare body parts
wheeled and rimmed
upon couches and crotches.

Understand, Taiwan
is a small island
near the equator shored up
by coral reefs and U.S. dollars.

---

30. wealthy housing enclave of Taipei, Taiwan

In all fairness, the Portuguese were right
when they named it Formosa,
beautiful island.
Between the hills and the sea,
shanties hug the dirt,
poor relations to mountains
of condos and mansions
which threaten to overwhelm them.

Boys and girls, here we go again,
high on imported alcohol,
airline tickets and altitude—
first class travelers who fly
the *hung kung syan*,[31]
International call line.
Roving the Pacific—
Taipei, Hong Kong,
Manila, Bangkok—we ply
German, Spanish, Dutch, British,
French, Japanese, and Americans
fresh from Nam on R and R.

A thousand and one tales
deflower the tropical night.
But for the children's sake,
keep the story simple:
shepherds and sheep
birds and lilies line the field.
Later, follow fishermen who drop
their nets and pants,
or fathers who trade in real
sons for real guns.
Ganbe.[32] Drink up.

God made the body of dust.

---

31. slang term referring to international prostitution
32. Chinese idom for "drink up."

10 WIND

I will try and do it.
I am trying to learn English.
He tried to escape,
But could not do it.

When I see
on the clothesline
my shirt moving in the wind,
I see Ba again,
his shoes, spit-shined; collar, point-starched;
ironing his speech for a *wuigoon*[33] clan meeting.

He climbs the stairs
and shuts the wooden doors to me.
But I know how the shots
of Johnny Walker, Seagram's, and black
watermelon seeds circulate the table
hand to hand, man to old man.

When I hear
my shirt moving in the wind
I hear his tenses again.
Whoosh of metal cleaver
flattened against palm,
eyes reversed in anger because I dared
to take my own life.

When I smell
my shirt moving in the wind
I smell his breath again
bitter with alcohol. Ma cursing.

Ba died three years ago.
His shirt is looser in the wind.
My shirt is dry, twisted on the rope.

---

33. Chinese fraternal class association, found both in China and immigrant
     communities in the United States

I tried to escape,
But could not do it.

11 CLAY

By feeling
We know if things
Are hard or soft,
Rough or smooth.

Across this hemisphere
I carry my body:
a brick of clay,
eight corners,
no match for the moon's curves.
Brick by clay,
a temple rises from the south,
by dusk, a roof shelters your spirit.

My feet are slate,
yet my tongue can taste
each morning that we have lived.
I curse my blood, clear before,
now spotted by the dust of death.

Who can see past this forest?
Branches, vines, birds
blind my eyes.
I follow my hands,
seek a ledge, a clearing,
where I can find your face
and face my own.

Limb and bone
fueled by air
form a pyre, break into flames.
I cannot quench my fear.

I cross a river place.
I touch you for the last time.
The sky holds your name
which I carry back
to my ancestors' village.

Who says a life is ever finished?
Who knows when it really began?
When does flesh decay or mud
awaken into breath?
Can bone burst into flame?
Can death be borne by love?
Not by words.

By feeling we know.

12 Dust

Now it is day.
The sun is red.
Why is the sun so red?

Ba ngoai.[34] Grandmother, I called her.
But she burnt all photos of me,
who brushed fingers and fate
with the stray soldier.

Falling faster after dusk
Saigon[35] fell through midnight.
By dawn we were delivered
into enemy hands.

He's a no-name man to her;
his name remains with me.
She put the photos in a brass basin.
They burnt to ashes with the incense.

---

34. Vietnamese word for grandmother on maternal side
35. former capital of South Vietnam

Smoke hid her face,
stole tears from mine.
"Burn the American papers
because they are leaving."

Yellow *mai*[36] flowers open,
then scatter in Spring;
down the *Cuu Long,*
we float toward colder continents.

I live alone.
Westminster, L.A., U.S.A.
Studio apartment. Three hundred
and ninety-five dollars a month.
I wear sun glasses
against Santa Ana[37] winds
and the dust of life.

Now, American husbands,
ex-G.I.s[38] like mine,
search for our smiles
in resettlement camps:
Thailand, Philippines, Guam.
His past bound by bent wire,
cardboard, expired stamps,
naivete.

Behind my sunglasses,
I tick to camp time—
an insect gone astray.
In Songfa[39] I saw
a buddhist nun kneeling
on the sand beside the sea;
her prayers eluding
the ears of Thai guards.

---

36. native tropical flower that blossoms in Spring
37. desert windstorms around Los Angeles
38. American soldiers
39. one of numerous refugee camps in Thailand for Vietnamese

Yesterday a middle-aged woman
in the mall walked up to me.
She asked if I wanted
permanent eyeliner on my eyes.
Many women were getting
that operation done.
"It's cheap and simple.
One steel needle etches
an eyeline of tattoo, black or blue
so that you look as complete
when you wake up
as when you put on make up.
Will you?"

"No," I said.
I told her that day and night
and whatever more
I would see or know
was the same to me, that
I could face my own life.

Hoa.
Phuong.
Mai.
Trang.[40]

Now it is day,
The sun is red.

13 NAME
What is your name?
My name is Ah Sam.
Where were you born?
In China.

---

40. common female given names

After Tiananmen,[41]
the plaster of Lady Liberty
crumbles. Speechless women
with bamboo brooms
sweep bloody concrete clean.
On television, Shanghai ruffians
are executed instead
of student rebels like me.

Bent on escape, I bribe and bootleg
my way across the continent.
Liquor, Levis and cigarettes
buy me the border
guards into Hong Kong.

Seeing that Chinese in this British[42] outpost
wear good tennis shoes and smart
haircuts,
I buy an expensive pair
and cut my hair to mode, knowing that
"head and feet are most important."[43]

Ox.
Man.
Woman.
Soldier.

In China it's a matter of position.
Top or bottom, you must salute
with your head
or follow with your feet.

Bare facts, blunt as they are
may determine my life.

---

41. the 1989 student prodemocracy protest movement against the Chinese government
    that took place in Tiananmen Square in Beijing
42. a British colony until 1997, when it reverts back to the People's Republic of China
43. Liu Xiang was a Tiananmen student activist who escaped through Hong Kong (*New
    York Times,* 1991).

My new colonial identity
might hang on a hairline
or fall short by a toenail.

Not that Hong Kongnese
are superficial people—
I, being from Beijing.
It's just that crowded
as they are,
shoulder to shoulder here
they will notice points north to south—
the shape of my head
my eyes, nose, mouth, cheekbones, jaw.
Beijing or Guangdong:[44]
native features can be reframed
by a permanent wave,
refined by a line of bangs,
concealed by a curve of black.

But no matter
whether my feet are large or small,
wide or narrow,
once they're laced up
in good tennis shoes—
white rubber, striped canvas,
neon-glo colours—
I can hide the dusty
tracks of my escape.
Bunions, corns, yellow dirt,
broken toenails.
Feet and head go first.

What is your name?
Where were you born?
In China.

---

44. Beijing is the capital of the People's Republic of China; Guandong is a southern
   Chinese province whose capital is Guangzhou, also called Canton.

14 FLUME

When they are at play,
Or in a rage from pain,
They lash the sea
Into a foam.

Sudden rills and rivulets
bend to brooks, and streams
enter rivers and seas
in which
all elements and myths
must finally meet.

Across my body spume
salt, sweat, saliva
tears, semen, opium.

Blue veins cross red arteries.
Impaled upon an ivory
dildo, upon an iron bed,
sell my sex for silver
my soul for pure pleasure.

Deposit dreams,

disasters, deaths, desires
in the flume
of history, flotsam
which furbishes itself.

Yellow River[45] reddens my eyes.
Boxer rebellions[46] inflame

---

45. main tributary of northern China
46. The Boxer Rebellions occurred from about 1898 to 1900. They were peasant revolts against the British and Western powers in China who had parceled up Chinese cities and lands after the Opium Wars of 1839–1842 and 1856–1860. By 1900, Beijing had become the center of the movement, which was subsequently crushed by Western and Japanese soliders with much bloodshed of Chinese civilians.

the hemorrhoids of holy pimps,
soothsayers, missionaries—
up their portals and treaty ports:

    Shanghai
Ningbo
    Amoy
Canton
    Hong Kong
Macao[47]

Let their blood flow from tongue to toe.

Time, bound on a rope,
hung from a tree on a river bank,
strangled by a tropic vine,
sunken in a marsh,
drowned in a lake,
buried in river beds.

As rivers must reach their mouths,
a hundred years of cold
grip the fingers
of Chinamen across the sea
who pan the Sacramento River[48]
sluice for gold.

North—
Cosumnes, Bear, Yuba, Feather.
South—
Calaveras, Stanislaus, Tuolumne
Merced, San Joaquin.[49]

Village roofs, shanty towns,
the delicate dregs

---

47. treaty port cities ceded to Western powers, including the U.S., France, and Britain,
    after the nineteenth-century Opium Wars
48. northern California's Mother Lode country
49. California rivers in which gold could be panned

of humans hands drift by.
A century later
the East is Red;
raw ideograms ride the waves
of a Chinese revolution[50]
stillborn, and still to come.

May the tide configure me
from the sediment
of eastern caves,
from the mud
of temples, casinos, bars,
basements and tenements.

Let western asylums release us—
a woman and a man,
who impress our poems
upon Angel Island[51] prison walls
before casting our shadows
blindly into the sea,
only to bubble
and surface again.

From pain
They lash the sea
Into a foam.

15 MINH[52]

Where did you go?
Where did you come from?
Where have you been?

---

50. refers to the 1949 Communist Revolution led by Mao Zedong
51. An immigration station on Angel Island in San Francisco Bay that detained
    thousands of Chinese immigrants between 1910 and 1930. In frustration and
    defiance, many of these immigrants chiseled poems on the barrack walls, many of
    which are still visible.
52. a male Vietnamese given name

Still it is in the air.
Color of this unspoken word.

You speak Vietnamese,
Cantonese, Khmer, French, Mon
to another by the Red River.[53]

Still it is in the air.
Cry of this unspoken word.
You look past my eyes.
Do you not know me?

Minh,
I am a stranger
in the story you remember.

No body or hand
can undo the pain
of bamboo cane scrolled
over your childhood back.

Know sometimes
that even monks must turn
their saffron shoulders away.

Still it is in the air.
This word, unspoken.

Your native tongue I do not speak.
Among missing
syllables
hear my voice.

Where did you come from?
Where have you been?

---

53. some common languages—both indigenous and colonial—used in Southeast Asia,
    including Vietnamese, Cantonese, Khmer, French, Mon, and others

16 ALOES

We must eat
And drink
In order to live.

The diving board
on which I sit
overhangs the edge
of the swimming pool,
drained of its water.
A concrete, kidney-shaped grave
swollen with the legs of odd chairs,
cracked tables
and a hundred aloe plants
in black plastic tubs.

This derelict yard
backdrops a yellow tract house
in Little Saigon: Minh-Quang,[54]
Temple of Light,
a freeway's turn from L.A.,
where helicopters buzz low,
overtake highways,
shopping malls, suburban tracts,
Mexican territories and
swoop down Hollywood.
Lowriders cruise the boulevards;
pickups flood the streets.
Driven by gunshots, I hit the floor.
Am I wounded too?

On the diving board, I unwrap
my legs, locate elements of myself
in air, earth and afternoon.

---

33. Vietnamese for "brightness"

Inside the temple
a monk is chanting.
His sutras[55] unlock doors,
release windows and walls,
sweep past wooden eaves
of the western house and alight
upon aloes in the yard.

I discard another layer
of my life. A friend tells me
that seven of his buddies
have died of AIDS.
No one wants to know.

In Asian families, you just disappear.
Your family rents a small room for you.
They feed you lunch.
They feed you dinner.
Rice, fish, vegetables.

At my feet
aloes thrust green spikes
upwards from black dirt,
promise to heal wounds and burns,
to restore the skin's luster.
Pure light will arise
over suburban roofs and power lines,
illuminating the path of green aloes
by which I return.

I drink snow water
that falls from high Sierra beaches,
bleached by white shellcaps
and whale bones. Petrified waves
fathom the past
and plumb the future.

---

55. Buddhist chant

Deer
   tigers
sables
   pandas
gibbons
   lynx
monkeys
bite their tongues,
rub their eyes in the red dust.[56]

The monk in the kitchen
is cutting cabbages
on the nicked formica table
for supper.

We must eat
And drink
In order to live.

---

56. "red dust", from the Chinese phrase "kan po hung chun," meaning to "see through the illusions (red dust) of the world"

Vince Gotera

(b. 1952)

Although Vince Gotera was born and raised in San Francisco, he also lived in the Philippines for several years as a young child. An award-winning poet who has received a National Endowment for the Arts creative writing fellowship and an Academy of American Poets Prize, Gotera's poetry has appeared in numerous literary journals and anthologies. In addition to his poetry, Gotera has published a book of literary criticism entitled **Radical Visions: Poetry by Vietnam Veterans** *(1994).*

Gotera graduated from Stanford in English and earned a master's in American literature from San Francisco State University and a master of fine arts in poetry as well as a doctorate in English from Indiana University. He presently teaches ethnic American literature and creative writing at Humboldt State University in Arcata, California.

The poems published here cover enormous ground, from the Philippines, to the story of two generations of immigrant Filipino men struggling to exist in America, and to Gotera's experience in the Vietnam War. In each one of the poems, Gotera's poetic voice is connected to his family and his family's past. Even in Vietnam, his allegiance is tied to his father, a veteran of Bataan in World War II, who tells him, "Just be a good son. Just do your job. If they send you, then they send. That's all." Gotera can't forget the face of his father in the same way Val in Bienvenido Santos's story "Quicker with Arrows" can't forget the face of his father.

Alan Valeriano Sees a Lynch Mob

This morning, Alan wraps a rust and verdigris
paisley scarf around his do, a bouffant
Elvis coxcomb. I'm sitting on
his bed with his little brother
Jose, my best friend in fifth grade.
On KDIA, the Temps croon about sunshine
on a cloudy day while Alan's getting on
his finest threads. Later, the requisite black
leather hip-length coat, but first,
starched Levi's steam-ironed between newspapers.
Jose asks about the cut on Alan's forehead.
Here's the thing, blood. I'm styling down Fillmore
yesterday. The old men, they standing round
the liquor store, and old Mr. Page, he ask,
"Where you going, my man?" But I keep on strutting.
Ladies on corners with they twenty dollars of White
Rain hair spray, they pivot to watch me go by, yeah.

Alan slips a flamingo knit over
a sleeveless turquoise undershirt. Then
silk stockings ribbed in maroon. In the mirror,
he rehearses the strut: left index finger
slung inside the pants pocket,
the other arm swinging free from right shoulder
cocked slightly lower than the left.
Anyway, I seen my partner Jackson
across the street, dig? And he yells,
"Say, Al! Check out my new ride, man!"
And his buddy Rolando, he yelling too,
"That's a '57 Chevy, nigger!
Sweet, sweet, sweet." So I yell back,
"Let's go for a spin, man," and Jackson,
he give me the wheel. We burning rubber
now, blood, heading for the Sunset.
Jose and I look at each other. Both
thinking the same thing: the Sunset District
might as well have its own white
pages—MacInerny, Petrovsky, Puccinelli, Ryan.
Well, maybe some Changs and Wongs. A Gomez or two.
We doing it, boy! Rubber smoking
every time we come round a corner.
But, hell, that cheegro Jackson, he got gypped.
Some mother-fucking thing wrong with the brakes, and boom!
the car's up against a garage door.
Jesus Christ, man. Got blood dripping
in my eyes, and we drawing a crowd now.
Blonde hair, freckles everywhere. Rolando
and Jackson, boy, they gone. And I'm seeing
axe handles, shotguns, a burning goddamn cross.
So I rip off my scarf, man, show them straight
hair. "I ain't a nigger! I'm flip! Filipino!"
Jose glances at me, but I'm
looking out the window. Now
Alan adds the final touches: sky-blue
Stacy Adams shoes, the leather coat,
one last glimpse into the mirror.

Aswang

Shooting marbles, Carding from across the street
and I knelt on gritty concrete in front
of his house. His mother and a couple of friends sat
on the steps, laughing and gossiping about *aswang,*[1]
those routine skulkers of the Philippine night. Carding's
mother had a pretty cousin who could
pierce your jugular with her hollow tongue
like sharpened bamboo, then delicately sip your blood,
her eyes darting crimson. One of the friends
had an uncle with fingernails hard as stone,
his breath reeking of damp earth, of human
flesh three days dead. They said Mang Enteng,
who sells baskets at market, changes into cat,
dog or boar at full moon and prowls *bundok*[2] roads.

That night, I was strolling by Carding's house,
and I saw his mother, a pretty *mestiza*[3] widow,
her face hidden by hair hanging down
as she bent far forward from the waist.
A *mananggal,*[4] the worst kind of *aswang:*
women who can detach themselves at the hips,
shucking their legs at night like a wrinkled slip.
They fly, just face and breasts, to prey on infants.
For a moment, a shadow like a giant bat
darkened the moon, then I ran to my friend's room.
He cried as we sneaked into his mother's bedroom
and sprinkled crushed garlic and holy water
on the legs propped up in the southeast corner. "She'll be free,"
I told his trembling shoulders. "She'll finally be free."

The next day, friends and neighbors gathered

---

1. witch
2. boondock or backwoods
3. mixed blood, multiracial
4. witch who is half-human and flies around in a caldron

at their house. The priest wouldn't let anyone
in the bedroom, they said. Then six men carried a pine
box into the light. I couldn't forget how his mother
flew in the window at dawn. Her face was white, her
lips full and red. She screamed when
she couldn't touch her legs. He rushed in,
began to brush away the garlic. His mother
like a trapped moth fluttering against the wall.
I leaped and wrapped my arms around Carding.
She swooped, we struggled until the first sunbeam
touched her. My friend sobbed as I wiped blood from
a cut on my arm. The funeral was a week ago, and all
I've dreamed the last six nights is neighbors standing

in a line—I'm running—they whisper, "*Aswang. Aswang.*"

Dance of the Letters

My father, in a 1956 gray suit,
had the jungle in his tie,
a macaw on Kelly green.
But today is Saturday, no briefs
to prepare, and he's in a T-shirt.

I sit on his lap with my *ABC
Golden Book*, and he orders the letters
to dance. The *A* prancing red
as an apple, the *E* a lumbering elephant,
the *C* chased by the *D* while the sly *F*

is snickering in his russet fur coat.
My mother says my breakthrough
was the *M* somersaulting into a *W*.
Not a mouse transformed into a wallaby
at all, but sounds that we can see.

Later, my father trots me out
to the living room like a trained *Z*.
Not yet four, I read newspaper headlines

out loud for Tito Juanito and Tita Naty
or for anyone who drops in.

Six years later, I am that boy
in a black Giants cap, intertwining orange
letters *S* and *F*, carrying my father's
forgotten lunch to the catacombs
of the UCSF[1] Medical Center,

and I love the hallway cool before the swirling
heat from the Print Shop door.
In his inky apron, my father smiles,
but his eyes are tired. The night before,
I pulled the pillow over my head, while he

argued with my mother
till two a.m. about that old double bind:
a rule to keep American citizens from
practicing law in the Philippines.
His University of Manila

law degree made useless.
But California's just as bad.
"You can't work in your goddamn
profession stateside either!" he shouts.
"Some land of opportunity."

There in the shimmer of the Print Shop, I can't
understand his bitterness. I savor
the staccato sounds. He leans
into the noise of huge machines, putting
vowels and consonants into neat stacks.

Fighting Kite

—1930—
Just outside Manila, it was my father's
ninth birthday, but all he could think about

---

1.   University of California at San Francisco

was his duel with fighting kite that afternoon.

For weeks, he'd been grinding glass between
rocks: green for luck. The kite string soaked in blue
then dipped in powdered glass. In the sun,

the string would gleam—filament of emerald.
His kite emblazoned with a vermilion hawk, talons
of shiny hooks and razors hammered from tin-can lids.

At 3 p.m. sharp, his hawk dancing
a red *tinikling* in the sun, my father stood
by the Pasig River,[1] his twelve-year-old opponent

on the other bank, the wind blowing downstream.
In the sky, the other kite was a silver mantis
with bat wings. The hawk and mantis swiveled

and faked like mongoose and cobra. My father
gauged the wind like a cat's paw on his cheek,
waiting for the breeze to hold its breath,

then the whiplash crack of his wrist.
Hawk whirled around mantis, razors flashing—
kite strings twining, sliced. The bat wings ripped

away in tatters. He'd won, my father had won.

　　—1989—
Swimming in that white hospital bed—IVs like
kite strings in reverse piercing his arms—

Papa must have longed to soar, to leave behind
his sick and scarred heart, his breath trapped

in emphysemic lungs … O to fly
like some red-feathered bird, to dance free

---

1.   a river that flows through Manila into Manila Bay

in lucid air above the sparkling Pasig.
How far, then, you could see: the jungle green

rock of Corregidor leaping from
Manila Bay, the Pacific stretched flat out,

an aquamarine mirror, endless and new.
The razors of Papa's soul slashed at his lines—

invisible strings tethered deep in the ground
—then Papa launched into gold and purple sky

like the sun's first flash breaking from the east,
his fingers uncurling slowly from a clenched fist.

Vietnam Era Vet

A fragrance remembered in Vietnam—
the acrid odor of gunpowder and tracer fire,
smudgy cooking fires in every hooch, the pungent scent
of *nuoe mam* and water buffalo shit, a father's
acid sweat as he searches for his lost son
in some ville, smoking from an H&I strike—all this was my wish.

I'd look at my class A's in their plastic bag in the closet and wish
sometimes I too had been to the 'Nam.
I remembered basic training at Fort Ord, double timing in the sun
to the range. "Ready on the left! Ready on the right! Fire
at will!" Late nights in the latrine, I wrote my father
long letters about being afraid I'd be sent

over there. Everyone in the platoon was afraid of being sent,
but not one of us admitted it. "Sure wish
they'd ship *me* over to that motherfucker,"
we said to each other in the noonday light, "Vietnam—
can't wait. Shoot me a fucking gook or two, fire
mortars all goddamn night." Papa'd write back, "Son,

let God's will be done. Just be a good son.
Just do your job. If they send you, then they send
you. That's all." And I'd lie on my dark bunk and smoke—the fiery
tip of the cigarette curling like a tracer ricochet—wishing
I loved it all. C-rations, the firing range, the memorized Vietnamese
phrases, my leaky shelter half on bivouac. All for Papa.

That was as close as I would get to my father's
war. I'm sure my grandfather called *him* a good son,
both in the U.S. Army, the Philippine Scouts. Their Vietnam
had been Bataan. When the sergeant would send
my father out on point, did he wish
even for a moment that he hadn't joined up? Did artillery fire

make him cringe in his foxhole? That time he was caught in crossfire,
did he try to will himself into a tree, a rock, a bird? Papa,
I knew only the mortar's *crump* and *whoosh*,
the parabolic path reaching up to California sun.
I never knew the shrapnel's white-hot whistle at arc's end.
Two nights ago, I dreamt I was in Vietnam:

a farmer runs for the tree line—I fire a crisp M-60 burst—Vietcong,
for sure, for sure. The LT sends me up to verify. In shimmering sun,
Charlie's face is the one I wash in my helmet. No. It's your face, Papa.

Marilyn Chin

(b. 1955)

Marilyn Chin has published two collections of poetry, **Dwarf Bamboo** *(1987) and* **The Phoenix Gone, the Terrace Empty** *(1994). She has won numerous awards and fellowships including a Stegner Fellowship and two National Endowment for the Arts creative writing fellowships. She graduated from the University of Massachusetts at Amherst in ancient Chinese literature and received a master of fine arts degree in poetry from Iowa in 1981. Born in Hong Kong and raised in Portland, Oregon, she currently teaches creative writing at San Diego State University.*

The three poems that follow are from **The Phoenix Gone, the Terrace Empty** *(1994). Chin is a natural storyteller whose wry sense of humor pushes the cultural boundaries of language, racial stereotyping, popular culture, and national origins.*

How I Got That Name

an essay on assimilation

I am Marilyn Mei Ling Chin.
Oh, how I love the resoluteness
of that first person singular
followed by that stalwart indicative
of "be," without the uncertain i-n-g
of "becoming." Of course,
the name had been changed
somewhere between Angel Island[1] and the sea,
when my father the person
in the late 1950s
obsessed with a bombshell blonde
transliterated "Mei Ling" to "Marilyn."
And nobody dared question
his initial impulse—for we all know
lust drove men to greatness,
not goodness, not decency.
And there I was, a wayward pink baby,
named after some tragic white woman
swollen with gin and Nembutal.[2]

---

1. U. S. immigration station for Chinese in San Francisco Bay, 1910–1940.
2. a sedative popular in the fifties and sixties, supposedly taken by Marilyn Monroe with alcohol, which led to her death

My mother couldn't pronounce the "r."
She dubbed me "Numba one female offshoot"
for brevity: henceforth, she will live and die
in sublime ignorance, flanked
by loving children and the "kitchen deity."[3]
While my father dithers,
a tomcat in Hong Kong trash—
a gambler, a petty thug,
who bought a chain of chopsuey joints
in Piss River, Oregon,
with bootlegged Gucci[4] cash.
Nobody dared question his integrity given
his nice, devout daughters
and his bright, industrious sons
as if filial piety were the standard
by which all earthly men were measured.

Oh, how trustworthy our daughters,
how thrifty our sons!
How we've managed to fool the experts
in education, statistics and demography—
We're not very creative but not adverse to rote-learning.
Indeed, they can *use* us.
But the "Model Minority" is a tease.
We know you are watching now,
so we refuse to give you any!
Oh, bamboo shoots, bamboo shoots!
The further west we go, we'll hit east;
the deeper down we dig, we'll find China.
History has turned its stomach
on a black polluted beach—
where life doesn't hinge
on that red, red wheelbarrow,
but whether or not our new lover
in the final episode of "Santa Barbara"
will lean over a scented candle

---

3. Chinese kitchen god
4. Italian fasion designer

and call us a "bitch."
Oh God, where have we gone wrong?
We have no inner resources!

Then, one redolent spring morning
the Great Patriarch Chin
peered down from his kiosk in heaven
and saw that his descendants were ugly.
One had a squarish head and a nose without a bridge.
Another's profile—long and knobbed as a gourd.
A third, the sad, brutish one
may never, never marry.
And I, his least favorite—
"not quite boiled, not quite cooked,"
a plump pomfret⁵ simmering in my juices—
too listless to fight for my people's destiny.
"To kill without resistance is not slaughter"
says the proverb. So, I wait for imminent death.
The fact that this death is also metaphorical
is testament to my lethargy.

So here lies Marilyn Mei Ling Chin,
married once, twice to so-and-so, a Lee and a Wong,
granddaughter of Jack "the patriarch"
and the brooding Suilin Fong,
daughter of the virtuous Yuet Kuen Wong
and G. G. Chin the infamous,
sister of a dozen, cousin of a million,
survived by everybody and forgotten by all.
She was neither black nor white,
neither cherished nor vanquished,
just another squatter in her own bamboo grove
minding her poetry—
when one day heaven was unmerciful,
and a chasm opened where she stood.
Like the jowls of a mighty white whale,
or the jaws of a metaphysical Godzilla,

---

5.   a fish of the genus stromatesoides

it swallowed her whole.
She did not flinch nor writhe,
nor fret about the afterlife,
but stayed! Solid as wood, happily
a little gnawed, tattered, mesmerized
by all that was lavished upon her
and all that was taken away!

A Break in the Rain

(or: Shall we meet again on Angel Island?)

Better squat
Better squat than sit—
    sitting is too comfortable.
Better squat than stand—
    standing is too expectant.
Better squat and wait—
    as many have done before you,
head bent, knees hugged, body curled.

Better play
And after all,
it is only Ping-Pong,
a game,
one to a side,
fixed points & boundaries,
a net that divides.
You needn't talent
or money,
only a green table
& white balls.
At first you play at the Y,
perhaps later
at Julie's or Mary's
in a freshly paneled room,
should you be invited.

Better dance

With the one named Rochester
who likes your kind.
Let us dub him
"the point of entry."
Suddenly, he noticed
your latticed hair.

Better wait
The queues are long
& the amenities spare.

But *do* play.
Play,
dance, sing,
wait for a break in the rain.

Elegy for Chloe Nguyen

(1955–1988)

Chloe's father is a professor of linguistics.
Mine runs a quick-you-do-it Laundromat in Chinatown.
If not pretty, at least I'm clean.

Bipedal in five months, trilingual in a year,
at eleven she had her first lover.

Here's a photo of Chloe's mother in the kitchen
making petit fours,[1] petit fours that are very pretty.
Here's my mother picking pears, picking pears
for a self-made millionaire grower.

The night when Chloe died, her father sighed,
"Chloe was my heart; Chloe was my life!"

One day under an earthen black sky

---

1.   small frosted and decorated teacakes

a star fell—or was it a satellite
exploding into a bonfire at the horizon?
Chloe said, "This is how I want to die,
with a bang and not with a flicker."

Oh, Chloe, eternally sophomore and soporific!
Friend of remote moribund languages!
Chloe read Serbo-Croatian, the Latin of Horace.
She understood Egyptian hieroglyphics, the writing of the tombs.
The tongues of the living, the slangs of the dead—
in learning she had no rival.

Then came the lovers of many languages
to quell her hunger, her despair.
Each night they whispered, "Chloe, you are beautiful."
Then left her with an empty sky in the morning.

Chloe, can you hear me? Is it better in heaven?
Are you happier in hell? This week I don't understand the lesson
being a slow learner—except for the one about survival.
And Death, I know him well...

He followed my grandfather as a puff of opium,
my father as a brand new car.
Rowed the boat with my grandmother,
blowing gales into my mother's ear.
Wrapped his arms around my asthmatic sister,
but his comforting never won us over.

Yes, Death is a beautiful man,
and the poor don't need dowries to court him.
His grassy hand, his caliph²—you thought you could master.

Chloe, we are finally Americans now. Chloe, we are here!

---

2. Caliph: A successor or supreme ruler in a Moslem state. Author's intention is to
    also invoke the word calligraphy.

Kimiko Hahn

(b. 1955)

Kimiko Hahn was born just outside of New York City to a Japanese American mother and German American father. Her collections of poetry include: **We Stand Our Ground: Three Women, Their Vision, Their Poetry**, *with Gale Jackson and Susan Sherman (1988);* **Air Pocket** *(1989); and* **Earshot** *(1992). Hahn's poetry is influenced by her study of classical Japanese literature, as well as American poetry, rock and roll, political work, and feminism. She has published her poetry in numerous literary magazines, journals, and anthologies and is the recipient of fellowships from the National Endowment for the Arts and the New York Foundation for the Arts. Hahn is an assistant professor at Queens College in New York and lives in Brooklyn with her husband and two daughters, Miyako Tess and Reiko Lily.*

The following poem, "Resistance: A Poem on Ikat Cloth" is excerpted from her book Air Pocket *(1989). The Poem defines the lives of Asian women and calls for a kind of mulitcultural voice rooted in one's native tongue, in slang, and in storytelling, where the different voices are woven like fabric and given to Hahn's own daughter at the end of the poem.*

Resistance: A Poem on Ikat Cloth

By the time the forsythia blossomed
in waves along the parkway
the more delicate cherry and apple
had blown away, if you remember
correctly. Those were days
when you'd forget socks and books
after peeing in the privacy
of its branches and soft earth.
What a house you had
fit for turtles or sparrows.
One sparrow[1]
wrapped in a silk kimono
wept for her tongue
clipped off by the old woman.

---

1. Sparrow references from the Japanes folk tale, "Shitakirisu-zume" (literally, "the tongue-cut"sparrow). The sparrow received the punishment after eating the old woman's rice starch. The sparrow got even.

You'll never forget that
or its vengeance as striking
as the yellow around your small shoulders.
         shitakirisuzume[2] mother called her.
         You didn't need to understand
         exactly.
a process of resistance
in Soemba, Sumatra, Java, Bali,[3]
Timor,
              Soon came mounds of flesh
              and hair here and there.
              Centuries earlier
              you'd have been courted
or sold.
              "Inu has let out my sparrow—the little one
              that I kept in the clothes-basket she said,
              looking very unhappy."[4]
For a Eurasian, sold.
              Murasaki[5]
mother
              She soaked the cloth
              in incense
              then spread it on the floor
              standing there in bleached cotton,
              red silk and bare feet.
And you feel in love with her
deeply as only a little girl could.
Pulling at your nipples
you dreamt of her body
that would become yours.
              "Since the day we first boarded the ship
              I have been unable to wear
              my dark red robe.

2.   see footnote 1
3.   Locations in Indonesia known for ikat. Ikat is the technique of resist-dying yarn
     before it is woven.
4.   from Genjimonogatari "The Tale of Genji" by Murasaki Shikibu, translated by
     Arthur Waley). This is the first time Genji hears the child Muraski who he later
     adopts, then marries.
5.   see footnote 4, Murasaki also means "purple"

That must not be done
out of danger of attracting
the god of the sea."[6]
red as a Judy Chicago[7] plate
feast your eyes on this
jack

"when I was bathing along the shore
scarecely screened by reeds
I lifted my robe revealing my leg
and more."[8]
roll up that skirt
and show those calves
cause if that bitch thinks
she can steal your guy
she's crazy

The cut burned
so she flapped her wings
and cried out
but choked
on blood.
The thread wound around your hand
so tight your fingers
turn indigo

Murasaki
The Shining Prince[9] realized
he could form her
into the one forbidden him. For that
he would persist
into old age.

rice starch
envelope, bone, bride

you can't resist
The box of the sparrow's vengeance
contained evils comparable to agent orange[10]

---

6. from Tosanikki ("The Tosa Diary" by Ki no Tsurayuki, translated by Earl Miner),
   written in the female persona
7. a contemporary American artist
8. see footnote 6
9. "The Shining Prince" refers to Genji.
10. refers to substance used in chemical warfare in the Vietnam War

or the minamata[11] disease. The old man
lived happily
without the old woman. But why her?
except that she was archetypal.
    She depended on her child
    to the point that when her daughter died
    and she left Tosa
    she could only lie down
    on the boat's floor
    and sob loudly
    while the waves
    crashed against her side
    almost pleasantly.
This depth lent the writer
the soft black silt
on the ocean floor
where all life, some men say, began.
    warp
"Mr. Ramsay, stumbling along a passage
one dark morning, stretched his arms out,
but Mrs. Ramsay, having died rather suddenly
the night before, his arms though stretched out,
remained empty."[12]
    when the men wove and women dyed
mother—
    mutha
Orchids you explained
represent female genitalia
in Chinese verse.
Hence the orchid boat.
Patricia liked that
and would use it in her collection
Sex and Weather.
the supremes soothed like an older sister
rubbing your back
kissing your neck and pulling you into

---

11. refers to a disease caused by toxic waste
12. from *To the Lighthouse*, Virginia Woolf

motor city, usa[13]
whether you liked it
or not that
was the summer
of watts[14] and though you
were in a coma
as far as that
the ramifications
the ramifications
bled through transistors
        a *class* act
blues from indigo, reds[15]
from mendoekoe root, yellows, boiling
tegaran wood
and sometimes by mudbath
        when you saw her bathing in the dark
        you wanted to dip your hand in
mamagoto suruno?[16]
        The bride transforms
        into water
        while the groom moves
        like the carp
        there just under the bridge—
        like the boy with you
        under the forsythia
        scratching and rolling around.
        No, actually you just lay there
        still and moist.
        Wondering what next.
    pine
        You're not even certain
        which you see—
        the carp or the reflection of your hand.

---

13 Diana Ross and the Supremes, a group from Detroit called "Motor City" or
     "Motown"
14. a section of Los Angeles, scene of a rebellion against poverty in the sixties
15. Colors refer to dyes used in Indonesia. (*Ikat Technique,* Charles Ikle, New York,
     1934).
16. Japanese, "playing house"

the forsythia curled
like cupped hands covering
       bound and unbound
As if blood
       "The thought of the white linen
       spread out on the deep snow
       the cloth and the snow
       glowing scarlet was enough
       to make him feel that"[17]
The sight of him squeezing melons
sniffing one
then splitting it open in the park
was enough to make you feel that
       Naha, Ryukyu Island, Taketome, shiga,
       Karayoshi, Tottori, Izo,[18]
resistance does not mean
not drawn it means
       sasou mizu araba
       inamu to zo omou[19]
bind the thread
with hemp or banana leaves
before soaking it in the indigo
black as squid as seaweed as his hair
       as his hair
       as I lick his genitals
       first taking one side
       deep in my mouth then the other
       till he cries softly
       please
for days
       Though practical
       you hate annotations

---

17. from Yukiguni "*Snow Country*," Kawabata Yasunari, a modern Japanese writer, translated by Edward Seidensticker).
18. locations in Japan known for ikat
19. *Sasou*, etc. is a quote from a waka (classical Japanese poem) by Ono no Komachi, a ninth-century court lady. Donald Keene translated these lines, "were there water to entice me/ I would follow it, I think." (*Anthology of Japanese Literature*, p. 79).

to the *kokinshu*;[20]
each note vivisects
a *waka*[21]
like so many petals
off a stem
until your lap
is full of blossoms.
How many you destroyed!
You can't imagine
Komachi's[22] world
as real. Hair
so heavy it adds
another layer of brocade
(black on wisteria,
plum—)
forsythia too raw
and the smell
of fresh *tatami*.[23]
But can you do without
kono yumei no naka ni[24]
Can you pull apart the line
"my heart chars"
      kokoro yakeori[25]
corridors of thread
    "creating the pattern from memory
    conforming to a certain style
    typical of each island"[26]
"K.8. Fragment of ramie kasuri, medium
blue, with repeating double ikat, and mantled
turtles and maple leaves of weft ikat.
Omi Province, Shiga Prefecture,

---

20. *Kokinshu* is the Imperial Anthology of poetry completed in 905.
21. see footnote 19
22. see footnote 19
23. straw matting for the floor in Japanese homes
24. *Kono* etc., Japanese, for "in this dream"
25. from another Ono no Komachi poem translated by Earl Miner (*Introduction to Japanese Court Poetry*, p. 82)
26. Ikle, p. 50

Honshu.[27]
L. 16.5 cm. W. 19.5 cm."
          "the turtle with strands of seaweed
          growing from its back forming a mantle,
          reputed to live for centuries,"
Komachi also moved
like those shadows in the shallows
you cannot reach
though they touch you.
Wading and feeling
something light as a curtain
around your calves you turn
to see very small scallops
rise to the surface
for a moment of oxygen
then close up and descend.
Caught, you look
at what he calls their eyes
(ridges of blue)
and are afraid to touch
that part.
          from memory or history
sasou mizu[28]
          Grandmother's *ofuro*[29]
          contained giant squid
killer whales
          hot
omou[30]
          You were afraid he would
          turn to the sea
          to say something
          that would separate you
          forever
          so kept talking.
          Of course he grew irritable

---

27. *Japanese Country Textiles*, Toronto, 1965, pp. 15,16.
28. see footnote 19
29. Japanese bathtub
30. see footnote 12

and didn't really want
a basket of shells
for the bathroom
"his arms though stretched out"
The line shocked you
like so much of Kawabata[31]
who you blame
for years of humiliation,
katakana, hiragana, kanji,[32]
at each stroke
You first hear the squall
coming across the lake
like a sheet of glass.
You start to cry and daddy
rows toward the shore and mother.
in the Malayan Archipelago[33]
Georgia O'Keefe's[34] orchid shocked you
so even now you can picture the fragrance
"Should a stranger witness the performance
he is compelled to dip his finger
into the dye and taste it. Those employed
must never mention the names of dead people
or animals. Pregnant or sick women
are not allowed to look on;
should this happen they are punished
as strangers."[35]
in the Malayan Archipelago
where boys give their sweethearts
shuttles they will carve, burn,
name,
"language does not differ
from instruments of production,
from machines, let us say,"[36]
knocked down

---

31. see footnote 17
32. *Katakana,* etc. are the Japanese syllabas and the Chinese characters, respectively.
33. location known for ikat
34. modern American painter
35. Ikle, p.51
36. Josef Stalin, *Marxism and the Problems of Linguistics*

knocked *up girl*
        "the superstructure"
he wouldn't stop talking
about *deep structure*
        and mention in prayer
but you need more than the female persona.
A swatch of cloth.
A pressed flower. The taste of powder
brushed against your lips.
        pine
matsu[37]
        The wedding day chosen
        he brought you animal crackers
cloths
        Pushing aside the branches
        you crawl in
        on your hands and knees,
        lie back,
        and light up.
tabako chodai[38]
        because the forsythia
        symbolizes so much
        of sneakers,
        cloth ABC books, charms,
sankyu[39]
        the "charred heart"
        would be reconstructed thus:
"Before the golden, gentle Buddha, I will lay
Poems as my flowers,
Entering in the Way,
Entering in the Way."[40]
        fuck that shit
Link the sections
with fragrance: *matsu*

---

37. Japanese for "pine tree" and "wait"
38. Japanese for "give me a cigarette [tobacco]"
39. Japanese pronunciation of "thank you"
40. Noh play by Kari ami Kiyotsugu, "Sotoba Komachi," supposedly about Ono no Komachi's repentance (Keene, p. 270)

                    shards of ice
The bride spread out her dress
for the dry cleaners
then picked kernels of rice
off the quilt and from her hair.
            bits of china
the lining unfolds
out of the body
through hormonal revolutions
gravity and chance
            lick that plate clean
can I get a cigarette
            got a match
click clack, click
clack
        chodai[41]
in this dream
            She wrapped the ikat
            around her waist and set out
            for Hausa, Yoruba, Ewe of Ghana,
            Baule, Madagascar, and Northern Edo[42]
I pull off my dress
and take a deep breath.
The cupped hands open then
onto the loom.
            click clack click
clack
            and in the rhythmic chore
            I imagine a daughter in my lap
            who I will never give away
            but see off
            with a bundle of cloths
            dyed with resistance

---

41. Japanese for "give me"
42. locations in Africa known for ikat

Cathy Song

(b. 1955)

Cathy Song was born in Honolulu to a Chinese mother and Korean father. Song is the author of two collections of poetry: **Picture Bride** *(1983), which won the Yale Series of Younger Poets Award in 1982, and* **Frameless Windows, Squares of Light** *(1991). She is a graduate of Wellesley College and Boston University and currently lives in Honolulu.*

As with many writers from Hawai'i, Song's poetry is deeply rooted to the landscape of Hawai'i. These three poems excerpted from **The Best of the Bamboo Ridge: The Hawaii Writers' Quarterly** *(1986) tell, in part, the story of three generations of her family from her immigrant Korean grandfather, who worked in the sugarcane fields in Hawai'i for eighteen years, to her own birth. The imagery in "Tribe" connects and even suggests a kind of christening of her birth by the Hawaiian landscape:*

> *I don't remember*
> *going there into the forest,*
> *although you must have taken me*
> *where the lilikoi vines*
> *dripped sticky sap passionately,*
> *their blossoms curling like bells or tongues.*
> *I heard my first story there.*

The Youngest Daughter

The sky has been dark
for many years.
My skin has become as damp
and pale as rice paper
and feels the way
mother's used to before the drying sun
parched it out there in the fields.

  Lately, when I touch myself,
my hands react as if
I had just touched something
hot enough to burn.
My skin, aspirin-colored,
tingles with migraine. Mother
has been massaging the left side of my face
especially in the evenings
when it flares up.

This morning
her breathing was graveled,
her voice gruff with affection
when I took her into the bath.
She was in a good humor,
making jokes about her great breasts,
floating in the milky water
like two walruses,
flaccid and whiskered around the nipples.
I scrubbed them with a sour taste
in my mouth, thinking:
six children and an old man
have sucked from these brown nipples.

I was almost tender
when I came to the blue bruises
that freckle her body,
places where she has been injecting insulin
for thirty years, ever since
I can remember. I soaped her slowly,
she sighed deeply, her eyes closed.

In the afternoons
when she has rested,
she prepares our ritual of tea and rice,
garnished with a shred of gingered fish,
a slice of pickled turnip,
a token for my white body.
We eat in the familiar silence.
She knows I am not to be trusted,
even now planning my escape.
As I toast to her health
with the tea she had poured,
a thousand cranes curtain the window,
fly up in a sudden breeze.

Easter: Wahiawa, 1959

1.
The rain stopped for one afternoon.
Father brought out
his movie camera and for a few
fragile hours,
we were all together
under a thin film
that separated the rain showers
from that part of the earth
like a hammock
held loosely by clothespins.

Grandmother took the opportunity
to hang the laundry
and mother and my aunts
filed out of the house
in pedal pushers and poodle cuts,
carrying the blue washed eggs.

Grandfather kept the children
penned in the porch,
clucking at us in his broken English
whenever we tried to peek
around him. There were bread crumbs
stuck to his blue-grey whiskers.

I looked from him to the sky,
a membrane of egg whites
straining under the weight
of the storm that threatened
to break.

We burst loose from Grandfather
when the mothers returned
from planting the eggs
around the soggy yard.

He followed us,
walking with stiff but sturdy legs,
curious at the excitement
shuddering through our small spines.
We dashed and disappeared
into bushes,
searching for the treasures;
the hard boiled eggs
which Grandmother had been simmering
in vinegar and blue color all morning.

2.
When Grandfather was a young boy
in Korea,
it was a long walk
to the river banks,
where, if he were lucky,
a quail egg or two
would gleam from the mud
like gigantic pearls.
He could never eat enough
of them.

It was another long walk
through the sugar cane fields
of Hawaii,
where he worked for eighteen years,
cutting the sweet stalks
with a machete. His right arm
grew disproportionately large
to the rest of his body.
He could hold three of us
grandchildren in that arm.

I want to think
that each stalk that fell
had brought him closer
to a clearing,
to that palpable distance.

From the porch
to the gardenia hedge
that day, he was enclosed
by his grandchildren,
scrambling around him
like beloved puppies
for whom he could at last buy
cratefuls of oranges,
basketfuls of sky blue eggs.

I found three that afternoon.
By evening, it was raining hard.
Grandfather and I
skipped supper. Instead,
we sat on the porch
and I ate what he peeled and cleaned
for me.
The delicate marine-colored shells
scattering across his lap
were something like what
the ocean gives
the beach after a rain.

Tribe

for Andrea

I was born
on your fourth birthday,
song of the morning dove
spilling from the guava trees.

Grandparents came to look at me,
the number two girl
with dumpling cheeks and tofu skin.
They pinched and cuddled,
affectionately gruff, blowing garlic breath
across my unflinching face.
Lifting me into their brown speckled arms,

you stood guard, proud and protective
of this new fat sister, stern
like a little buddha

I rolled and rebounded,
gravity nestling its fist
in the center of my stubborn belly
whereas you were lithe
with the speed of a rabbit,
quick and cunning.
You hopped to errands,
fetching this and that.

We shared papaya boats
Mother emptied of tiny black seeds
that resembled caviar
and egg shells Father hollowed for whistles.
Our lungs expanded
as though they were balloon fish
fluttering out noiseless tunes.
We blew our songs to the gulch
that brought the eucalyptus smell of rain.

I don't remember
going there into the forest,
although you must have taken me
where the lilikoi vines
dripped sticky sap passionately,
their blossoms curling like bells or tongues.
I heard my first story from you.

Waving good-bye
at the edge of the grass,
you disappeared into the bushes
like a huntress, the only girl
in a gang of boys.
I knew bravery then
and what it meant to belong to a tribe
when you returned triumphant

just as the afternoon showers broke,
with all their marbles
bulging in the pockets
of your leopard spotted pedal pushers.
I heard your slippers slapping the mud
and running to meet you
at the screen door,
I saw you laugh, tossing up something
sunlit and flashing into the air:
you told me how Arnold had cried
to lose his precious tiger's eye.

Myung Mi Kim

(b. 1957)

Myung Mi Kim was born in Seoul, Korea, and emigrated to the United States at age nine. She has received degrees from Oberlin College, John Hopkins University, and the University of Iowa, where she received a master of fine arts. Her first book of poetry, **Under Flag,** *was published in 1991 and her second,* **The Bounty,** *will be published soon by Chax Press. She currently is an assistant professor in the creative writing program at San Francisco State University.*

The two poems published here first appeared in **The Forbidden Stitch: An Asian American Women's Anthology** *(1989). Both poems pursue the loss of a sense of self and culture through immigration, naturalization, and assimilation. In the process there is the potential for the denial of one's origins and language. In the poem "Into Such Assembly," Kim asks "Who is the mother tongue, who is the father tongue?"*

Into Such Assembly

1.
Can you read and write English? Yes__. No__.
Write down the following sentences in English as I dictate them.
    There is a dog in the road.
    It is raining.
Do you renounce allegiance to any other country but this?
Now tell me, who is the president of the United States?
You will all stand now. Raise your right hands.

Cable car rides over swan-flecked ponds
Red lacquer chests in our slateblue house
Chrysanthemums trailing bloom after bloom
Ivory, russet, pale yellow petals crushed
Between fingers, that green smell, if jade would smell
So-Sah's thatched roofs shading miso hung to dry—
Sweet potatoes grow on the rock-choked side of the mountain
The other, the pine wet green side of the mountain
Hides a lush clearing where we picnic and sing:
    Sung-Bul-Sah, geep eun bahm ae[1]

---

1.   Transliteration of Korean composer Hong Nahm Pah's song, "Night at Sung-Bul-Sah." The line may be translated as "Sung-Bul-Sah, in the depth of night."

Neither, neither

Who is mother tongue, who is father country?

2.
Do they have trees in Korea? Do the children eat out of garbage cans?

We had a Dalmatian
We rode the train on weekends from Seoul to So-Sah where we grew grapes

We ate on the patio surrounded by dahlias

Over there, ass is cheap—those girls live to make you happy

Over there, we had a slateblue house with a flat roof where I made many snowmen, over there

No, "th," "th," put your tongue against the roof of your mouth, lean slightly against the back of the top teeth, then bring your bottom teeth up to barely touch your tongue and breathe out, and you should feel the tongue vibrating, "th," "th," look in the mirror,
that's better

And with distance traveled, as part of it

How often when it rains here does it rain there?

One gives over to a language and then

What is given, given over?

3.
This rain eats into most anything

And when we had been scattered over the face of the earth
We could not speak to one another

The creek rises, the rain-fed current rises

> Color given up, sap given up
> Weeds branches groves what they make as one

This rain gouging already gouged valleys
And the fill, fill, flow over

> What gives way losing gulch, mesa, peak, state, nation

Land, ocean dissolving
The continent and the peninsula, the peninsula and continent
Of one piece sweeping

One table laden with one crumb
Every mouthful off a spoon whole

Each drop strewn into such assembly

A Rose of Sharon[1]

Is it because my hair is golden brown that even when I wear it in pigtails like them they still snicker and push me away from the twirling rope?

By the time I finish my newspaper cone of fried sweet potatoes you will be standing on the corner wearing spit-shined shoes. By the time I choose the shape I want and watch the old man pour the brown melted sugar into the hot mold, when I'm about to lick the bronze candy rabbit on a stick you will wave to me getting off a crowded bus.

I will know it is you because you will be tall and you will be handsome. You will know it is me because my eyes are round and big like a doll's that other girls buy.

Do you have a dog? When's your birthday?

---

1.   Rose of Sharon is the Korean national flower.

After mom leaves, grandmother fixes my supper. Was he kind? Tell me one little thing he said. I don't remember, she says. Where did he come from? I don't know, she says, gnashing on tidbits of pickled roots, a fish head. What color hair? Just an American, a Big Nose—eat that soup.

I could tell you how many apples the fruit vendor has piled on his cart, how the holes in front of the house fill, thick with mud. I'll tell you what they are saying today.

They say two Big Noses threw her out a window. They say her hands were tied, and she had no clothes on. It is well after noon. She would have washed her hair by now and lain down. I would be fanning the dust, heat, or stray fly away from her, watching her sleep.

Li-Young Lee

(b. 1957)

Li-Young Lee was born to Chinese parents in Jakarta, Indonesia, in 1957. Lee's father fled from Indonesia in 1959 after spending a year as a political prisoner during President Sukarno's regime. For the next five years, the family traveled through Hong Kong, Macau, and Japan, eventually arriving in America to settle in Pennsylvania. Li-Young Lee studied at the University of Pittsburgh, the University of Arizona, and the State University of New York at Brockport. His first book of poetry, **Rose** (1986), won New York University's Delmore Schwartz Memorial Poetry Award. His second volume of poetry, **The City in Which I Love You** (1990), was the 1990 Lamont Poetry Selection of the Academy of American Poets. A memoir entitled **The Winged Seed** was published in 1994. He has also received numerous other honors, including a John Simon Guggenheim Memorial Foundation fellowship, the Writer's Award from the Mrs. Giles Whiting Foundation, and a fellowship from the National Endowment for the Arts. He lives in Chicago with his wife Donna and their two children.

"The Cleaving" comes from Lee's collection of poems **The City in Which I Love You**. In this poem Lee focuses on his family's ancestral roots and the discovery and preservation of that knowledge feeds the soul and feeds the act of naming all those who came before him:

> ... this Jew, this Asian, this one
> with the Cambodian face, this Vietnamese face, this Chinese
> I daily face,
> this immigrant,
> this man with my own face.

The Cleaving

He gossips like my grandmother, this man
with my face, and I could stand
amused all afternoon
in the Hon Kee Grocery,
amid hanging meats he
chops: roast pork cut
from a hog hung
by nose and shoulders,
her entire skin burnt
crisp, flesh I know
to be sweet,
her shining

face grinning
up at ducks
dangling single file,
each pierced by black
hooks through breast, bill,
and steaming from a hole
stitched shut at the ass.
I step to the counter, recite,
and he, without even slightly
varying the rhythm of his current confession or harangue,
scribbles my order on a greasy receipt,
and chops it up quick.

Such a sorrowful Chinese face,
nomad, Gobi, Northern
in its boniness
clear from the high
warlike forehead
to the sheer edge of the jaw.
He could be my brother, but finer,
and, except for his left forearm, which is engorged,
sinewy from his daily grip and
wield of a two-pound tool,
he's delicate, narrow-
waisted, his frame
so slight a lover, some
rough other
might break it down
its smooth, oily length.
In his light-handed calligraphy
on receipts and in his
moodiness, he is
a Southerner from a river-province;
suited for scholarship, his face poised
above an open book, he'd mumble
his favorite passages.
He could be my grandfather;
come to America to get a Western education
in 1917, but too homesick to study,

he sits in the park all day, reading poems
and writing letters to his mother.

He lops the head off, chops
the neck of the duck
into six, slits
the body
open, groin
to breast, and drains
the scalding juices,
then quarters the carcass
with two fast hacks of the cleaver,
old blade that has worn
into the surface of the round
foot-thick chop-block
a scoop that cradles precisely the curved steel.

The head, flung from the body, opens
down the middle where the butcher
cleanly halved it between
the eyes, and I
see, foetal-crouched
inside the skull, the homunculus,[1]
gray brain grainy
to eat.
Did this animal, after all, at the moment
its neck broke,
imagine the way his executioner
shrinks from his own death?
Is this how
I, too, recoil from my day?
See how this shape
hordes itself, see how
little it is.
See its grease on the blade.
Is this how I'll be found
when judgement is passed, when names

---

1.   a dwarf

are called, when crimes are tallied?
This is also how I looked before I tore my mother open.
Is this how I presided over my century, is this how
I regarded the murders?
This is also how I prayed.
Was it me in the Other
I prayed to when I prayed?
This too was how I slept, clutching my wife.
Was it me in the other I loved
when I loved another?
The butcher sees me eye this delicacy.
With a finger, he picks it
out of the skull-cradle
and offers it to me.
I take it gingerly between my fingers
and suck it down.
I eat my man.

The noise the body makes
when the body meets
the soul over the soul's ocean and penumbra
is the old sound of up-and-down, in-and-out,
a lump of muscle chug-chugging blood
into the ear; a lover's
heart-shaped tongue;
flesh rocking flesh until flesh comes;
the butcher working
at his block and blade to marry their shapes
by violence and time;
an engine crossing,
re-crossing salt water, hauling
immigrants and the junk
of the poor. These
are the faces I love, the bodies
and scents of bodies
for which I long
in various ways, at various times,
thirteen gathered around the redwood,
happy, talkative, voracious

at day's end,
eager to eat
four kinds of meat
prepared four different ways,
numerous plates and bowls of rice and vegetables,
each made by distinct affections
and brought to table by many hands.

Brothers and sisters by blood and design,
who sit in separate bodies of varied shapes,
we constitute a many-membered
body of love.
In a world of shapes
of my desires, each one here
is a shape of one of my desires, and each
is known to me and dear by virtue
of each one's unique corruption
of those texts, the face, the body:
that jut jaw
to gnash tendon;
that wide nose to meet the blows
a face like that invites;
those long eyes closing on the seen;
those thick lips
to suck the meat of animals
or recite 300 poems of the T'ang;[2]
these teeth to bite my monosyllables;
these cheekbones to make
those syllables sing the soul.
Puffed or sunken
according to the life,
dark or light according
to the birth, straight
or humped, whole, manqué, quasi, each pleases, verging
on utter grotesquery.
All are beautiful by variety.
The soul too

---

2. T'ang Dynasty, 618–907

is a debasement
of a text, but, thus, it
acquires salience, although a
human salience, but
inimitable, and, hence, memorable.
God is the text.
The soul is a corruption
and a mnemonic.

A bright moment,
I hold up an old head
from the sea and admire the haughty
down-curved mouth
that seems to disdain
all the eyes are blind to,
including me, the eater.
Whole unto itself, complete
without me, yet its
shape complements the shape of my mind.
I take it as text and evidence
of the world's love for me,
and I feel urged to utterance,
urged to read the body of the world, urged
to say it
in human terms,
my reading a kind of eating, my eating
a kind of reading,
my saying a diminishment, my noise
a love-in-answer.
What is it in me would
devour the world to utter it?
What is it in me will not let
the world be, would eat
not just this fish,
but the one who killed it,
the butcher who cleaned it.
I would eat the way he
squats, the way he
reaches into the plastic tubs

and pulls out a fish, clubs it, takes it
to the sink, guts it, drops it on the weighing pan.
I would eat that thrash
and plunge of the watery body
in the water, that liquid violence
between the man's hands,
I would eat
the gutless twitching on the scales,
three pounds of dumb
nerve and pulse, I would eat it all
to utter it.
The deaths at the sinks, those bodies prepared
from eating, I would eat,
and the standing deaths
at the counters, in the aisles,
the walking deaths in the streets,
the death-far-from-home, the death-
in-a-strange-land, these Chinatown
deaths, these American deaths.
I would devour this race to sing it,
this race that according to Emerson[3]
managed to preserve to a hair
for three or four thousand years
the ugliest features in the world.
I would eat these features, eat
the last three or four thousand years, every hair.
And I would eat Emerson, his transparent soul, his
soporific transcendence.
I would eat his head,
glazed in pepper-speckled sauce,
the cooked eyes opaque in their sockets.
I bring it to my mouth and—
the way I was taught, the way I've watched
others before me do—
with a stiff tongue lick out
the cheek-meat and the meat
over the armored jaw, my eating,

---

3.   Ralph Waldo Emerson, U.S. essayist and poet, 1803–1882

its sensual, salient nowness,
punctuating the void
from which such hunger springs and to which it proceeds.

And what
is this
I excavate
with my mouth?
What is this
plated, ribbed, hinged
architecture, this *carp head*,
but one more
articulation of a single nothing
severally manifested?
What is my eating,
rapt as it is,
but another
shape of going,
my immaculate expiration?

O, nothing is so
steadfast it won't go
the way the body goes.
The body goes.
The body's grave,
so serious
in its dying,
arduous as martyrs
in the task and as
glorious. It goes
empty always
and announces its going
by spasms and groans, farts and sweats.
What I thought were the arms
aching *cleave*, were the knees trembling *leave*.
What I thought were the muscles
insisting *resist, persist, exist*,
were the pores
hissing *mist* and *waste*.

What I thought was the body humming *reside, reside,*
was the body sighing *revise, revise.*
O, the murderous deletions, the keening
down to nothing, the cleaving.
All of the body's revisions end
in death.
All of the body's revisions end.

Bodies eating bodies, heads eating heads,
we are nothing eating nothing,
and though we feast,
are filled, overfilled,
we go famished.
We gang the doors of death.
That is, our deaths are fed
that we may continue our daily dying,
our bodies going
down, while the plates-soon-empty
are passed around, the true
direction of our true prayers,
while the butcher spells
his message, manifold,
in the mortal air.
He coaxes, cleaves, brings change
before our very eyes, and at every
moment of our being.
As we eat we're eaten.
Else what is this
violence, this salt, this
passion, this heaven?

I thought the soul an airy thing.
I did not know the soul
is cleaved so that the soul might be restored.
Live wood hewn,
its sap springs from a sticky wound.
No seed, no egg has he
whose business calls for an axe.
In the trade of my soul's shaping,
he traffics in hews and hacks.

No easy thing, violence.
One of its names? Change. Change
resides in the embrace
of the effaced and the effacer,
in the covenant of the opened and the opener;
the axe accomplishes it on the soul's axis.
What then may I do
but cleave to what cleaves me.
I kiss the blade and eat my meat.
I thank the wielder and receive,
while terror spirits
my change, sorrow also.
The terror the butcher
scripts in the unhealed
air, the sorrow of his Shang[4]
dynasty face,
African face with slit eyes. He is
my sister, this
beautiful Bedouin, this Shulamite,[5]
keeper of sabbaths, diviner
of holy texts, this dark
dancer, this Jew, this Asian, this one
with the Cambodian face, Vietnamese face, this Chinese
I daily face,
this immigrant
this man with my own face.

---

4. Shang Dynasty, 1765–1122 B.C.
5. Bedouin: nomadic desert Arab; Shulamite: epithet of the brides from the Bible,
    Song of Solomon 6:13.

DRAMA

Wakako Yamauchi

(b. 1924)

Wakako Yamauchi was born in Westmoreland, California. Her mother and father, both issei, or first-generation immigrants from Japan, were farmers in California's Imperial Valley. Many of her stories and her first two plays, **And the Soul Shall Dance** and **The Music Lessons**, are set in the same dusty, isolated settings. In 1942, Yamauchi and her family were interned at the concentration camp in Poston, Arizona. Her first play, **And the Soul Shall Dance**, adapted from her short story of the same title, was first performed at the East/West Players in Los Angeles and won the Los Angeles Critics' Circle Award for best new play of 1977. It was produced for public television.

The Music Lessons, like her first play, explores the suffering and hardships of the first-generation issei women who came to America in the early part of the 1900s. These women not only had to adjust to their settlement in America, but also to an often bitter arranged marriage. Chizuko, the thirty-eight-year-old widowed mother of three, explains, "When I left Japan I never knew it would be like this.... Never thought my life would be so hard. I don't know what it is to be a ... a woman anymore ... to laugh ... to be soft ... to talk nice ... " Yamauchi also touches on the American-born nisei children of the issei who live by different cultural imperatives brought on by an American education and an ability and desire to assimilate. The isolation of the agricultural landscape is a metaphor for Chizuko, who is isolated in marriage, within the family, and obviously from Japan.

The Music Lessons

Time: September 1935
Place: Imperial Valley, California

CHARACTERS

KAORU KAWAGUCHI, thirty-three, Japanese male, itinerant
CHIZUKO SAKATA, thirty-eight, Issei widow farmer, mother
AKI SAKATA, fifteen, daughter of Chizuko
ICHIRO SAKATA, seventeen, son of Chizuko
TOMU SAKATA, sixteen, son of Chizuko
NAKAMURA, forty-five, male, Issei farmer
BILLY KANE, fifteen, white, friend of the children
WAITRESS, middle-aged, non-Asian

Act One

Scene 1

Time: September 1935

At rise: Center stage left is the interior of the Sakata kitchen. It is spare, almost stark. There is a table with at least three chairs, some crockery (water pitcher, glasses) on a cupboard. An upstage door leads to the bedrooms. Upstage left is a screen door leading outside.

Stage right is a tool shed. There is a cot turned on its side, crates and some tools. The interior of the shed is kept dark until it is used.

Nakamura, Issei farmer, dressed in farm clothes of the era, and Kaoru Kawaguchi, Japanese itinerant, in a sport coat, hat, and carrying a violin case and an old-fashioned suitcase enter from stage left.

NAKAMURA: I don't see the truck. Maybe she's not home.

KAORU: You're sure she'll hire me?

NAKAMURA: Well, I'm not *sure*. You said you're looking for work and I thought, well, maybe Chizuko. She runs this farm all by herself and … Chizuko-san! One thing you ought to know about farming; there's always work to be done; the problem is money. There's not a lot of it around these days. (*he opens the door and peers in*) I guess she went out. Depression's still here for us farmers, you know.

KAORU: Yes, I know.

NAKAMURA: (*looking at his pocket watch*) Well, I gotta be going. (*Kaoru picks up his violin case, continuing; stopping him from following*) You ought to wait for her. She'll be back (soon) …

KAORU: (*quickly*) You do all your own work? I'd like to … you know, you don't have to pay me right (away)…

NAKAMURA: (ha-ha) I got two grown sons to help me. Now Chizuko, her boys are still young, and well, it's hard for her. It's hard for *me*; it's gotta be rough for her. You wait here. She'll be back soon. (*Kaoru puts down his violin and wipes his brow.*) Not used to the heat, eh? N'other thing: I'd hide the violin if I was you. (*he almost takes the case from Kaoru*) No good to look too … You gotta look like you can *work*. You know what I mean?

KAORU: I see.

NAKAMURA: Why don't you mosey around while you're waiting? See what people do on a farm. (ha-ha) Maybe you won't *want* to work here.

KAORU: Yes, I'll do that.

NAKAMURA: I live about a mile down this road. If Chizuko doesn't want you, come on down and I'll give you a lift back to town.

KAORU: Thank you. Thank you for being so kind to a stranger.

NAKAMURA: Japanese stick together, eh? (*he stops on his way out*) Oh, you tell her you picked grapes in Fresno and cut lettuce in Salinas. Tell her I sent you.

KAORU: Yes, I will. Thank you.

NAKAMURA: Good luck.

Nakamura exits left. Kaoru puts his suitcase in an inconspicuous place and still carrying his violin, he walks upstage center and exits behind the tool shed.

The Sakata offspring: Ichiro, son, in cotton twills and plaid shirt, hair cut short; Tomu, son, similarly dressed, and Aki, daughter, hair clasped with one metal barrette at her neck, dressed in a cotton dress of the period, have just returned from shopping for staples. They enter from the left carrying the groceries.

AKI: It's no fun shopping: shoyu, rice, miso … Always the same old stuff.

ICHIRO: Stop complaining. Next time, don't go.

AKI: Boy, Ichiro, you're getting just like Mama. Wouldn't even give me a quarter. You could have loaned it to me. I would have paid you back.

ICHIRO: With what? Tomatoes?

AKI: I could do extra work for Mama.

ICHIRO: Who gets paid for extra work?

TOMU: Ma doesn't pay for work. Period.

ICHIRO: You get food in your belly, consider yourself paid.

Chizuko Sakata, Issei, gaunt and capable-looking, hair bunned back, wearing her dead husband's shirt, pants, heavy shoes and hat, enters from stage right. She does not see the suitcase. She carries a basket of peas.

Aki comes downstage to the yard.

AKI: He wouldn't even give me a quarter, Mama.

CHIZUKO: What do you want a quarter for? (*They enter the kitchen.*)

AKI: I just wanted a small book, Mama.

ICHIRO: (*giving Chizuko the bill and change*) It's all there.

CHIZUKO: (*counting the change and putting it away in a jar*) Money has to last until spring.

AKI: But Mama, a quarter ...

CHIZUKO: A quarter buys two pounds of meat.

TOMU: We ought to be able to spend for something else besides just keeping alive.

ICHIRO: Quit complaining, will you?

CHIZUKO: After harvest you can have treats.

AKI: I won't want it then.

TOMU: She only wanted a quarter, Ma.

ICHIRO: (*silencing the two*) Hey!

CHIZUKO: I told you we don't spend right now.

TOMU: Yeah, Ma.

AKI: It was different when Papa was here.

ICHIRO: Well, Pop's not here.

AKI: He always brought stuff for us. Remember that dog, Tomu?

TOMU: Oh, yeah, Maru.

ICHIRO: Well, it's different now. You might as well get used to it.

Kaoru enters from upstage center. He picks up his suitcase. Ichiro notices him in the yard and goes out.

KAORU: Oh, hello.

ICHIRO: Hello.

CHIZUKO: Who is it, Ichiro? (*she comes to the yard*)

KAORU: Oh. You are ... Sakata-san?

CHIZUKO: Yes.

KAORU: Ah! I am Kawaguchi.

Kaoru extends a hand and Chizuko reluctantly takes it. It's not a Japanese custom to shake hands.

CHIZUKO: Kawaguchi-san?

KAORU: Kaoru. I was ... a ... with Nakamura-san a little while ago. He brought me here. He said you might be needing help and I...

Aki and Tomu come out. Visitors are few and they are very interested.

CHIZUKO: Nakamura-san brought you? (*she feels obligated to invite Kaoru in*) Sah, dozo ...[1]

Chizuko opens the door and everyone enters the house. Ichiro pulls out a chair for Kaoru.

KAORU: Yes, yes. I was looking for work and he thought you might be able to use me.

CHIZUKO: I don't know why he'd do that. He knows I don't have the money to hire. There's plenty of work here, but I just don't have the money right now.

KAORU: We can talk about that later ... when the crop (is harvested) ...

CHIZUKO: Well, we never know how it turns out. Sometimes it's good; sometimes, bad. A lot depends on weather, prices ... things like that. Besides ... (*She looks him over shamelessly.*) I need a man who can work like a horse.

KAORU: Ma'am, I know how to work. I come from peasant stock.

CHIZUKO: Then sometimes, when it rains, there's nothing to do.

KAORU: Pay me what you can.

CHIZUKO: (*dubiously*) You look like a city man.

KAORU: (*pressing*) If you put me up, I'll only need a little now and then—not right away—for cigarettes and things, you know.

CHIZUKO: Well ...

KAORU: If you do well with the harvest, we can settle then. I promise you I won't be idle. When there's time I can ... (*he brushes the dust from his violin case, and changes his mind*) Can I help your boys with their math work?

---

1. please

TOMU: Boy, I can sure use some help there.

AKI: Maybe you'll make a "C" this year.

KAORU: I can keep books for you. That's what I did in the city—bookkeeping.

CHIZUKO: (*starting to shell peas*) Looks like you're a man of talent—culture.

KAORU: (ha-ha) Well, I came to America as a boy. I finished high school here. You know, school boy—live in. I lived with rich white folks and did the gardening and cleaning while I went to school. The lady I worked for was a musician. She taught me to play this. (*he laughs wryly*) She wanted me to be a musician

CHIZUKO: Oh? What happened?

Aki gives Kaoru a glass of water. Kaoru gratefully drinks it.

KAORU: Thank you. Well, I don't know. As soon as I was able, I left them. I wanted to be on my own. But there's no chance for a Japanese violinist in America.

CHIZUKO: You worked in the city all the time?

KAORU: Most of the time, yes.

CHIZUKO: What did you do?

KAORU: This and that. Waited tables, cooked—worked as a fry cook. And bookkeeping. I did that the last few years.

CHIZUKO: Maybe better you stay at a nice clean job like that than work on a dirt farm like this. Why did you want to come out here?

KAORU: Oh, I didn't get fired. To be honest, I wanted to ... start something new. I was tired of city life. I wanted a change.

CHIZUKO: I want a change too. But some of us ... (*she glances at her children*) we're not free to do that. Change.

Kaoru sees the futility of going on. He just about gives up but gives it one last try.

KAORU: I understand your doubts about me. I have no references or recommendation, but I'm an honest man and I'll work hard for you. I give you my word.

Chizuko looks quickly at Ichiro. The children are excited.

CHIZUKO: All right. But no pay until after the harvest.

KAORU: You won't regret this, Ma'am.

From stage left, Billy Kane, white neighbor, pedals his bicycle into the yard. It's equipped with a raccoon tail, reflectors, stickers, etc.

BILLY: Tomu! Hey, Tomu!

TOMU: That'll be Billy.

KAORU: (*to Chizuko*) You have another son?

ICHIRO: It's Billy Kane. He lives down the road.

AKI: He comes over a lot. They're rich.

Tomu goes downstage to meet Billy.

TOMU: (*to Billy*) Hi.

ICHIRO: They're not that rich. His father works for the American Fruit Growers. On salary.

BILLY: (*astride his bicycle*) Guess what? We went to Yosemite[2] last week.

The conversation is heard in the kitchen.

TOMU: Oh, yeah?

CHIZUKO: (*to Kaoru*) My boys spent summer here—flooding, plowing, getting ready for planting. It was hot. Hundred ten degrees.

ICHIRO: We bought the seed today. Cash.

BILLY: (*in the yard; to Tomu*) There was a stream just outside the tent. It was cold!

TOMU: That right? (*he gets on Billy's bicycle*)

BILLY: (*showing Tomu a postcard*) See this?

CHIZUKO: (*to Ichiro*) You and Tomu clean the tool shed. Aki, get blankets and sheets for Kawaguchi-san.

Aki exits through the upstage doorway and Ichiro goes outside to join Tomu and Billy.

BILLY: We cooked over a fire. You know, the fish Dad caught.

ICHIRO: Come on, let's get this done. (*to Billy*) You too.

---

2.   Yosemite National Park

CHIZUKO: (*to Kaoru*) Looks like an act of Providence. We start planting tomorrow. If we get through in a week, the boys can start school together this year. I don't want them to get behind.

Aki appears with a pillow, sheet, and blanket.

AKI: They're both in the same class.

CHIZUKO: (*impatiently*) They have to be so they can teach each other.

KAORU: How's that?

AKI: They take turns going to school and the one that goes, teaches the other what he missed.

CHIZUKO: Not all the time. Only when work piles up here. Some things just have to be done on time.

Chizuko waves Aki away. Aki joins the boys in the shed.

CHIZUKO: When did you say you came to America?

KAORU: Nineteen nineteen. I was sixteen.

The children are in the shed putting hoes, rakes, etc., out and making the bed.

CHIZUKO: I'll call you when supper's ready.

KAORU: (*taking this cue to leave*) Yes, thank you.

He follows the children's voices to the shed. Chizuko begins chopping vegetables. Aki returns to the kitchen.

AKI: (*peering over Chizuko's shoulder*) Oh, don't make that again, Mama.

Fade out

Fill-in to make time for costume changes before Act I, Scene 2, and also to indicate the passage of time.

The stage is dark. Kaoru is in the shed changing. Country western music of the thirties plays from a radio (suggestions: "Now and Then") and the announcer makes a weather report.

ANNOUNCER: This is Bucky Burns with the extended forecast for Saturday through Monday. Fair weather except for some night and morning clouds. A slight warming trend with highs ranging from seventy-five to eighty degrees. Low in the upper sixties. North-westerly winds at five to ten miles. Generally fair for the next three days. Now back to your old favorites.

Country music continues until costume changes are made.

Scene 2

Time: October—afternoon

At rise: In Kaoru's shed. Kaoru has just returned from town. He's dressed in his good clothes. It's his day off and on the edge of the bed is a paper bag containing a small book of poems, magazines, some candy, and a pretty chiffon scarf. Kaoru's door is closed. Nakamura enters from stage left. He carries a small bottle of wine in his back pocket.

NAKAMURA: Chizuko-san … (*he opens the kitchen door and peers in*) Chizuko-san!

KAORU: (*opening his shed door*) Hello!

NAKAMURA: Oh! Chizuko told me she hired you.

KAORU: Come in. Come in. (*Nakamura enters the shed.*) Been almost a month now. Today's my day off.

NAKAMURA: (*looks for a place to sit and picks up the paper bag*) Been to town already, eh? Been shopping.

KAORU: Just some things for the kids. They don't have much fun.

NAKAMURA: You're a good man, Kawa. (*he looks inside the bag*)

KAORU: For the girl. She likes to read. (*Nakamura pulls out the scarf and looks questioningly at Kaoru. The scarf should convey the kind of woman Kaoru loved.*) Oh, that. Reminded me of someone I once knew. I'm thinking of sending it to her.

NAKAMURA: Oh, yeah? (*he drinks from his bottle*)

KAORU: Maybe it's foolish.

NAKAMURA: No-no. (*he offers Kaoru a sip*) Where's Chizuko-san?

KAORU: (*refusing the drink*) I don't know. I just got back from town.

NAKAMURA: (*looking around and lowering his voice*) That woman never lets up. Works like a man. Maybe better, eh?

KAORU: Maybe.

NAKAMURA: Says she found a good man, Kawa. Thanked me for sending you down. (*he laughs raucously*) Yeah. She thinks we're old friends.

KAORU: I'm working hard. I'm going to try to get her a good harvest so I can make some money too.

NAKAMURA: *(laughing hard)* You think all you got to do to make money is to work hard? If that's the way, I'd be a millionaire now.

KAORU: You don't have to be a millionaire to have a farm. I want to save some money and start my own place. (*Nakamura laughs again.*) Sure. I'll work here for a while and get the feel of it; save my money and ...

NAKAMURA: "Save," horseshit! Only way to do is borrow money.

KAORU: Who's going to lend me money? I got no collateral.

NAKAMURA: Well, first you get some names together. Good names. You can use mine. Sponsors, you know? Then you go to a produce company—in Los Angeles—put on a good suit, talk big ... how you going to make big money for them. Get in debt. Then you pay back after the harvest. (*the futility of it occurs to him*) Then you borrow again next year. Then you pay back. If you can. Same thing again next year. You never get the farm. The farm gets you. (*he drinks from the bottle*)

KAORU: You never get the farm?

NAKAMURA: 'S true. Orientals can't own land here. It's the law.

KAORU: The law? Then how is it that (you) ...

NAKAMURA: Well, I lease. If you have a son old enough you can buy land under his name. He's American citizen, you see? That's if you have enough money.

KAORU: I'll apply for citizenship, then.

NAKAMURA: There's a law against that too. Orientals can't be citizens.

KAORU: We can't?

NAKAMURA: That's the law. Didn't you know?

Nakamura again offers Kaoru a drink. This time he accepts and drains the bottle. Nakamura looks at the empty bottle.

   Hey, let's go to town.

KAORU: I just came from there.

NAKAMURA: Yeah, me too. Come on, we'll get some more wine. (*he moves to the door, lowering his voice*) You know, Chizuko doesn't like drinking. Her old man used to (ha-ha) drink a little. Like me. He drowned in a canal, you know. Fell off a cat-walk.

KAORU: (*putting on his coat*) Is that right?

NAKAMURA: Yeah, six ... almost seven years ago.

KAORU: That long?

NAKAMURA: Yeah. She got lucky with tomatoes a couple of years ago and paid back all her old man's debts. People never expected to see their money again, but she did it. She paid them back. Now she never borrows—lives close to the belly—stingy, tight. That's the way she stays ahead. Not much ahead, but ...

They exit talking.

KAORU: That so?

NAKAMURA: What's she planting this year?

KAORU: Squash, tomatoes ...

NAKAMURA: Tomatoes again?

Fade out

Scene 3

Time: Shortly after

At rise: On stage right there is a set-up for a pool hall. There is a table, two chairs, and a beer sign on the wall.

Waitress, heavily made-up, non-Asian, sits on one of the chairs, her feet propped on the other. She files her nails. Faint sounds of country music come from a radio off-stage.

Nakamura and Kaoru enter talking.

NAKAMURA: And the day after he was buried, she's out there plowing the field. (*he addresses the waitress rudely*) Oi!

WAITRESS: Oi???

NAKAMURA: I couldn't believe it. The day after she buried him. (*to the waitress*) Wine!

WAITRESS: (*shining up to Kaoru*) What kind of wine.

NAKAMURA: (*oblivious*) Red wine. (*to Kaoru*) Can you believe it? A woman behind the ass of a horse the day after her man's funeral. It ain't right.

The waitress brings the wine to the table and Kaoru pays her in small change while Nakamura fumbles with his wallet (a pinch purse).

WAITRESS: *Arigato!*[3]

Kaoru looks the waitress over. Nakamura is irritated and waves the woman away. Since they are speaking in Japanese, the waitress doesn't understand them except when they talk directly to her.

NAKAMURA: She'll give you a disease, Kawa. You don't want to fool around with that kind. (*Kaoru laughs.*) I mean it. They can get you in a lot of trouble.

KAORU: (*laughing*) I know, I know.

NAKAMURA: Japanese stick to Japanese. Better that way.

KAORU: Yeah.

NAKAMURA: So I tell her, "Chizuko-san, you got a right to cry. Take time out to cry." She says no. So I say, "I'll do your plowing. Stay home for a while." And you know what she said?

KAORU: What'd she say?

NAKAMURA: She says that's the way she cries … by working. (*he calls for the waitress*) Oi!

KAORU: I guess there're all kinds of ways.

NAKAMURA: She must be crying all the time, the way she works.

They both have a good laugh on Chizuko.

NAKAMURA: Too bad. She's getting all stringy and dried up. Heh, I remember when she was young—kinda pretty—but she's getting all … oh-oh …

———————————

3.   thank you

The waitress pours again and Nakamura makes a feeble attempt to reach for his purse. Kaoru pays again.

WAITRESS: *(to Kaoru)* You're a real gentleman. Thank you. *(she winks at him and leaves)*

NAKAMURA: Bet you had plenty of them, eh? All kinds?

KAORU: *(laughing)* All kinds.

They're feeling loose and happy from the wine.

NAKAMURA: Yeah? Bet you been in heaps of trouble, eh?

KAORU: Oh-yeah. *(he pushes up his sleeve)* See this? Bullet went clean through this arm.

NAKAMURA: Ever get one in trouble?

KAORU: Hunh?

NAKAMURA: Ever get one pregnant?

KAORU: Yeah, I did.

NAKAMURA: Liked her a lot, eh?

KAORU: Yeah.

NAKAMURA: I never been that way. A woman's a woman to me. Never been that way. *(he feels sad)* What's it like, Kawa? Never been that way. Must be a good feeling.

KAORU: Sometimes.

NAKAMURA: Old bastard like me, been married, the same woman—picture bride—twenty years. Still don't know that feeling. *(he drinks)* Is it good? Kawa, what's it like?

KAORU: Sometimes it hurts like hell. Rather be shot, sometimes.

NAKAMURA: Why's it gotta hurt like that?

KAORU: I don't know. Sometimes they're married. Then everybody gets hurt.

NAKAMURA: Married! What kind of woman's that?

KAORU: That's the way it happened.

NAKAMURA: What's the matter you do like that?

KAORU: I don't know ...

NAKAMURA: The baby. What happened to the baby.

KAORU: No baby. Aborted.

NAKAMURA: Waaah! You lucky to get away from that kind.

KAORU: Yeah, I know. (*he is still morose*)

NAKAMURA: No good, Kawa! You got twenty-thirty more years. Let a woman
grab your balls and you good for nothing. 'Specially that kind.

KAORU: You're right.

NAKAMURA: Sure, I'm right. I'm right. Oi! (*he calls the waitress*)

KAORU: No-no. No more for me. Well, maybe I'll take one with me.

NAKAMURA: Get my friend a bottle.

WAITRESS: To go?

NAKAMURA: Sure, I'm right. Laugh about it; you got to move on.

KAORU: 'S what I'm trying to do.

NAKAMURA: (*reluctantly standing*) You think 'bout what I said.

WAITRESS: (*to Kaoru*) You're going already?

KAORU: Pretty soon.

WAITRESS: (*whispering*) I'll be off in a couple of minutes.

NAKAMURA: Kawa, you coming?

KAORU: (*his attention on the waitress*) Pretty soon.

NAKAMURA: Come on, come on.

KAORU: All right. (*but he doesn't stand*)

NAKAMURA: (*noticing what's happening*) Well, I'll pick you up later.

KAORU: That's fine.

Light fades on Kaoru and the waitress sitting together and whispering.

Fade out

Scene 4

Time: That evening

At rise: Interior of the Sakata kitchen. Dinner is just over; Ichiro and Tomu are seated at the table. Aki is clearing the dishes and Chizuko puts out text books. A place is still set for Kaoru.

TOMU: (*picking his teeth*) The food is getting better around here.

ICHIRO: What you call company dinner.

AKI: It was good.

TOMU: Too bad Kaoru-san couldn't eat with us.

CHIZUKO: (*worried*) Maybe something happened.

TOMU: Maybe he couldn't get a ride back.

ICHIRO: Maybe he's looking around town.

AKI: Not much to look at. Five blocks and you're out of it.

TOMU: Why don't we go pick him up?

ICHIRO: Aw, he'll find his way back.

TOMU: But it's getting late. Eight miles is a long ...

ICHIRO: No one ever worried about me walking eight miles. He'll catch a ride.

CHIZUKO: Ichiro's right. He'll get a ride.

AKI: There're hardly any cars on the road at night, Mama.

CHIZUKO: He'll find his way back.

ICHIRO: Or maybe he won't come back.

TOMU: He'll come back.

CHIZUKO: He'll come back.

TOMU: Besides, where would he go? Ma didn't give him much money.

CHIZUKO: I gave him as much as I could. After the har(vest) ...

AKI: Yeah, we know. After the harvest.

CHIZUKO: Well, we'll make it up to him later.

Billy drives into the yard on his bicycle. He bleeps his new horn. The boys look up from their books.

BILLY: Tomu ...

ICHIRO: Your friend, Tomu.

AKI: *(to Ichiro)* I suppose he has something else to show us. *(Tomu goes downstage.)*

TOMU: *(to Billy)* Hi!

ICHIRO: The bicycle horn. Didn't you hear it?

Billy and Tomu can be heard in the kitchen. The yard remains dark.

BILLY: *(honking the horn again)* Look at this.

TOMU: Swell! Did you buy it?

BILLY: Sold twenty-four Wolverine salves for it.

TOMU: Salves?

BILLY: Yeah. You can get one too. Just sell the salves. My dad bought all mine.

TOMU: No thanks. I might get stuck with them. What'd I do with twenty-four salves?

ICHIRO: *(leaning toward the window)* What'd you do with a bicycle horn? You ain't even got a bicycle.

BILLY: *(to Tomu)* You can give them away. My mom's going to give them to friends for Christmas. *(Tomu bonks the horn several times.)*

CHIZUKO: *(leaning out the door)* Shhh!

TOMU: My mom'd hit the ceiling.

AKI: *(to Ichiro)* Maybe he'll get one one day. How do you know?

ICHIRO: Yeah, when he's fifty.

Billy and Tomu walk into the kitchen. Billy gives Chizuko a quick nod.

BILLY: Hi! Want to see what I got, Ich?

ICHIRO: Don't have time.

BILLY: Aki?

AKI: I'm busy.

BILLY: Busy, busy, busy. This family's always busy. What do you do for fun?

ICHIRO: Oh, we have fun. We ... we seed, we weed, we irrigate, and in winter we light smudge pots.

BILLY: That's fun?

ICHIRO: Lots of fun. Two o'clock in the morning ... cold as hell. And pretty soon we'll be doing brush covers.

Aki snickers. Chizuko shrinks in pain.

TOMU: Yeah, and all the other times we study, study, study. That's the kind of fun we have.

CHIZUKO: It'll be better this year.

BILLY: (*to Aki*) Aren't you going to ask me to sit down?

AKI: Sit down.

TOMU: Come on, Billy, let's go to my room.

But Billy sits down. Of stage we hear the sound of a car driving into the yard. Nakamura and Kaoru enter from left with a bottle. They sing and laugh. The family sits frozen and listens.

KAORU AND NAKAMURA: Oyu no naka ni mo / Korya hana ga saku go / Choyna, choyna ... [4]

KAORU: Oh-oh.

NAKAMURA: You all right?

KAORU: Sure. Thanks a lot. Appreciate it.

NAKAMURA: 'S all right. We do it again sometime, eh?

AKI: (*at the window*) He drinks, Mama.

CHIZUKO: That's not your business, Aki.

Nakamura exits left and Kaoru goes into his shed, sees the paper bag with the presents, picks it up and with his bottle, crosses the yard and enters the kitchen. His laugh is still on his face.

KAORU: (*he steps back to look at the family*) Hello-hello. What a nice picture.

CHIZUKO: (*dispassionately*) Did you eat?

---

4.   old Japanese drinking song

KAORU: Oh-yeah. Ate, drank, and (ha-ha)...Got a ride back with Nakamura-san. Very friendly, nice man. Spent most of the day with him.

CHIZUKO: With a family waiting supper for him.

KAORU: (ha-ha) Got some things here.

He spills the presents, candy, magazines, and book on the table—all but the scarf. If the scarf happens to fall partially out, Kaoru will put it back in the bag. He distributes the magazines to the boys.

ICHIRO: What for? What's this for?

KAORU: They're presents.

The children come alive. Billy is happy for them. The bag with the scarf falls to the floor. The children's talk overlap.

BILLY: How about that?

TOMU: Gee, thanks.

ICHIRO: Thanks a lot.

Kaoru gives the book of poems to Aki with exaggerated gallantry.

KAORU: And ... for Aki-chan!

AKI: Oh! Thank you!

KAORU: Now would you get me a small glass, Aki-chan?

AKI: Oh, sure.

Chizuko gets the glass for Kaoru and plants it firmly in front of him.

KAORU: (*elaborately*) Thank you, Chizuko-san.

CHIZUKO: (*clearing away Kaoru's dishes*) You sure you don't want something to eat?

KAORU: No-no, nothing. (*he pours his wine and lifts the glass as though to make a toast. The family stares at him—Chizuko with disapproval. There is an uncomfortable silence*) Well, I'd better go.

AKI: (*holding her book to her breast*) Thank you, Kaoru-san.

KAORU: Goodnight.

ICHIRO AND TOMU: Yeah, thanks.

BILLY: Goodnight.

Kaoru leaves. The children look at their magazines.

TOMU: Look, Billy.

BILLY: Oh! Hey, can I borrow that?

TOMU: (*kidding*) No.

BILLY: Man-o-man. (*to Aki*) Let's see the book.

Aki flicks it briefly in front of Billy. Tomu catches a look.

TOMU: Sonets from the ... What are sonets?

AKI: Sonnets. Poems, dopey.

ICHIRO: Poems?

BILLY: Oh-boy.

AKI: (*reading from the book*)

> "What can I give thee back, O liberal
> and princely giver, who has brought the gold
> and purple of thine heart ... "

TOMU: What's she talking about?

BILLY: Beats me.

AKI: " ... unstained, untold,

> And laid them on the outside of the wall
> For such as I to take or leave withal
> In unexpected largesse? am I cold ...   "

ICHIRO: Largesse?

TOMU: Woo-woo!

AKI: (*continues to read as much of the poem as it takes for Kaoru to get to his shed and start playing the violin*)

> "Ungrateful that for these most manifold
> High gifts, I render nothing back at all?
> Not so; not cold—but very poor instead
> Ask God who knows. For frequent tears have run
> The colors from my life, and left so dead
> And pale a stuff, it were not fitly done
> To give the same as pillow to thy head
> Go farther! let is serve to trample on."[5]

---

5.   Elizabeth Barrett Browning, *Sonnets from the Portuguese*

From the shed comes beautiful violin music that breaks the stillness of the desert (Bach?). Everyone is still for a while. Then Aki closes her book and starts out the door.

BILLY: Hey, where you going?

ICHIRO: I think they're playing our song.

TOMU: (*teasing*) That's our song?

BILLY: Aki, is that *our* song?

ICHIRO: "When I'm calling you ooooo ... "

AKI: I'm going to the toilet!

BILLY: Don't forget to request some potty music. (*Aki is already out the door.*) Just kidding, Aki. Aki ... ? (*Aki stands at Kaoru's door and listens to the music.*) I think I'll go home now.

TOMU: Yeah? Well, okay. (*he's engrossed in his magazine*)

Billy leaves. Downstage is dark. There's a light in the kitchen and we see the boys reading and Chizuko standing by the window. In the shed, Kaoru plays the violin.

There is a narrow cot, a few upturned crates, a bottle of wine, and a glass near his bedside. The room is neat.

BILLY: (*to Aki*) What're you doing out here?

AKI: (*moving downstage*) Shhh!

BILLY: I'm going home now.

AKI: (*listening to the music*) Okay.

Billy gets on his bicycle, bleeps his horn and exits to the left. Kaoru hears the horn and comes out. Billy is gone.

KAORU: Oh. Aren't you cold out here, Aki-chan?

AKI: The music is so beautiful.

KAORU: Come inside. I'll teach you to play this. (*he holds the door open for her*)

AKI: (*hesitantly entering*) Oh, I don't know if I can ...

KAORU: Sure, you can. (*Kaoru tucks the violin under Aki's chin and shows her how to hold the bow and lets her draw her own sounds. The noise is terrible.*) Put your chin ... that's right. Elbow in ... unhunh.... Hold your fingers ... now draw down. Up ... down ...

In the kitchen Chizuko and the boys hear the sounds and sit there shocked. Then they start to laugh.

ICHIRO: Sounds like a cat with a belly-ache.

TOMU: Ooooo—eeeee … (*imitating*)

ICHIRO: That's what you call the horse's tail hitting the cat gut.

TOMU: Maybe something under the horse's tail, huh?

CHIZUKO: (*stifling her laughter*) Well, she's got to start somewhere.

ICHIRO: Yeah, but why here?

TOMU: Why not in Siberia?

CHIZUKO: You have to hand it to her. Walking right in and asking to learn.

TOMU: You think she walked in his room and asked him to teach her?

ICHIRO: What else?

TOMU: I don't think Aki would do that. (*The music stops.*)

ICHIRO: You just don't know that girl. She'll do anything.

Chizuko glances at Ichiro. In the shed Aki hands Kaoru the violin.

AKI: It sounds awful. Would you play something for me?

KAORU: All right. What would you like to hear, Aki-chan?

AKI: Oh, I don't know. Something romantic. (*she touches her book of poems*) Something … something that will remind you of me … no matter where you are.

Kaoru takes a moment to consider the implication. He plays "Two Guitars." In the house the boys return to their books. Chizuko goes to the window; she appears happy. She walks on the downstage side of the table and notices the paper bag. She picks it up. Light slowly fades in the shed and focuses on Chizuko as she holds the scarf and returns it to the bag.

Fade out

Act Two

Scene 1

Time: The next day

At rise: The Sakata yard. Kaoru and Chizuko enter from upstage right (behind Kaoru's shed), carrying hoes.

CHIZUKO: We got lots of work done. Almost half the field.

KAORU: I could have moved faster, but ...

CHIZUKO: You did good. There's a big difference between the work of a man and the work of boys.

KAORU: *(has a terrible hangover)* I'm not so good today. Don't feel so good.

CHIZUKO: Maybe too much wine last night.

Kaoru laughs weakly. Chizuko grows self-conscious and smoothes her hair. She looks better these days.

CHIZUKO: *(continuing)* Well, we'll stop for today. You want something to eat?

KAORU: No-no. I'm not hungry.

Kaoru starts toward his shed. Chizuko follows him.

CHIZUKO: How about coffee?

KAORU: That sounds good. I could use that.

Kaoru lies down on his cot as Chizuko goes to the kitchen to heat the coffee. She lights the stove and looks into the paper bag that Kaoru left the night before. She takes out the scarf, returns it to the bag and carries it to Kaoru.

CHIZUKO: Kaoru-san. Thank you for all the gifts last night. You did too much.

KAORU: No-no. It's nothing. Unless you don't want me to.

CHIZUKO: It's not that. I didn't give you much money and it's not right for you to spend it all on the children.

KAORU: Just cheap presents.

Chizuko tentatively takes a step into Kaoru's room.

CHIZUKO: You left this bag last night.

Puzzled, Kaoru looks into the bag. He sees the scarf he'd bought for someone else. He pushes the bag back to Chizuko.

KAORU: Oh. You can have it.

CHIZUKO: (*not accepting the bag*) Didn't you buy it for someone?

KAORU: No. No one. It's for you. (*he takes the scarf out and hands it to her*)

CHIZUKO: But it's too …

KAORU: It's yours.

CHIZUKO: Too nice for me.

KAORU: Not at all. Please keep it. Wear it. (*he hangs it on Chizuko's neck*)

CHIZUKO: (*embarrassed*) I'll have to find someplace to wear it to. Oh! Coffee! (*she rushes back to the kitchen*)

KAORU: Don't hurry.

Kaoru slowly leaves his quarters and sits on the bench outside as Chizuko enters the kitchen, hums a small tune, touches the soft fabric of the scarf, picks up the coffee pot (with a cloth) and a cup and returns to him in the yard. She pours the coffee.

This will make me like new. I can still get in a few hours of work.

CHIZUKO: We'll stop for today.

KAORU: There're three good hours of daylight left.

CHIZUKO: Please, Kaoru-san, I … (*she watches him drink*) Thank you for the scarf.

KAORU: Nnn.

CHIZUKO: You're so kind. My children, my boys … they do good work in school now.

KAORU: That's good.

CHIZUKO: And Aki ... you teaching Aki to play music. Thank you, Kaoru-san.

KAORU: You don't have to say anything.

CHIZUKO: She seemed so happy last night.

KAORU: Aki is, you know, very sensitive. She's a lonely little girl.

CHIZUKO: They miss their father.

KAORU: Yes, of course.

CHIZUKO: They miss him *(her voice does dead)* Funny. He never paid attention to them—to any of us. Well, I guess this work wasn't suited for him. He was always too late or too early for everything: planting, harvesting ... And dying like that—so soon. Leaving us with ... But the children miss him.

KAORU: *(reluctantly)* It must be lonely for you too.

CHIZUKO: When I left Japan I never knew it would be like this. The babies came so fast ... and me, by myself, no mother, no sister—no one—to help. I was so young ... never dreamed it would be like this. Never thought my life would be so hard. I don't know what it is to be a ... a woman anymore ... to laugh ... to be soft ... to talk nice ... *(she can't look at Kaoru)*

KAORU: Well ... (ha-ha)

CHIZUKO: I hear myself: "Don't do this; don't do that. Wear your sweater; study hard ... " I try to say other things: "How smart you are; how pretty you look ... " but my mouth won't let me. I keep thinking, life is hard. I shouldn't let them think it would be easy.

KAORU: That's true.

CHIZUKO: Well, they're used to me like I am. If I change now, they'd think I went crazy.

KAORU: The important thing is, you're here. It's no good without a mother, Chizuko-san. I know.

CHIZUKO: You ...

KAORU: My grandfather brought me up. My father was always in the rice paddy. He was a bitter old man. Old and bitter on a rice paddy. Growing old in the mud. I didn't want to die like that too.

CHIZUKO: And you never married? (*Kaoru gets another cup of coffee. Chizuko rushes to pour for him.*)

KAORU: When you're young, you think youth will last forever. You throw it away foolishly. When you finally decide you want more—a family, maybe, it's too late. Family means roots, money, and you're like one of those tumbleweeds out there. Seeds all run out of your pockets and you have no roots. No one wants a tumbleweed.

CHIZUKO: But you're not a (tumbleweed) ...

KAORU: There're lots of tumbleweeds out there. Some have wives in Japan; some even children. Some—well, like me—never got started. Before they know it, time passed them by and nothing can bring it back. (*he moves away from Chizuko*) The stories are always the same. You hear them all over—in bars, gambling dens ... forgotten men laughing at their lost dreams.

CHIZUKO: I'm forgotten too. My dreams are lost too. And my stories are all the same—one year following another, all the same.

KAORU: You have lots to look forward to: fine sons, a nice daughter.

CHIZUKO: I wonder sometimes, if it will not be the same for them too.

KAORU: (*trying to change the mood*) Cheer up, Chizuko-san. One of these days it will be time to harvest. Say! Nakamura-san told me yesterday he thinks you ... you're getting quite pretty.

CHIZUKO: (*covering her embarrassment*) Nakamura-san's an old goat.

KAORU: He's all right. I like him.

CHIZUKO: (*trying to get back to a certain topic*) I don't know how I managed all these years by myself. I don't know how I did it. It's been a hard seven years. I don't think I can do it again.

KAORU: (*laughing*) Sure, you can.

CHIZUKO: I've been thinking ... ah, wondering how you would feel about ... what you think about staying on ... on this farm, I mean. With us. (*she waits; Kaoru is silent*) I mean, share the profits ... a partnership.

KAORU: I have no money, Chizuko-san.

CHIZUKO: (*quickly*) Oh, you pay nothing. I mean a joint venture. More or less. This farm is too much for a woman alone and I ...

KAORU: Well, to be honest, I planned to work on a piece of land for myself one day.

CHIZUKO: You don't have to. You can stay right here.

KAORU: (*drawing away*) Well ...

CHIZUKO: You don't like it here? You mean you ...

KAORU: (*quickly*) No-no. Don't think me ungrateful. I mean, right now, I don't have anything to offer.

CHIZUKO: You give only what you can. (*Kaoru is silent.*) We like you, Kaoru-san. All of us. As a family, well, the children are quarrelsome sometimes, but they're good kids. They're not mean ... no trouble ...

KAORU: They're fine. You should be proud.

CHIZUKO: I ... I promise to do my best to make it nice for you. (*with some discomfort*) I know I'm not an easy woman to get along with—being so set in my ways.

KAORU: You're a fine person.

CHIZUKO: (desperately) I'm so tired. Sometimes I wish ...

KAORU: Chizuko-san, this is not a day to be so solemn. Look, the sun is shining, birds are singing ...

CHIZUKO: (*depressed at not getting through*) Yes.

KAORU: Don't worry. Everything's going to be all right. (*it's a line that's got him by many times before*) Another couple days and the weeding will be done. I think you'll have a great harvest.

CHIZUKO: If this weather holds.

KAORU: It will. Nakamura-san said it'll be a mild winter. His son heard it over the radio.

CHIZUKO: They have a radio?

KAORU: A crystal set. Maybe I can get one for Ichiro to assemble. Then you ... we can get the weather reports.

CHIZUKO: Ichiro can do that?

KAORU: Sure, he can. He's smart.

CHIZUKO: (*she brightens*) After harvest, we can buy a small radio for everyone to enjoy. We can listen to it in the evenings.

KAORU: That would be nice.

CHIZUKO: Maybe we can get a bicycle for Tomu. A used one.

Aki enters from stage left. She wears school clothes and carries books. She comes bounding into the yard.

AKI: A used what? Are we buying something? Hi!

Chizuko hurriedly pulls the scarf from her neck and stuffs it into her pocket.

KAORU: Hello there, Aki-chan.

CHIZUKO: Where are your brothers, Aki?

AKI: They're coming.

CHIZUKO: You got home early today.

AKI: I took a short cut.

KAORU: (*laughing*) Your face is flushed.

AKI: I ran all the way.

CHIZUKO: Go change your clothes, Aki.

Kaoru heads toward his shed, unbuttoning his shirt, preparing to start back to town.

AKI: Where are you going, Kaoru-san?

KAORU: I thought since we stopped work for today, I'd go (into town) …

CHIZUKO: Maybe this is a good time to repair the barn. There's a big hole in the north wall.

AKI: That's been there before Papa died.

CHIZUKO: Change your clothes, Aki.

KAORU: Yes, I noticed it. I'd better fix it. Winter's coming and the wind will blow right through.

Chizuko pushes Aki toward the house. Aki sulkily goes in. Ichiro and Tomu enter from the left. Kaoru, with a tool box in his hand, sees them.

Hello, boys. How's school. Is the math any easier?

TOMU: A lot easier.

ICHIRO: (*overlapping*) Not bad, not bad.

TOMU: (*to Chizuko*) Did Aki get home?

CHIZUKO: She's inside. What's the matter with you, Ichiro? I told you always to walk together. You're the oldest and ...

TOMU: She ran away from us, Ma.

Kaoru exits to the right. The boys and Chizuko enter the house.

ICHIRO: God, she's a big girl now. I can't watch her all the time.

CHIZUKO: I want you to walk together. I told you that. Anything can happen.

ICHIRO: Like what?

CHIZUKO: Anything. Snakes, scorpions ...

ICHIRO: Snakes? Scorpions?

TOMU: How about spiders and lizards?

ICHIRO: (*overlapping*) Yeah, and man-eating ants.

AKI: (*off stage, reading*)

"A heavy heart, Beloved, have I borne

from year to year until I saw thy face

Tomu and Ichiro groan and exit through the upstage door. Aki continues reading as the light slowly fades on Chizuko taking the scarf from her pocket and looking at it.

AKI: And sorrow after sorrow took place

of all those natural joys as lightly worn"

Fade out

Scene 2

Time: A month later

At rise: Kaoru, Ichiro, and Tomu sharpen tools downstage. The sun is setting, there is an orange glow that slowly turns dark as the scene progresses.

TOMU: (*to Kaoru*) Is this sharp enough?

KAORU: (*feeling the edge*) Just a little more.

ICHIRO: (*teasing*) That'll cut butter real good ... in summer. (*he takes the hoe from Tomu*) Here, I'll do it.

Nakamura enters from stage left.

TOMU: (*imitating Nakamura*) Nakamura-san's here. Haro-haro.

NAKAMURA: Haro-Haro. You can stop now. Sun's gone down, you know.

KAORU: (ha-ha) How are you?

NAKAMURA: You caught it from Chizuko-san, eh? I didn't know work was catching.

KAORU: Just honing tools for tomorrow.

NAKAMURA: Go easy. You'll be all worn out by harvest time.

Aki comes out of the house and walks downstage.

NAKAMURA: Oh, Aki-chan.

AKI: Hello, Oji-san.

KAORU: (*to Aki*) Go on and start. I'll be there soon.

AKI: Okay. (*she enters Kaoru's shed and prepares to practice*)

NAKAMURA: (*watching her pass him*) They grow up before you know it, eh?

KAORU: Sometimes *they* don't even know it.

NAKAMURA: Yeah. Before you know it. Next year my son—the oldest—be twenty. If it was the old country, I would think about ... about giving him a parcel of land ... (*he laughs dourly*) Well, maybe in a couple of years I can get together a down payment for ... maybe ten acres. Put it in his name ... (*Aki starts practicing. Nakamura is surprised.*) Ah! She can play the violin!

ICHIRO: No, she can't.

KAORU: Well, I've been trying to teach her.

NAKAMURA: Oh, yeah?

KAORU: She's not a good player, but she's smart. She ...

ICHIRO: (*to Tomu*) Let's get out of here.

TOMU: Yeah, let's go to Billy's.

They exit left.

NAKAMURA: Chizuko's kids are all smart. Nice boys too. Nice family.

Chizuko appears in the yard with a basket of laundry. Nakamura sees her first.

Ah! Chizuko-san! Nice, eh? Nice evening. I'm enjoying the nice music.

CHIZUKO: She's just a beginner. Sometimes I wish I were deaf. (*Aki hits some sour notes.*)

NAKAMURA: You know, Chizuko-san, when I first saw him in town—no job, nothing—just a suitcase and a violin—I felt sorry for him, then (I thought of you) ...

CHIZUKO: Nakamura-san, did you ... How is your family.

NAKAMURA: Fine, fine.

Aki's playing grows progressively worse. She tries to get Kaoru's attention. Nakamura winces at the sour notes. He prepares to leave.

Well, I better ... Eh! I almost forgot what I came for. Chizuko-san, I'm irrigating tomorrow. You want water too? Might as well order same time, eh?

CHIZUKO: Well ...

NAKAMURA: No trouble for me.

CHIZUKO: Kaoru-san, what do you think?

KAORU: Maybe we ought to finish the thinning first.

CHIZUKO: Yes. We'll wait a few days. Thank you anyway.

KAORU: (*shaking his head over Aki's bad playing*) I'd better get in there.

Aki stops playing.

NAKAMURA: That's better.

KAORU: (*in the shed, softly*) You're going to drive visitors away with your playing.

AKI: Why, thank you sir.

CHIZUKO: (*to Nakamura*) That was nice of you to ask.

NAKAMURA: Oh. Yeah. It's all right.

CHIZUKO: Would you like a cup of tea?

NAKAMURA: Tea? No-no. No tea (heh-heh). (*There's an awkward silence.*) Aki-chan's growing up fast, eh?

CHIZUKO: No, not so.

NAKAMURA: They're like weeds. You don't give them water but they grow anyway.

CHIZUKO: That's true.

NAKAMURA: Pretty soon the yard be full of young men. Maybe my sons come too, eh? Chizuko-san, you chase them out with your broom, eh? (*he laughs heartily but Chizuko doesn't find it funny*) I better be going. Goodnight. You're sure about the water?

CHIZUKO: I'm sure. Goodnight.

Nakamura exits left.

NAKAMURA: Goodnight.

CHIZUKO: (*without looking at the shed*) Kaoru-san, you want ... would you like some tea?

KAORU: (*calling out*) No tea, thank you.

Aki and Kaoru laugh softly. Light fades on Chizuko still holding her basket of laundry.

Fade out

Scene 3

Time: Winter night—a few months later

On rise: In the Sakata kitchen, the lantern is dimly lit. Ichiro sits at the table reading. Tomu has already retired.

Aki practices in Kaoru's shed standing over a music sheet. There is a bottle of wine and a glass on an up-turned crate. Kaoru sits on the cot listening. The music can be heard in the kitchen. Chizuko, in a robe, sweeps the floor. She opens the door to sweep out the dust. The door closes; the music stops. Chizuko grows restless and steps to the window. She returns to the table to work out some figures. The music starts again.

ICHIRO: (*looking at Chizuko*) So long as she keeps playing, eh, Ma?

CHIZUKO: What do you mean?

ICHIRO: Want me to talk to her?

CHIZUKO: About what?

ICHIRO: Okay.

Ichiro shakes his head and exits through the upstage door. Light fades in the kitchen and turns up in the shed.

Kaoru sits on the cot and watches Aki. It's been a bad day for both of them.

KAORU: (*pointing to the music sheet*) See this symbol? That's a sharp. You know all the f's are sharped. I told you that.

AKI: I know. I forgot.

KAORU: Now. The last three measures again.

AKI: The last three?

KAORU: That's what I said.

AKI: (*muttering and finding her place*) The last three ...

She starts playing and makes another error. Kaoru jumps to his feet.

KAORU: Those are all eighth notes. One half of a quarter. Quarters go: one, two, three, four. Eighths are: one and two and three and four and. (*he taps it out*) We went through this before. (*Aki starts over, making another error.*) Sharp! Sharp! (*he takes the violin from her*) Here! (*Aki starts to cry. Kaoru reconsiders.*) I'm sorry, Aki-chan. I guess I'm tired. Here. Lie down. (*Aki is sullen and hesitant.*) Go on. Lie down. Close your eyes. Now this is how it should sound.

He plays the exercise. He stops and taps her knees with the bow. He plays something beautiful, possibly "Two Guitars."

Think of yourself as the violin. Feel the music coming from deep inside. Listen to it. Does it tell you what you want to hear?

AKI: No.

KAORU: (*patiently*) You see, Aki-chan, this instrument is not so different from people. The songs that come from us depend on how we are touched. If you want sweet music, you must coax and stroke—coax and stroke.

AKI: I can't do it.

KAORU: Yes, you can. If you hear it ... and feel it, then it's only a matter of time. I know you can do it. Tell me why you want to play this, Aki-chan.

AKI: (*warming up*) Because ... oh, because when I hear your music, I feel another world out there ... full of romance and mystery. I feel like I'm missing so much. I want to know what it's like, I want to be a part of it; I want in ... but ... the door won't open for me.

KAORU: It will open. You have to keep at it and keep at it and one day ...

AKI: How long will it take?

KAORU: I don't know. That depends on you.

AKI: Five years?

KAORU: More than that.

AKI: Ten? Twenty?

KAORU: Maybe. Maybe more. Depends on how hard you want to work.

AKI: I don't want to work twenty years just to be a second-rate fiddler.

KAORU: (*suddenly depressed*) I see.

AKI: It's only for fun anyway, isn't it?

KAORU: That's right. Only for fun.

AKI: Then why do we have to be so ... serious? Why do we have to be so strict?

KAORU: That's right. Why? What does it matter?

AKI: I love the book you gave me.

KAORU: (*putting the violin away*) That's good.

AKI: (*taking the book from her pocket*) Listen Kaoru-san: "The face of all the world is changed, I think, Since first I heard the footsteps of thy soul. Move still, oh, still, beside me, as they (stole) ... " Do you like it?

KAORU: We'll practice again next week.

Kaoru does not turn. Aki waits. He does not face her. She finally leaves the shed.

Fade out

Scene 4

Time: Shortly after

At rise: Interior of the Sakata kitchen. Chizuko sits at the table deep in thought.

Aki, after waiting in the dark, contemplating what had transpired in the previous scene, finally enters the kitchen. She is careful to close the door quietly. She discovers her mother.

AKI: Oh. You're still up.

CHIZUKO: (*casually*) That was a long lesson.

AKI: (*trying to get away*) Un-hunh.

CHIZUKO: I didn't hear you play much tonight.

AKI: We talked. I guess he knows I'll never make a good player so he just talked to me tonight. About music. That's just as important.

CHIZUKO: For playing the violin?

AKI: We do have to talk, you know.

CHIZUKO: About what?

AKI: Things.

Aki starts for the bedroom.

CHIZUKO: What kind of things?

AKI: Music, composers, what kind of music they write ... why ... where they come from. We talk about other things too. Books, writers. He's been to high school, you know. Why do you ask?

CHIZUKO: I ... I don't like you staying up so late. (*she starts to fold clothes*) You have a hard time in the morning ... getting up. You know that.

AKI: Tomorrow's Saturday!

CHIZUKO: Shhh!

AKI: Then why do I have to go to bed so early?

CHIZUKO: The boys have to go to bed early because they work on Saturday. It's not fair to them.

AKI: *They* don't care!

CHIZUKO: Kaoru-san works in the morning too.

AKI: I know that.

CHIZUKO: Then you shouldn't keep him up so late.

AKI: I'm not keeping him up!

CHIZUKO: Shhh!

AKI: Well, if he wanted me to leave, he'd tell me.

CHIZUKO: He's too polite to tell you.

AKI: It's not that late anyway. God, he's a grown man. He can stay up as long as he wants and still work in the morning. That's all you think about: work, work, work!

CHIZUKO: (*warning*) Aki ...

AKI: Well, it's true. You're always telling me what to do and how to do it. You're always trying to tell everyone what to do around here.

CHIZUKO: I'm not trying to tell everyone ...

AKI: You're going to drive Kaoru-san away from here—bossing him like you do.

CHIZUKO: Take care how you talk to me.

AKI: Nobody likes that. Especially a man like Kaoru-san.

CHIZUKO: Enough. I'm not trying to tell everyone what to do.

AKI: Yes, you are! You're trying to control everything. It's a free country. If we want to talk, what's wrong with that?

CHIZUKO: You can talk in the kitchen.

AKI: We *can't* talk in the kitchen.

CHIZUKO: (*looking innocent*) Oh? Why?

AKI: Ma, you *know* why. Ichiro and Tomu sitting around all the time and making all those cracks ... and you sitting there listening and making those faces ... like telling me what I should say and when I should say it—when I should shut up and ...

CHIZUKO: You don't want me to listen? You saying things you don't want me to hear?

AKI: No! But I try to talk about ... about ... *things*, and there's Ichiro and you sitting there. I know you're thinking: "How stupid!" (*she stands up for herself*) Yes! I don't want you to hear what I say!

CHIZUKO: You think you're the only one with feelings? You don't think anyone else has feelings they want to talk about?

AKI: Well, let them talk about it then. I don't care. (*she again starts toward the bedroom door*)

CHIZUKO: You don't care!

AKI: No! I don't care who talks to who!

CHIZUKO: That's what I mean. You don't care about anyone but yourself. You don't care *how* anyone else feels.

AKI: You mean *you*? (*she turns back*)

CHIZUKO: I mean other people! How do you think it looks: you all the time in a man's room?

AKI: I don't care how it looks.

CHIZUKO: (*lowering her voice*) I'm not saying you're doing anything wrong. I'm saying (that) ...

AKI: You're saying *you* don't like it. No one else cares. You're saying ...

CHIZUKO: Aki-chan. It's not like that. You don't understand. Kaoru-san is a grown man.

AKI: I just told you that.

CHIZUKO: Kaoru-san's twice your age.

AKI: He is not!

CHIZUKO: If you want a friend to talk to, find someone your age who can understand you.

AKI: Who? Name me one.

CHIZUKO: There're lots of boys—*and* girls. Friend doesn't have to be a man. Nakamura-san has two sons.

AKI: Hunh!

CHIZUKO: There's Billy.

AKI: He's a baby!

CHIZUKO: He's your age.

AKI: You think he understands me? Ma, you don't even know what I'm talking about, do you?

CHIZUKO: Kaoru-san is (old) ...

AKI: I don't care!

CHIZUKO: I know you don't care ... right now. I'm just saying you shouldn't let your emotions run away with you.

AKI: Emotions? What do you know about emotions?

CHIZUKO: How can you say that?

AKI: I'm not going to live like you. I'm not going to live all tied up in knots like you: afraid of what people say, afraid of spending money, afraid of laughing, afraid (of) ...

CHIZUKO: Do you understand my problems?

AKI: Afraid you're going to love someone. Afraid you're (going) ...

CHIZUKO: I have lots to worry about. I got to see you have enough to eat, give you an education, see you're dressed decent—so people won't say. "Those kids don't have a father." See you're not left with debts, like what happened to me. See you don't make a mess (of) ...

AKI: I know you work hard. I'm grateful. But I can't ... you can't tell me how to feel, how to live ...

CHIZUKO: Aki, I don't want you to get hurt.

AKI: It's *my* life!

CHIZUKO: Your life is my life. We're one.

AKI: No! We're not! We're not the same!

CHIZUKO: I mean, when you hurt, I hurt.

AKI: That's not true. I hurt when I see how you live—dead! Nothing to look forward to. You think that's good. You want me to live like that. Well, I won't! I want more.

CHIZUKO: You will have more. Things are not the same as they were for me. You're young—you have lots to look forward to. I just don't (want) ...

AKI: God, you never give up.

CHIZUKO: Someone more your age ...

AKI: (*it dawns on her*) You're jealous!

CHIZUKO: Jealous?

AKI: Yes, because he ...

CHIZUKO: What're you talking about?

AKI: Yes, because he pays attention to me ...

CHIZUKO: That's ridiculous! He likes all of us. He told me!

AKI: It's more!

CHIZUKO: (*screaming*) No! No more!

Ichiro enters from the bedroom door. Both women stop talking.

ICHIRO: (*commanding*) Go to bed, Aki!

Aki exits through the bedroom door. Ichiro stands looking at Chizuko who avoids his eyes.

We hear Kaoru's violin ("Two Guitars") and we know he also does not sleep.

Fade out

Scene 5

Time: Spring—Evening

At rise: Interior of Kaoru's quarters. A bottle of wine and a small glass sit on an up-turned crate. The rest of the stage is dark.

Aki is practicing. Kaoru lies on the cot after a hard day's work. He appears to be listening, keeping time with his foot.

Aki's playing is improved but not much. She stops momentarily.

KAORU: Go on. Continue. (*Aki resumes. Kaoru looks at the ceiling and tries to keep awake.*) Getting old. (*he falls asleep*)

Aki watches Kaoru and her playing grows slower and finally stops. She quietly sits on the floor, opens the violin case, and starts to put the violin away. She holds it a moment.

AKI: (*stroking the violin*)

"My cricket chirps against thy mandolin

Hush, call no echo up in further proof

Of desolation! There's a voice within

That weeps ... as thou must sing ... alone, aloof"

KAORU: You know so little about life. What do you learn from those words? (*Kaoru sits up. He reaches over and pours a drink.*) Love is beautiful?

AKI: Of course.

KAORU: (*teasing*) Tell me about it, Aki-chan. What do you know about it?

AKI: Love is ... Oh, you wake up in the morning knowing good things are going to happen. It's making ... making people like me—nobodies—feel special. You *know* there's a heart beating inside—pumping, singing—and you *know* this is what people are born to feel. Everyone. It's sublime; its eternal and forever (and) ...

KAORU: (Ho-ho) So that's what it is: beating and singing and eternal and forever.

AKI: Don't laugh at me.

KAORU: Let me tell you something, Aki. Love doesn't always sing. Sometimes it pulls you to the bottom. It drags everything along with it. Then all sense of right or wrong goes too.

AKI: I don't believe you.

KAORU: You don't know. It turns sour and pretty soon you start enjoying the sick smell of it.

AKI: That's not love. Love isn't like that.

KAORU: I loved someone once. (*he drinks wine*) Her name was Yoko. She didn't want me to leave. She begged me to stay.

AKI: (*angry and jealous*) Well, why'd you leave then? Why didn't you stay with her?

KAORU: She wouldn't marry me.

AKI: Well, why not? If she loved you, why wouldn't she marry you?

KAORU: She had a husband. A family.

AKI: That's awful!

KAORU: Things like that happen sometimes.

AKI: That's no excuse!

KAORU: Sometimes you meet someone you can love at the wrong time. Too late. She was already married.

AKI: (*jealous and hurt*) You shouldn't have let that happen!

KAORU: What does it matter? It's past. Gone. (*he drinks*) I've never been long with a woman. Even my mother left me. Every time I saw a pretty lady, I thought maybe she was my mother. I thought she was waiting for me somewhere. Somehow I wouldn't believe she was dead.

AKI: Was she?

KAORU: Who knows? Maybe she did die. Maybe she ran away with another man. No one talked about it.

AKI: (*sympathetically*) Oh ... Kaoru-san.

KAORU: I never stayed long in one place. Always wandering away; always running. With Yoko was the longest. She was ... warm, sweet ... she was evil. (*he buries his face in his hands*) Too much wine. I'm a little drunk. (*he sits on the cot*)

Aki watches him for a moment, then sits on the cot and slowly, tentatively puts her arm around him. Kaoru shrugs her off.

Don't. (*Aki persists.*) Don't do that ...

Aki will not let him go. His vision blurs, he sees Aki's innocent longing and responds to her embrace. They kiss and hold for a long moment before Kaoru puts her down on his cot. The embrace becomes sensual.

Chizuko who has been sitting in the kitchen gets up and walks to the shed. She listens for sounds of music and not hearing any, she flings open the door.

CHIZUKO: What's this? What are you doing?

Kaoru and Aki jump apart.

KAORU: Chizuko-san ...

CHIZUKO: (*overlapping to Aki*) Get in the house. (*she pushes Aki out of the shed*)

AKI: Mama ... (*she starts to cry*)

KAORU: Chizuko-san, please let me explain. Please ...

CHIZUKO: "Please-please-please." Don't beg now! Pack your things and get out! (*she pulls shirts and things off the pegs and throws them on the bed*)

KAORU: Chizuko-san!

AKI: (*overlapping*) Mama! Don't!

Chizuko finds the violin case on the floor and picks it up. Kaoru holds her to prevent her from throwing it.

KAORU: Chizu(ko-san)

CHIZUKO: Don't touch me! Don't call my name!

KAORU: Calm down; please calm down.

CHIZUKO: You thought you could fool me. You … you violated my trust. You violated my daughter!

KAORU: Vio …? I did nothing. Believe me, I did nothing.

AKI: Ma! Nothing! We did nothing!

CHIZUKO: Get in the house!

AKI: It's not his fault!

CHIZUKO: I'll fix you. I'll get the police!

KAORU: Be reasonable. Let's talk this over.

CHIZUKO: I said out! Tonight! Now! (*she pulls Aki downstage*)

AKI: (*balking*) Mama! Don't do this to us!

CHIZUKO: "Us? What is "us"?

KAORU: Believe me. I meant no harm …

CHIZUKO: What did you do to *me*?

AKI: I'm sorry, Mama. It was my fault. All of it. *I* did it. *I* started it. It was me, Mama. Blame *me* …

CHIZUKO: I know his kind, Aki. He preys on women with his talk … his gifts. (*she tries to touch Aki but Aki draws away*) That's what I tried to tell you. How many women do you think he's lured with his … his sweet talk. Little country girls like you …

KAORU: I've made no pretenses. From the beginning, I told you …

Chizuko stops him before he says the terrible words that would prove how foolish she had been to dream.

CHIZUKO: I trusted you, I trusted you.

KAORU: I'm sorry. I didn't betray that trust. Tonight I … I had too much to drink. I know that's no ex(cuse) …

CHIZUKO: Get out. Get out!

KAORU: I have no money.

CHIZUKO: I'll give you money! (*she starts toward the house dragging Aki with her*)

AKI: Don't! Don't, Mama, I love him!

CHIZUKO: (*the word "love" stops her*) Don't say that. Don't say that word! You're confusing it with something else.

AKI: I do. I love him.

CHIZUKO: Do you really believe this ... this old man loves you? (*Aki looks at Kaoru. He avoids her eyes.*) He doesn't know the meaning of the word. I know his kind. Where do you think he goes on his days off? To women! He goes to women, Aki.

AKI: I don't care. I love him.

CHIZUKO: (*contemptuously*) Where is your pride, Aki?

AKI: If you send him away, I'll go with him.

CHIZUKO: You don't know what you're saying, Aki.

AKI: I will. I'll go with him.

She runs to Kaoru's side and holds his arm. Kaoru reacts, drawing away from her.

CHIZUKO: (*pulling Aki away*) You know what you're asking for? From town to town ... no roots ... no home ... nothing. Maybe one day, he'll get tired of you ... throw you out ... leave you in some dirty hotel for another fool woman. Think, Aki. And you'll come crawling (home) ...

AKI: I'll never come home! I'll never come back to you! You're not a mother. You're a witch!

Kaoru goes back to his quarters and starts packing.

CHIZUKO: Witch? Who you calling witch? Someone who sacrificed a life for you?

AKI: You didn't sacrifice for me.

CHIZUKO: No? No? You think I like this life? You think I like grubbing in dirt and manure (and) ...

AKI: That's the only way you know to live. You don't want to change your life.

CHIZUKO: You believe that? You believe this is all I want? That I lived with a man I hardly knew, didn't understand, didn't respect because (I) ...

AKI: You didn't love him! You didn't love him, did you?

CHIZUKO: How could I love him—I didn't know him. All the time I was keeping our heads above water ... single-handed! Yes! While he was still alive, until the merciful day he drowned! Growing old before I was ready—dying before I ever lived ...

AKI: Then you've never loved. Then you don't know anything about love.

CHIZUKO: I do! *You* don't know! What do you know about my feelings?

AKI: I know about them and I don't want to stick around and become the kind of woman *you* are.

CHIZUKO: (*in a towering rage*) (Annngh!) Go then. Go! Go! You'll find out. And when things get rough, remember tonight!

AKI: I'll never forget.

CHIZUKO: You think you know all the answers. You think everything's so simple. You haven't even tasted pain yet. You'll find out.

AKI: So I'll find out! (*she walks to the kitchen door*)

CHIZUKO: Aki ...

AKI: Leave me alone!

Aki slams the door behind her. Chizuko is stunned. She sits on a bench until Ichiro comes out (in the next scene).

Fade out

Scene 6

Time: Immediately after

At rise: Awakened by the sound of angry voices, Ichiro, in pajamas, enters from the bedroom (upstage door). He peers through the screen door.

ICHIRO: You all right, Ma?

CHIZUKO: (*getting up and entering the kitchen*) Everything went wrong. Get the money jar.

ICHIRO: What?

CHIZUKO: Kaoru-san's leaving.

ICHIRO: What happened?

CHIZUKO: I don't know. I don't know what happened. Suddenly ... everything happened and ... and he's leaving us. Aki too.

ICHIRO: Aki? Goddamn kid.

Tomu enters from the upstage door. He wears p.j.'s and rubs his sleepy eyes.

CHIZUKO: I don't know what happened. Suddenly ... Ichiro, what went wrong? She's going with him. How can things turn so bad?

TOMU: What turned bad? What happened to Aki? Where's she going?

ICHIRO: She's going with him. That stupid brat!

TOMU: Why?

ICHIRO: Never mind why.

TOMU: What's going on?

CHIZUKO: Get the money, Ichiro. I have to give them money.

TOMU: Don't let her go, Ma.

CHIZUKO: She wants to leave. We have to let her go.

TOMU: You can stop her, Ma. Stop her!

CHIZUKO: I can't. I can't anymore.

ICHIRO: Never mind, Ma. Give them some money and let them go. (*he gets the money jar*)

TOMU: Ma, stop her. Stop her! (*he starts toward the upstage door*)

ICHIRO: Tomu! Get back here, dammit!

CHIZUKO: Don't get mad. Let's not fight any more.

ICHIRO: (*counting the money*) I knew what was going on. I should have knocked some sense ...

CHIZUKO: No. If ... no. I was thinking of myself all the time ... the farm. It was easier with a man helping. I was thinking ... I'm getting old... tired ...

TOMU: Why can't they both stay then?

CHIZUKO: That's not possible.

ICHIRO: Shut up, Tomu.

CHIZUKO: We can't stay here anymore. It will be too hard for us.

ICHIRO: Don't worry, Ma. We can make it. I'll quit school and ...

CHIZUKO: No. It's no good. We have to move.

TOMU: Ma ...

CHIZUKO: You can't quit school.

ICHIRO: Where will we go? The crop ...

CHIZUKO: After the harvest. I was thinking ... maybe San Pedro.

ICHIRO: Where?

CHIZUKO: Terminal Island. I hear there're lots of Japanese there. And the canneries. You boys can get part-time work. After school. That way you don't miss school so much ... like you've been doing.

TOMU: We didn't miss this year.

CHIZUKO: We sell everything. Maybe just keep the truck and the beds ... some furniture. Rent an apartment ...   How much should we give them?

ICHIRO: Just enough to get out of town.

CHIZUKO: Aki will need too. Poor Aki ...

ICHIRO: Don't waste any sympathy, Ma. She asked for it. She's no good.

CHIZUKO: She's a good girl, Ichiro. She's not to blame.

TOMU: She's a good girl.

ICHIRO: She's a selfish brat. (*he finishes counting the money*) This should be enough. (*Chizuko adds the rest of the bills.*) That doesn't leave us much.

CHIZUKO: That's all right. We can get credit at the store. Ishi-san will give us credit.

Aki comes out of the bedroom with her clothes in a pillow case.

ICHIRO: You spoiled everything for everybody.

Ichiro follows Aki downstage hoping to say a few more things but he sees Kaoru waiting with his violin case and bag and he stops. He slams the money on the bench.

Here. Give him that.

Aki gives Kaoru the money; Kaoru looks at it and slips it in his pocket. Aki takes his arm preparing to leave with him.

KAORU: (*gently detaining her*) I can't take you with me; you can't come with me, Aki-chan. You know that, don't you?

AKI: But I have to! I can't stay here.

KAORU: You understand why don't you?

AKI: But what will I do here all by myself? You got to take me. Please take me with you ...

KAORU: (*gently*) I can't.

AKI: Please take me ... take me with you ... (*she tries to embrace him but he will not permit it*) I'm going to die, Kaoru-san.

KAORU: (*firmly*) No, you won't.

AKI: Take me ...

KAORU: Now go inside and apologize to your mother. Try to explain ...

AKI: She won't understand; she won't take me back. Please, Kaoru-san ... please ...

KAORU: She *will* take you back. In time you'll both forget.

AKI: I'll remember all my life. (*she tries to embrace him again*)

KAORU: (*stopping her*) You must stop this.

AKI: Please ...

KAORU: Stop it!

AKI: (*after a moment*) What will you do? Where will you go?

KAORU: I don't know. First to the bus depot. This time of year there'll be harvesting all along California. Grapes ... peaches ... Like she said: another town, another job.

AKI: Another woman?

KAORU: Another? You're not a woman yet. When you grow up to be a real woman, I'll be an old man. You'll be all right. Now be a good girl and say good-bye.

Aki embraces him and he permits it without responding. She releases him. He prepares to leave.

AKI: Will you write me?

KAORU: (*without turning*) You know I can't do that.

Kaoru exits left. Aki stands dejected and watches him go.

Tomu comes from the house. He reaches in his pajama pocket and gives Aki some money.

TOMU: Take this with you, Aki.

AKI: I'm not going.

TOMU: You're not going? (*We hear the sound of a truck approaching from a distance.*) Ma! Did you hear that? She's not going! (*he runs in the house pulling Aki with him*)

ICHIRO: He won't take you, eh? You should have figured that out yourself.

Chizuko hushes him.

The family is quiet. Kaoru hails the truck.

KAORU: (*off stage*) Hey … stop. Stop … (*The truck stops.*) Can you give me a lift to town?

TRUCK DRIVER: (*off stage*) Yeah. Hop in.

Aki walks to the screen door as the truck starts up again. She stands there until she can no longer hear it. Then she moves toward the bedroom door.

CHIZUKO: It's better this way, Aki, better.

Light fades slowly out.

Fade out

The End

Alternate Table of Contents
by Theme

Selected Bibliography

I. Critical Readings in Asian American Literature

Chan, Jeffery Paul, Frank Chin, Lawson Fusao Inada, and Shawn Wong, eds. *The Big Aiiieeeee! An Anthology of Chinese American and Japanese American Literature*. New York: Meridian, 1991.

Cheung, King-Kok. *Articulate Silences*. Ithaca, NY: Cornell University Press, 1993.

Chin, Frank, Jeffery Paul Chan, Lawson Fusao Inada, and Shawn Wong, eds. *Aiiieeeee! An Anthology of Asian American Writers*. New York: Mentor, 1991.

Houston, Velina Hasu, ed. *The Politics of Life: Four Plays by Asian American Woman*. Philadelphia: Temple University Press, 1993.

Kim, Elaine H. *Asian American Literature: An Introduction to the Writings and Their Social Context*. Philadelphia: Temple University Press, 1982.

Lim, Shirley Geok-lin, and Amy Ling, ed. *Reading the Literatures of Asian America*. Philadelphia: Temple University Press, 1992.

Moy, James S. *Marginal Sights: Staging the Chinese in America*. Iowa City: University of Iowa Press, 1993.

Sumida, Stephen H. *And the View from the Shore: Literary Traditions of Hawai'i*. Seattle: University of Washington Press, 1991.

Uno, Roberts, ed. *Unbroken Thread: An Anthology of Plays by Asian American Women*. Amherst: University of Massachusetts Press, 1993.

Wong, Sau-ling. *Reading Asian American Literature: From Necessity to Extravagance*. Princeton: Princeton University Press, 1993.

II. Critical Readings in Asian American Literature

Asian Women United of California, eds. *Making Waves: An Anthology of Writings by and about Asian American Women*. Boston: Beacon Press, 1989.

Bacho, Peter. *Cebu*. Seattle: University of Washington Press, 1991.

Bulosan, Carlos. *America Is in the Heart*. Seattle: University of Washington Press, 1973.

Chang, Diana. *The Frontiers of Love*. Seattle: University of Washington Press, 1994.

Chin, Frank. *The Chickencoop Chinaman and the Year of the Dragon*. Seattle: University of Washington Press, 1981.

_____. *Donald Duk*. Minneapolis, MN: Coffee House Press, 1991.

_____. *Gunga Din Highway.* Minneapolis, MN: Coffee House Press, 1994.

_____. *The Chinaman Pacific & Frisco R. R. Co.* Minneapolis, MN: Coffee House Press, 1988.

Chin, Marilyn. *Dwarf Bamboo.* Greenfield Center, NY: The Greenfield Review Press, 1987.

_____. *The Phoenix Gone, The Terrace Empty.* Minneapolis, MN: Milkweed Editions, 1994.

Chin, Woon Ping. *The Naturalization of Camellia Song.* Singapore: Times Books International, 1993.

Chock, Eric, and Darrell H. Y. Lum, eds. *The Best of the Bamboo Ridge.* Honolulu: Bamboo Ridge Press, 1986.

Chu, Louis. *East a Bowl of Tea.* New York: Lyle Stuart, 1961.

Gonzalez, N. V. M. *Bread of Salt and Other Stories.* Seattle: University of Washington Press, 1993.

Hagedorn, Jessica, ed. *Charlie Chan Is Dead.* New York: Penguin, 1993.

_____. *Danger and Beauty.* New York: Penguin, 1993.

Hahn, Kimiko. Air Pocket. Brooklyn, NY: Hanging Loose Press, 1989.

_____. *Earshot.* Brooklyn, NY: Hanging Loose Press, 1992.

Hom, Marlon K. *Songs of Gold Mountain.* Berkeley: University of California Press, 1987.

Houston, Jeanne Wakatsuki, and James D. Houston. *Farewell to Manzanar.* Boston: Houghton Mifflin, 1973.

Inada, Lawson Fusao. *Before the War.* New York: William Morrow, 1971.

_____. *Legends from Camp.* Minneapolis, MN: Coffee House Press, 1992.

_____. *Dogeaters.* New York: Penguin, 1990.

Jen, Gish. *Typical American.* Boston: Houghton Mifflin, 1991.

Kingston, Maxine Hong. *Chinaman.* New York: Vintage, 1989.

_____. *The Woman Warrior: Memories of a Girlhood Among Ghosts.* New York: Alfred A. Knopf, 1976.

_____. *Tripmaster Monkey: His Fake Book.* New York: Alfred A. Knopf, 1989.

Kogawa, Joy. *Itsuka.* New York: Anchor Books, 1994.

_____. *Obasan.* New York: Anchor Books, 1994.

Kohl, Stephen W. *An Early Account of Japanese Life in the Pacific Northwest: Writings of Nagai Kafu.* Pacific Northwest Quarterly (April, 1979): 58–64.

Lee, Gus. *China Boy.* New York: Dutton, 1991.

Lee, Li-Young. *Rose.* Brockport, NY: BOA Editions, 1986.

_____. *The City in Which I Love You.* Brockport, N: BOA Editions, 1990.

Leong, Russell. *The Country of Dreams and Dust.* Albuquerque, NM: West End Press, 1993.

Louie, David Wong. *Pangs of Love.* New York: Alfred A. Knopf, 1991.

Lum, Darrell H. Y. *Pass On, No Pass Back.* Honolulu, HA: Bamboo Ridge Press, 1990.

Minatoya, Lydia. *Talking to High Monks in the Snow.* New York: HarperCollins, 1992.

Mirikitani, Janice. *Awake in the River.* San Francisco: Isthmus Press, 1978.

_____. *Shedding Silence.* Berkeley, CA: Celestial arts, 1987.

Miyamoto, Kazuo. *Hawaii, End of the Rainbow.* Rutland, VT: Charles E. Tuttle, 1964.

Mo, Timothy. *Sour Sweet.* New York: Vintage, 1985.

Mori, Toshio. *Yokohama, California.* Seattle: University of Washington Press, 1985.

_____. *The Chauvinist and Other Stories.* Los Angeles: Asian American Studies Center, 1979.

Mukherjee, Bharati. *The Middleman and Other Stories.* New York: Ballantina Books, 1988.

Murayama, Milton. *All I Am Asking for Is My Body.* Honolulu: University of Hawaii Press, 1988.

Ng, Fae Myenne. *Bone.* New York: Hyperion, 1993.

Okada, John. *No-no Boy.* Seattle: University of Washington Press, 1983.

Okubo, Mine. *Citizen 13660.* Seattle: University of Washington Press, 1993.

Pak, Ty. *Guilt Payment.* Honolulu, HA: Bamboo Ridge Press, 1983.

Ronyoung, Kim. *Clay Walls.* Seattle: University of Washington Press, 1989.

Sasaki, R. A. *The Loom and Other Stories.* Saint Paul, MN: Graywolf Press, 1991.

Santos, Bienvenido. *Scent of Apples.* Seattle: University of Washington Press, 1979.

Song, Kathy. *Frameless Windows, Squares of Light.* New York: W. W. Norton & Co., 1988.

_____. *Picture Bride.* New Haven, CT: Yeale University Press, 1983.

Tan, Amy. *The Kitchen God's Wife.* New York: G. P. Putnam's Sons, 1991.

_____. *The Joy Luck Club.* New York: G. P. Putnam's Sons, 1989.

Watanabe, Sylvia. *Talking to the Dead.* New York: Doubleday, 1992.

Watanabe, Sylvia, and Carol Bruchax. *Home to Stay: Asian American Women's Fiction.* Greenfield Center, NY: The Greenfield Review Press, 1990.

Wong, Jade Snow. *Fifth Chinese Daughter.* Seattle: University of Washington Press, 1989.

Wong, Shawn. *American Knees.* New York: Simon & Schuster, 1995.

_____. *Homebase.* New York: Plume, 1991.

Yamamoto, Hisaye. *Seventeen Syllables and Other Stories.* Latham, NY: Kitchen Table: Women of Color Press, 1988.

Yamauchi, Wakako. *Songs My Mother Taught Me.* New York: The Feminist Press at the City University of New York, 1994.

Yep, Laurence. *Child of the Owl.* New York: Harper &Row, 1977.

_____. *Dragonwings.* New York: Harper & Row, 1975.

Index of Author Names, Titles, and First Lines of Poems

Acknowledgments

Carlos Bulosan. "The Romance of Magno Rubio." From the Carlos Bulosan Papers, University of Washington Libraries, Seattle, WA 98195. Used by permission.

Jeffrey Paul Chan. "Sing Song Plain Song" from <u>Amerasia Journal</u> 3:2 (1976). Copyright © 1976 by Jeffrey Paul Chan. Reprinted by permission of the author.

Diana Chang. "Falling Free", a short story originally published in <u>Crosscurrents: A Quarterly</u>, Vol. 5, No. 3, pp. 55-72 (1985), © 1985 Diana Chang. Reprinted by permission of the author.

Frank Chin. "Rendezvous." From <u>Conjunctions: Credos Issue</u> (1993) published by Bard College. Copyright © 1993 by Frank Chin. Reprinted by permission of the author.

Marilyn Chin. "How I Got That Name," "A Break in the Rain," and "Elegy for Chloe Nguyen" were originally published in <u>The Phoenix Gone, The Terrace Empty</u> by Marilyn Chin (Milkweed Editions, 1994). Copyright © 1994 by Marilyn Chin. Reprinted with permission from Milkweed Editions.

Woon-Ping Chin. "The Naturalization of Camillia Song," "In My Mother's Dream," and "Seven Vietnamese Boys" from <u>The Naturalization of Camellia Song</u> published by Times Editions, Singapore. Copyright © 1993 by Woon-Ping Chin. Reprinted by permission of the author. "In My Mother's Dream" originally appeared in <u>The Kenyon Review</u>, Vol. 14, No. 1, Winter 1992.

Vince Gotera. "Alan Valeriano Sees a Lynch Mob," © 1989 by Vince Gotera. Originally published in <u>The Madison Review</u>, Spring 1989. "Aswang," © 1990 by Vince Gotera. Originally published in <u>Zone 3</u>, Spring 1990. "Dance of the Letters," © 1989 by Vince Gotera. Originally published in <u>Ploughshares</u>, vol. 15, no. 1 (1989). "Fighting Kite," © 1992 by Vince Gotera. Originally published in <u>Hawaii Pacific Review</u>, Fall 1992. "Vietnam Era Vet," © 1993 by Vince Gotera. Originally appeared in <u>The Journal of American Culture</u>, Fall 1993. All reprinted by permission of the author.

Jessica Hagedorn. "The Blossoming of Bongbong" from <u>Danger and Beauty</u> by Jessica Hagedorn. Copyright © 1993 by Jessica Hagedorn. Used by permission of Viking Penguin, a division of Penguin Books USA Inc.

Kimiko Hahn. "Resistance: A Poem on Ikat Cloth" from <u>Air Pocket</u> (Hanging Loose, 1989). Copyright © 1989 by Kimiko Hahn. Reprinted by permission of the author.

Bharati Mukherjee. "The Management of Grief." From <u>The Middleman and Other Stories</u> by Bharati Mukherjee. Copyright © 1988 by Bharati Mukherjee. Used by permission of Grove/Atlantic, Inc.

Fae Myenne Ng. "Backdaire." Reprinted by permission of Doandio & Ashworth, Inc. Copyright 1989 by Fae Myenne Ng. Originally published in <u>Harper's</u> April 1989.

Bienvenido N. Santos. "Quicker with Arrows" from <u>Scent of Apples: A Collection of Stories</u> by Bienvenido N. Santos. Copyright 1955, 1957 by Bienvenido N. Santos. Reprinted with permission of the University of Washington Press.

R. A. Sasaki. "First Love" copyright © 1991 by R. A. Sasaki. Reprinted from <u>The Loom and Other Stories</u> with the permission of Graywolf Press, Saint Paul.

Connie Ching So, "The Color Yellow" working Class Asian American Women and Feminism." Copyright © 1995 by Connie Ching So. Used by permission of the author.

Cathy Song, "the Youngest daughter," "Easter: Waihiawa, 1959," and "Tribe" from <u>Picture Bride</u> by Cathy Song. Copyright © 1983 by Cathy Song. Reprinted by permission of Yale University Press.

Carol Roh-Spaulding. "Waiting for Mr. Kim." Copyright © 1900 by Carol Roh Spaulding. Reprinted by permission of the author. Originally appeared in <u>Plowshares</u>, vol. 16, nos. 2 and 3, Fall 1990.

Amy Tan. "Mother Tongue" First published in <u>The Threepenny Review</u>. Copyright © 1990 by Amy Tan. Reprinted by permission of the author.

O. Wini Terada. "Intermediate School Hapai." Copyright © 1980 by O. Wini Terada. Originally published in <u>Bamboo Ridge: The Hawai'i Writers' Quarterly</u>, #5, 1979-1980. Reprinted by permission of the author.

Monique Thuy-Dung Truong. "Kelly." From <u>Amerasia Journal</u> 17:2 (1991). Reprinted by permission of the publisher and the author.

Sylvia Watanabe. "A Spell of Kona Weather," from <u>Talking to the Dead</u> by Sylvia Watanabe. Copyright © 1992 by Sylvia Watanabe. Used by permission of Doubleday, a division of Bantam Doubleday Dell Publishing Group, Inc.

Traise Yamamoto. "Different Silences." Copyright © 1994 by Traise Yamamoto. Used by permission of the author. A version of this essay "Different Silences" appeared in <u>The Intimate Critique: Autobiographical Literacy Criticism</u> edited by Diane P. Freedman, Olivia Frey, and Frances Murphy Zauhar, 1993: Durham, Duke University Press. Reprinted with permission.